Restless Pilgrim

Restless Pilgrim

Andrew Jenson's Quest for Latter-day Saint History

REID L. NEILSON AND
SCOTT D. MARIANNO

UNIVERSITY OF
ILLINOIS PRESS
Urbana, Chicago, and Springfield

Manufactured in the United States of America
1 2 3 4 5 C P 5 4 3 2 1
♾ This book is printed on acid-free paper.

Library of Congress Cataloging-in-Publication Data
Names: Neilson, Reid L., 1972– author. | Marianno, Scott D., author.
Title: Restless pilgrim: Andrew Jenson's quest for Latter-day Saint history / Reid L Neilson and Scott D Marianno.
Description: Urbana: University of Illinois Press, [2021] | Includes bibliographical references and index.
Identifiers: LCCN 2021031550 (print) | LCCN 2021031551 (ebook) | ISBN 9780252044229 (hardback) | ISBN 9780252086267 (paperback) | ISBN 9780252053184 (ebook)
Subjects: LCSH: Jenson, Andrew, 1850–1941. | Church of Jesus Christ of Latter-day Saints. Church Historian's Office—Employees. | Church of Jesus Christ of Latter-day Saints—Historiography. | Religion historians—United States—Biography. | Mormon converts—Biography. | Danish Americans—Biography. | Mormon missionaries—Scandinavia—Biography. | LCGFT: Biographies.
Classification: LCC BX8695.J46 N45 2021 (print) | LCC BX8695.J46 (ebook) | DDC 289.3092 [B]—dc23
LC record available at https://lccn.loc.gov/2021031550
LC ebook record available at https://lccn.loc.gov/2021031551

For President Russell M. Nelson, Elder Jeffrey R. Holland, Elder Quentin L. Cook, and Elder Dale G. Renlund

—RLN

For my grandfather, David Marianno Sr., the grandson of a Portuguese immigrant, a rancher, a friend.

—SDM

Contents

Acknowledgments

We are grateful for the support of the Church Historian and Recorders as well as the Assistant Executive Directors of the Church History Department of The Church of Jesus Christ of Latter-day Saints, including Elders Marlin K. Jensen, Paul K. Sybrowsky, Marcus B. Nash, James J. Hamula, J. Devn Cornish, Steven E. Snow, and LeGrand R. Curtis Jr. A number of our Church History Library colleagues, especially Christopher J. Blythe, Justin R. Bray, Peter Crawley, Jo Lyn Curtis, Matthew Geilman, Silvia Ghosh, Matthew J. Grow, Claire Haynie, Ronald Young, Jed Woodworth, Alan D. Johnson, Robin S. Jensen, Kelley Konzak, R. Mark Melville, Brandon J. Metcalf, Jennifer L. Lund, Elizabeth Pinborough, Mitchell K. Schaffer, and Riley M. Moffat helped prepare or review portions of this manuscript. Matthew Marianno also graciously reviewed the manuscript and provided insightful feedback. We also received valuable translation assistance on Danish sources from Julie K. Allen and her students at Brigham Young University. Julie also generously shared her scholarship with us and helped us improve our own. We would also like to express gratitude for the support and sources we received from Jenson family descendants, including Theresia May, Susan May, and Angela Kinsley.

The librarians, archivists, and professional staffs of the Archives and Special Collections and the Pacific Islands Reading Room at Brigham Young University–Hawai'i; the L. Tom Perry Special Collections; the Utah Valley Regional Family History Center and the Harold B. Lee Library at Brigham Young University; the Church History Library and the Family History Library at The Church of Jesus Christ of Latter-day Saints; the Special Collections and the J. Willard Marriott Library at the University of Utah; the Special Collections and Archives at Utah State University; the Lone Tree Branch of the Douglas County Libraries, Parker, Colorado; the Napa County Library; the Riverton Historical Society; and the Doe

Memorial Library and Moffit Library at the University of California, Berkeley; and the Research Library and Collections at the Utah State Historical Society, all provided helpful guidance and access to needed primary source documents and secondary research along the way.

Many thanks are also due to the leadership and faculty of Brigham Young University's College of Religious Education, where Reid began his scholarship on Andrew Jenson, including Terry B. Ball, Alexander L. Baugh, Scott C. Esplin, J. Spencer Fluhman, Arnold K. Garr, Steven C. Harper, Richard Neitzel Holzapfel, Kent P. Jackson, R. Devan Jensen, Dennis L. Largey, John P. Livingstone, Robert L. Millet, Brent R. Nordgren, Paul H. Peterson, Joany Pinegar, Brent L. Top, Thomas A. Wayment, and Dennis A. Wright. Reid's BYU student research assistants, including Ashley Gentile, Krystyna Hales, Landon Lisonbee, Paul Olson, Adam Prestidge, and Christopher Rawlins, helped with early work on this project. We received help on several of the previous Jenson publications from Religious Studies Center student employees, including Alex Masterson, Hadley Griggs, Allyson Jones, Kimball Gardner, Leah Welker, Lauren Whitby, Aleesha Bass, Austin Ballard, Juliana Cox, and Rachel Ishoy.

Several of the themes and conclusions in this biography were explored and developed by Reid and his collaborators in the following articles and books: Reid L. Neilson, "Enlarging the Memory of Mormonism: Historian Andrew Jenson's Tales from the World Tour, 1895–1897," *International Journal of Mormon Studies* 2 (Spring 2009): 42–61; Reid L. Neilson and Riley M. Moffat, eds., *Tales from the World Tour: The 1895–1897 Travel Writings of Mormon Historian Andrew Jenson* (Provo, UT: Religious Studies Center, Brigham Young University, 2012); Reid L. Neilson, "Around the World a Second Time: The 1912 Travel Writings of Mormon Historian Andrew Jenson," *Mormon Historical Studies* 14, no. 1 (Spring 2013): 45–65; Justin R. Bray and Reid L. Neilson, "Looking Beyond the Borders of Mexico: Historian Andrew Jenson and the Opening of Mormon Missionary Work in Latin America," *Mormon Historical Studies* 14, no. 2 (Fall 2013): 1–27; Justin R. Bray and Reid L. Neilson, eds., *Exploring Book of Mormon Lands: The 1923 Latin American Travel Writings of Mormon Historian Andrew Jenson* (Provo, UT: Religious Studies Center, Brigham Young University, 2014); Reid L. Neilson, Justin R. Bray, and Alan Johnson, eds., *Rediscovering the Historic Sites of the Restoration: The 1888 Travel Writings of Mormon Historian Andrew Jenson, Edward Stevenson, and Joseph S. Black* (Provo, UT: Religious Studies Center, Brigham Young University, 2015); Reid L. Neilson and R. Mark Melville, eds., *A Historian in Zion: The Autobiography of Andrew Jenson, Assistant Church Historian: Revised and Enhanced Edition* (Provo, UT: Religious Studies Center, Brigham Young University, 2016); and Reid L. Neilson and Scott D. Marianno, eds., *A Voice in the Wilderness: The 1888–1930 General Conference Sermons of Mormon Historian Andrew Jenson* (New York: Oxford University Press, 2018).

As we published this material on Jenson, we were also able to present our evolving ideas at a number of academic conferences and historical gatherings, including the annual meeting of the European Mormon Studies Association, Turku, Finland, 2008; the annual Church History Symposium, Brigham Young University, Provo, Utah, 2009; the Faculty Forum, College of Religious Education, Brigham Young University, Provo, Utah, 2012; the annual meeting of the Brazilian Mormon Studies Association, Sao Paulo, Brazil, 2013; the Men and Women of Faith Lecture Series, Church History Department, Salt Lake City, Utah, 2014; and the spring meeting of the American Society of Church History, Berkeley, California, 2017. We are grateful for the support of all of our colleagues and friends who have allowed us to share our working drafts in the various venues.

Finally, Reid dedicates this biography of his fellow Assistant Church Historian Andrew Jenson to then Elder Russell M. Nelson, Elder Jeffrey R. Holland, Elder Quentin L. Cook, and Elder Dale G. Renlund, the apostolic advisors to the Church History Department during his decade-long tenure there as managing director. Their personal goodness and professional excellence continue to inspire Reid's life and scholarship.

Scott dedicates this biography to his grandfather, David Marianno Sr. His work ethic and commitment to building a legacy carries echoes of Jenson's own remarkable life.

Restless Pilgrim

Prologue

On the morning of July 24, 1934, Andrew Jenson, Assistant Church Historian for The Church of Jesus Christ of Latter-day Saints (hereafter "the church"), boarded a United Airlines plane at the Omaha, Nebraska, airport bound for Salt Lake City, Utah. He was in town to promote his newspaper column Day by Day with the Utah Pioneers, which had recently been serialized in the *Salt Lake Tribune*. The 111 articles of Jenson's column coincided with the 111 days the vanguard company of Latter-day Saint pioneers traveled along the Mormon Trail, from the Midwest to the Salt Lake Valley, which they reached in July 1847.[1] To promote his column, Jenson had traveled by train to Omaha, where he spent a week researching pioneer history and giving lectures.[2]

Sixty-eight years earlier, at the age of fifteen, Jenson himself, along with his family, had walked the length of the Mormon Trail from Nebraska to Utah, over sixty-two grueling days, as part of a pioneer wagon company. That year, 1866, was the last summer Latter-day Saint pioneers like Jenson would travel all the way from the Missouri River to the Salt Lake Valley by foot and wagon. As the Transcontinental Railroad inched westward, pioneers took advantage of more western waystations to launch their travel across the trail, until the completion of the railroad three years later made travel by wagon obsolete. Between 1847 and 1868, more than sixty thousand Latter-day Saints crossed the US plains by wagon train as part of the church's mass migration westward.[3]

Now, at age eighty-three, Jenson was completing the same journey by airplane. He left on Utah's Pioneer Day, July 24, which in 1934 commemorated the eighty-seventh anniversary of the Latter-day Saint pioneers entering the Salt Lake Valley. This time he would cross the thousand-mile distance in just a few hours. As he sped through the sky at 165 miles per hour, he found it "difficult to realize that he was covering as much distance in a little over five minutes as the pioneers covered in a day behind their lumbering oxen." The flight marked his thirty-third trip over the Mormon Trail.[4] The trip exemplified just how much the world around Jenson had advanced over his eighty-three years of life. Technology and travel had changed as had the Latter-day Saint people, but Jenson's lifetime commitment to documenting church history remained as steady as ever.

Born to a peasant family in rural Denmark on December 11, 1850, Andreas Christiansen Jensen (later Andrew Jenson) was christened into the Danish Lutheran Church only months after Latter-day Saint missionaries first reached Danish soil to preach the restored gospel.[5] When the Jensen family converted in 1854, their new church significantly disrupted their lives. The new religion suggested a reordering of Danish social and cultural norms, claiming that God could speak personally to a Danish peasant through revelation, not only through priestly channels; that new (American) scripture repaired the corrupted traditional Christianity; and that a Zion was being built in the American West. Enthused by the promise of prophets, democratized religious authority, and economic opportunity, the Jensens abandoned their ancestral home and journeyed to the Latter-day Saint kingdom in the Great Basin.

Much had transpired for the Latter-day Saints prior to the conversion of the Jensens. Organized in a log home in the burned-over district of upstate New York during the Second Great Awakening, the movement founded by Joseph Smith had grown from a handful of members in 1830 to over fifty thousand by 1850. The church had moved from New York, to Kirtland, Ohio, to counties in Missouri, and to Nauvoo, Illinois—each migration forced by political pressure and occasional violence. Despite opposition, in just a decade and a half, Smith translated the Book of Mormon—an ancient account of a New World people—dictated dozens of revelations, built one temple and started constructing another, and created a Latter-day Saint city on the banks of the Mississippi River. The church's strained relationship with the larger American society, however, ultimately culminated in the 1844 murder of Joseph Smith while he was jailed in Carthage, Illinois. A short time later, in 1846, tensions with the surrounding community drove adherents into the Iowa wilderness and eventually further westward. While the Jensens converted in Denmark, Brigham Young, Smith's successor, was working to colonize the desert in the West, attempting to create an insular kingdom where Latter-day Saints could practice their religion unmolested.

Andrew Jenson lived in a time of remarkable change for the Latter-day Saints. Just years before Jenson's birth in 1850, the church had 51,839 members, spread across one stake and nine missions.[6] By the time his family reached Utah Territory in 1866, plural marriage was practiced committedly in Latter-day Saint settlements, communal economic arrangements and storehouses were commonplace, and the Transcontinental Railroad was nearing completion.[7] Jenson was a faithful witness of the period that followed, a time that historians have called the church's era of "transition" or "Americanization."[8] Jenson's career as a historian for the church blossomed in the 1890s, just as the institution was on the precipice of unprecedented change and growth. He sought to document it all. By Jenson's death in November 1941, there were 892,080 Latter-day Saints of record, organized into 139 stakes and 36 missions worldwide.[9]

Initially disappointed by the economic realities of life in nineteenth-century Zion, Jenson developed skills as an entrepreneurial historian. He roved the western landscape, documenting its development from Arizona to Idaho, capturing the memories of settlers and immigrants, and encouraging better record keeping. Tutored in a hardscrabble frontier print culture, Jenson learned from the literature and newspapers of the Great Basin. He got his start as a translator and journalist following the nineteenth-century subscription model of publishing. Jenson and local agents pushed his Danish translation of the History of Joseph Smith (*Joseph Smiths levnetsløb*) and later his Danish magazine, *Morgenstjernen* (Morning star) to Scandinavians in rural Utah communities. His journalism, however, soon morphed into a full-scale historical operation that transformed him into a historian before the Latter-day Saint public. When Jenson was finally invited to work for the Church Historian's Office as a diplomat of the office's initiatives, most of the church's wards and stakes, located in the Intermountain West, were reachable within a few days of travel. His work only expanded from there.

The Historian's Office on the south side of South Temple Street, the site of Jenson's hopes, dreams, and sometimes disappointments, lacked systemization and resources for much of the nineteenth century. As its Church Historians and Assistant Church Historians attempted to fulfill the divine mandate given to Joseph Smith to keep a record of the church's history, they were often pulled away by other ecclesiastical responsibilities.[10] In support of the office, Jenson traveled to gather and appraise Latter-day Saint records in the scattered ecclesiastical units of the church. This first assignment from the Historian's Office launched a lifetime quest to render the church's historical record complete and comprehensive. This meant in part writing a chronological history of every branch, ward, and mission of the church, the entirety of the church's organizational units. In addition, it meant writing biographies of prominent men and women in the church, including all of its General Authorities and general officers. It also meant compiling a chronological history of major events contributing to the church's development and growth.

Jenson borrowed his narrative and chronological style from the popular histories of his day. Professional historians were not commonplace in the American West when he began writing history. Instead, he learned from prominent amateurs like Hubert Howe Bancroft or John Clark Ridpath, as well as those who wrote from within his own faith like Parley P. Pratt, George Q. Cannon, and Orson F. Whitney.[11] He eschewed the romantic and flowery style of certain popular histories of his day and instead hoped to produce fact-based and definitive histories of the Latter-day Saint movement. Jenson's career ended before he could drink deeply from the skepticism of postmodernist scholars and their challenge to the definitive claims of "scientific" history. For Jenson, the sources he gathered made historical events absolutely discernible.

While Jenson's work lacked analytical heft, he was not out of place in the field until much later in his career, two decades into the twentieth century, when professional historians began to achieve prominence in Utah. His newspaper columns on historical subjects were widely read, and his public lectures were well attended. Jenson was emblematic of the local historian who performed many roles. He gathered, organized, and compiled historical data but also contextualized it for the Latter-day Saint public.

His efforts made his presence irreversible in the developing Latter-day Saint archive. He obsessively gathered records to add to the Church Historian's Office the world over, but this was according to his own determination on what qualified as historical and worth keeping. Jenson sought the names of local ecclesiastical leaders, dates of important events, the founding details of Latter-day Saint settlements, and church ordinance data, to name a few. He then culled the data from these sources to produce manuscript histories, adding another layer of his historical perspective to histories presented as comprehensive, complete, and reliable. Jenson, of course, was careful in verifying historical facts, but he wrote and gathered from the perspective of a Danish immigrant convert, a journalist-turned-historian, and a defender of the faith. Jenson feared historical silences—the silence of the faithful Latter-day Saint who, without learning and retelling the true story of the church, would be influenced by the church's critics, and the silence of the historical record if documents went missing or remained ungathered. His perspective also did little to resolve other silences. His histories were often male-centered, absent of details about indigenous populations, and short on church history subjects seen as controversial, all tendencies that his contemporaries were also not immune to.

The tasks of writing a complete church history and improving church record keeping were not easy, since the process for doing so relied generally on untrained volunteer labor. Jenson's attempts to systematize ecclesiastical record keeping were met with breakthroughs and disappointments. Yet, he initiated a slow administrative modernization over the course of his four decades as Assistant Church Historian, a position he was appointed to in 1897. By the end of Jenson's life, local church clerks sent annual histories to church headquarters in Salt Lake City and most domestic ecclesiastical units followed standardized guidelines for recording ordinance and priesthood ordination data as well as other historical facts. While Jenson continued to lament shortcomings in Latter-day Saint record keeping until late in his life, it was his advocacy and persistence that fixed historical record keeping as a critical duty for faithful Latter-day Saints. Such routinization led to the preservation of volumes of historical data that would have been lost to time if not for Jenson's foresight at a time when church administration often had other priorities.

Though Jenson saw himself as on the church's errand, others struggled to see him similarly; separating his histories from the personality that produced them was a challenge. The passion and zeal he sometimes displayed in his calls for improved record keeping stemmed from a deeper, spiritual understanding of what it meant to be a record keeper. He believed Latter-day Saint doctrine supported the notion of a parallel record in heaven: "Whatsoever you record on earth shall be recorded in heaven, and whatsoever you do not record on earth shall not be recorded in heaven."[12] Thus, for Jenson, record keeping ideally was a community project uniting Latter-day Saints both past and present. Creating a complete historical record was a race against time, as early documents were eroding and the memories of the founding generation of the church were expiring with their aging authors. Jenson's historical project was ultimately about recovering memory and narrative and was a broad, spiritual endeavor to offer an eternal record of the restored gospel of Jesus Christ as an ultimate accounting to God. Such a belief shaped his perception of his calling; he felt he possessed a divine mandate to produce a history of the Latter-day Saint people that would forever influence how they viewed their religious heritage.

To Jenson's recurring disappointment, the position of Assistant Church Historian was a general-officer station that lacked any formal ecclesiastical authority. For much of his career, Jenson agitated for improved standing, authority, respect, and resources from his General Authority colleagues. As church administration expanded, modernized, and grew in its bureaucratic layers, Jenson felt increasingly removed from the day-to-day decisions of his ecclesiastical superiors. He held dear his friends in the church's hierarchy and asked a lot of them—Apostle Erastus Snow, Apostle and Church Historian Franklin D. Richards, President Joseph F. Smith, and First Presidency Counselor and Church Historian Anthon H. Lund.[13] Jenson's allies within church administration proved invaluable in steadying his emotions in the Historian's Office, though he nearly quit multiple times. He rubbed shoulders with and occasionally upset or challenged some of the central characters of the twentieth-century church. Jenson's life and career crescendoed with, moved against, and sometimes deflated with the concerns, challenges, priorities, and decisions of church leaders.

Ultimately unbordered and curious, Jenson was comfortable pushing to new frontiers. Church leaders knew he did better on the road than he did at home, and Jenson enjoyed playing the role of a pilgrim to new lands. During his two world tours as a representative of the Historian's Office, he recovered the records of the establishment of the gospel in missions around the world. Jenson hoped to render the peoples, places, and events he documented visible to his superiors and to church members. His frequent travels on behalf of church history—covering over one million miles by the end of his life—transformed Jenson into a global representative of the church. By his tally, from the documents he gathered, he compiled and wrote, with the assistance of the Historian's Office staff, 850 volumes of manuscript history, which were subsequently filed at the Historian's Office. Jenson was a forerunner to an increasingly global church, turning the church's attention to its people abroad and recovering memories that otherwise may have been lost to time.

Jenson's Prophetic Legacy

In his imagination, Jenson assumed a role just below the prophets and spotted parallels between the visionary role of seer and that of a historian. When he published his autobiography, condensed from his voluminous journals, he viewed himself as similar to the Book of Mormon prophets Mormon and Moroni, the primary abridgers of that sacred text.[14] We give Jenson many titles in the chapters that follow, but perhaps he would have been more inclined toward ones he used to describe himself: dreamer, creator, and poet. "I am impressed with the thought that certain spirits were selected to come down and mingle with these leaders and rulers in mortality as poets and historians to record the work to be done by these great and noble ones," he wrote in his last published book, *Encyclopedic History of the Church* (1941).[15]

Jenson desired to see ahead and write history to be used by future generations. He thought of himself as akin to Abel, of whom the Apostle Paul remarked "He being dead yet speaketh."[16] At the 1930 general conference, in the church's centennial year, he similarly spoke on the prophetic legacy of the faithful historian in what became his final conference address: "There are many things that a real historian can see and understand which perhaps are not generally seen and comprehended by his contemporaries, but which will be better understood and appreciated by future generations—perhaps hundreds of years hence. Some of us, pioneers in new fields, must necessarily live ahead of our time, in order to accomplish work in the interest of yet unborn millions."[17]

As Jenson prepared to make his publicized flight above the Mormon Trail in 1934, the local *Omaha Bee-News* published a portrait of a smiling, aged Jenson under the headline "Oxen Driver Will Fly."[18] The Pioneer Day flight proved an apt metaphor for Jenson's historical career. His rags-to-riches life had come full circle. An unassuming Danish immigrant with the dream of a literary career had been carried to the Great Basin on the promises of Zion. Since then, he had done more to fill in the institutional record of the globalizing church than any other person in history. Self-taught, determined, and restless, Jenson felt he was always one step ahead of institutional priorities and a faithful steward of the burden and blessing of the historian's perspective. And on that Pioneer Day, he marveled at the familiar trail of his youth while thousands of feet in the air. He cherished the Latter-day Saint past from a broader vantage point, one unseen by many of his fellow church members.

1 Danish American Emigrant

The lush pastoral landscape of Denmark was ablaze with political and social change by December 11, 1850, when Andreas Jensen was born in the small rural parish of Torslev, outside of Hjørring, in the North Jutland region of Denmark. Despite the national transformation underway, the parish of Jenson's birth still bore the longtime markers of his Danish ancestry—it was impoverished, agrarian, and inconsequential to elite Scandinavian society. Jenson described his forebears as "hard working people—tillers of the soil—with honest and determined traits."[1] Agrarian reforms in the late eighteenth century had restructured Denmark's traditional class system, weakening the feudal arrangements that had exploited the Danish peasantry for centuries. Private farm ownership offered some the opportunity to move into the newly forged middle class. Still, a majority of Danish society remained immobilized in the peasantry, conscripted as either itinerant or tenant farm laborers and held at the mercy of private farmers or large landholders. As reforms slowly disrupted agrarian villages—the traditional social and cultural centers of Danish society—the geographic and economic divide between the peasantry and the upper classes widened.[2] Jenson's immediate family struggled to navigate this transforming world of nineteenth-century Denmark.

Jenson's father, Christian Jensen, was born into a life with "slim opportunities" to "accumulate means, or even to become comfortable in life."[3] One of eight children born to Jens Jakobsen and Johanne Andersdatter, Christian fell into the cycle of poverty common to the Danish peasant class. Andrew Jenson's paternal grandfather was an anxious nomad who failed to retain claim on any family land, leaving his posterity essentially "penniless" and in search of work. Christian, thus, had to work at a young age to offset his father's struggles.[4] Other branches of his extended family were able to climb in status, but Christian's immediate family remained on the lowest rung of the social, political, and economic ladder. The financial situation of Andrew Jenson's mother, Kirsten Andersdatter was no different.[5] Her parents, Anders Christensen and Inger Marie Pedersdatter, lacked the means to fully support a family, so Kirsten began working young for meager wages. Christian labored as a carpenter "on a large estate or farm known as Haven, in the parish of Hørby," where he met Kirsten, who worked as a maid on the estate.[6] The two were married in the Danish Lutheran Church in December 1848 and settled on a small farm on the estate of Ormholt in Torslev.

Andrew Jenson reflected on his birthplace in his memoir: "It consisted of a house with two or three rooms, and was surrounded by a few acres of land, upon which a cow and a few sheep could be kept, while some of the land, if cultivated with care, was capable of producing rye, oats, and potatoes. The house was situated in a snug little vale running east and west with an average width of about 100 yards, the west end terminating in a mill point which occupied a portion of another narrow vale running north and south." Encompassing "meadow land which looked green and lovely during the summer months," the pastoral setting of Jenson's early childhood would have appeared idyllic if not for the family's financial struggles.[7]

The prospect of running an independent farm was a dream held by most Danish peasants, but reality often fell short of expectations, a fact that Christian and Kirsten's young family soon found to be true. The land at Ormholt was not productive enough to support the family, forcing Christian to hire out as a farmhand to his wealthier neighbors. Jenson recalled: "This was a hard experience for father whose natural abilities ran in the mechanical direction, and hired hands on these farms were put to the hardest kind of manual labor."[8]

To add to the family's financial troubles, Jenson's father was conscripted by the Danish army in August 1850 to fight in the First Schleswig War (or Three Years' War). Inspired by revolution in France, the economically strategic southern duchies of Schleswig and Holstein rebelled against the Danish crown. Ethnic Germans predominated in Schleswig and Holstein and sought a closer affiliation with the neighboring German confederation. The war was nearing its end when Christian was called away to Fredericia, in southeastern Jutland, to join the Danish forces. After Denmark's victory, with national pride at a near fever pitch, Christian returned home on December 23 to find Kirsten had given birth to a second son, Andrew.[9]

Weeks after their son's birth, Christian and Kirsten took Andrew to the local Lutheran church to have him christened.[10] The Jensen family's roots in the Danish Lutheran Church went back generations, as they did for most native Danes. Ever since the Protestant Reformation, which had swept across Catholic Europe in the sixteenth century, the Danish state had maintained a firm alliance with the Lutheran tradition. For the next three centuries, Lutheranism was sovereign on

Danish soil. Denmark's monarch reigned as head of state and head of church.[11] Church attendance and confirmation were generally required. Clergymen also occupied dual roles as ecclesiastical leaders and local magistrates who enforced the will of the state. Danish citizens who converted to a new religion were forced to forfeit their property and were banished from the country.[12] With most facets of life structured by the Danish Lutheran Church, newcomers to Denmark's religious scene were not just threats to political, social, and cultural norms, but to national identity and tradition.[13]

The First Latter-day Saint Missionaries in Denmark

By the time Apostle Erastus Snow began preaching in Copenhagen, Denmark, with missionaries John E. Forsgren, Peter O. Hansen, and George P. Dykes in June 1850, recent political reforms suggested that a new religious plurality might challenge the homogenous Lutheran establishment in Denmark.[14] Two years before the arrival of Latter-day Saint missionaries in Denmark, political forces in favor of liberal reforms replaced Denmark's absolutist monarchy with a bicameral parliamentary system. The reforms culminated in the 1849 June Constitution, which included provisions that opened the door for religious plurality in Denmark.[15] In theory, Snow and his missionary companions arrived at a fortuitous moment in Danish national history, but Danish culture proved to be somewhat impervious to religious pluralism. The new constitution remained equivocal on protections for religious freedom and failed to sever state ties with the Danish Lutheran Church. Instead, the state church was rebranded as Folkekirken (lit., People's church), and an officially appointed minister for church affairs remained influential in the new government.[16] Belonging to the People's Church ensured one was seen as a proud Danish citizen; conversion to another faith, while technically legal, moved a person outside of the boundaries of Danish respectability.[17]

The Latter-day Saint faith caught on quickly in some regions of Denmark, sparking both fear and resentment among locals.[18] To Danes immersed in the Christian tradition of the Old World, Latter-day Saint missionaries were foreign invaders from the New World who sought to challenge their established brand of Christianity. In the absence of specific laws supporting religious freedom, local government authorities, clergymen, and police continued to enforce old legal restrictions on public worship and proselytizing.[19] But through private, inconspicuous meetings, the missionaries gained converts. By August 1850, twenty-six Danes, mostly Baptists, had been baptized.[20] Just a year later, Latter-day Saints in Denmark numbered around 260.[21]

Part of the early success of Snow and his group of missionaries grew out of the excitement their message stirred among the peasant class. While daily life for the rural peasantry in Denmark still revolved significantly around the local Lutheran parish, the prospect of religious freedom opened a new avenue for subverting Denmark's traditional social hierarchy.[22] These missionaries offered a fresh form of antiauthoritarian expression, one that empowered the peasantry to be participants in the restoration of "true" Christianity. This new religion had the potential to challenge the social hierarchy by subverting the state-supported Folkekirken, the religion of the powerful elites. In this way, the spread of the Latter-day Saint faith across Denmark exacerbated a national identity crisis for the modernizing Danish state.

Jenson and the Early Church in Denmark

Surrounded by social and political change, Andrew Jenson's family heard the message of the Latter-day Saint missionaries near Vendsyssel in 1854. Outside of Copenhagen, northern Jutland proved quite fruitful for converts, in part, according to missionary reports, because of the "liberality, kindness, and freedom of spirit" that prevailed.[23] In Aalborg, to the south, Latter-day Saint missionary Christian Madsen reported success among the region's rural lower class: "The country people, who are almost the only ones to receive the Gospel here, furnish themselves with food and clothing, with an average expenditure of about *two pence* daily for each individual." Despite widespread poverty, the people were "contented, and willingly divide[d] their scanty means, being kind, warm-hearted, devoted, obedient, and faithful."[24] The missionaries preached and held meetings in any space that would accommodate them, often in private homes, barns, or other farm structures.

It was in this environment that Andrew Jenson's parents "were won for 'Mormonism.'"[25] Elder Christen Hansen baptized Jenson's mother and father in December 1854. The Latter-day Saint church in the Vendsyssel Conference had grown significantly throughout that year. At the time of the Jensens' conversion, the conference had eight branches, 257 members, and ten missionaries laboring in the region.[26] The next year, Christian Jensen was ordained to the office of a deacon in the Aaronic Priesthood and called to serve in the Taars Branch.[27] The family moved a few miles away in fall 1856, and in the first part of 1857, Jenson's father took on several local church leadership positions. Christian presided over the Hørmested Branch of the Vendsyssel Conference beginning in March 1857 and after three months became president of the Skjæve Branch.[28] In October 1857, he received a mission call to Læsø, an island in the Kattegat, where he evangelized by offering his services repairing clocks, a trade he learned after an injury left him unable to perform farm labor.[29] As he worked, he would "introduce religion and commence explaining the principles of the gospel to the household." In two years of intermittent preaching on the island, Christian not only baptized the island's inaugural converts but also organized the first congregation, the Byrum Branch, in March 1859. He served as president of the branch until the conclusion of his mission in September 1859.[30]

Though the young Andrew Jenson was surrounded by reminders of his Lutheran roots, including while he was at school, he anticipated the day he could formally join his parents in their faith.[31] When Jenson turned eight, the age appointed by Latter-day Saint scripture for adherents to be baptized, no priesthood holders were in the immediate vicinity of his home to perform the ordinance. Christian was still away on a mission, forcing Jenson to wait until missionaries returned to the area in February 1859, two months after his birthday, to be baptized.[32]

The Jensen family members were active participants in the Latter-day Saint church in Denmark, often traveling long miles to hear from visiting church leaders from Utah. As he grew up, he also traveled with his father to conference meetings, and on August 25, 1861, Jenson heard apostles for the first time—Elders Amasa M. Lyman and Charles C. Rich—at a meeting in the Tidemandsholm, Taars, parish.[33] On that occasion, Lyman issued a pointed reminder to the Danish Saints: "In your associations you must cultivate a spirit of forbearance. . . . If you live as Saints and seek to save men . . . it will make a favourable impression on all good men; it will burst asunder the clouds of prejudice that are between us and them."[34]

Lyman's sermon was perhaps an attempt to foster a truce between new converts and the agitated Lutheran establishment. Latter-day Saint missionaries used Lutheran doctrine to draw distinctions between it and their restoration message, and Danish parishioners heard repeatedly from missionaries that their country was locked in the grips of a corrupted brand of Christianity and in need of rescue. Lyman's advice to forge a friendship with their fellow Christians came after nearly a decade of public outcry, verbal and written polemics, disrupted meetings, and occasional violence against the Latter-day Saints. The Lutheran clergy had induced pledges not to materially assist Latter-day Saint missionaries, printed attacks against the church in local newspapers, and circulated tracts quoting disenchanted converts who had already emigrated. In addition, they disrupted Latter-day Saint meetings and pulled financial support from parishes whose members were baptized into the Latter-day Saint faith. Some clergymen also reevaluated and recommitted to pastoral outreach to counteract the influence of Latter-day Saint missionaries.[35] Danish Latter-day Saints knew they were being watched closely by their curious and anxious Lutheran countrymen, who believed their traditional Christian ritual and doctrine were under assault.

The simmering religious conflict touched the daily life of the Jensen family on a few occasions. Although attending public school was mandatory for students between ages seven and fourteen, Danish parents could educate their children at home with some restrictions. Like many other Latter-day Saint converts, Jenson's parents opted to educate their three sons at home because of conflict with instructors and students at the local parish schools.[36] Arguments between Jenson's parents and the local instructor in Trye centered predictably "on points of religion." Jenson said that the educator "would denounce Joseph Smith and 'Mormonism' in a way that ill befitted a man of education and one who called himself a gentleman." In opting to teach their children at home, Jenson's parents sought to protect them from those who would "poison their minds against 'Mormonism.'"[37]

Jenson did end up attending the Trye village school during the winter of 1862–63 and passed his spring examination.[38] Young Jenson was a devoted student who possessed a natural interest in learning—"since my earliest recollection," he noted, "I have been of a studious disposition." He also reported that his "own aptitude to learn and advance in the common rudiments of education without going to school somewhat astonished the examiners as I could sometimes answer questions that other and older students attending school regularly could not comprehend at all." His mother would occasionally become upset with him for always having his nose in a book. Jenson wrote, "The fact is that I was fond of studying and acquiring knowledge, and when I had learned to read, my greatest desire was to obtain books from which to glean further information."[39]

Having reached the head of his class, he received a certificate saying that he could discontinue his studies. But, since Jenson's older brother, Jens, needed another year of schooling, it was agreed that Jenson would attend school for another winter. According to Jenson, classmates "would often torment and abuse us because we were 'Mormons,' and many a little rumpus did I have with my schoolmates because I was a Mormon, as I would occasionally defend myself against their attacks, and retaliate." Despite these occasional fights, Jenson apparently had no lasting ill will toward his classmates: "I loved my studies and had become somewhat attached to the schoolteacher and my schoolmates." He concluded his formal educational training in 1864.[40]

Jenson's inclination toward history and impulse to defend the church were born from his childhood education at home and in the Lutheran parish. He frequently read articles from the Scandinavian Mission periodical, *Skandinaviens Stjerne*. Reading these Danish-language articles piqued his interest in Latter-day Saint history. This initial exposure to history prompted him to memorize "as many dates as possible, from which [he] subsequently derived much satisfaction when matters pertaining to Church history would be discussed in [his] presence." With little financial means, the Jensen family owned only a few books outside of scripture. Jenson recalled having "a Bible, a Book of Mormon and other Church works in the house," which he "read with interest." He also noted being intrigued by the historical parts of the Bible and the other Latter-day

Saint scripture. As a young man he created a Bible chronology before he knew that such a thing as a Bible timeline existed. When he compared his work with that of other scholars, he "was pleased to discover that [his] feeble effort at chronology making was in the main correct." When he was thirteen, he began a journal. Jenson was later somewhat dismissive of his early musings, saying that "most of these notes were not important," but he did say that "they pointed toward the future historian."[41]

As Jenson matured in his faith, the pressure to immigrate to "Zion," which Latter-day Saints had established in the American West, increased. In September 1862, Jenson traveled twenty-five miles from home with his father to attend a church conference at Aalborg. The General Authorities in attendance included Apostle George Q. Cannon, who was then president of the European Mission, and missionaries from Utah, including Joseph F. Smith.[42] This was the first time Jenson saw Smith, a future church president and eventual friend and in-law. Smith gave a short address, but it was the words of Cannon that were the most notable of the Aalborg conference. "The nations of Christendom are waxing strong in iniquity and corruption," he told the congregation through a translator. "The Lord will in his just wrath and judgment sweep the earth of wickedness, and dash the nations to pieces." The only way for the righteous to avoid this destruction was to join with the Latter-day Saints, who were, according to Cannon, "united in that love and confidence."[43] The apocalyptic rhetoric from Latter-day Saint leaders, commonplace also in Utah Territory during this period, only heightened the urgency felt among Danish converts, including the Jensen family, to gather to the valleys of Utah Territory.

Preparing to Leave for Zion

In February 1864, Prussian forces crossed the border into the Danish duchy of Schleswig in the country's southern region, supporting German occupiers who had already assumed control of the neighboring duchy of Holstein. Though the Danish military had fended off German and Prussian forces years earlier (1848–52), they failed to repel invasion on this occasion. By August 1864, the Danish government, with the king of Denmark, Christian IX, had surrendered the duchies of Schleswig, Holstein, and Lauenburg to Prussia and Austria, effectively ending Danish rule over that region. The defeat was devastating to Danes living among the ethnic Germans in the region, and many elected to emigrate. Over the next forty years, an estimated sixty thousand people left northern Schleswig, many heading for the United States.[44]

According to Jenson, the war "caused the deepest consternation throughout Denmark" and significantly impacted the daily lives of Jenson and his family. Early in the war, as Danish forces retreated before the Austrian army, Jenson's uncle (his mother's brother) Niels Christian Andersen died in battle.[45] The personal loss was made worse by the brief Prussian occupation of North Jutland. Throughout the later portion of the war, Prussian and Austrian officials exacted heavy taxes on the Danish people to pay their war debts. Jenson, at the age of fourteen, was hired to collect the war taxes in his home district. "While this tax collecting was an unpleasant task for a boy loyal to his country," Jenson remarked, "I always felt a little proud to think that I was trusted so early in life with considerable sums of money."[46]

The sweeping defeat of the Danish army tempered much of the nationalistic fervor that had come in the wake of the June Constitution and its liberal reforms. Denmark ceded 40 percent of its territory to Prussia and Austria, along with 30 percent of its population. The large concessions were a major blow to Denmark's already declining influence on the world stage and prompted a nationwide discussion on what composed a national identity for the Danish people.[47]

Amid these political and diplomatic challenges, Denmark's economy diversified and expanded. Denmark was beginning to urbanize, creating new job opportunities for Danes willing to abandon their agrarian roots. Still, the growing economy failed to keep pace with demographic changes and the nation's rapidly growing population, leaving a sizable class of landless laborers forced to travel the countryside looking for work.[48] Jenson's father Christian's employment as a clock repairer was not always steady, leaving the financial situation of the family unpredictable.[49] Jenson wrote: "Father's lameness returned and our financial circumstances became more trying, so that my parents could not afford to keep me at home. Hence, in the summer of 1861 I had my first experience in serving other people, being engaged to herd sheep on the neighboring estate of Riis. For my season's work I received three Danish rigsdaler (less than two dollars American money)."[50]

In 1864, Christian moved to the seaport town of Sæby, where he established himself as a skilled watchmaker; his wife, Kirsten, and two-year-old son, Joseph, eventually joined him. As Christian's reputation and business grew, he was able to amass enough money to cover the expenses of his household and to begin to save for his family's emigration, but fourteen-year-old Andrew Jenson and his older brother, fifteen-year-old Jens, still had to work to support themselves and the family.[51] After watching the aftermath of his father's injury, Jenson refused to rejoin other poorly compensated, landless farm laborers. He determined to find new opportunities to support himself. Jenson recalled that he possessed "a natural desire to travel" and began selling "tin wares and other small articles needed by the peasantry." In comparison to farming, this work was "more agreeable and withal more profitable" to him. Jenson soon became proficient in selling pictures created by a German lithograph company. He "learned to associate freely with the people" and "earned considerably more means than [he] used for [his] traveling expenses," which allowed him to begin saving for his personal immigration to Utah.[52]

The vast American West appealed even to those Danes who did not convert to the church, and the outmigration from Denmark in the latter half of the nineteenth century was substantial. They were fed reports of available and affordable land from fellow countrymen who had immigrated to the United States in search of a more profitable life. Included among the immigrants was a sizable number of the landless farmers, who sailed to America, buoyed by promises of cheap land. The US Homestead Act of 1862 offered prospective settlers the chance to own land in the West for a minimal fee, feeding the dreams of immigrants who had lost hope for such a prospect in their crowded homelands. Forty-three percent of Danish immigrants to America in the second half of the nineteenth century belonged to the non-land-owning laborer class. During the 1870s and 1880s, 120,000 Danes left for the States. The bulk of those who chose to leave Denmark never ventured as far west as the Latter-day Saint immigrants. Most, including some disaffected Danish Saints, settled in the midwestern United States.[53] For Latter-day Saint converts in Denmark, however, the allure of Zion shifted their sights toward Utah Territory. Once the church was established in the Intermountain West, the Latter-day Saints invited all converts across America, Europe, and elsewhere to join them.

Danish Saints followed developments in Zion closely through reports in *Skandinaviens Stjerne*.[54] Among the *Stjerne*'s pages were translations of the First Presidency's general epistles, which offered firsthand accounts of settlement in the US West. Outside of the providential boosterism that sometimes filled the epistles were details of Indian raids, illnesses, harsh weather, food and supply shortages in the Great Basin, and decisions made by the territorial legislature and the US government.[55] The *Stjerne* offered a primer on the hardships and demands of establishing a frontier settlement in the American West and connected Danish Latter-day Saints to the body of church members gathering in the Utah valleys.[56]

The first company of Danish converts to heed the call to gather to Zion left Denmark in early 1852. After their arrival in the Salt Lake Valley, the *Stjerne* reported: "They are all alive and well satisfied and they urge their friends to follow them."[57] The information that flowed across the Atlantic from Utah Territory often romanticized the Latter-day Saint gathering.[58] Land in Zion was depicted as being fruitful, plentiful, and obtainable. As summarized by P. C. S. Kragskov to the readers of the *Stjerne*, the valley held "the healthiest air, the clearest water" and provided "the best place for the Saints I have ever seen. . . . But the greatest joy for me is that I can see and hear prophets and apostles Sunday after Sunday who teach us Christ's pure gospel."[59] The refrains of Zion colored the accounts of Danish immigrants and often obscured the harsher realities of frontier life.

Enthusiastic reports from the Salt Lake Valley also infused the gathering with a millenarian sense of urgency. With wars, dissensions, sicknesses, and "divisions among professing Christian parties," the Second Coming was "near at hand."[60] The only place where Latter-day Saints could find refuge and the complete ordinances for salvation and exaltation was in Utah Territory. The First Presidency declared, "Gather yourselves together; come home!"[61] From 1850 to 1905, over twelve thousand of the approximately twenty-three thousand Danes who converted to the church immigrated to Utah.[62]

The Jensen family absorbed the excitement and prophetic counsel to gather to the Salt Lake Valley. Entering his sixteenth year, on New Year's Day in 1866 Andrew Jenson was filled "with hope for the future, and . . . fully expected to see the land of America before another New Year's Day." He had saved enough money to take him "to the frontiers in America."[63] The expense of overseas and overland travel weighed heavily on larger families. Costs were somewhat more manageable for solo travelers: about $75 to $100 (150 to 200 rigsdaler) would cover travel from Copenhagen to Salt Lake City. But multiplied across a family, the cost of traveling to Zion was steep.

Occasionally, families divided up or postponed emigration until a later date. In the case of the Jensen family, the eldest son, Jens, remained behind until he could earn enough money to follow the family. Andrew and the rest of his family (his father, mother, and younger brother) decided to "emigrate to Utah at once."[64] The average cost for steamship passage was approximately $30 for adults, and train fare from New York or Philadelphia to the staging outpost on the frontier was another $12 to $14.[65] Thus, the cost of Jenson's travel to the frontier town of Wyoming, Nebraska, was about $42 (82 rigsdaler). Short about 5 rigsdaler, Jenson borrowed the remainder of his fare from his brother Jens, with the promise that he would send money from Utah Territory as soon as he was employed.[66]

For each Latter-day Saint emigrant, explaining the decision to leave Denmark to Lutheran family members was challenging. Such a decision often left Danish Latter-day Saints socially isolated in their homeland. The Danish relatives and friends of Jenson and his family resented their religious switch and subsequent decision to immigrate to the United States. The Jensen family, however, "rejoiced exceedingly, and," according to Jenson, "it seemed no great sacrifice to us to leave our native land, relatives, and friends to go to the gathering place of the saints." Despite the best efforts of his parents and siblings, none of Jenson's relatives was interested in hearing their testimonies of the church but rather, wrote Jenson, they "looked upon us as fools because we had joined so unpopular a sect as the 'Mormons.'" Jenson posited that much of his family's resistance derived from their affluence. While Jenson watched others in his lower economic class warmly accept missionaries, his "wealthier relatives rejected the gospel because they had too much of this world's goods." Others were too secular, and others still "loved the ways of the world too much to repent of their sins."[67]

The family's impending emigration, while filled with anticipation and anxiety, was neither improvised nor solitary. By 1866, church leaders had installed infrastructure on either side of the Atlantic to aid immigrant converts and to remedy the common pitfalls previous immigrants to the United States had experienced. The system had been fine-tuned two decades before as scores of British converts traveled to America. This system included traveling in companies, which mitigated travel costs by allowing the emigrants to charter transportation. Each company was led by a Latter-day Saint familiar with the emigrant route, who could provide guidance and leadership along the way.[68] Cash shortages were offset by assets from the Perpetual Emigrating Fund, a communal trust authorized by Brigham Young in 1849 to assist in bringing impoverished Latter-day Saints to the Salt Lake Valley.[69] Every stage of the journey to the United States was planned for and executed with precision by missionaries in Denmark who also acted as emigration agents.[70]

Traveling to Zion

Christian, Kirsten, Andrew, and Joseph Jensen departed from the city of Sæby on May 8, 1866, following the well-trodden course of previous Danish Latter-day Saint emigrants. "Bright and early in the morning," Jenson recalled, "a one-horse vehicle driven by a good natured old farmer, made its way slowly toward the city of Aalborg, distant about thirty English miles. . . . Our baggage consisted of the usual emigrant equipment averaging about one hundred pounds to each person." The Jensens' first destination, Aalborg, was the appointed gathering place for Latter-day Saints from the Aalborg and Vendsyssel Conferences. While at Aalborg, Jenson's family, with the rest of the emigrants from Vendsyssel, lived in a hired hall. Emigrants continued to gather throughout the week, their number reaching almost two hundred.[71]

Meetings were held in Aalborg to further orient Jenson and the other Latter-day Saints on the journey ahead of them. On May 16, they departed on the SS *Dania* to join with Latter-day Saints from other conferences in Copenhagen, where they arrived the next day. Life in the city of approximately 180,000 people was foreign to the life Jenson knew in the parish villages of Vendsyssel. "I was too deeply interested in the grandeur of the city to remain quietly in one place," Jenson wrote, "and so, notwithstanding the protests of my parents, I walked all about the city, promenaded on the ramparts, visited the principal squares and churches and enjoyed myself immensely."[72]

The immigrating party soon proceeded from Copenhagen to the German city of Kiel, where Jenson again disembarked and explored "different parts of the city with its beautiful parks and gardens." The group then traveled to Altona on the Elbe by rail (Jenson's first railroad journey) before heading to the emigration house in the adjacent city of Hamburg, the last leg of their European journey. Insatiably curious, Jenson ventured into Hamburg, where he got lost, only returning to the emigration house with "considerable difficulty."[73] In Hamburg, the company spent a few days preparing for their Atlantic voyage. They boarded their sailing vessel, an English packet called the SS *Kenilworth*, with two decks that had been fitted with bunks to accommodate passengers. At the time of Jenson's departure on May 25, 1866, the immigrant travelers onboard had increased to 684.[74] The Latter-day Saint company consisted of forty-two divisions, each overseen by a president, who received and distributed provisions to the families in their care, presided over evening and morning prayers, and enforced cleanliness and order.[75]

Although ships carrying emigrants from continental Europe usually followed a course through the English Channel, the *Kenilworth* traveled north around Scotland. Day-to-day life aboard the ship proved tedious. Jenson recorded his daily routine: "At 6 o'clock in the morning we arose at the signal of the bugle and washed ourselves, and soon afterwards ate breakfast. . . . At 8 A.M. prayers were held in each district by itself. At 11:30 A.M. we ate dinner, which generally consisted of good and solid food. After dinner we were generally permitted to amuse ourselves by dancing or engaging in diverse plays on the deck in order to keep the humor, and counteract the tediousness which is natural in so long a voyage."[76]

Though his account of nineteenth-century immigrant travel suggests it was pleasant, the voyage resulted in tragedy for some. Jenson tallied a dozen or so deaths while the company crossed the Atlantic, most of them infants and children. While the deaths were disturbing for immigrants far from home, many also witnessed other, more celebratory life events. On the *Kenilworth*, for example, at least two children were born and seven marriages performed.[77]

After a journey of nearly two months, the European company finally spotted the shores of Long Island, New York, on July 15, 1866. Relief and exuberance spread throughout the ship. "Perhaps only those who for weeks and months have been tossed about upon the face of a troubled sea can appreciate the pleasure of seeing land again," Jenson remarked. The site of the American continent filled the immigrants with renewed "hope for a good future." As Long Island came into view, the vivid descriptions of the United States imagined by the seekers of Zion for the first time became real. "To us Latter-day Saints the first sight of the coast of America had even more than ordinary significance, as this was the land of promise, the land of Joseph, about which we had sung and talked for many years, before beholding it," Jenson wrote.[78]

The *Kenilworth* cast anchor off Staten Island, and the following day a doctor came aboard to screen for contagious diseases, after which the Jensen family disembarked for Castle Garden, on the south end of Manhattan Island.[79] A steamship then transported the Jensen family and their fellow immigrants to New Haven, Connecticut, where they boarded a train, eventually making their way to Quincy, Illinois.[80]

A ferry transported Jenson's company across the Mississippi River to the Missouri shore, where the company of immigrants witnessed firsthand the hostility some Missourians harbored against the Latter-day Saints. Locals congregated at stations, eager to catch a peek at the allegedly deluded and impoverished converts heading to the Latter-day Saint kingdom in the West: "Some of the worst men in the crowd gave the impression by their movements that they would have taken delight in treating us similar to the treatment that was given our coreligionists years ago. The conductor of our train appeared to be one of our bitter enemies. In starting the train and in quickening or lessening speed he treated us to such jerks and violent shocks as ordinarily are experienced only on freight trains. Fortunately, none of us were seriously hurt, but some of our more delicate women were threatened with nervous breakdowns."[81]

The Jensen family eventually arrived at St. Joseph, Missouri—the last stop on their ten-day railroad journey covering seventeen hundred miles. There they boarded the steamboat *Denver* and traveled up the Missouri River to the Territory of Nebraska, where Latter-day Saints were being outfitted for their westward trip across the plains.[82] Jenson's family arrived near the village of Wyoming in Nebraska, on July 28, 1866.

Wagons, oxen, and teamsters sent from the Salt Lake Valley for the immigrating Saints had already been encamped at Wyoming for a number of days, awaiting their arrival. Six years earlier, in the final stages of the 1860 immigration season, church leaders decided to abandon one short-lived method for traveling across the western plains, handcarts, in favor of a new "down-and-back" system. With prices for provisions, wagons, and livestock steadily climbing in the Midwest, church leaders opted to send their own outfitted teams directly from the Salt Lake Valley to an established post on the plains. This new strategy limited the need for cash and reinforced self-sufficiency. The entire round-trip was made in one season; the expedition gathered in Salt Lake City in April and reached the outfitting post in July. From 1861 to 1868, nearly two thousand wagons were sent from the Salt Lake Valley to shuttle sixteen thousand European immigrants back to Utah.[83]

The Nebraska outfitting scene was an inspiring sight for the Jensens, who for the first time since their conversion felt surrounded by friends. "At Wyoming we could breathe the air of freedom more fully than upon any previous occasion since we commenced our journey," Jenson wrote. Everywhere around them the "hill-sides showed quite a camp, as the tents and family boweries were being pitched and erected by the weary pilgrims."[84] Here, the Jensens drew on church resources to restock their provisions for the final leg of their journey and awaited an opportunity to depart with one of the church wagon trains.

Jenson's family set out for the Salt Lake Valley on August 8, 1866, under the leadership of Captain Andrew H. Scott, with George M. Brown as their spiritual leader. Their wagon train had approximately three hundred emigrants from Britain, Norway, and Denmark, traveling in forty-nine wagons. Once Jenson acclimated to the physical challenges of trekking across the plains and mastered the skills of cooking on an open fire, he found life on the pioneer trail to be quite liberating and enjoyable.[85]

Scott and other company leaders frequently gave encouragement and instruction, which Brown interpreted for the Scandinavian-language-speaking emigrants. (By the time Jenson and his company arrived in the Salt Lake Valley, he claimed he was able to understand English well enough that he no longer needed a translator, though he could still hardly speak the language.)[86] The company traveled along the Oregon Trail before following the Mormon Trail into Utah Territory. Along the journey, Jenson marveled at their mostly positive interactions with Native Americans. "After we had subdued our fear and timidity," Jenson journaled, "they became the object of our greatest attention and curiosity and as they were a friendly band, a number of them soon appeared in our camp. Some of the young warriors entertained us by showing us their skill as marksmen with their arrows. Most of them were scantily clad, and some of the young boys were entirely naked, a feature which was rather shocking to us people from the north who had never seen anything like it before."[87]

Despite Jenson's positive experiences, the customary travails of the pioneer journey hit the Scott Company. Harsh, snowy weather strained the company's food and fuel supplies. Near the infamous Rocky Ridge in Wyoming, the company was stalled in six inches of snow in freezing temperatures. Eight oxen died, and fifty more were injured, prompting Scott to send a swift message to church leaders in Salt Lake City, notifying them of the hardships.[88] Just weeks before, Jenson had been bedridden with cholera and forced to ride in the back of a wagon for a few days.[89]

On October 7, 1866, the Scott Company finally reached the Salt Lake Valley via Parley's Canyon.[90] Hope and optimism returned to Jenson as it had for many other immigrants when they first spotted the Latter-day Saint stronghold. "Climbing a hill on the right, I obtained my first view of Salt Lake City," Jenson wrote. "It appeared grand and beautiful as it nestled in the full blaze of the afternoon sun. With my companions I almost shouted with joy at the realization of our fondest hearts desires. . . . Our dreams were about to be realized in entering the chief city of the Saints—the home of Prophets and Apostles."[91] For most immigrants, however, arriving in Zion did not complete their transition into their new world. Integration into Utah society would be a long process, one often rife with struggle and occasional disillusionment.

Life in Zion

The immigrants' first task in the Great Basin was to find a place to settle. For a few days, the Jensen family watched as members of their wagon train and others departed Salt Lake City for settlements to the south. Despite intentions to settle in Pleasant Grove, about thirty-five miles south of Salt Lake City, the family continued south to Ephraim, in Sanpete County, which had been largely settled by Scandinavians. Surrounded by fellow countrymen, Jenson found work tending livestock over the winter, but the family soon discovered that the entire region was embroiled in a war against a coalition of Native Americans, led by a band of Utes. Jenson's ranch work placed him close to what became known as the Black Hawk War, in which Native Americans countered settler attacks by plundering livestock.[92] The conflict, as well as the fragile physical health of Jenson's father, Christian, forced the family back to Pleasant Grove, where they lived in a small dugout before erecting an adobe home and orchard on an acre of land.[93]

The romanticized American West that had buoyed Jenson's hopeful expectations failed to materialize in the first years after his arrival. Instead, Jenson fell into an unpredictable and nomadic cycle of employment, characteristic of the immigrant experience in the West. To be sure, the West offered unmatched opportunities for social mobility, but achieving rapid prosperity was not the common experience. Migrant labor, often provided by immigrants, propped up the western economy and led to a concentration of wealth in the hands of a few, but new workers rarely enjoyed stable employment. As Jenson navigated the western working class, he found little difference between his early employment in his Danish homeland and his current American situation. Unskilled wage work was his lot, and he traveled the intermountain region looking for suitable employment to eke out a living and help support his family's new homestead.[94]

Jenson pursued several occupations as a frontiersman in Utah. He herded cows over the summer of 1867 but found the job "distasteful . . . tedious and irksome." He received payment in livestock and produce, of which he sold a portion for money to send to Denmark to support the immigration of his brother Jens.[95] In June 1868, Jenson joined seven other men as grade workers in Echo Canyon to complete a railroad contract that Brigham Young had negotiated with the Union Pacific in May 1868. The 150-mile track, part of the Transcontinental Railroad, would stretch from Echo Canyon to the Great Salt Lake and required five thousand workers to complete. Young hoped the contract would infuse Latter-day Saint communities with cash profits to pay off debts and stimulate the development of industries throughout the territory. The work seemed a safe bet for the now-seventeen-year-old Jenson, who joined other Latter-day Saint workers in a company that avoided the harsh and unprincipled conditions of other railroad encampments. Jenson and his fellow workers expected to earn within the range of $1.50 to $2.00 a day.[96] After finishing the initial contract, Jenson traveled throughout the region, hiring out for other rail jobs.[97]

When Jenson returned home, he found his family divided between two locations. His mother, Kirsten, and younger brother, Joseph, remained in Pleasant Grove in Utah Valley, but his father had elected to return to Ephraim in the Sanpete Valley after tensions there with the Native Americans had subsided. The move made Jenson's "family affairs . . . not very pleasant," and, as Jenson observed, "the best understanding did not exist between father and mother." Despite a trip to Sanpete County to petition his father's return, the family remained in separate towns except for a brief period of reconciliation.[98]

As the only consistent breadwinner in his family, Jenson continued to work in the rail camps to the north throughout 1869. He worked as a timber cutter initially, but with the Transcontinental Railroad nearly completed to its endpoint in Promontory, Utah, he found employment opportunities less consistently by April.

The challenges of manual labor in tough conditions also began to wear on him. At a Union Pacific Railroad camp, Jenson found that "drinking and fighting were matters of daily occurrence." He was "looked upon by some of the camp rowdies as an innocent 'Mormon' youth who knew not the ways of the world," but they respected him for it and "would consider it sin to do . . . harm" to him.[99] After a few lonely nights in the wilderness, supervising camp mules and horses, Jenson returned to the camp and was met by what could have been a fatal accident when a frightened horse broke his jaw with a kick, knocking him unconscious. Injured and unable to perform his normal tasks, he took on work as a camp cook.[100] In part because of his injury and the failure of his other contracts to pay out in a timely manner, Jenson eventually departed the railroad camps for the season penniless in August 1869. "And here I was on my way home without a single dollar on hand," Jenson wrote, "my clothes almost in rags, my toes sticking out of my shoes and a bandage around my head to protect the wound on my chin which had not entirely healed up yet. Was it any wonder then that I left Salt Lake City homeward bound with a heavy heart and very much ashamed and humiliated at the plight I was in." The journeyman lifestyle of the American West wore heavily on Jenson, yet he felt "the Lord had a work for [him] to do," which kept him from indulging in the normal activities of youth.[101]

Soon after returning to Pleasant Grove, Jenson was reunited with his older brother, Jens, who had finally immigrated from Denmark. The reunion lifted Jenson's spirits: "My adventures on the railroad and my association with men of the world had not changed my faith in 'Mormonism' or destroyed my confidence in the providence of the Lord. . . . My brother had also been faithful. . . . Hence to meet in Zion under these conditions sent a thrill of joy to our hearts."[102]

Anxious to make something more of his life and to demonstrate an ability to navigate adulthood, the restless Jenson determined to set out back across the plains to earn money in the East. His mother protested, but Jenson insisted.[103] He embarked on an adventure that would give him a better understanding of the general American experience, far away from Zion.

His search for employment took him through Wyoming and then on to Omaha, Nebraska. He presented himself as being capable at diverse frontier jobs, including masonry and saw work on ice blocks. At Omaha, he attempted work on a railway bridge spanning the Missouri River but found the frigid temperatures difficult to withstand, and, with both feet frostbitten, he resigned. Fearing his body would succumb to more challenging manual labor, Jenson resumed his pre-immigration business of selling lithographs. He sold his prints with some success in parts of Nebraska and Missouri until supplies ran short. He then acquired a job at Fort Leavenworth, a US Army installation in Kansas. His adventures during this period at times tested his moral resolve, though he later viewed them as an excellent tutelage in living faithfully as a Latter-day Saint. At one point, his non-Latter-day Saint companions at Fort Leavenworth duped the unsuspecting Jenson into entering a brothel, where he was solicited but quickly exited the establishment. On another occasion, Jenson entered a saloon with a group from the fort who intended to get him drunk. He reluctantly partook of a few rounds of beers before excusing himself and returning somewhat disoriented back to the fort. Navigating the hardscrabble frontier proved to be a challenging task for a young Latter-day Saint, but Jenson took pride in rejecting worldly influences.[104]

Jenson's experience at Leavenworth prompted him to turn his focus back westward with hopes of returning home. In Abilene, Kansas, he joined a group of cattle ranchers who were preparing to drive a herd west. The cattle drive took him as far as Corinne, just outside of Brigham City, in Utah Territory, where he purchased a horse to ride south to his home in Pleasant Grove.[105] In Jenson's estimation, his experience wandering the American frontier was pivotal to his future life as a solitary globetrotter and committed ambassador of the Latter-day Saint gospel.[106]

Jenson's itinerant lifestyle continued in 1872 as he sampled the various industries in Utah and the surrounding region. He tried his hand as a storekeeper, fisherman, smelter, and miner. The frequent rotation through jobs was partially the result of Jenson's restless spirit and curiosity but was also caused by his acute sense of responsibility for his family's welfare. With his father in Richfield, separated from the family, the task of building and maintaining the family's home and land in Pleasant Grove fell upon Jenson and his brothers and mother. Jenson sent home much of his wages immediately after collecting on his contracts, while his mother performed the hard labor of working the fields and harvesting crops. This arrangement was less than ideal for members of the Jensen family, who loathed the frequent separation and the unpredictability of harvests and the labor market.

The strain caused by his father's desertion matured Jenson faster than many of his peers around him. By June 1872, Jenson's parents had divorced and his father quickly remarried. Details on the split are scarce in Jenson's personal record, but it caused him severe heartache, especially since the family had left their homeland for Zion intact, with great anticipation for Utah's peaceful, spiritual, and hospitable conditions. In the midst of these challenges, Jenson, now twenty-two years of age, anticipated a missionary assignment.

A Mission Call to Denmark

The April 1873 general conference of the church was surrounded by the usual fanfare, as Latter-day Saints from around Utah Territory crowded the Salt Lake Tabernacle on the Temple Block to hear from church leaders. Among the customs of the conference proceedings, which were held semiannually, church members anticipated the calling of missionaries, who would be assigned their field of labor and sustained by the congregation. Missionary service was a rite of passage for many young Latter-day Saint men, and at this time calls could be issued to men both young and old, married and unmarried. The calls were often anticipated but not solicited. Jenson was prepared for such service: he spoke both Danish and English, had some means to support himself and his family, was an experienced traveler, and had no serious health problems, though at twenty-two he was on the younger end of the church's missionary force; the average age for Latter-day Saint missionaries in the 1870s was approximately forty.[107]

Jenson attended the 1873 general conference on April 8, when mission calls were issued to five men to serve in the Scandinavian mission.[108] Though he had anticipated a similar call, Jenson could not be called until he had formally become a US citizen. Citizenship was required to avoid being conscripted into the Danish army while serving there as a missionary. After receiving his US citizenship papers on April 9, the next day he went to the Endowment House in Salt Lake City, where he participated in the covenantal endowment ceremony, a sacred temple ordinance that most men received before serving missions.[109] Jenson's name was then put forth as a missionary to Scandinavia and presented for a sustaining vote at an adjourned session of general conference on May 3, 1873.[110]

Jenson followed in the footsteps of hundreds of other Scandinavian Latter-day Saints who had been called back to their native lands to serve as missionaries during this era. Church leaders hoped converts-turned-missionaries could capitalize on their kinship networks to bring in more converts.[111]

In a council meeting on May 30, the day Jenson arrived at mission headquarters, he received his official appointment as a traveling elder in the Aalborg Conference, in the heart of North Jutland, the region of his birth.[112] Jenson's exodus from Denmark came full circle when he returned to Vendsyssel. "I beheld the well known places from the days of my childhood and recognized almost every hillock, bush, valley, creek, pond, etc.," Jenson reflected in his journal. Jenson recalled fondly his "happy glee as a child playing on the hillsides with [his] comrades" in Vendsyssel, where he also "first learned to understand the Gospel" and felt his "heart first beat warm for Zion."[113]

Despite these pleasant memories, his missionary experience reflected the uncomfortable middle ground occupied by most Danish Latter-day Saint emigrants who returned to Scandinavia. Their ethnic and ancestral heritage linked them to Denmark, but their conversion to a distinctly American faith moved them to the margins of Danish society. As before, Jenson's extended family cared nothing for his gospel message.[114] The experience of proselytizing to his Danish relatives and associates became the most vulnerable and heart-wrenching aspect of his first mission, leaving the generally confident Jenson "quite miserable." "I had perhaps feasted on the possibility of posing as a great orator before my former friends and neighbors," Jenson reflected, "and the thought that I had made a failure, at least in part, caused me to retire to a lonely place . . . where I poured out my heart's feelings unto the Almighty."[115]

Jenson was also sobered by the economic devastation in parts of his homeland. "Nearly all the Saints that I visited on this trip were very poor," he wrote, "and I could only feel sorry for them when I became acquainted with their temporal condition." Despite Jenson's early struggles in Utah Territory, he felt that his immediate family had been "blessed with abundance" by comparison to what he saw around him. It had been only seven years since Jenson departed Denmark, but his perception of his new and old homelands were also colored by his gospel perspective. "Would that our wealthy Saints in Zion could witness the poverty of their brethren and sisters in Babylon," he wrote. Though there was little financially rich about the fledgling Latter-day Saint kingdom in the Great Basin to draw new converts, his missionary errand increasingly took on the tone of reclamation as he sought the "deliverance of good, faithful Saints from thraldom."[116]

The prospect of better opportunities in Zion and the persistent emphasis on emigration from church leaders and missionaries strained local church resources. Hjørring, for example, near the region where Jenson's immediate family had embraced the gospel, used to boast a "flourishing branch" but was now depleted of Latter-day Saints; "the decrease of the membership of the branch during the past few years, by emigration and removal" created a dire financial situation, with the very poor, who lacked the means to emigrate, along with those who refused to emigrate, bearing the responsibility of paying rent on the local meeting hall. Jenson, with Branch President Fred Jensen and Elder Peter O. Hansen, elected to forfeit the lease on the hall and move their meetings into the homes of local members, which at this point included "only one single family of saints and four single sisters," with "only about 90 members in the whole branch embracing the whole upland."[117] Hjørring's residents had since grown cold toward the missionaries, and Jenson felt that they "have perhaps been sufficiently warned," as "there are not many places in Denmark where our Elders have preached so continuously as they have in Hjørring during the past 24 years."[118]

Missionaries had now been on Danish soil for more than two decades, which resulted in a degree of familiarity between the Danish people and the church. Jenson understood the explicit disdain many Danes held for his faith—he had witnessed the tension firsthand as a young boy. As a mature adult missionary, Jenson became a student of the contours of Danish Lutheranism and experienced much abuse and vilification from the religious establishment. When no Latter-day Saint services were available to attend during his travels, Jenson elected to attend a Lutheran parish church. After reexperiencing Lutheran services, Jenson was unrestrained in his disdain: "They teach perverted doctrines and one of their special objects seems to be to keep the peasantry in ignorance. . . . 'Mormonism' is declared, the Priests oppose it with all their might why because it is a light which lies bare their deceptions and dishonesty." "These Sectarian Priests," he concluded, "know very well that 'Mormonism' is a menace to their temporal advantages, for when their false doctrines become known to the people, they of course will withdraw their confidence from the priests and denounce their intrigues."[119]

Jenson sought to understand the various intellectual movements within the wider Folkekirken. He particularly detested the theological innovations of N. F. S. Grundtvig, a poet, scholar, and theologian who hoped to inspire a resurgent Danish nationalism that would open the church to a broader Danish audience, even as he sought to separate the church from the state. To Jenson, and even Grundtvig's Danish critics, the movement seemed too expansive.[120] Early in his mission, Jenson lodged with some "so-called Grundtviganere" whom he labeled the "most peculiar specimens and religious cranks that I had hitherto met." He took issue with their brand of "easy and happy Christianity" and its broad opportunities for salvation. "It is not necessary for anyone to put forth any effort to be good or to live righteous lives, for Christ has done all," Jenson assessed. He attempted to bait his hosts into a debate from the Bible, but they declined his invitation. Instead, Jenson privately railed against the movement and its appeal to "patriotism toward their king and fatherland" over true Christianity.[121]

The pietistic and conservative Lutheran organization known as the Indre Mission (Home mission) also inspired a number of conflicts between Latter-day Saint missionaries and Lutheran clergy. Adherents of the Indre Mission downplayed Lutheran sacraments and instead opted for a less rigid quest for personal holiness. Its proponents were unrelenting in their zeal and often distributed tracts and preached in much the same way as Latter-day Saint elders.[122] The competition in Danish villages left Jenson frustrated. "It is a deceptive plan laid by the Devil to hold the people in darkness and get them to reject the truth," Jenson concluded. In contrast to the Latter-day Saint missionaries, who traveled without sufficient monetary means, "the so-called Indre Missionaries," Jenson noted, "are well paid, like other priests of the old school and travel extensively through the country holding meetings in the school houses." This network of "awakened Christians" was hard to combat; Latter-day Saint elders struggled to get permission to hold public meetings in the same manner.[123]

Jenson's indictment of his fellow countrymen suggested changing fortunes for the once fruitful Scandinavian Mission. The incredible success of the 1850s and 1860s was not to be repeated in the ensuing decades, and with the massive outmigration of converts to the Great Basin, Danish American missionaries at times felt isolated in their inhospitable homeland.[124] Jenson was a foreigner in his Danish homeland and became increasingly grateful during his missionary service for his adopted spiritual home in the US West.

Returning Home

On June 5, 1875, just under a month before a company of Scandinavian Saints were scheduled to leave for America and the Utah Territory, Jenson received word that he had been "honorably released" from his mission. Mission President Christian G. Larsen expressed "entire satisfaction" with Jenson's missionary work and remarked on the many "good and warm-hearted friends" Jenson had made in his travels.[125] Indeed, despite his occasional abrasiveness in squaring off against Lutheran opponents, Jenson displayed a remarkable ability to grow a network of Danish members and missionaries who supported him in his persistent pamphleteering and travels. He also had thoroughly reacquainted himself with his former Danish culture, a learning experience that would serve him well in future endeavors.

But the mission was not immediately over for Jenson and other Scandinavian missionaries released to return home. As experienced immigrants, the departing elders helped organize the travel for the company of emigrants heading to Utah that season. Jenson collected funds in Aalborg and purchased steamer and train fare for the company.[126] In late June, Jenson again boarded a ship in Copenhagen and bid farewell to his homeland. He and the emigrating Latter-day Saints crossed the North Sea to the British Isles and then traveled overland to Liverpool to prepare for the transatlantic crossing. About two weeks later, Jenson and his fellow travelers landed in Manhattan. From there, they enjoyed the comfort of locomotion as they traveled across the breadth of the nation. Jenson soon arrived at the train depot in Salt Lake City, where he was met by family members from Pleasant Grove.[127]

Jenson's first trip back to Denmark had renewed a wave of nostalgia for the rural Danish landscape he had traversed as a child, but it was clear that his conversion and departure had effected a change that would forever separate him from the culture of his homeland. Jenson's early life epitomized the tension in and the transformation of the typical Latter-day Saint emigrant. His integration into Utah culture was painstaking and incomplete, and the final stage of assimilation into his new home involved retracing steps back to his former one. While proselytizing in his native Denmark, Jenson fully realized he was a misfit among his fellow countrymen—neither wholly Danish nor wholly American, but a Latter-day Saint who had chosen to live in a new spiritual community.

The American church had brought him to heaven's door; it was infused with traditional Christian elements, such as prophets, revelation, authority, ordinances, and new scripture. His conviction of the gospel message was strong, and when it was rejected he felt authorized to condemn his native land, to write off its citizens as a wicked manifestation of the deteriorating world prior to the Second Coming of Jesus Christ. Whatever kinship he had lost in Denmark was replaced by full citizenship in the church's spiritual and millennial project in the Great Basin, and when he returned from his first mission, he was inspired to become more involved in forging a cohesive Latter-day Saint kingdom in the West.

2 Entrepreneurial Chronicler

When Andrew Jenson arrived home from his mission to Scandinavia in July 1875, he confronted the lingering effects of a global financial downturn. Economic depression brought on by the Panic of 1873 had exposed Utah's economic vulnerability and revived calls from Latter-day Saint leaders for the faithful to join in communitarian economic arrangements. Jenson's father, Christian, lived with his second wife, Jensine Madsen, since 1872 in Richfield. This forced Jenson's mother, Kirsten, to wade through economic hardship on her own. Kirsten had acquiesced to Christian's invitation to remarry as his plural wife while Jenson was away; they were remarried in February 1875. Kirsten, however, remained in Pleasant Grove, somewhat defiant of the new marriage arrangement. With her upbringing in the Danish peasantry, Kirsten was well prepared for the challenges of frontier life, and she tilled and planted like others in her agrarian community. Upon his return to their family home in Pleasant Grove, Jenson found that "the garden looked lovely, the fruit trees were loaded with the most delicious fruit, a part of my little farm was sown and planted with wheat, corn and potatoes. Mother had done all within her power, according to her circumstances, to have everything in as good condition as possible on my return."[1]

Even with his family's "temporal affairs in good condition," Jenson internalized the calls from church leaders for repentance and reform that echoed in meeting halls throughout Utah Territory.[2] A week after arriving home, he traveled south to Provo to attend a two-day conference, at which church president Brigham Young and other church leaders spoke. According to Jenson, the "Saints were chastised considerably because of their transgressions on general principles, or for neglect of duty, and the cry for reform and repentance was sounded in high notes."[3] Church leaders urged the church members to put aside self-interested economic arrangements and join the United Order, a cooperative and communal economic system established in some Latter-day Saint settlements in the 1870s.[4] The utopian arrangement, inspired by the church's past consecration practices, was short-lived but was promoted by Young and other leaders as a way to combat an increasing reliance in Utah Territory on outside goods, capital, and businesses. Fearful that traditional Latter-day Saint communal bonds were eroding in the midst of encroaching capitalism, Young hoped to inspire a retrenchment.[5]

Jenson quickly obeyed prophetic counsel and joined the first United Order in Pleasant Grove through rebaptism.[6] The United Order was intent on fostering not only economic unity but also personal and family purity. Jenson, however, was inadequate at least in one way in the eyes of the most faithful Latter-day Saints. He had yet to marry and participate in the sacred sealing ritual in the Endowment House, one of the crowning ordinances in Latter-day Saint practice and one that bound couples together for eternity. He would quickly fulfill this doctrinal and cultural obligation. While on his mission, Jenson had met Kirsten Marie (Mary) Pedersen (age sixteen) in the vicinity of Hjørring, and she emigrated with his company on his return trip home.[7] Mary was baptized into the same United Order as Jenson, and on August 30, 1875, the two were married in a ceremony performed by Daniel H. Wells at the Endowment House.[8]

In Search of Stability

The responsibilities associated with having a family renewed his commitment to his faith and made him determined to ease the temporal burdens of his young family. At the close of 1875, Jenson had amassed meager resources: he owned two oxen, an old wagon, a cow, a heifer, a calf, modest furniture, and kitchen utensils; and he had placed ninety dollars in the bank.[9] By March of the next year, Jenson had purchased a lot in Pleasant Grove with an existing adobe home, and he and Mary moved from Jenson's mother's home into their own private residence. "Truly we commenced at the bottom of the ladder," Jenson remarked in his journal.[10]

While remodeling his first home, Jenson tried his hand at farming to provide income for his family and food for their kitchen table. To supplement his farming income and pay off his real-estate loan, Jenson joined many other Latter-day Saint Scandinavian immigrants in working for a construction company with a contract to build a tramway up Little Cottonwood Canyon. Each man was paid two dollars a day for their hard labor. Now more experienced as a laborer, Jenson found "the mountain life, coupled with camping out" to be "not at all distasteful." His past experiences on the frontier, however, also had made him less tolerant of poor working conditions and mistreatment by his superiors. According to Jenson, the foreman on the tramway project "treated his men in a rather uncivil and unbecoming manner." His "tyrannical conduct" caused the "independent nature" of Jenson to rebel against the "repeated insults," and Jenson soon resigned his position and returned to Pleasant Grove.[11]

Jenson then spent his time tending to his land and preparing for the arrival of the couple's first child. On November 24, 1876, he left for Salt Lake City to procure a stove and other household articles needed for the coming winter. While he was away, Mary went into labor and delivered their firstborn, a son they named Andrew. But the childbirth nearly cost Mary her life, and she remained in bed for weeks afterward, with Jenson doing the best he "knew how to nurse and take care of her."[12]

The frequent seclusion in the mountains and his time at the bedside of his wife gave him time to contemplate his "condition in life," and he started to wonder if there was not a more worthwhile occupation for him. He was not "a natural farmer, nor a mechanic like [his] father." After he finished his daily work in the canyon, he often "would go out alone in the evening and reflect . . . upon [his] present situation and [his] prospects for the future." "Had the Lord nothing else for me to do," he asked, "than to labor at this common, ordinary manual labor, something that anyone with physical strength and ordinary intelligence could do?" In this distraught state, Jenson remembered turning to prayer while in the mountains and receiving a distinct response: "the answer came; the Lord spoke peace to my anxious soul and seemed to say: No, the Lord has something of greater importance for you to do in life, be of good cheer." Through "direct inspiration from heaven," Jenson claimed, came the concept for a project that would take his life in a new direction.[13]

The allure of earning a more substantial living and an unrelenting belief in himself nudged Jenson slowly away from the communal United Order (which was on the wane by 1876 because other participants similarly struggled). "I had intended to join the Order with heart and soul," he remarked, "but I soon discovered that I, with my ambition and aspiration, could not prosper in the Order under present conditions and therefore I withdrew quietly from it without contention."[14] Jenson had learned by now that capitalism reigned supreme in the West and could often betray the wage laborer. Monetizing his natural talents became the most pressing task of his young life. Jenson had his eye on the literary field, a growing but still young industry in Utah Territory and a crucial component of the church's gathering and missionary enterprise.

A Historian by Yearning

In November 1876, during the tenure of Church Historian and Apostle Orson Pratt, Jenson wrote a letter to First Presidency counselor Daniel H. Wells, who had recently performed his marriage, seeking approval to publish the Prophet

Joseph Smith's history in the Danish language. While still a young church member living in Denmark, Jenson was "of a studious nature" and "had read, re-read and digested to the best of [his] understanding, the historical parts of the Bible and the Book of Mormon." He had also read extracts of the "History of Joseph Smith" (first published in the 1840s and later called the Manuscript History of the Church), which had been translated into Danish and published in the *Skandinaviens Stjerne*.[15] Jenson's renewed interest in Smith's history was inspired by the recent serial publication of abridged sketches of the life of Joseph Smith in the church's Sunday School periodical, the *Juvenile Instructor*.[16]

Weeks after he mailed his translation proposal to church headquarters, Jenson received a thoughtful reply from Wells. Wells supported Jenson's project but also gently expressed doubt that Jenson could support himself or his family with the history's publication and subsequent sales, whether in Utah or even back in Denmark. Despite Wells's caution, the approval to publish the history gave Jenson hope for his professional future.[17]

After receiving Wells's somewhat encouraging response, Jenson traveled to Salt Lake City to meet with the church leader and seek his further counsel. Since arriving in the valley ten years earlier as a young immigrant with few personal connections, Jenson had learned to broaden his relationships. In Wells, he saw an important gatekeeper and potential mentor within the church hierarchy. He met with Wells and more precisely laid out his plans for producing a compelling translation of Smith's history. He intended to work in part from the translation published in the *Skandinaviens Stjerne* to create an "abbreviated form" of the history.[18] Though Jenson's translation initially followed the structure and content of the *Stjerne* translation, he made significant revisions to the *Stjerne* version, and as his translation progressed, he summarized and abridged content more liberally.[19] Jenson's *Joseph Smiths levnetsløb* (History of Joseph Smith) was thus part translated institutional history and part historical product—the first of a number of chronologies on Latter-day Saint history that Jenson would produce.

Jenson's meeting with Wells apparently went smoothly enough, since Wells was thereafter willing to share Jenson's translation project with the elderly President Brigham Young, who was then spending the winter months in the warmer climate of southern Utah. Jenson gave Wells a copy of a portion of his translation to send to the church president with an explanatory cover letter. Young then passed the proposal and translation along to Apostle Erastus Snow, who had opened Latter-day Saint missionary work in Scandinavia in 1850 and could read and speak Danish, for his appraisal.[20]

Jenson soon corresponded with Snow about his proposed translation project, and in the process, further expanded his ecclesiastical contacts. The apostle would become another one of Jenson's trusted mentors in the years to come. Snow hoped Jenson could differentiate his translation from the *Stjerne*'s by making it "a short, clear and concise" history, "adapted to the general audience." Jenson too felt the translation needed to "be made in a plain, easy style in the pure native tongue as far as practicable."[21] His entire translation would be subdivided into monthly installments and sold as a subscription.

Jenson worked to improve his English-language skills and historical knowledge by subscribing to the *Juvenile Instructor*. He also cherished a growing collection of books that included volumes purchased from roving book agents. In the isolated and expansive American West, agents—paid by large eastern publishers—commonly canvased rural frontier towns selling multivolume or installment subscriptions to literature-starved residents. Most of the popular history books of the day were sold in this manner, and a growing Latter-day Saint print culture in the Great Basin relied on the same subscription model.[22] With no prior publishing or journalism experience, Jenson was nonetheless confident that he could make the business model work.

His confidence likely stemmed from his mild success as an itinerant salesman in Denmark and on the American frontier. Salesmanship was key in gaining subscribers. Publishers or their agents were required to cultivate a readership, take orders, and deliver regular issues, while collecting pledged fees. Jenson spent much of his initial year—and the next decade—traveling the breadth of Utah Territory to solicit individual subscriptions from cash-strapped Latter-day Saints living in a largely barter and agricultural economy. Often gone from his family for weeks at a time, he traveled to small pioneer towns and held history meetings in local church ward houses or community centers. To the gathered crowds, he introduced historical or gospel subjects and invited potential patrons to support his literary work by subscribing to his monthly installments. On his methods of attracting subscribers, Jenson commented, "Usually I was blessed under the influence of the spirit of the Lord to preach gospel sermons or enlarge upon the history of the Church and other things, . . . and then usually towards the close of my remarks I would mention my literary venture."[23] In this practice, he followed nineteenth-century Latter-day Saint preaching conventions in which speakers delivered sermons extemporaneously, with "liberty" and "freedom" to let the Spirit dictate their words in the moment.[24]

Before moving on to the next settlement, Jenson would appoint an agent in the town to collect payments and distribute the published monthly issues.[25] He often traveled by foot or wagon and relied on the hospitality of old friends and new contacts for meals and a place to sleep at night. Sometimes he received small cash donations to help offset his travel expenses. During these many visits, he established an expansive network throughout Utah of friends and supporters for his historical projects and publications. His first trip, completed in April 1877, to Latter-day Saint settlements in southern Utah to gain support for his *Levnetsløb* netted 650 subscribers.[26] By August, his subscriber base ballooned to 1,400.[27]

While on his first southern Utah tour in search of subscribers, Jenson became reacquainted with Johan A. Bruun, a fellow Scandinavian whom Jenson had met on his first mission to Denmark. Bruun had worked as a translator for the *Skandinaviens Stjerne* before immigrating to Utah in 1876. With some persuasion, given the unsettled financial state of the *Levnetsløb*, Bruun agreed to join Jenson in a partnership, and the pair began to work on revising Jenson's translation. While in southern Utah, Jenson also found opportunities to mingle with Latter-day Saint leaders who were in town for the general conference, to be held in conjunction with the St. George Temple dedication. After one meeting, President Brigham Young, who had already approved the translation project, questioned Jenson specifically on his "literary undertaking" and again seemed satisfied by the plan.[28] Jenson later expanded his reflection on his first and only meeting with President Young: "He seemed to size me up with his piercing eyes, as if he would question me by saying 'Do you think you can do it?' He did not say that, but I thought I could read his thoughts in his countenance."[29]

The historical project appeared to be off to a fortuitous start. Nearly a third of the entire run was ready for printing by February 1877, and the *Deseret News* published Jenson's introductory letter to the work in the paper's April 25 edition, increasing the visibility of his campaign for subscribers.[30] The letter introduced the goal of the publication: "to promote the welfare of the kingdom, and especially to benefit those of the Scandinavian Saints who are not capable of reading the English language."[31] The concise introduction was followed by a recommendation from Snow, encouraging Scandinavian Latter-day Saints to donate money to the project.[32]

Despite offering Jenson no monetary support from church coffers, Latter-day Saint leaders still held an intellectual stake in the printed material consumed by the general church membership. In the late 1870s especially, with public interest and outrage over the Latter-day Saints' practice of plural marriage on the rise, printed material on the Latter-day Saints was divided along polemical lines. Even within territorial borders, the church was subject to printed attacks against the church's intervention in the territory's politics and economy.[33] Introducing more inspiring literary offerings, supportive of the church, was important to church leaders. Snow was appointed to oversee the quality of Jenson's translation and to verify that the entire publication met the standards of church leaders.[34] The *Levnetsløb* benefited from the consent and praise of Snow and other presiding officers, which, in a crowded publishing scene, elevated the status of the publication, casting it as a work that was worthwhile and faith promoting.

The Scandinavian Audience

As interest in his historical project grew, Jenson's value to the church and the Scandinavian community in Zion increased as well. The mass emigration from

Scandinavia and Britain transformed the Utah Territory citizenry into a diverse, multilingual community. The ethnic diversity was not lost on outside observers. Existing animosity against Latter-day Saints, mixed with popular nativist sentiment against foreign-born immigrants, stirred accusations that the church was recruiting the lowest segments of society overseas to further what others perceived as religious delusions.[35] In contrast, church leaders welcomed as fellow Christians the immigrant converts who contributed skilled labor to their wilderness settlement. In the face of stigmatizing press reports and lingering religious and ethnic prejudice, however, assimilation into American society could be challenging.

Jenson understood firsthand the struggles of the immigrant. In his own experience, he had found an impressive institutional infrastructure to aid the arriving Latter-day Saint immigrants but less assistance in laying down firm roots in Zion. New immigrants had to find stable housing and employment while attempting to learn a new language. Despite the growing ethnic diversity in Utah Territory, English remained the official language of Zion. Immigrants were encouraged to take local English language classes, some of which were taught by Jenson, to ease the transition, and by most accounts, efforts to integrate immigrants into local Latter-day Saint communities were eventually successful.[36]

Integration was not immediate, however, and despite pushes for cohesiveness, immigrants were permitted to retain cultural traditions and attend special church meetings in their native tongue.[37] Jenson was very active in the Pleasant Grove Scandinavian community. With over one hundred Scandinavian families in the city's limits—approximately a third of Pleasant Grove's population—Scandinavian Latter-day Saints decided to divide into three districts and hold three separate Scandinavian meetings on nights throughout the week.[38] Official Scandinavian meetings were held in other Utah communities with enough interest. The meetings were distinct from the regular Sunday worship services (which Scandinavian Latter-day Saints were still obligated to attend) and operated with their own presiding officers, distinct from those of other ecclesiastical jurisdictions. They represented a committed institutional attempt to ease the transition of Scandinavians into a new, homogenous religious community.[39]

Challenges in the Publishing Market

Jenson firmly believed in the intellectual and spiritual value of the *Levnetsløb* for the Scandinavian community. Subscription numbers were not necessarily an indicator of success for the amateur publisher. Indeed, in tabling his itinerant wage work for itinerant literary work, Jenson felt he was more ably building and contributing to Zion.[40] "I acknowledge, the hand of the Lord in the success that has attended our labors," he wrote in 1879. "It has given to the Scandinavian Saints a better understanding of the divine mission of the Prophet Joseph

Smith and has greatly strengthened the faith of many."[41] And though his family continued to struggle to make ends meet, Jenson found satisfaction in work of a more spiritual and enduring nature and took pride in compiling the first foreign-language book to be printed in Utah Territory.[42]

The first year of his work as an entrepreneurial historian introduced Jenson to the grim financial realities of the publishing world. "Means are coming in quite slowly," Jenson remarked at the end of 1877. He had recruited 1,825 subscribers to his *Levnetsløb* and mailed out the first 112 pages. However, the pledged subscribers fell well short of the 2,400 copies Jenson had printed in anticipation of higher demand. Though he devised a plan to take the remaining print run and bind the sections into single volumes to sell, the unsold copies left an enormous burden on his fledgling publishing establishment.[43] Jenson's contract with Bruun, in theory, awarded him an extra 25 percent of the initial net profits, after which the pair would split the remaining profits evenly.[44] Their agents in the various cash-poor Scandinavian communities, however, struggled to collect payment from subscribers, forcing Jenson to forgo his contract provisions in order to give Bruun "some money to assist him in living," while Jenson took "next to nothing" from the endeavor.[45]

Over the next two years, Jenson redirected small amounts from *Levnetsløb* subscriptions to support his family, but the printing debt with the Deseret News continued to mount.[46] When the twenty-eighth and final installment of the *Levnetsløb* was nearly off the press and Jenson and Bruun prepared to bind the 550 surplus sets of the history into complete volumes, they owed the press $675, more than half the total printing cost of $1,159. In addition, they had amassed postage and traveling expenses of close to $400. Jenson estimated that nearly $1,800 still needed to be forwarded from subscribers, but if the sale of the remaining volumes at three dollars apiece attracted interest, the venture might soon give Jenson and Bruun a respectable payoff.[47]

With limited cash flow, Jenson sought to supplement his meager earnings with other business ventures. In 1878 he began helping fellow Scandinavian immigrant Anders W. Winberg with the translation of *Bikuben* (the Beehive), Salt Lake City's weekly Danish Norwegian–language newspaper since 1876. Winberg was a Swedish blacksmith and now merchant, who sensed a market need for a Scandinavian paper faithful to the Latter-day Saint cause, but he lacked any formal experience in the publishing world. The newspaper's competitor, the *Skandinav*, issued weekly vitriol against the church from its press. Winberg, as president of Salt Lake City's Scandinavian Meeting, stepped into the publishing arena with *Bikuben*, to counterbalance the *Skandinav* and to promote the interests of Latter-day Saint Scandinavians.[48]

Jenson, however, was critical of the amateur style of *Bikuben* almost from the beginning. The Danish Norwegian newspaper had numerous advantages that might have predicted its future success if it had been in expert hands. It benefitted from its location in Salt Lake City and its proximity to church headquarters. With a solid subscriber base, *Bikuben* could disseminate accurate information on the church to Scandinavians throughout Utah Territory and facilitate their assimilation. But in its first two years of existence, the paper was struggling to turn a profit and needed help.

Jenson and Bruun were now quite familiar with the subscription model of publishing and maintained their own network of subscribers, which overlapped with those interested in *Bikuben*. Both also sought an opportunity to shift their publishing and writing endeavors from Pleasant Grove to Salt Lake City to align more easily and closely with the interests of the church. While attending the April 1878 general conference, Jenson met with Apostle Erastus Snow to discuss future opportunities, and both Bruun and Jenson soon found themselves in front of President John Taylor, Brigham Young's successor, laying out the prospects of reorganizing *Bikuben*'s staff. Lacking confidence in Winberg's ability to edit and manage *Bikuben* as a solo endeavor, both Taylor and Snow encouraged the trio to form a firm that would benefit from the more experienced Jenson and Bruun.[49]

The new business partners rented office space in Salt Lake City's Constitution Building on Main Street, and Jenson worked long hours to prepare content for future issues, often sleeping in the newspaper's office to avoid paying for lodging. Their first published work was volume 2, number thirty-three of *Bikuben*, but there was little cause to celebrate. The new enterprise seemed doomed from the start. Winberg had been relegated to treasurer when the firm was organized (presumably because of his lack of literary experience), and Bruun took over the editorial duties, a move that caused some resentment and tension. Jenson, as business manager, set out on a quick tour of the southern Utah settlements in May to generate subscriptions. When he returned, he found Bruun and Winberg "in a serious state of disagreement" over the main operations of the paper. The tension was made worse by the fact that "no means to speak of was coming in for the paper."[50] Costs were offset using personal funds and by transferring money from *Levnetsløb* accounts, which only further complicated the partnership. Jenson assessed the situation realistically: "The greatest difficulty is undoubtedly this[:] that we are three men of three very different characteristics and in all our thoughts, planning and movement we seemed to go in opposite directions."[51]

The firm limped along for another month, but the disagreement between Bruun and Winberg was irreconcilable. Jenson and Bruun returned to President Taylor's office in early July to report their failure. Taylor, clearly disappointed, called a meeting with the three partners and rebuked them for their "antagonistic feelings toward one another." He also declared "in the name of the Lord" that, if they did not put their pride aside to continue the publication of *Bikuben*, they would "sooner or later have occasion to regret it."[52] Taylor's refusal to let the partnership dissolve and his prophetic promise troubled Jenson.

Despite Taylor's warning, Bruun was determined to end the partnership, and Jenson, not wishing to jeopardize the future of the *Levnetsløb*, was forced to oblige, though it caused him great pain "to consider the President's words with indifference."[53] The affairs of *Bikuben* went before arbitrators, and the firm was disbanded, though Jenson remained on as an assistant to Winberg until the second volume of *Bikuben* was completed in September in an attempt to obey President Taylor's counsel and to prevent the newspaper from folding.

The dissolution of the Bikuben Publishing Company was a notable setback in Jenson's early publishing career. His reputation among the Scandinavian community and with church leaders suffered a blow, and Jenson was reminded that he still had a great deal to learn about the business. His interest in *Bikuben* as the primary newspaper for Utah's Scandinavian population remained, despite his withdrawal from its day-to-day operations. Three years later, he again met with President Taylor and weighed in on the newspaper's imperfections: "The 'Bikuben' is and has always been, as an organ for the Scandinavians in Utah a disgrace for us as a nationality. Bro. A. W. Winberg, the publisher of the paper is undoubtedly a good man, but as he has no education to speak of and is entirely incapable as a Swede by birth to write any thing correctly in Danish, we had suggested that it would be better for himself and the community at large if he returned to his old handicraft as a blacksmith."[54] But Taylor was suspicious of Jenson's motives. At the expense of Winberg, Jenson seemed to be ingratiating himself with his ecclesiastical leaders. His frequent critiques of *Bikuben*'s quality eventually led to a long-standing editorial arrangement to fix the paper's problems.[55]

A Second Mission to Denmark

In January 1879, six months after the dissolution of the Bikuben Publishing Company, Jenson received his second official mission call from President John Taylor. With Jenson so active in Utah's Scandinavian community, he was an obvious choice to fulfill another mission to Denmark.[56] The call filled Jenson with a "peculiar and strange impression."[57] His relationship with Taylor was professional but not particularly cordial or personal. At a time when Jenson felt his value to the church was increasing domestically, his talents were needed abroad. Taylor sensed that Jenson had potential to assist the church in the literary field but still needed polish and experience. Jenson later reflected on the reason behind his sudden call to serve in Denmark: "The authorities of the Church desired that I should obtain a better knowledge of the Danish language, so that I might be used by the Church in the future as a writer and translator."[58] Jenson's Danish-language skills, especially when it came to producing polished translations, had waned since immigrating. His apprenticeship would be short, however. Pamphlets and periodicals were central to missionizing on European soil, and Jenson's publishing experience, though limited, filled an immediate and valuable need in the Scandinavian Mission.

The new missionary assignment forced Jenson to pause his work on the *Levnetsløb* and to rush renovations on his home in Pleasant Grove.[59] After arranging the remaining *Levnetsløb* business with Bruun, Jenson departed Salt Lake City on May 21, 1879, for the East, leaving behind his wife, Mary, and two young children—Andrew, now two years old, and Parley, not yet one. Jenson's departure took an immediate financial toll on his young family. Mary, with the assistance of her mother and father, ran the household and took on domestic chores and sewing jobs to support the family. Despite her best efforts, she was frequently "hard up for money," with no means of subsistence coming from Jenson. Even with financial challenges, Mary enrolled at Brigham Young Academy in Provo. Her coursework forced her to spend many nights away from home "awful lonesome," by her account, when she thought of her children.[60] She corresponded with Jenson in the mission field regularly and also built a wide social circle in Utah County in his absence.

Jenson and his traveling companion, Paul D. S. Lund, reached Copenhagen on June 11 during the mission presidency of Nils C. Flygare.[61] Though convert baptisms were in decline in Scandinavia, when compared with the mission's first two decades of success, the mission still featured its highest number of Utah missionaries (forty-seven) and facilitated the emigration of hundreds of converts each year.[62] Church membership in Denmark, a steady group of faithful Latter-day Saints who largely lacked the means or ability to immigrate to Zion, hovered around two thousand.[63] To keep Jenson close to mission headquarters, where he could take lessons in Danish and translate, he was assigned to preside over the Copenhagen branch.[64]

Jenson took pride in his proximity to the church's senior brethren, an honor achieved after launching the *Levnetsløb*. But he also nurtured an inflated sense of importance that poisoned his early experiences during his second mission. "I had expected to be appointed assistant at the mission office on my arrival in the mission, and when that did not occur I sometimes thought that I had arrived either too soon or too late," he wrote after being called as branch president in Copenhagen.[65] A troubling letter from home added to his disappointment—he learned that his partner Johan Bruun had possibly appropriated for his personal expenses the remaining funds needed to pay off the *Levnetsløb* debt. Making matters worse, the final installments of *Levnetsløb* were delayed in reaching subscribers.[66] In reality, Bruun was struggling to collect funds from his agents, who in turn were struggling to collect from subscribers.[67] Despite these frustrations, Jenson wrote, "I am beginning to learn that such an experience," like not being selected as a leader in the mission office, "was beneficial to me. It taught me humility and brought me to my knees in prayer to God for strength."[68]

As he ministered in Copenhagen, Jenson was able to observe conditions on the ground of "the ordinary Saint and the public generally."[69] What he witnessed in Copenhagen and around the mission was captured in the sentiments of President Flygare, who called the Scandinavian Saints "truly a good people" and noted that "the great question among the Saints is 'How shall we get to Zion?'"[70] The Copenhagen branch, while relatively large for a branch outside of Utah, with 390 members, bore little resemblance to the vibrant and growing Pleasant Grove community from which Jenson had departed, but he felt privileged to minster at the epicenter of the mission's emigration system.[71] While there, he discerned the needs of Danish Latter-day Saints and reacquainted himself with the poverty that sometimes beset converts in his homeland. As Jenson's leadership and editorial skills matured, he gave voice to these challenges in the pages of Scandinavian mission literature.[72] He also introduced his homeland to the church's recently created and expanding organizations. In November 1879, he helped establish Denmark's first Female Relief Society and Young Men's Mutual Improvement Association (YMMIA).[73]

Andrew Jenson on his second mission to Denmark, 1880. Courtesy Church History Library.

To improve his Danish-language skills, Jenson negotiated a trade with a scholar from Copenhagen, L. Moth Iverson. Apparently, Iverson had fallen in love with a Latter-day Saint woman who would not date or marry him unless he was baptized. In exchange for lessons in his native tongue, Jenson taught the principles of Latter-day Saint doctrine to Iverson, who was soon baptized.[74] Jenson's Danish quickly improved, which allowed him to pick up more literary assignments at the mission office.

One of his first assignments was translating a new monthly periodical targeted at the youth and issued by the Sunday School and YMMIA called *Ungdommens raadgiver* (Counselor of youth).[75] He also began editing a new edition of the Bible-reference volume for missionaries, *Bibelske henvisninger* (Bible references).[76] After February 1880, Scandinavian Mission president Niels Wilhelmsen, who had arrived in late summer 1879 to replace President Flygare, required Jenson's literary services full-time and released him from his responsibilities as branch president.[77] On his call to full-time literary work, Jenson wrote, "I shall be able to meet a want that long has been felt in the Church in Scandinavia as well as among the Scandinavia Saints in the valleys, namely, a lack of men with literary ability who also harbor in their bosoms a love for the gospel."[78] Soon after, on May 1, Jenson was also called to be the assistant to the mission president and took over as assistant editor for the *Skandinaviens Stjerne*.[79]

When Jenson joined the staff of the *Stjerne*, the average circulation was around 1,500, down from its peak of over 2,700 in 1861, a side effect of Danish Latter-day Saint emigration.[80] As Jenson knew from his youth, the *Stjerne* was Danish Latter-day Saints' main point of contact with the Utah church. Jenson translated material for the *Stjerne* from Utah publications and from the British *Millennial Star*. The responsibility of keeping the scattered membership in Denmark united and informed fell in part on the editors of the *Stjerne*, who also abridged and published correspondence from church leaders and meeting minutes from around the mission. In addition, the *Stjerne* was still the principal source for travel information for prospective emigrants. Jenson's upstart literary career had placed him in a role in which he partially controlled the primary intellectual medium for the Danish Latter-day Saints, a prestigious position with which he could establish solid credentials in the literary field.

To further capitalize on Jenson's talents, President Wilhelmsen commenced the daunting task of updating old mission literature, some of which had not been retranslated or reprinted in decades. For the next year, Jenson and Wilhelmsen partnered on the sensitive but pressing responsibility of revising the Danish edition of the Book of Mormon. The first edition had been published in 1851, one year after the arrival of the first missionaries to Denmark. The edition was primarily the product of missionary Peter O. Hansen, who like Jenson was a Danish emigrant whose language skills had suffered by the time he returned to

Denmark.[81] Erastus Snow had aided Hansen in correcting the Danish translation, the first foreign-language translation of the Book of Mormon, and sent the work to press, thus publishing *Mormons Bog*.[82]

Though Hansen's initial translation had been a remarkable service to the first generation of Danish Latter-day Saints, by the time of Jenson's second mission to Denmark, thirty years later, it seemed unpolished given the native language abilities of the large quantity of Danish Latter-day Saints freshly converted to the church. In addition, the supply of the first two editions was exhausted, and missionaries in Denmark needed copies to sell and proselytize with.[83]

Jenson and Wilhelmsen reformatted the Danish edition with shorter chapters, new versification, and new footnotes and cross-references, based on the recent reformatting of the English-language Book of Mormon by Orson Pratt.[84] The pair also felt revisions were needed because the "Danish language, both as regards orthography and style, had undergone material changes since 1851." In accounting for modern linguistic changes, Jenson and Wilhelmsen reviewed every sentence and verse of Pratt's English edition against the current Danish edition, "marking off the book into chapters and verses" and adjusting the text when needed. Jenson described the arduous work: "Thus we often sat from early morning till late at night and were so industrious and careful in our work that we scarcely took time to receive visitors or to attend the meetings. . . . Midnight often found us busily at work, long after the other brethren at the mission office had retired. And when we finally laid down to rest our minds were frequently so tired that our natural rest was denied us."[85] After two comprehensive reviews, Jenson and Wilhelmsen felt confident in their new translation of the Book of Mormon text. The translation was finished on April 1, 1881, and two thousand copies were printed and bound by June.[86]

In retranslating and reprinting the Danish Book of Mormon, Jenson ensured that the most visible evidence of the restored gospel's divinity was accessible to another generation of Latter-day Saints in his homeland. Jenson knew that the Book of Mormon had been a lightning rod for criticism from the predominating Danish-Lutheran community since its 1851 publication. The Lutheran opposition took exception to Latter-day Saint claims of continuous revelation and modern prophets, and the Book of Mormon served as evidence of both. As the most distinctive product of a new American religion now on Danish soil, the Book of Mormon was part conversion tool and part literary defense, used to combat traditional Christianity's assault on Latter-day Saint truth claims. In the eyes of Danish Lutherans, the book was pulling Danes away from their homeland to the American Zion. Jenson's publishing work for the Scandinavian Mission placed him at the frontlines of the church's defense in Denmark as he issued and reissued not only scripture but also tracts and periodicals to further missionary efforts.

Becoming an Ecclesiastical Leader

Jenson's close work with President Wilhelmsen in the mission office and on the new Danish edition of the Book of Mormon fostered an intimate friendship and trust between the two missionaries. Jenson later commented on Wilhelmsen: "I soon learned to love him with a devotion similar to that of a son for an affectionate father, and he seemed to fully reciprocate my feelings."[87] As the summer of 1881 wore on, the joy of their joint literary successes gave way to anxiety when Wilhelmsen was hospitalized in Copenhagen with a gallstone. On July 24, he underwent surgery to remove the stone, and Jenson and his fellow elders were confident that he would make a full recovery. In Wilhelmsen's absence, Jenson ran the day-to-day affairs of the mission in addition to visiting the president daily.

By July 31, Wilhelmsen was in poor health and prone "to most serious reflections which caused him" to give Jenson "instructions concerning himself, his family and the mission affairs in general, in case anything serious should happen to him." After another evening visit, Jenson returned home in a somber state and spent a sleepless night "with the most peculiar and sad feelings in regard to Prest. Wilhelmsen." On a few occasions that night, he pled with the Lord to "spare his life," but on returning to the hospital the next morning around nine o'clock, he was given tragic news.[88] Over two years into his missionary service, and only months away from returning to his home in St. Charles, Idaho, the beloved president of the Scandinavian Mission was dead.

The passing of Wilhelmsen was perhaps the most heart-wrenching experience of Jenson's young life. "Oh Lord, how strange and mysterious are thy ways in dealing with thy servants! Why should thy faithful servant thus pass away, while he was so far away from his family and friends in Zion?" Jenson lamented. "Never before had I labored with a man, either in the missionary field or elsewhere, with whom I have been so intimate and confidential as I had been with him. I could not love my own father with a greater devotion than I loved this man, but now he is gone and we cannot call him back."[89] Wilhelmsen's sudden death left Jenson at the helm of the mission, responsible for planning the funeral and informing his fellow missionaries, as well as Wilhelmsen's family in Idaho, of the tragedy.[90]

These unfortunate circumstances made an ecclesiastical leader of Jenson, who acted decisively in his new role. He next wrote quickly to the conference presidents scattered throughout the mission, inviting them to gather for the funeral and for a special meeting. At the hastily called conference meeting, the affairs of the mission were reviewed as was the need for a temporary mission president. Peter O. Hansen, serving his third mission to Scandinavia at the age of sixty-three, spoke out and nominated Jenson because he "did not believe that there were any better fitted or entitled to take temporary charge of the affairs of the mission." A number of other mission leaders from the various conferences throughout the mission agreed, and they collectively sustained Jenson "as director of the Scandinavian Mission until another man is sent here from home or until our superiors in the priesthood should de[c]ide otherwise."[91]

Jenson was initially unsure how long he would remain in his temporary position, but church leaders in Salt Lake City spared little time in appointing an official successor. Christian D. Fjeldsted, a fifty-two-year-old native Dane who lived in Logan, Utah, was called as mission president and arrived in Copenhagen on September 1, 1881.[92] Jenson's literary and proselytizing work in his Danish homeland came to a close as he transferred mission accounts and business over to the new president and departed for home. Jenson was "unable to hold back tears" as he left Copenhagen.[93]

Church leaders, including the First Presidency—John Taylor, George Q. Cannon, and Joseph F. Smith—were pleased with Jenson's service on his second mission, especially his astute and skillful performance as interim mission president after Wilhelmsen's death. By all accounts, Jenson's mission was a success. It had allowed him to acquire the needed literary and linguistic experiences to return home an experienced Scandinavian writer and publisher, and it also gave him unexpected training in ecclesiastical and administrative leadership. Such valuable experience encouraged Jenson to expand his publishing ventures in the coming years.

A New Danish-Language Periodical

His short stint with *Bikuben* aside, most of Jenson's prior publishing work in Utah Territory involved translating existing content into Danish rather than creating original content. After reimmersing himself in Danish culture overseas and improving his language abilities, Jenson felt confident he could produce content that would meet the needs and demands of the growing Scandinavian audience in the Great Basin. Past challenges, however, still haunted the amateur publisher, and the months after Jenson's return from his mission were spent addressing the debt incurred from his *Levnetsløb* project.

An outstanding printer's debt of $300 was owed to the Deseret News for the *Levnetsløb*, and Jenson lacked the means to pay it.[94] Forecasting Utah Territory's unpredictable market forces proved risky for the budding entrepreneur. Few Latter-day Saints were flush with cash, and the little cash that circulated in their settlements was used to purchase needed household goods and supplies. Jenson's publications, while valuable, strained the average household budget of Utah's immigrant population. Eager to see his publications succeed, Jenson's initial business model operated on faith in shared ethnic ties and promises from subscribers. Many people, however, pledged subscriptions too optimistically and could not pay by collection time, shrinking Jenson's growing network down to a small group of Scandinavian stalwarts who could afford to pay.

Some of Jenson's appointed collection agents, however, were less than diligent, which forced him to travel to the settlements himself to try and recoup owed subscription fees (which totaled approximately $600).[95] He traveled first through Utah, Sanpete, and Sevier Counties, popular regions of settlement for Scandinavian immigrants. As he tracked down his agents, Jenson discovered that some had failed to deliver finished copies of the *Levnetsløb* to subscribers or had taken and spent more than their allotment of the collected fees.[96] Jenson also discovered it was almost impossible to recover outstanding payments that were nearly two and a half years old, and in some cases debtors or agents had moved or could not be found. The delinquent agents were "enough to make the publishers of papers and books desperate," Jenson concluded.[97] In the twenty-five-day trip south, Jenson managed to collect only $30.[98] The Deseret News printing office cut Jenson a deal, given the fact that 432 unbound copies of *Levnetsløb*, as well as a number of bound copies, still sat unsold in its office. If Jenson could pay off $200 of the debt by the end of the year, the office would remit the remaining $130.[99] He failed to meet that deadline but was able to repay the debt over the next year.[100]

The challenges of the *Levnetsløb*, including meager personal earnings, did little to dissuade Jenson from his chosen literary career, but unreliable financial returns did prompt him to try to secure more stable employment. Shortly after his return home from his second mission to Denmark, Jenson wrote to John Taylor in hopes of securing employment and a salary with the church. "During my stay abroad I improved almost every spare moment I could get for gathering historical information in regard to the History of the church," he wrote. While perusing mission records, he had found "several of these records were about to be destroyed, or at least were fast decaying because of neglect. . . . This inspired me to get facts from them while they yet were in existence." Jenson offered to publish a serialized history of the Scandinavian Mission on behalf of the church for the benefit of Scandinavian Latter-day Saints and included a gracious offer to furnish the Church Historian's Office with the most important historical details from his research. Jenson also alluded to his desire to work at the Historian's Office: "To translate so much matter, however, will take considerable time . . . perhaps it would be . . . the best if I did the labor right at the Historian's Office where I could have access to all the printed authorities, or the sources for at least that part of the information." Jenson intended his temporary project to be a trial run to show off his capacity as a historian. "Nothing would please me better than to be employed by the church at the Historian's Office," he stated.[101] President John Taylor, however, did not officially respond to Jenson's request for months.

Apostle Erastus Snow became the intermediary between Jenson and the First Presidency in regard to Jenson's proposal. While Jenson was in St. George in November, collecting on funds for the *Levnetsløb*, he heard from Snow briefly about his proposal via telegram: "No decision reached. . . . He (Taylor) was unfavorably impressed with your criticism of 'Bikuben.'"[102] Jenson had indeed criticized the literary quality of *Bikuben* and Winberg's editorial eye before his mission and had reluctantly voiced the same opinions the previous September during an interview with church leaders to report on his mission.[103] Taylor was reticent to pit various Scandinavian publishing ventures against one another and thus wanted to further discuss Jenson's proposal with Snow. At last, in December, Jenson received a positive letter from Snow, delivering news of Taylor's approval for a new Danish-language publication to be privately issued by Jenson without "detracting from Bro. Winberg" and *Bikuben* so that each might "build up the other rather than pull down."[104]

It was not the historian position Jenson had hoped for, but the approval was enough to encourage him to begin once again seeking subscribers and publicizing his new endeavor. The prospect of an entirely new publication was risky for Jenson. His personal finances were depleted, and he still carried a debt for the *Levnetsløb*. Yet, he persisted, confident that his own historical abilities and his persuasiveness among the Scandinavian Latter-day Saints would eventually yield substantial financial returns.

Jenson's initial efforts to compose a history of the Scandinavian mission soon morphed into a historical Danish periodical titled *Morgenstjernen* (the Morning star), likely a reference to the early Latter-day Saint periodical *The Evening and the Morning Star*, published in both Missouri and Ohio. But the title was also symbolic of the dawning of a new era for Jenson, one in which his hard work and careful literary translations would finally pay off. Erastus Snow gave Jenson a letter of recommendation to print in the first issue and to show to potential subscribers. The recommendation also ran in the *Deseret News*.[105]

The initial print run, produced through the Deseret News office, was ambitious, given that Jenson had secured few subscribers when the first number was issued. With an anticipated subscribership of two thousand for both *Morgenstjernen* and a freshly envisioned 252-page chronology titled *Kirkens historie* (church history, covering the Restoration from the 1844 martyrdom of Joseph Smith to the early Latter-day Saint settlement in Utah), Jenson ran up a personal debt of close to $1,000.[106] By March 15, 1882, when the Deseret News office had finished printing 2,400 copies of the first issue, Jenson had acquired only three hundred subscribers, at a rate of $1.25 for a yearly subscription.[107]

The slow growth of interest in his literary work did nothing to injure his confidence. In fact, he hoped to relocate his family near church headquarters to be closer to where he performed his business. In February, he purchased a building lot in the Seventeenth Ward in Salt Lake City, only a few blocks away from the Salt Lake Temple Block. With no excess cash on hand, Jenson borrowed from friends in Pleasant Grove to pay for the lot and materials for a new house and began construction in the spring.[108] The home loan from friends set him back $540 with an interest rate of 8 percent, a sizable loan for someone with a steady income, let alone Jenson, who lacked such reliable funding.[109] He estimated his total personal debt at $922. "I have been compelled to use about all the money which I have collected in subscriptions for my paper, toward my building," he remarked in his journal. "I have the best prospects for pulling through the hole successfully," he believed, if his anticipated subscriptions panned out.[110] Jenson was back in business as a fledgling historian, but the upcoming year would either prove successful at last or ruin him financially.

Jenson, like others hoping to grow their industry in the immature western economy, had to accumulate investments and oversell to generate initial interest. In Jenson's case, he bet on the quality of his historical content and its appeal to Scandinavians, who he felt were largely unimpressed by the quality of *Bikuben* and might desire a more polished paper. His first issue contained a glowing biography of his mentor, Erastus Snow, who also carefully reviewed some of his translations and approved them for publication.[111] The issue also included a comprehensive statistical report of the Scandinavian Mission and a historical chronology of the church for the year 1881. In addition, Jenson promised subscribers his *Kirkens historie* free of charge.[112] *Morgenstjernen* became fertile ground for a number of Jenson's future historical projects, including a church chronology, a published history of the Scandinavian Mission, and a multivolume series of biographical sketches. Jenson was testing the market among his religious peers for his nascent historical ideas. They responded favorably.

Jenson traveled through Latter-day Saint settlements, advertising his periodical and also securing historical sources from which to create future content.[113] Reviews also began to flow in. The *Deseret News* labeled *Morgenstjernen* a "good periodical" that was "highly spoke of by parties who are its constant readers."[114] Erastus Snow, too, continued to encourage Latter-day Saints to patronize the paper, which could combat "Scandinavian papers and magazines from abroad, published by our enemies" that "circulated freely throughout the whole Territory." Jenson was producing content intended to "expound the Gospel, defend correct principles, and furnish news and intellectual food for the people."[115]

By November 1882, the full print run of *Morgenstjernen* had sold out, forcing Jenson to temporarily stop taking new subscribers.[116] Payment on subscriptions was still slow to come in as he waited for his subscribers to reap profits from the fall harvest. The delay forced his family "to live very ecconomically [*sic*]," he recorded in his journal, "in order not to increase our debt, which is at present very considerable."[117] By the year's end, however, he had collected nearly $900, and the prospects for the future appeared bright for Jenson's new enterprise.[118]

Over the next several years, he would continue publishing *Morgenstjernen*, which would include a revised Danish-language translation of the Pearl of Great Price—a combination of revelations, narratives, and translations from Joseph Smith that had recently been canonized as scripture in 1880. After its canonization, Danish Latter-day Saints wanted the benefit of immersing themselves in the scripture in their own language, and Jenson asked the First Presidency for permission to translate and publish the work.[119] President Taylor quickly approved Jenson's proposal.[120] In the span of three years, Jenson had thus produced reputable translations of both the Book of Mormon and the Pearl of Great Price—two pillars of the Latter-day Saint scriptural canon. In the hierarchy of texts central to the Latter-day Saint tradition, scripture was far more important than the historical texts Jenson traditionally worked with and created. If his increased subscriber base failed to demonstrate his value to the Latter-day Saint Scandinavian community, his efforts to bring sacred scripture to the Danish Saints in their own tongue at least pointed to a growing trust between Jenson and church leaders and predicted a robust future for the entrepreneurial historian. Later in 1883, *Den Kostelige Perle* (The Pearl of Great Price) was issued as a stand-alone volume.[121]

Over the four-year print run of *Morgenstjernen*, Jenson published sixty issues for a total of 960 pages of historical text.[122] To save on costs, in 1884 Jenson started to typeset *Morgenstjernen* out of his Seventeenth Ward home in Salt Lake City. "I secured a little handcart," Jenson reflected in his autobiography, "on which we wheeled the forms to the Deseret News office where the press work was done. . . . The printing . . . looked fine and hence the mechanical part of the work on the periodical received considerable praise."[123] Jenson also made periodic visits to the Historian's Office on South Temple Street, opposite the Lion House, to gather historical sources to create new content for his periodical.

With his literary work in full swing, Jenson's hardscrabble life as a frontier wage laborer was firmly in the past. He was an immigrant turned entrepreneur, who through ingenuity and determination, had forged a network of fellow Scandinavians to prop up his business. Jenson was entirely reliant on community for his sustenance. Jenson profited as a trustworthy and church-sanctioned voice of the Scandinavian Latter-day Saints. He forwent a place in the church's communal revival, the United Order, to forge a life as an independent historian and editor. Such a choice represented tensions that were changing Utah culture in the late nineteenth century—those between individual profit and communal gain and assimilation and Latter-day Saint distinctiveness. Jenson nurtured his new venture carefully, seeking always to stay in the good graces of his ecclesiastical superiors as he helped his fellow countrymen acclimate to Zion and their new life on the American continent.

His life as an entrepreneur was not without unavoidable costs. Jenson's business was built on itinerancy. He was frequently away from home, gathering new subscribers and collecting from old ones. While he relished his expanding stature in the territory, he lamented the boom-or-bust cycle of his subscriber-based business, and his frequent absence from his Seventeenth Ward home. Though he attempted to maintain religious and ethnic bonds with his fellow immigrants, his Scandinavian associates now represented both patrons and potential profits, which occasionally strained their previously friendly alliance that had aided Jenson during his own adaptation to Zion. Though Jenson was still involved in the scattered Scandinavian Latter-day Saint settlements as he grew his historical work, over time, his enterprises would start to pull him away from these familiar roots. With his close association to the church leadership, Jenson was evolving into an unofficial representative of the church, a role that was at once exhilarating and lonely and at times frustrating for the new historian.

3 Historian's Office Affiliate

On the south side of South Temple Street in Salt Lake City, across from the famed mansion of the late church president Brigham Young, sat an unassuming adobe residence. The home lacked the eye-catching ornamentation of Young's Lion House and now, nearly a quarter century old, was beginning to show the effects of age and the harsh Utah elements. The two-story Church Historian's Office, completed in 1856, was a vestige of early territorial life, when resources were scarce and infrastructure projects abundant. The building had predominantly served the purpose of housing official documents and the church's fledgling historical enterprise.[1] It was a central hub in the nineteenth century for church administration as well as historical and doctrinal documentation and preservation.

Only a few blocks to the northwest sat Andrew Jenson's Seventeenth Ward residence. He was within walking distance of the Historian's Office and its clerical staff, archival records, and library. This closer proximity facilitated more frequent engagement with the office's record keepers, including Church Historian and Recorder Wilford Woodruff and Assistant Church Historian Franklin D. Richards. Jenson was still a private entrepreneur who shared the passion of the Church Historians for Latter-day Saint history but lacked the official title to guide and expand the projects of the Historian's Office. Jenson's "calling" as a historian came not from formal ecclesiastical endorsement but from personal ambition and a spiritual sense of purpose. Yet the private nature of his literary work increasingly failed to satisfy his personal and career expectations. Jenson was a committed writer, translator, and recorder of Latter-day Saint history, but he longed to be consecrated as an official church record keeper.

The Beginnings of the Church Historian's Office

Record keeping and history writing were important enterprises for the church from its beginning. On the day Joseph Smith organized the church, April 6, 1830, he also dictated a revelation to guide the new faith: "Behold, there shall be a record kept among you."[2] Early church record keepers included Oliver Cowdery, the "second elder" of the church, and John Whitmer, who was commanded in a March 1831 revelation to "to keep the church record and history continually."[3] Whitmer did keep a history of the church, though it, as well as Smith's private attempts at record keeping, were done largely in fits and starts.[4]

As the body of the church underwent several large-scale migrations, which created new pressing priorities for church leaders, the work of gathering and writing history struggled for stability. Several men served formally as either Church Historian or Church Recorder during these tumultuous times.[5] Smith finally appointed Apostle Willard Richards to be both the Church Historian and Church Recorder in Nauvoo, Illinois.[6] When the Latter-day Saints were forced from Nauvoo, Richards and his clerks packed up their paper records into wooden boxes and freighted them west to Utah. But with the demands of settlement in the Great Basin, other apostolic duties, and health challenges, the Church Historian did not unpack the historical records until June 1853—six years later.[7]

A month after Richards's death in March 1854, Apostle George A. Smith, first cousin of the martyred prophet, was appointed Church Historian and Church Recorder.[8] This appointment further established the tradition of calling apostles to the ecclesiastical office of Church Historian.[9] Smith moved the historical records from Richards's office to the Council House, but he was soon forced to move operations to the neighboring Tithing Storehouse. Smith described the poor condition of his work environment and records in a late February 1855 letter: "Many records are nearly obliterated by time, damp and dirt. Others lost. Some have worked into mouse nests, and many important events were never written except in the hearts of those who were concerned."[10]

President Brigham Young determined that Smith's family and his small staff warranted better accommodations, and in 1855, workmen finished construction on Smith's residence and adjoining structure—the Historian's Office. Smith was soon elected to petition the US Congress in Washington, DC, for Utah's statehood, leaving Apostle Wilford Woodruff, one of the foremost diarists of the early church, in charge of the church's record-keeping operations.[11] Finally, beginning on September 10, 1856, Woodruff and the clerks moved all the records into the new Historian's Office.[12] During that October's general conference, church leaders sustained Woodruff as the first Assistant Church Historian, a new official position within the church's hierarchy.[13]

Smith, who returned to Utah by June 1857, served as Church Historian until October 1870.[14] The First Presidency appointed Apostle Albert Carrington as the next Church Historian in October 1870. But when Carrington was called to be one of Young's counselors in the First Presidency in May 1874, he was released and succeeded by Apostle Orson Pratt, who led the Historian's Office until his death in 1881. The office of the Church Historian then sat vacant for two years until Woodruff was finally promoted to the position in 1883.[15]

All four Church Historians and their Assistant Church Historians had also served in church leadership. These dual roles, as well as outside persecution and the early struggle to properly house the documents, resulted in disorganization and inefficiencies.[16] The chaos continued into the 1880s, when Andrew Jenson began frequenting the Historian's Office semi-regularly, searching for historical material to support his publications and inserting himself into the quotidian activities of the office.

Tensions between Latter-day Saints and the federal government ratcheted up as new legislation more effectively targeted polygamists in Utah Territory for prosecution. In the 1870s, church leaders floated a test case before the territorial courts that resulted in the first upheld conviction of a Latter-day Saint polygamist. The federal government, emboldened by its victory in the *Reynolds v. United States* case, strengthened its anti-polygamy legislation with broad enforcement powers that sent many Latter-day Saint polygamists underground to avoid prosecution and imprisonment for "unlawful cohabitation." Federal prosecutors responded with "raids," as they became known in Latter-day Saint circles, targeting high-profile church leaders.[17] Assistant Church Historian (since 1884) and Apostle Franklin D. Richards administered the church from the Historian's Office while supporting (generally with documentation) the efforts of his lawyer-son Franklin S. Richards, who was the church's main legal counsel and tasked with defending indicted polygamists. The Historian's Office soon became a target of federal authorities who sought access to records that might shed light on the church's marriage practices and economic holdings. In late 1887, when it became clear that the anti-polygamy campaign would not relent, Richards began to move church records from the Historian's Office in case federal marshals assumed control of church property.[18] During the decade when Jenson became more affiliated with church leaders, the crisis of anti-polygamy legislation and enforcement would touch many aspects of his own life.

Ecclesiastical Aspirations

The appointed ecclesiastical offices of Church Historian and Assistant Church Historian fell under the umbrella of the larger priesthood hierarchy of the church. The First Presidency, led by the prophet and president (the most senior apostle), was the church's governing council. The second-highest presiding body, the Quorum of the Twelve Apostles, served under the First Presidency's direction. Collectively, these fifteen or so men became known as the "presiding brethren." Beginning in 1876, when Jenson sent his initial letter to First Presidency counselor Daniel H. Wells about his proposed Danish translation and revision of the history of Joseph Smith, Jenson cultivated a number of relationships with apostolic leaders, especially Erastus Snow, John Taylor, and Franklin D. Richards. As an immigrant-convert who lacked familial ties or social networks in Utah's power structure, he quickly appreciated the importance of developing friendships with church leaders above him who could potentially aid his professional progress and aspirations.

His frequent interactions with some in church leadership likely stoked his private desire for ecclesiastical appointment. The death of Elder John Van Cott, one of the Seven Presidents of the Seventy, in February 1883 left an open position.[19] The Quorum of the Seventy, a third tier of general church leaders, was created in 1835 under the direction of Joseph Smith in Kirtland, Ohio.[20] By the mid-1880s, there were seventy-six quorums of the Seventy spread throughout the Intermountain West.[21] But only the Seven Presidents of the Seventy, who were responsible for leading Latter-day Saint men—including Jenson—ordained to the priesthood office of seventy, were considered "General Authorities" (a term used in Doctrine and Covenants 102:32) with the members of the First Presidency, Quorum of the Twelve, and Presiding Bishopric.[22] These appointed men were called to minister for the church full time, with a limited living allowance, for the remainder of their lives.[23] In Utah, whose population was overwhelmingly Latter-day Saint, few individuals were held in higher esteem—or to superior standards—than the General Authorities of the church.

Full-time church service appealed to Jenson. His livelihood currently depended on his personal ambition and ingenuity as well as on erratic market forces. Having attended Van Cott's funeral, he began to ruminate about the president's replacement.[24] He recorded his private hopes in his journal: "I was led to ask the Almighty for special blessings, and I felt at the time that my desires should be granted, if I continue faithful, which may God enable me to, is my earnest prayer." His aspiration was further fueled by the comments of his associates. "When I went up in the centre of town in the evening," he wrote, "I learned from one of my good friends that about the time I was praying one of the leading men of the Church had been making diligent inquiries in regards to my faithfulness, trait of character, family affairs etc. What does it mean? The future will undoubtedly unfold the mystery."[25] It possibly meant that church leaders were considering him for another proselyting mission, but Jenson hoped a formal General Authority calling might be in his future. However, church leaders made no announcement weeks later during the April general conference meetings, leaving Van Cott's successor a mystery to church members.

On April 14, 1883, President John Taylor shared new organizational "instructions" regarding the Seventy quorums; among other counsel, the instructions advised that the vacancy "occasioned by the death of Elder John Van Cott" be filled by "one from among the Scandinavian brethren."[26] Latter-day Saint leaders published these instructions in a pamphlet and distributed three thousand copies to general church members.[27] The announcement was so meaningful to the Danish Jenson that he pasted an entire copy into his journal.[28]

The public pronouncement likely fueled the secret hopes of many Danish, Norwegian, and Swedish priesthood holders in Utah. Jenson was no different. His name was perhaps brought up unprompted by friends and colleagues to church leaders, but he also made his own recommendation. In May 1883, a joint letter with his mentor Apostle Erastus Snow was sent to Apostle Wilford Woodruff, putting forward Jenson's name as one qualified and willing to fill the vacancy in the Seven Presidents of the Seventy. According to Franklin D. Richards, who was present in a meeting of the First Presidency and Quorum of the Twelve when the letter was read, the letter's contents described Jenson's "fitness for & dream of being called to fill vacancy caused by [the] death of John Van Cott."[29] It's unclear how seriously church leaders considered Jenson's self-recommendation, but he was certainly anxious to be seen by his leaders as one prepared for a higher calling.

In what was likely an agonizing waiting period for Jenson, Van Cott's position remained open for a year. Unknown to Jenson, Wilford Woodruff, president of the Quorum of the Twelve, and Horace S. Eldredge, president of the First Council of the Seventy, had made a joint recommendation to the First Presidency in June 1883, which President Taylor and the rest of the First Presidency had privately approved.[30] Almost a year later, at general conference on April 6, 1884, church leaders finally announced fifty-five-year-old Christian D. Fjeldsted, a Dane and then serving as president of the Scandinavian Mission, to fill the open position.[31] Jenson was devastated. "Thus exploded, at least for the time being, the realization of my expectation to become one of the seven presidents of the seventies, notwithstanding I had every reason to expect that I would be called to fill that position," he grieved in his journal. Jenson, just thirty-two years old at this time, searched for a reasonable explanation for his missed appointment, theorizing that it was because he, unlike Fjeldsted, was a monogamist: "The reason why I was slighted and another man, who by the way, was considered too old for the position at first when his name was suggested, is more than I can tell, but the supposition is, that it was because I have not yielded obedience to the principle of plural marriage."[32]

The most probable explanation for Jenson being passed over for a General Authority position, however, was his lack of administrative or leadership experience. The predecessor Van Cott was of Dutch descent but had presided over the

Scandinavian Mission twice (1853–56, 1859–62).[33] Jenson had served as a mission president on only a short interim basis before Fjeldsted's appointment as mission president and still had much to learn. If he had not noticed before the disappointing rejection, he surmised now that presiding over the Scandinavian Mission offered a possible route into the presiding quorums of the church.

Dejected, Jenson walked home from the Tabernacle and did not return that evening for the general priesthood meeting because he felt "bad and tired." Ironically, he missed "some excellent instructions . . . in regard to plural marriage" from church leaders that night. Days later, Jenson met with one of his advisors and shared his disappointment about not being called as a General Authority: "Erastus Snow told me not to feel bad about it for the Lord had a better position reserved for me."[34] The consoling words from his apostle mentor did little to relieve Jenson's anxious spirit.

A Postlude in Scandinavian Publishing

Without the anticipated added ecclesiastical responsibilities, Jenson's focus remained on serving as a historian and champion for Scandinavian Latter-day Saints. For years, Jenson's frustrations with *Bikuben*'s lack of literary and professional quality had been simmering. By the summer of 1884, Jenson was considering publishing a competing newspaper alongside his historical magazine, *Morgenstjernen*. Even as he struggled to keep *Morgenstjernen* solvent, Jenson proved unafraid of taking on more publishing risks. In August, he entered an agreement with fellow Dane Christian A. F. Orlob to begin presswork on a newspaper the next December.[35] The paper reprised the title of *Utah Posten*, a now-defunct creation of Peter O. Thomassen, a Norwegian Latter-day Saint, who gave Jenson approval to use the name of his former paper.[36]

The new competition did not sit well with Jenson's former publishing partner, Anders W. Winberg, who continued to sustain *Bikuben*. Jenson's new venture threatened to further divide the already limited Scandinavian subscriber base, initiating a newspaper war between the two publications. Jenson and Orlob approached Winberg with a proposal to combine the two newspapers, but Winberg firmly declined. Instead, Winberg hired Thomassen, who was a gifted writer and could improve the literary appeal of *Bikuben*. *Bikuben*'s masthead still billed itself as "the best Scandinavian paper" in the territory, while Jenson attempted to appeal to "intelligent Scandinavians" throughout Utah. In addition, Jenson suggested that his paper carried the coveted sanction of church leaders.[37]

The first number of *Utah Posten* came off the press and was mailed to subscribers in early January 1885.[38] By the end of February, Jenson had gathered nearly five hundred subscribers, likely because he tapped into his existing subscriber base for *Morgenstjernen*. He also witnessed the anticipated division among Scandinavian Latter-day Saints. "There are, however, a great many who think that the opposition between our papers and 'Bikuben' should not exist, as it has a tendency to divide the people in parties, a fact that perhaps can not be successfully denied," Jenson wrote to Apostle Erastus Snow. "The collision had to come," according to Jenson, because Winberg refused to reconcile the two newspapers into one. Jenson felt that he was being treated as an enemy at a time when Scandinavians should be "united in the common defence" of the church, given its current political and legal challenges. In his letter, Jenson was essentially asking Snow to pick sides in the affair. "We need your full hearted support," he told Snow, "for it is a true fact that there is not element enough in our Territory to sustain two papers of the same kind."[39] But Snow refused to select and endorse a side.[40] Embittered against Winberg, Jenson intended to initiate the demise of *Bikuben*, but he needed church leaders to sign off on his paper with a more decisive public endorsement.

Instead, financial struggles forced Jenson to reconcile. With Thomassen's help, the increased quality of *Bikuben* stayed the mass exodus of subscribers Jenson had initially anticipated, and he never received the full endorsement of his ecclesiastical superiors for *Utah Posten*. In early April 1885, Jenson negotiated a truce with Winberg, agreeing to start a joint-stock venture under the Scandinavian Publishing Company, officially folding *Utah Posten* into *Bikuben*. However, further disagreement on the terms of the merger prevented the company from ever launching, and Jenson resumed editing *Bikuben* with Winberg under a private arrangement.[41]

The reconciliation with Winberg and *Bikuben* was also perhaps caused by Jenson's sense that his relationship with Snow was growing strained, given Jenson's repeated requests of the apostle. A letter from Snow just prior to Jenson's suspension of *Utah Posten* had censured him for some of the content printed in the paper. The withdrawal of Snow's support caused Jenson to "kindly ask to be excused from having any thing to do with Scandinavian literature . . . in Utah."[42] Humbled, Jenson began to contemplate and question his future in the Scandinavian publishing business. He needed a wider reach for his historical publications and more financial and ecclesiastical support to breathe life into his struggling career as an entrepreneurial historian.

Affiliating with the Historian's Office

In the summer of 1884, Assistant Church Historian Franklin D. Richards encouraged Jenson to more closely affiliate with the Historian's Office. The apostle "intimated to me," wrote Jenson, "that it might be better for me to be engaged at the Historian's Office to work in connection with him and Woodruff, instead of pushing my historical labors on in a private way, to which I consented."[43]

The invitation from Richards was at least partially self-interested. Since 1880, the Historian's Office, and Richards in particular, had assisted Hubert Howe Bancroft, the renowned historian of the American West, with a volume on the history of Utah. Bancroft, stationed in San Francisco, needed direct assistance from the Historian's Office in gaining access to valuable manuscripts and early territorial documents. The First Presidency saw an opportunity in helping Bancroft: balanced histories of the Latter-day Saints were in short supply as the church continued its public fight with the federal government over polygamy. A praiseworthy history from the respected Bancroft could shift the critical tides.[44]

By 1884, Richards, while supportive of Bancroft's project, was starting to grow weary of the frequent requests for material. Thus Jenson stepped in to help service Bancroft's research requests.[45] On November 20, Jenson commented in his journal, "I worked my first day at the Historian's Office, making extracts of Church History for Bancroft's History of the Pacific States. The labor pleased me."[46] In between prolonged periods of absence, Jenson would also fulfill small tasks as assigned to him by Woodruff and Richards. His infrequent presence in the Historian's Office was perhaps caused by his continued preoccupation with *Morgenstjernen* and his new work on *Utah Posten*. When he accepted the temporary work at the Historian's Office, he told Woodruff and Richards that he still needed part of his time at his "own command" until he had his "publishing business properly wound up."[47] Jenson had to earn a living. By year's end, his compensation from the Historian's Office was a lowly $10.15 (compared to the $1,287 netted from *Morgenstjernen*).[48]

The temporary arrangement with the Historian's Office did little to inspire Jenson's confidence that he would one day obtain a permanent role there. Thus, he continued to imagine new private enterprises through which to support his family. Jenson had contemplated shifting away from Scandinavian publishing for a time, and with the church facing serious external threats, he felt the time was right to expand his audience (and he received approval from Erastus Snow to do so).[49] Jenson believed he had "published in Danish all in the historical line that can be deemed necessary for the present."[50] After four years of editing and publishing *Morgenstjernen*, he transformed the periodical into an English-language historical magazine, beginning in January 1886, a decision that would increase his contact with the Historian's Office as he used its holdings to create content for his new publication.[51]

To generate interest in his new historical venture, Jenson issued a bold prospectus in the *Deseret Evening News*, which introduced English-speaking Latter-day Saints to his future publishing projects. "After being engaged in historical labor for nearly nine years, during which we have published a condensed history of the Prophet Joseph Smith, reminiscences from the Scandinavian mission, etc., in the Danish-Norwegian language, we have finally concluded to enter into a more extended historical field," he announced. Jenson planned to continue publishing a variety of church history and statistics, which could later be gathered into a comprehensive encyclopedia. He promised his readers a grand overview of the leading people, places, and events important in Latter-day Saint history; mission histories along with histories of individual church units; histories of church historical sites as well as sacred structures, like temples and tabernacles; and a chronology of Latter-day Saint history from 1805 to the present. Regarding his literary style, Jenson promised, "No attempt will be made to use flowery language, as the main object is to present facts in truth and simplicity. Accuracy as to dates and figures will be a predominant feature, so that the entire work may be considered good authority in all matters upon which it treats."[52] He announced that the first issue of the monthly *Historical Record* would soon appear at the continued annual subscription price of $1.25.

As promised, Jenson published the inaugural issue of the *Historical Record* in January 1886. Volume 5 (continuing the numbering where *Morgenstjernen* had left off) surveyed a range of topics on church history, sometimes relying on the work of others while occasionally featuring Jenson's own historical spadework. That January and February he focused on early church history, reprinting the writings of George A. Smith and Orson Pratt, both former Church Historians, and inaugurated a long-standing series of articles on members of the Quorum of the Twelve. He also added a "Miscellaneous" section, a collection of geographical and biographical entries that he was collecting for later compilation and publication.[53] That March he continued "The Twelve Apostles" sketches and "Miscellaneous" biographies and ventured into a project on church historic sites that would eventually take him on a historical tour in 1888.[54]

His foray into English-language publishing confirmed what Jenson had privately feared—that Latter-day Saints lacked a firm understanding of the historical details related to the people, places, and events of the Restoration. Jenson offered chronologies, biographies, and documents related to the development of the church to Latter-day Saints in the Great Basin in order to preserve public memory of their history. Latter-day Saints could celebrate their "Historical Record," which reinforced their distinctiveness and divine favor as a people and their ability to overcome external persecutions for the restored gospel's sake. Jenson witnessed the rise of Latter-day Saint struggles, particularly over the practice of plural marriage, firsthand as he made his transition from Danish publisher to church historian and weighed his own entrance into the practice.

Entering into Plural Marriage

In the years since Jenson's marriage to Mary, the couple had fallen into a routine. Jenson was frequently away supporting his literary and historical ventures, leaving Mary home to tend to the household and children alone. She proved equal to the task while also becoming involved in humanitarian causes, including helping coordinate multiple excursions for the "poor, orphans, fatherless and motherless children of both sexes, children of newly arrived emigrants, and poor children of Salt Lake City generally."[55] She also filled Jenson's absence with social activities, hosting and attending parties and building a network of friends that elevated her influence in the Salt Lake community. Mary found enjoyment in her work, and all appeared well for the married couple. In August 1885, they welcomed a daughter, Eleonore.[56] Fortunes, however, would change quickly for the young family.

On May 2, 1885, Jenson attended a mass meeting for Salt Lake County church members to approve a declaration of grievances in support of plural marriage and religious liberty intended for US president Grover Cleveland. Similar assemblies were occurring in counties throughout Utah Territory on the same day.[57] Jenson remarked in his journal, "This is no doubt to be considered an important day in Church History." Jenson attended as a committed church member, not as a polygamist in fear of prosecution.[58]

These were dangerous times for polygamists. Salt Lake Stake President Angus M. Cannon, for instance, was currently being prosecuted in a high-profile case for unlawful cohabitation.[59] Polygamists were encouraged to remain in hiding, but church leaders showed no signs of suspending the practice. Instead, they were resolute, even defiant in their beliefs that the principle was ordained by God and that federal marshals were infringing on constitutional liberties. A frenzied political and legal climate contributed to an end-times atmosphere in the territory.[60] Jenson absorbed the strident rhetoric of church leaders about entering plural marriage.

Over a year later, on September 10, 1886, Jenson and another male member of his ward visited and blessed a sick neighbor, Emma Howell, then twenty-four years old and living only two houses down from the Jenson family.[61] Emma, her mother, Fanny, and her younger sister, Bertha, had emigrated from Great Britain earlier in the year. Emma's father, James Howell, had passed away from consumption in 1873, leaving Emma, as the eldest daughter, and her mother in search of work. The Howells first heard of the church from a relative, Joseph Bodell, who was serving in England as a missionary. While Emma and Bertha both converted, Fanny still clung to her faith in the Church of England.[62] To Jenson, Emma seemed to possess the refinement and interests of high Victorian society, and he learned quickly of her skills as a homemaker, acquired during her tenure as a lady's maid among England's leisure class.[63] He "began to feel considerable affection" for her and at the same time spent much of his time at the bedside of Mary, who had been sick the entire summer of 1886 from tuberculosis.[64]

Bertha Howell and Emma Howell in England, circa 1883. Courtesy Church History Library.

As Emma began to recover, Mary grew increasingly ill. Jenson informally proposed plural marriage to Emma on October 27, making it clear that the marriage would need to remain private, "submitting to the conditions and restrictions necessitated by the pressure of the present unhallowed persecutions against the Saints."[65] Plural marriages during this period were performed in secret and not publicly announced to avoid federal prosecution. The prospect of a second marriage put Jenson's personal and public life at risk. A conviction for unlawful cohabitation carried a prison sentence of up to six months and a fine of three hundred dollars.[66]

The following week Jenson formally approached Emma's mother and asked for her permission to proceed with the marriage, which she reluctantly gave after much protest.[67] Jenson, however, still had not received the consent of his wife, Mary, to take another wife. According to a revelation dictated by Joseph Smith, men entering the order of plural marriage were required to ask for the consent of their first wife but could proceed without consent if their first wife rejected the principle of plural marriage.[68] Mary Jenson was "indirectly opposed" to the practice, according to Jenson.[69] She, however, understood the ecclesiastical and social pressure he, along with other monogamist Latter-day Saint men, faced to obey "the principle" and perhaps suspected, as did Jenson, that his General Authority ambitions had been hindered because of his monogamist status. Mary eventually eased her spousal opposition with a compromise. "On Saturday morning," presumably November 6, she told Jenson that "she had covenanted with the Lord that if He would spare her life and restore her to health and strength, she would obey all His commandments and allow her husband to take another wife." Jenson promised her "that she should recover if it was the Lord's will which may God grant."[70] Perhaps fearful that she was being punished with illness by God for her reticence, Mary's exclusive relationship with Jenson became her sacrificial offering as she prayed for a miraculous healing.

Days later, Jenson wrote to Emma under a pseudonym: "I am happy to be able to inform you that my wife is better, and is improving daily, and furthermore that she will give her full-hearted consent—so far as it is possible for a woman—to your union with the family." "I love you," he wrote, "and am willing to take chan[c]es with you to obey the law of God in preference to the unjust laws passed by a wicked and fallen nation." "It must not be forgotten," he reminded Emma, "that my action is owing to my belief in a principle that I know comes from God."[71] He began making preparations with his local bishop for Emma to head to the recently completed temple in Logan, Utah, to receive the endowment ordinance so that they could be married.[72]

Mary's health, however, soon turned for the worse, proving resistant to both her and her husband's frequent pleadings to God and Jenson's priesthood blessings to her.[73] On December 8, he called upon John Henry Smith, of the Quorum of the Twelve, and their ward bishop to bless Mary again. "But it did not seem to have much effect," Jenson lamented.[74] At this point he hired a doctor to look after Mary, and the physician promised a full and speedy recovery.[75]

Even with Mary's health failing, Jenson was still determined to proceed with the marriage to Emma. On December 10, he took Emma to the Salt Lake Endowment House, where they were married by sealing ordinance by Apostle Franklin D. Richards. The only other person present was Seventy Joseph W. McMurrin, who served as a witness.[76]

Little changed in the closing weeks of 1886. Emma returned to live with her mother down the street from Jenson's home, and the marriage was met with no celebration or announcement to friends and family. His time and attention continued to be occupied by Mary. By January 3, 1887, it became clear that Mary's fate was sealed. "I felt it my duty to let her go, for her sufferings were almost unendurable, but she still desired to live," Jenson wrote. While Jenson attempted to ease Mary's final moments in mortality, she pleaded with her husband, "No, don't give me up." Despite her protest—her last words to the family—she died in Jenson's arms that afternoon, surrounded by their young children Andrew, Parley, and Minerva (baby Eleonore was with Mary's parents) and other loved ones. Jenson inscribed a benediction to his wife's life in his journal: "Goodbye, my beloved Mary, wife of my youth, my first love, until we shall meet again in the resurrection of the just, never more to part."[77]

Jenson's religious world was briefly shaken by the death of his wife. He vented the feelings of his heart and his anguish to God. "O Lord," he grieved, "why am I called upon to sustain this great loss? Why did you not prolong her days upon the earth for which we had prayed so earnestly? Why allow the destroyer to slay her thus in the prime of youth, and leave my four children without a mother? How incomprehensible are thy ways, O Lord, but I will not murmur. When my eyes are opened so that I shall see and understand as God, I shall no doubt understand that Thou had a purpose in thus calling her away. But O, how lonesome I feel."[78] Sorting out his own desires and what he discerned as God's will became one of the major tensions of his life. On the evening of Mary's death he penned, "When I am writing these lines at 10 o clock at night, while I am watching over the earthly lifeless tabernacle of my beloved One, I feel that the world is so empty, that there is a vacancy which never can be filled, and that my loss is great indeed."[79] The Jensons buried their wife and mother, dressed in her temple clothes, in the Salt Lake City Cemetery, in the middle of a snowstorm.[80]

In early January, Jenson's three youngest children—Parley (age eight), Minerva (age three), and Eleonore (age sixteen months)—were sent to Pleasant Grove to live with Mary's sister Christine and her husband while Andrew (age ten) remained at home to help his father. Over the next month, Jenson brought the children home to live with him, with the exception of Eleonore, who stayed in Pleasant Grove until June.[81] The burden of keeping a household and tending to the children quickly overwhelmed Jenson, and he decided to invite Emma into the home in early February under the guise of being his housekeeper. Still almost no one knew that they had been married secretly nearly two months earlier.[82]

By the end of February, however, Andrew and Emma Jenson determined to solemnize in public their earlier private sealing in the Endowment House. Though Jenson was once again a monogamist and unlikely to be arrested, he and Emma took precautions to avoid prosecution for his brief participation in plural marriage. On February 28, the couple traveled to Ogden, Utah, to feign the performance of an actual marriage ceremony. Instead, they merely stayed for a few days at the home of his former mission president, Nils C. Flygare.

The marriage, wrote Jenson, "subjected me to criticism on the part of some who thought it improper for me to marry so soon after Mary's death."[83] The most strident critique came from Mary's family members, who were "cross and ugly" about the prospect of Mary being replaced so quickly.[84] When Jenson and Emma returned to Salt Lake City, they presented themselves as husband and wife to those in their community. Emma's mother, Fanny, was also baptized a Latter-day Saint about this time.[85] For the time being, Jenson watched from the sidelines as his polygamous friends and leaders faced the perils of living as polygamists. His committed private testimony of the practice would soon turn into a public defense.

Defending Plural Marriage

Within a week of his "honeymoon," church leaders invited Jenson to speak to two hundred Latter-day Saints incarcerated at the Utah Penitentiary south of Salt Lake City for their defiant practice of plural marriage. It was a sobering moment for Jenson. "To see our brethren, many of whom I was personally acquainted with, clad in the striped garb of the prison and mingled with criminals of the worst kind was too humiliating a sight for my sympathetic nature. I found tears coursing their way down my cheeks." He preached again at the penitentiary in June of that same year.[86]

Witnessing firsthand the effects of the federal raids on Latter-day Saint polygamists may have provoked Jenson to eventually publicly defend the practice, even as other Latter-day Saints fell silent on the issue. By 1887, the federal government's prosecution of polygamists in Utah had reached a fever pitch with the passage of the Edmunds-Tucker Act. At the same time, leaders and missionaries of the Reorganized Church of Jesus Christ of Latter Day Saints (RLDS Church) and other Restoration movements were publicly attacking the church, charging Brigham Young—not Joseph Smith—with instituting plural marriage in the 1840s to satisfy his own carnal desires. As public opinion sharpened and legal attacks on Latter-day Saint polygamists increased, church leaders attempted to downplay in public discussion the furtherance of plural marriage in the territory, even as they still privately encouraged its practice.[87] Silence on the topic was observed in Latter-day Saint meetings and publications.

The immediate rationale for suspending any public defense of plural marriage related directly to new efforts to achieve statehood for Utah. A constitutional convention was held in late June, and the selected delegates took a test oath as required by the Edmunds-Tucker Act, to demonstrate their loyalty to federal law and to certify their monogamist status. Jenson was selected to participate. The most provocative aspect of the convention was an adopted clause to the proposed state constitution criminalizing polygamy and prohibiting the union of church and state. While outsiders doubted the sincerity of the new provisions, they addressed the major sticking points of prior statehood attempts and were meant to mitigate the potentially disastrous effects of the Edmunds-Tucker Act on the church and its leaders. Jenson was invited to speak at the convention, where he made clear his pride in his new adopted country: "Many of the people of Utah had come from the Scandinavian nations, but they were not Scandinavian to-day," the *Deseret News* summary read. They were now "American citizens, honest and true."[88]

Church leaders, despite their relative absence from public life, attempted to orchestrate the bid for statehood behind the scenes, a move that, if successful, would take the reins of governance out of the hands of federally appointed officials and place them in the hands of local legislators who, in theory, would be more sympathetic to the church's political aims. Church leaders invited Jenson and many of the other delegates to a private meeting at the President's Office to counsel them on how to represent their labors to the public. First Counselor George Q. Cannon told the delegates "not to argue with the people" but to give the church's endorsement on the new anti-polygamy provisions. "The Lord was in the movement," Jenson recorded Cannon as saying.[89] Jenson left the meeting with a new appreciation for the delicate public-relations task before them. Voters in the territory overwhelmingly ratified the new constitution in August, and it went before Congress the next year. However, despite the added anti-polygamy statutes, the continuance of plural marriage in the territory delayed congressional action on the new statehood bid.[90]

With his fellow religious adherents in peril, Jenson longed to take a more active role in their defense. His new periodical, the *Historical Record*, offered a suitable platform for a long-form defense of plural marriage. Unlike *Morgenstjernen*, there was no apostolic oversight of the *Historical Record*, so he was free to prepare and issue content as he saw fit. In June, he began to research the plural wives of Joseph Smith for a forthcoming article. He spent the better part of a week interviewing "ladies who had formerly been sealed to Joseph Smith the Prophet as wives."[91] His primary confidantes were Malissa Lott Willes and Eliza R. Snow.[92] Willes, a resident of Lehi, a city south of Salt Lake City, had been sealed to Smith in late September 1843 at the age of nineteen, and Snow, a gifted writer and thinker who was well-known throughout Utah Territory, was president of the Relief Society.[93] She had been sealed to Smith in 1842 (and later to Brigham Young).[94]

Jenson also sent out letters soliciting information from former spouses of Smith. This included one to Willes, who sent him back a document that helped him create his list of plural wives.[95] It also seems likely that Jenson showed his provisional list to Snow, who offered more names and improvements.[96] He wrote or spoke to a number of others, including Mary Elizabeth Rollins Lightner and Zina D. H. Young (plural wives of Smith), Emmeline B. Wells (widow of Bishop Newel K. Whitney and a prominent Relief Society leader), Marietta Welling (the daughter of Smith's plural wife Elvira A. Cowles), John Lyman Smith (son-in-law of Smith's plural wife Sarah M. Cleveland), Levi W. Richards (a nephew of Smith's plural wife Rhoda Richards), and others.[97] Jenson also combed existing affidavits, testimonies, and newspaper accounts for information. The scope of Jenson's sleuthing in a short amount of time was remarkable.[98] While Joseph Smith's practice of plural marriage was occasionally discussed openly by his former wives, an authoritative list with documentation had not yet been published.[99]

The list that Jenson published accounted for twenty-seven of the names found on two of his earlier drafts, but these preliminary lists and his notes suggest that he was aware of at least three other potential plural wives not included in his published version.[100] In the introduction to his list of Joseph Smith's plural wives, which appeared in the July issue of the *Historical Record*, Jenson laid out his logic for making the list public. He felt "apostates and other opponents of the truth" were "attempting to deny certain facts connected with the introduction of plural marriage among the Latter-day Saints by Joseph Smith." Thus Jenson "deemed proper" his effort to "compile and republish in the *Record* the . . . statements, testimonies, affidavits, etc., from truthful and reliable parties, who have been eye and ear witnesses to the circumstances and incidents of" Smith's practice of plural marriage.[101]

Without question, the resulting fifteen-page article on the origins of plural marriage became Jenson's most controversial piece of writing. His essay showcased one of the earliest published lists of Joseph Smith's plural wives together with affidavits and testimonies from several of these women and their family members that documented their marital status to the church's founding prophet. Jenson provided concise biographical details for most of the plural wives on his list and more detailed biographies for the rest of them. He concluded his lengthy defense of plural marriage with his own conviction and testimony of its righteous origins and rationale: "We could produce hundreds of other testimonies of a similar nature to these given above, were it necessary, but what we have already given must be deemed fairly sufficient to prove, beyond a shadow of doubt, that Joseph Smith, the Prophet, did teach and practice the principle of plural marriage in his lifetime."[102]

Jenson's documentary disclosure of Joseph Smith's practice of plural marriage likely further flamed attacks from the church's critics. Church leaders were concerned that Jenson's article would hinder them in their critical battle with the federal government and their latest bid for statehood. "We do not question your good desires in making these names public," Church Historian Wilford Woodruff wrote to Jenson, "but we are led to question the propriety of giving this publicity to them at the present time."[103] With the bid for statehood on its way to Congress, the church needed to appear as if it were distancing itself from the practice of plural marriage. In addition, Woodruff feared Jenson had made Smith's surviving wives the potential targets of prying reporters and gawking onlookers who might do them harm. Woodruff's fears aside, only a month later the *St. Louis Globe-Democrat* printed a candid interview with Zina D. H. Young, Emmeline B. Wells, and Eliza R. Snow about their experiences with plural marriage. The article, titled "Two Prophets' Widows," reprinted and made frequent reference to Jenson's list of Smith's plural wives in the *Historical Record* (which Wells supplied to the correspondent during the interview).[104] The women had given their sanction to Jenson's work and apparently did not share Woodruff's fears.

Jenson felt misunderstood and worked to explain his misstep. He wrote a response to Woodruff, assuring him that he had received the consent of all of the women and their families who might be impacted by his article. In cases where "parties themselves did not wish the circumstances of their having been sealed to the Prophet made public," Jenson had not published their names. In addition, he felt at liberty to release the information because much of it had been published before. He was simply aggregating content into a singular source and releasing it for the benefit of a limited Latter-day Saint audience. Indeed, on this one occasion, Jenson felt the small circulation of the *Historical Record* worked to his advantage by reaching only its intended audience. Church leaders also later noted that they had derived at least a small victory from Jenson's article. Richards privately recorded that Jenson's list was "causing extensive schisms in the ranks of Young Joseph's followers." Joseph Smith III, and his RLDS Church publicly denied that Joseph Smith ever practiced or taught plural marriage. According to Richards, RLDS adherents were disturbed to "find that [Joseph Smith III] and his mother have lied to them & that Joseph had plurality of wives."[105] Jenson ultimately conceded to Woodruff's wishes and promised not to release any additional names (which suggests that he may have added to his published list in the ensuing months).[106] After being questioned and admonished by church authorities, Jenson resumed his next issue with staider and less controversial topics.

His public defense of plural marriage turned into private observation over the next year as he grew emotionally closer to Bertha, his new wife's twenty-two-year-old younger sister, who, together with their mother, had become de facto members of his household. There was increasing personal intimacy between Jenson and Bertha through the shared rhythms of daily life. Jenson finally asked to marry her, and she consented. The marriage had to be hidden from the public eye and out of the reach of the federal marshals around the Salt Lake area. Jenson devised a plan to leave the city separately from Bertha. He went by horse and buggy, and she traveled by train southward to Manti, Utah. Still uneasy that federal authorities might catch on to his marriage plans, Jenson arranged for Bertha to lodge at a friend's home while he slept on the limited comfort of a haystack a mile away. On July 18, 1888, at a predetermined time, Jenson took

The Jenson family, circa 1888. (Left to right) Mary Minerva Jenson, Andrew Alexander Jenson, Emma Jenson with child, Fanny Howell, Andrew Jenson, Bertha Howell, Parley P. Jenson, and Eleonore Elizabeth Jenson. Courtesy Church History Library.

Bertha to the recently completed and dedicated Manti Temple to be sealed to her in a private marriage ceremony performed by Apostle Daniel H. Wells. The pair immediately set out on an overnight trip home, but after a close encounter with federal marshals, they determined it was safer to travel home separately.[107]

The marriage put Jenson and his family at incredible risk of prosecution and complicated the dynamics of his household for years to come. At the time of his plural marriage to Bertha, Jenson had four living children from his first marriage to Mary—Andrew, Parley, Minerva, and Eleonore—and one child with Emma, Alfred, born earlier that year. For now, Jenson's historical labors and frequent travels helped mask his polygamist lifestyle, and given his already close attachment to the Howell family, nothing appeared out of the ordinary.

Striving for an Official Historical Voice

Still searching for inclusion, praise, and status, Jenson was disappointed when he continued to largely be an outsider to the Historian's Office in 1886 and 1887 as he persisted in publishing the *Historical Record*. His historical work brought him increased recognition and speaking opportunities among the general body of the church but initiated little change in the professional opportunities available to him. Jenson understood the respectability a formal attachment to church headquarters would give him and invited the First Presidency, especially President John Taylor, to offer a positive endorsement of his *Historical Record*. Such a recommendation, he hoped, would increase his magazine's circulation and alleviate pressing financial burdens.[108] In reviewing issues of the *Historical Record*, a project that he admitted knowing little about initially, Taylor found errors that concerned him. He gave Jenson a conditional recommendation, not wishing yet to stake his own reputation by endorsing a publication he did not find accurate.[109]

As church president, Taylor, had more pressing problems than the success of Jenson's magazine. Beginning in 1885, he went into hiding to avoid prosecution for plural marriage. Administering the church became increasingly challenging as he worked primarily through clandestine meetings and correspondence, which rendered Jenson's request only one among many sent to the aging prophet.[110] A year later, in February 1886, Jenson helped Apostles Wilford Woodruff (by dressing him in a disguise) and Erastus Snow escape from federal marshals encircling the Historian's Office. The marshals, in search of both Presidents Taylor and George Q. Cannon, also raided the residence of John Taylor, the Tithing Office, and other church offices.[111] Less than a week later, Cannon was arrested.

The unrelenting outside pressure on Latter-day Saint leaders failed to dissuade Jenson from asking for internal recognition and support. Prior to his letter to Taylor, Jenson had pleaded with Franklin D. Richards to broker the church's formal acquisition of his *Historical Record*. Jenson reminded Richards that he stood "ready at any time to deliver up every document or note of historical value that I have, if the authorities so desire, and continue my labors for the Church." Jenson felt that if his *Historical Record* was published as an "authentic Church publication," its circulation would expand. Furthermore, Jenson proposed a full tour of Latter-day Saint historic sites to gather information that would enhance his paper's contents, but he needed the financial support of the church to do so.[112] As Jenson's historical skills matured, he imagined a new role for himself—that of a traveling historian who would gather historical information for the church from the road. Church leaders made no immediate decision to acquiesce to the request, but his proposal formed a vision for the church's future historical work.

Jenson wrote again to Taylor in October 1886, laying before the prophet his financial struggles and his dedicated labors of the last decade. Disappointed with Taylor's earlier tepid recommendation, Jenson hoped a more "full and hearty approval could better be given" now that he had published more of the *Historical*

Record, including more of his church chronology. He also again boldly invited himself into the Historian's Office: "nothing would please me better than to be employed by the Church, as an assistant to its Historians."[113] A more supportive relationship with the Historian's Office would grant Jenson space to pursue more research on the scattered missions of the church, something he was now contemplating in addition to a tour of the church's historic sites. Taylor fell silent for a time, so in early 1887 Jenson repeated his request to George Q. Cannon.[114] Finally, in February he heard again from Taylor, who, citing practical reasons, politely declined to give Jenson's publications the full sanction of the church: "It is out of our power," he continued, "to examine the voluminous works which are published by one and another and pronounce upon their correctness, or give an unqualified opinion concerning them."[115]

Jenson remained persistent on his quest for more stable employment. Only weeks after Taylor's death in July 1887, he repeated his request for a formal church endorsement of the *Historical Record*, this time to Wilford Woodruff, now the senior member of the Quorum of the Twelve. Jenson's vision as expressed to Woodruff, if approved, would have placed the *Historical Record* as the de facto periodical of the Historian's Office, permitting him to work closely with the church's historians, improving the accuracy of his publication, and giving him a formal place at the Historian's Office.[116] Woodruff predictably declined, still put off by Jenson's public list of Joseph Smith's plural wives, but the Church Historian was ultimately sympathetic to historical work. For the first time, the church had a leader at its head (Woodruff would be sustained as church president in 1889) with personal experience in the Historian's Office. Woodruff eventually compromised with Jenson, and the Quorum of the Twelve approved a monthly stipend from the General Tithing Office for the equivalent of fifty dollars to compensate Jenson for his traveling expenses and time spent working on church history.[117] "This help came very handy as I am at present indebted to the amount of $1,000 to the Deseret News Company for printing," Jenson noted in his journal.[118]

The stipend was more than just monetary remuneration for the struggling historian. It was a sign to Jenson that his labors were appreciated and valued by his ecclesiastical leaders. This impression was reinforced by his first invitation to speak at general conference, during the opening session in April 1888. The invitation came "very unexpectedly" from Apostle Lorenzo Snow, just days after Jenson had received word of his stipend from the Historian's Office.[119] The call for the layman Jenson to address the churchwide congregation dispensed with the usual protocol of having mostly General Authorities address the congregation, but the number of General Authorities available to speak had been significantly decreased by the federal hunt for polygamists in the territory.[120] The private historian felt inadequate to "say anything that could edify this congregation unless the Spirit of God shall sustain me."[121] His address featured a mixture of testimony and church history, which was well suited to the ecclesiastical setting of general conference and suggested Jenson's future value to his superiors. A capable speaker, Jenson could communicate the church's historical interests to the Latter-day Saints.

The invitation to speak in general conference marked a transition then underway for the self-trained historian. Jenson agitated to be a historian for the church en masse, but he also learned the hard way that such an affiliation allowed church administration and leadership to closely direct his work at any time. Nonetheless, he continued to painstakingly produce and curate historical content for the general church membership while remaining faithful to church leaders. Such tireless effort paid off as church leaders realized Jenson's allegiance could benefit the church. Yet, he needed something beyond his existing publications to extend his reach and cement his position as an authoritative spokesperson on Latter-day Saint history.

Rediscovering the Sacred Sites of the Restoration

Ironically, Jenson, as a new polygamist, was safer in the provinces of former church persecution—New York, Ohio, Missouri, and Illinois—than he was in Utah Territory. Like some other Latter-day Saint polygamists, rather than conceal away underground, Jenson decided to travel, feeling the time was now right for his trip, contemplated two years prior, to the church's historic sites. For the Danish immigrant and convert, the historic sites of the Restoration were only adopted memories, an intellectual inheritance that informed his and other church members' shared religious heritage, but he longed to witness them in person. His trip, however, had a greater purpose. His tour was not merely a pleasure trip or an assignment from the Historian's Office but a formal mission for which he was set apart—along with his two companions, pioneers and fellow polygamists Edward Stevenson and Joseph S. Black—by Assistant Church Historian Franklin D. Richards.[122] Richards blessed Jenson that he might "write competently and creditably and faithfully of the doings of the Lord on the earth in the latter days, and of the doings and experiences of His people."[123] His divine errand included producing historical content that would capture the early experiences, persecutions, and triumphs of early Latter-day Saints. Similar to most departing missionaries, Jenson collected financial support from friends and family prior to leaving for his mission.[124]

Jenson's tour of the sacred places of the Restoration, none of which were then owned by the church, attempted to return the church's providential deliverance and its persecuted past to the public memory. Jenson and his traveling companions wrote of "the waste places of Zion" to uplift and encourage Latter-day Saints back home. Indeed, it was the absence of Latter-day Saints from the eastern and midwestern landscape—and the deterioration of their former homelands—that underscored God's presence with his people in the Great Basin. Before leaving on their journey, Jenson and his companions entered into an agreement with the church-owned *Deseret News* to publish their ongoing adventures. Over the next month, the three correspondents would send a flurry of eighteen letters, all of which were published on the pages of Utah's largest newspaper.

On September 6, 1888, Jenson and Black departed by train from Salt Lake City. Jenson was accompanied by both of his wives—Emma and Bertha—as he waited to leave at the train platform. Stevenson, a well-known polygamist, did not join Jenson and Black until they were farther south, "he being rather under cover—in danger of being arrested on a charge of unlawful cohabitation."[125] The three men traveled by rail from Utah to Missouri, where they visited several historic church sites before continuing eastward through Tennessee and to the seaport of Norfolk, Virginia. They then steamed up the Atlantic coast to New York City and then headed to Rochester, New York, and the cradle of the Restoration in nearby Palmyra. The trio next traveled to Kirtland, Ohio, and to Chicago, before turning south to Nauvoo, Illinois.

In Missouri, the men visited the site of the old temple lot in Independence, which Joseph Smith in 1831 had prophesied would be the "center place'" of Zion and the site of a new temple.[126] After Missouri mobs drove Latter-day Saints out of Jackson County in 1833, Smith received another revelation promising that one day "they that remain, and are pure in heart, shall return . . . to build up the waste places of Zion."[127] The current situation in Utah returned the minds of the travelers to the promises of their late prophet. Jenson, Black, and Stevenson kneeled at the dedicated temple site and prayed: "O Lord, remember thy words, and let not Zion suffer forever. Hasten her redemption, and let thy name be glorified in the victory of truth and righteousness over sin and iniquity." Jenson reminded *Deseret News* readers that God provided for "Israel to return to Jerusalem from their captivity in Babylon" and could perform the same miracle in modern times.[128]

Other visited sites included the jail in Liberty, Missouri, where Joseph Smith and other leaders had been imprisoned in late 1838; the site of the Hawn's Mill Massacre; the Hill Cumorah in New York; the church's former temple in Kirtland, Ohio; and sites in Nauvoo, Illinois. In lucid detail, Jenson and his traveling companions described the contemporary state of these places. Only a few Utah Saints had returned to these sites since the exodus from Nauvoo, beginning in 1846. Through the published accounts, readers could reacquaint themselves with early church prophecies and sacrifices and learn of the current state of the former homes and buildings of notable Latter-day Saint leaders.

In addition, the travelers reported on encounters with schismatic groups and enemies of the Utah church. The trio visited the office of the notorious editor and critic of the Latter-day Saints, Thomas C. Sharp, still the proprietor of a local newspaper. Sharp was unavailable, but they engaged in a cordial conversation with his son William, who allowed them to peruse the office's collection of papers critical of the Latter-day Saints in Nauvoo, including Sharp's *Warsaw Signal* and the *Nauvoo Expositor*, whose press was destroyed by order of Joseph Smith and the city council in June 1844, in the buildup to the prophet's murder.[129] Such intimate encounters with the infamous actors of the Martyrdom gripped readers back in the Great Basin even though Jenson's journalistic style refrained from overt sensationalism about contemporary and past scenes; instead, his columns were a "where are they now?" status report on the characters, events, and places that informed the collective historical memory of the Latter-day Saints. It was enough to pique the curiosity of church members currently engaged in another battle for their religious liberty.

With their monthlong tour nearly over by early October, Black returned alone to his home in Deseret, Utah. Jenson and Stevenson, on the other hand, had unfinished business in Richmond, Missouri. Weeks earlier, while visiting Missouri, the three missionaries had called on John C. Whitmer, the presiding elder of the Church of Christ (a schismatic branch of the early church whose members were sometimes known as Whitmerites) and nephew of the early Church Historian John Whitmer. During this initial visit, the three missionaries had hoped to see "the Church history kept by John Whitmer," a narrative account of the first eight years of the church's history.[130] (After Latter-day Saint leaders excommunicated John Whitmer in 1838 at Far West, Missouri, he refused to hand over his history, and it stayed in his possession until he died in 1878.)[131] To their disappointment, however, the record book had been locked up by John J. Snyder, a former scribe of John Whitmer's brother, David Whitmer, who was the founder of the Church of Christ (Whitmerite). Snyder had secured the record book while away on out-of-state business. John C. Whitmer promised the three Utah-based missionaries that they could see the history if they passed through Richmond again, since Snyder would be back by that time. Jenson and Stevenson took Whitmer up on the offer.[132] The chance to see and possibly bring home at least a transcription of the original records kept by John Whitmer was thought to be worth the trouble.

Sadly, Jenson and Stevenson never caught a glimpse of the Whitmer history. After making the necessary arrangements and returning to Richmond, John C. Whitmer "had gone back on his word in relation to letting [them] see the old Church record." After pleading their case to Whitmer and Snyder and realizing their efforts were futile, Jenson and Stevenson left. With obvious disappointment, Jenson wrote in his journal that night, "Thus we had come several hundred miles out of our way for nothing."[133] After traveling west through Kansas City, Denver, Cheyenne, and Ogden, Jenson and Stevenson finally arrived back in Salt Lake City on October 15, 1888.

Despite some disappointments along the way, the tour boosted Jenson's historical credentials before the Utah public. The following week Jenson spoke in the Salt Lake Tabernacle and in the Seventeenth Ward on his church history travels. He also visited with the editors of the *Deseret News*, who told Jenson that his first sixteen letters from the trip "have been read with the greatest interest by the people."[134] As fall turned to winter, Jenson and Stevenson delivered several sermons on their travels. After a few months they decided to create more formal and professional lectures, using commissioned paintings of the historic sites.[135] Based on popular demand for their travel accounts, Jenson and Stevenson eventually compiled their eighteen dispatches into a single volume. The volume was published as a stand-alone supplement to the *Historical Record* and titled *Infancy of the Church: An Elaborate and Detailed Description of Persons, Places and Incidents connected with the Early Rise and Progress of the Church of Jesus Christ of Latter-day Saints: A Series of Letters* (1889).

Ultimately, the attention Jenson's tour received was not so surprising given the unique and polarizing climate of Utah Territory in the late 1880s. During this time, Latter-day Saints rallied behind their distinctive heritage, searching for signs that God would not forsake his people in their current struggle. Jenson's tour underscored the seemingly deafening silence of the federal government when Latter-day Saints' constitutional liberties had been threatened in the past. The historical parallels seemed to affirm that Latter-day Saints were participants in a providential march toward the redemption of Zion and the millennial return of Jesus Christ. Recapitulating the tragedy and triumphs of the early church redirected Latter-day Saints' public memory to their shared cultural heritage as a distinctive minority who were persecuted for the gospel's sake. For a month in the fall of 1888, Jenson offered faithful Latter-day Saints historical context for their misfit status in the American nation and hope for their eventual deliverance.

Ongoing Affiliation with the Historian's Office

When Jenson returned from the Midwest that October, he resumed writing for the *Historical Record*. But now he wrote with the additional authority that comes from personal experience and a better appreciation of the actual sites and places that informed the content of many of his articles.[136] This trend would continue over the next several months. The December 1888 issue featured major events and atrocities from the Latter-day Saint experience in Missouri during the 1830s.[137] The January 1889 issue continued the focus on Missouri, while the March and June issues focused on Illinois.[138] For December 1889, Jenson's attention shifted to a new structure for his latest work, which he titled "Church Encyclopaedia," featuring short encyclopedic entries of different places and events in church history.[139]

That spring he expressed his ongoing hopes that he would be able to merge his personal desires with his professional future: "How I wish that I could devote my whole time to the history of the Church—something that has interested me since the days of my early childhood. And I think I will get there by and by. I may [get] to work for the Church soon."[140] Leadership changes in the Historian's Office may have increased Jenson's optimism that he might obtain permanent status there. In April 1889, Assistant Church Historian Franklin D. Richards succeeded Wilford Woodruff as Church Historian when the latter was named president of the church. Breaking with over three decades of tradition, John Jaques, a longtime clerk, was appointed as Assistant Church Historian. This marked the first time a non-apostle had been named to this office, a shift that would become the norm.

That September, Jenson wrote to the new First Presidency—Wilford Woodruff, George Q. Cannon, and Joseph F. Smith—about the publishing status of his *Historical Record* and his ongoing hopes to work full time at the Historian's Office. The letter shared similarities with his prior requests, but by this time, Jenson had grown bolder: "I am now prepared to continue, or discontinue, my publication according to your counsel, but I am under the impression now, more than ever, that my work ought to be published by authority, or not at all. And in order to make myself plain I will state that I am willing to *devote my entire future life in the interest of Church history, and offer you my services from the 1st of January next [1890] with or without compensation of a material nature*." Jenson's *Historical Record* would continue only with the official endorsement and supervision of the church, to lend it the authority it needed to survive. Jenson proposed full-time employment either at the Historian's Office or as a traveling historian to collect and preserve history in the church's stakes and missions. As a sign of good faith, he also offered to donate to the church his previous scholarship and writings, including his meticulously prepared indexes of the *Millennial Star*'s reprinting of the "History of Joseph Smith." In summary, he placed at the feet of church leaders his entire professional life for them to examine and hopefully deem worthy for employment as a church historian.[141] After waiting two months for an answer, Jenson tried to gain an audience with the First Presidency to no avail. He sensed they intended to dodge his requests.[142] Finally, on the last day of 1889, Jenson met with the Church Historian and left with the impression that he would be employed full time by Richards beginning in January 1890.[143]

The sluggish pace of church business was understandable—the First Presidency was spending much of its time working to keep the church intact in the face of the devastating financial, political, and legal ramifications of the federal anti-polygamy campaign. Unbeknownst to Jenson, however, the First Presidency was vetting his application carefully behind the scenes. In February 1890, Church Historian Richards and Assistant Church Historian Jaques offered their opinion in a fourteen-page letter to the First Presidency. They acknowledged the seeming generosity of Jenson's offer to donate the *Historical Record*, his subscriber list, his past work, and so forth as a "free gift" to the church. "But to this proposition another is attached, which is that he be taken into the employ of the Historian's Office, and this latter proposition, in its various bearings, has caused the most anxious thought," they wrote.[144] Both had worked with Jenson since the mid-1880s and knew well his strengths and weaknesses, which they candidly rehearsed to Woodruff and his counselors.

The current leaders of the Historian's Office harbored specific concerns about Jenson's character and work style. His blatant office-seeking stirred fears that he "would make much of his authority and position" and would soon grow more eccentric in his requests so that beyond "regular compensation," he "would expect R[ail] R[oad] passes, travelling expenses, . . . or a sort of virtual *carte blanche* to ask local aid in his labors." The current dynamics of the office lacked the ability to support one who "has repeatedly said that he does not want . . . to be in the office much, but he wants to have a desk here, so that he can have free run of the papers and documents in the office, but he would like most of the time to travel about the country, in and through the various stakes and wards, to collect historical information." Past experiences also informed the opposition expressed by Richards and Jaques. They had struggled to manage former employee Milando Pratt, who floated in and out of the Historian's Office with little accountability. They worried that Jenson would cause similar problems among the established staff and disrupt the status quo: "His ambition reaches forth in other directions, and consequently he would chafe and be ill-suited and dissatisfied under the restriction of steady daily clerk work."[145]

Jenson's penchant for self-promotion in building a subscriber base for his historical products also bothered the Historian's Office staff: "He is such a persistent pusher of himself and his projects. . . . He is the kind of man who wants to pry into the bottom of everything, to know just what everybody else in the office was doing."[146] Even with the very limited role Jenson currently occupied as an affiliate of the Historian's Office, his controlling nature created friction and an inhospitable work environment, causing Richards and Jaques to question if he could work under a hierarchical and administrative system without the freedom to control his own projects and movements.

The larger problem with Jenson's plan was that it anticipated a fully mature and staffed Historian's Office, not one that had largely limped along during the federal raids. "At present little more than ordinary current work can be done," Richards and Jaques lamented, "the main object being to take care of what we have and obtain from time to time, and keep the old ship off the breakers,. . . . rather than to be spreading out sail and unnecessarily increasing work and expenses." Jenson's intention to explore and gather more history would stretch the financial limits of the office's resources. They closed their letter with a recommendation to decline his proposal: "It would require considerable branching out into labors and expenditures at an exceedingly inopportune time and under peculiarly forbidding circumstances. A competent, discreet, and trustworthy clerk of all work, rather than a specialist, is the best kind to have in the Historian's Office now." With the political climate decidedly against even average Latter-day Saints, Jenson's proposal seemed imprudent for the foreseeable future.[147]

Days after receiving the candid assessment from Richards and Jaques, President Woodruff drafted his own response to Jenson, declining his application for full-time employment with the church.[148] Anxious that he continue to receive his monthly stipend from the church, Jenson asked the First Presidency to confirm that ongoing arrangement, which they did, to Jenson's relief.[149]

Rebuffed again by the First Presidency and the Historian's Office leadership for a permanent position, Jenson, in March 1890, seriously considered organizing a private publishing company.[150] By early April he had prepared the articles of incorporation for his "Deseret Historical Company" and shared them with Franklin D. Richards.[151] The following week Jenson met with the church president to discuss his historical ventures. "In my conversation with Prest. Woodruff he said I had been doing a noble work in the historical field. I am inviting the leading authorities of the Church to take a controlling interest in the contemplated historical company, and Prest. Woodruff seemed to be in favor of it, but kept the documents which I had submitted to lay the matter before his counselors and others."[152] In the middle of June, Jenson wrote again to the First Presidency, seeking further counsel on his contemplated publishing company, but again, they had cooled on another of Jenson's ventures that required their endorsement and guiding hand.[153]

The tireless entrepreneur and historian began to fatigue. With the *Historical Record* still struggling for stability, Jenson grew "tired of publishing, mainly because there was too much expense and trouble attached to collecting dues from subscribers and furthermore because people generally do not seem to appreciate literature of an historical nature."[154] Jenson concluded his periodical with volume 9 (1890). In his "Publisher's Valedictory," he expressed his bittersweet feelings: "For thirteen years we have labored faithfully and true in the interest of Church history, and have succeeded in gathering considerable historical information (only a part of which has been published), which we hope will prove beneficial to future generations, as well as the present one." Although some church members had exhibited interest and provided financial support for his periodical, "the majority of the Saints have not manifested that interest for our labors," Jenson stated, "which we had fondly anticipated."[155] He encouraged delinquent subscribers to settle their accounts but gave no hint at what he would do next other than continuing to gather church history.

His fortitude was admirable. Jenson's work life to this point assumed a cyclical rhythm of imaginative projects, extensive promoting, and invitations for ecclesiastical recognition, followed by counsel and rejections from his leaders. Below the surface, however, his historical proposals were not wholly driven by egotistical delusion or personal avarice. He was a vulnerable and budding intellectual in search of validation. And he began to believe deeply in the vitalness of his vision of serving as a roving church historian, documenting the development of the church and its members, so he held tightly to that vision.

The political, social, and economic conditions in the Great Basin began to evolve after President Wilford Woodruff issued a Manifesto in 1890, initiating the beginning of the end of the Latter-day Saint practice of plural marriage. The Manifesto declared the church's intent to obey anti-polygamy legislation, eventually easing federal pressure on the church and initiating a slow cultural evolution in Utah Territory. The Latter-day Saints' insularity and autonomy in the Great Basin appeared no longer practical or sustainable. The church nurtured a complicated and contentious relationship with US Protestantism, but over the next few decades Latter-day Saints would work tirelessly to demonstrate their worth, progress, and successes to the American people and to prove their staying power in a political and social system that had largely shunned them.

In the meantime, the anti-polygamy crusade sent a jolt through the church's system and a recovery was far from immediate. With church records scattered and finances in disarray, church leaders began to refocus on their ecclesiastical units and their global ecumenical and missionary objectives. In this environment, institutional record keeping would suddenly take on a new urgency. Jenson's imagined role for himself now appeared prescient. Jenson's persistence pulled Richards and the Historian's Office from the past into the future.

Finally, in February 1891, the First Presidency interviewed Jenson about his willingness to work full time as an "attaché" for the Historian's Office, at a doubled salary of one hundred dollars per month to offset the traveling expenses Jenson would incur as he traveled to Latter-day Saint settlements in search of stories and documents.[156] "I had always kept myself in readiness to comply with any call that might be made upon me, and that I would be satisfied with whatever they wanted to give me," Jenson rejoiced in his journal. "Thus I am permanently engaged as a historian to labor in connection with the Church Historians."[157] A month later Jenson received his first monthly payment from the General Tithing Office: $25.00 in cash, $64.50 in produce orders, and $10.50 in meat orders.[158]

His new post as an attaché for the Historian's Office was a deliberate choice on the part of church leaders. They wanted a status report on the state of their ecclesiastical units, including their neglected record books, which contained information on sacred ordinances and priesthood ordinations, as well as reports on membership. Jenson's title signaled a change in strategy for documenting the church and its growth in the future. He was now a diplomat for the Church Historian, and in the coming years his role as an ambassador of record keeping would take him to the scattered wards, stakes, and missions of the church. He would arrive on the global scene when the church was still young or unsettled in many regions and lay the framework for documenting the Restoration around the world.

4 Itinerant World Traveler

Andrew Jenson's career took a turn for the better on April 16, 1891. Church Historian Franklin D. Richards invited Jenson to come to the Historian's Office to discuss his professional future. Earlier, in February, the Danish American historian had been hired as a full-time employee at church headquarters after years of angling for a position. Richards, who a year earlier had cautioned against hiring Jenson in the Historian's Office, now laid his hands on the top of Jenson's head and consecrated him as a "historian in Zion." The Church Historian also assured Jenson that some future day, when "the books should be opened to view, the importance of [his] labors should become apparent and the good work done by [him] should bring its benefits and blessings to all Israel." Richards also counseled him to "cultivate a spirit of humility and meekness" so that he "might gain the love, good will and confidence of the saints."[1] This instruction was not surprising given Richards's earlier assessment of Jenson's complex character.

Following the priesthood blessing, Richards handed Jenson a formal letter outlining Jenson's official charge on behalf of the Historian's Office. He was to personally visit the North American branches, wards, and stakes of the church to examine and collect records, ideally during their quarterly conferences, when the local Latter-day Saints were gathered together and could verify their personal and local histories. A week earlier, President Wilford Woodruff had advised North American stake presidents on church record-keeping practices and informed them that a historian would soon visit their church units to audit the preservation of their ecclesiastical records and encourage improvements where needed.[2]

Though his commission came formally from the First Presidency, his assignment was one he had essentially created for himself, born originally out of his work with the *Historical Record* and distilled in his repeated requests for employment at the Historian's Office. His special mission began the regular collection of local ecclesiastical records at the Historian's Office. Shortly after its inception, the church made earnest attempts to inscribe many of its sacred records into ledger volumes for permanent safekeeping. In theory, as the church expanded and created new ecclesiastical units, these record-keeping practices would be replicated and perpetuated at the local level.[3] With a divine commandment to keep a record, Latter-day Saint record keeping was always meant to be a democratized task, not just for the select few appointed to do so.[4] But despite divine directive, six decades into the church's history, the Latter-day Saints' record keeping lacked standardization and a perceived importance.

In addition, the federal raids of the last decade left the church's record books scattered and in disarray. Volumes with ordinance and property information housed at the Historian's Office had been moved by Richards to avoid seizure by the federal government. Anticipating the passage of certain punitive provisions of the Edmunds-Tucker Act, church leaders in 1887 placed some of the church's property in newly created nonprofit ecclesiastical corporations, managed by loyal local leaders, as well as into the custody of private church members.[5] Gathering the dispersed documents became a near impossible task.

Other books maintained in the ecclesiastical units of the church were in the private custody of former ward and stake clerks who never returned them when they were relieved of their duties. Clerks, generally with no designated space at local meetinghouses to store their records, maintained church books in their homes. No accurate accounting of membership totals, priesthood ordinations, ordinance data, leadership succession, or other historical facts could be gathered for use at church headquarters with the records so scattered. Also, church members who moved wards frequently lacked documentation of their membership status, which hindered their acceptance into their new ward or their entrance into the temple. In an era when the church was working to accurately appraise its current state, church record books became of paramount importance.

Jenson's blessing as "a historian in Zion" also reinforced a reality that the church would confront in the ensuing decades. In the past, Zion had been designated as a specific gathering place for the Latter-day Saints; whether in Ohio, Missouri, or Utah, Zion had always been near church headquarters, where the Latter-day Saint prophet presided. Zion's ideals, enshrined in Latter-day Saint scripture, remained unchallenged, but the idea of Zion as a singular, physical place began to change and expand as the physical gathering to the Great Basin lost importance. Thus, Jenson's call to labor in Zion meant he would have to depart the church's main stronghold to perform his duties.

As church leaders began to emphasize the development of Latter-day Saint ecclesiastical units the world over (instead of a literal gathering to Utah), Jenson intended to establish local record-keeping practices to document this new growth. He worked initially to capture the experiences of every branch, ward, and stake of the church in North America, foreshadowing a future where Historian's Office collections reflected a worldwide church. From aging pioneers and local church leaders, he gathered narratives of Latter-day Saint colonization and the development and growth of the church outside the Salt Lake Valley as much as he recorded the facts and data of ecclesiastical administration. In doing so, Jenson reconfigured the dynamics of Latter-day Saint institutional and social memory. For now, the record holdings of the Historian's Office reflected the provincial nature of the church, with a heavy emphasis on its administrators—church leaders—centered in North America. But Jenson eventually reconfigured Latter-day Saint memory to include the church's regional and even global presence. If the archival record could be expanded, he reasoned, the institutional "church," as reflected in its documentary record, would include information on the church's hierarchy as well as its members in branches, wards, and stakes.

Long before professional standards were commonplace in public archives throughout the United States, he was commissioned by church leaders to impose rational order and standardization on the church's record books to ensure the systematic recording of historical and administrative data. But record keeping to Jenson was not just about training local clerks to serve the administrative needs of the church. He conceived of the archive as a potential knowledge center, where a comprehensive historical record could be filled in, preserved, and then accessed by future church historians. Jenson's work over the next decade would be a race against time to capture Latter-day Saint memories before they expired or deteriorated.

Touring the North American Stakes of Zion

Having been charged, blessed, and recommended by the Church Historian, Jenson soon embarked on his first official stake visit on behalf of the Historian's Office. In late April 1891, he boarded a northbound passenger train in Salt Lake City for Brigham City, Utah, the center of the Box Elder Stake. There, he interviewed Apostle Lorenzo Snow and other local church leaders. He also reviewed church-related records at the county courthouse and the church's tithing office. Jenson attended the stake conference meetings held that weekend and was invited to speak to the assembled Saints about their shared record-keeping duties. He also preached to the Scandinavian Latter-day Saint community at a local chapel. According to Jenson, "After the conference I resumed my historical labors and besides perusing records I visited a number of old residents and obtained from them valuable information. In the many special meetings which were held in the different settlements I gave instructions on the proper method of making stake and ward records."[6] Afterward, he visited Latter-day Saint villages elsewhere in Box Elder County.

Andrew Jenson, circa 1890. Courtesy Church History Library.

From late May until early July 1891, Jenson made a similar tour of the Panguitch and Sevier Stakes in Utah.[7] In August, he toured the Summit and Morgan Stakes in northern Utah over a three-week period, gathering historical material from twenty-one wards.[8] During September and October, Jenson traveled throughout the Bear Lake Stake in Idaho and returned again to the Summit Stake in Utah.[9] Jenson's fifth and final record-keeping visit in 1891 was to the Cache Stake in northern Utah. The six-week tour lasted from late October through mid-December.[10] After each church history tour, some of which he conducted with Bertha or Emma, Jenson would travel back to Salt Lake City and assemble his notes and observations at the Historian's Office and then report to the First Presidency.[11]

Jenson settled on a preferred method of visiting and teaching the stakes. Upon reaching a stake headquarters, he would call a meeting with the stake presidency to sketch out his plan for traveling through the respective wards and branches of the stake. He would hold a general meeting the same evening to introduce himself and to outline for local settlers the main goals of his trip. The next morning, he would convene an exclusive meeting with "old settlers, ward clerks and secretaries of the different associations"—the main keepers of local history and church records. The meetings would last between three to six hours, which gave Jenson enough time to painstakingly appraise existing records, gather historical information from old settlers, and push for better practices. He reported to the First Presidency, "Almost universally the leading brethren, and people generally have responded cheerfully when called upon to give information."[12]

Jenson encouraged local church clerks and church members to record traditional genealogical information along with blessing, baptism, confirmation, and priesthood ordination information. He anticipated a day when, to defend the church, members would need to prove their claim to priesthood authority before enemies of the church. He witnessed cases in his travels where members were unable to recount who ordained them to the priesthood or when their vital ordinances were performed. To guard against the loss of important membership data, Jenson urged families to keep personal journals and record books so that their records could supplement the imperfect volumes maintained by the church's ecclesiastical units.[13] Every member was enlisted in the safeguarding of historical and administrative records.[14]

In the course of his work, he also developed questions to ask "old settlers, ward clerk[s], quorum clerks, and association secretaries" to begin a historical sketch of the wards he visited.[15] His questions centered on the founding members of Latter-day Saint settlements and wards, meetinghouse information, ward boundaries, priesthood and auxiliary organizations, bishop and stake president succession, and major church history events in the area. He immediately began to compile the historical information as he gathered it and showcased some of his sketches for Latter-day Saint audiences in the *Deseret News*.[16]

His schedule was demanding. but his prior itinerant lifestyle made his travels feel manageable. The work of the Historian's Office had never before been as visible to scattered Latter-day Saints outside of Salt Lake City as it was on Jenson's initial tour in 1891. By this point, over the course of his career with the Historian's Office, Jenson had visited sixteen stakes, which totaled about half of the stakes that existed in 1892 and comprised 248 Latter-day Saint settlements. His visit to just eleven of those stakes required 4,684 miles of travel—including 942 miles by rail, 3,737 by horse and buggy, and 5 by foot. He generally paid his own fare and relied on the hospitality of local church members for food and board. Through his travels, Jenson received an unparalleled look at the state and growth of settlements across the Latter-day Saint cultural region. And he felt confident that he had gathered enough information to begin his histories of the stakes and settlements that he had visited to that point.[17]

The unprecedented nature of his historical tour did not obscure the sobering realities plaguing local church records, and Jenson relayed that information to the First Presidency. "I am sorry to report that in most places I have found the Church records in a very deplorable, neglected condition; in many instances no regular records are being kept at all, and those few which are kept are as a rule kept without system or order," he wrote. "Nearly all the early records kept in the several wards and branches have long ago been lost, misplaced or destroyed entirely, and consequently about half the members of the Church are in perfect ignorance today as regards the dates of their blessings, baptism, confirmations, ordinations, etc., as most of them have relied on the public records that are lost."[18]

During the summer of 1892, Jenson followed his established pattern in touring the Malad Stake in Idaho and the Juab, Wasatch, and Uintah Stakes in Utah.[19] In 1893, he continued his tour through Utah counties, visiting the Weber, Tooele, Millard, Davis, and Utah Stakes. That August he reported on his annual labors to the Church Historian, informing Richards that he only had six stakes left to visit in the entire United States (four stakes in Arizona, the San Luis Stake in Colorado, and the San Juan Stake in southeastern Utah).[20] In November and December 1893, Jenson traveled to the San Luis and San Juan Stakes over a five-week period. His round-trip route took him over fifteen hundred miles. Despite the relative isolation of the two stakes, Jenson found the Latter-day Saints there accommodating: "They are as a rule very hospitable and treated me very kindly, giving me the best accommodations they had."[21]

The hospitality was appreciated by Jenson, whose personal finances were in dire shape in 1893. Beginning that summer, the United States confronted a serious economic depression, causing numerous businesses and banks to shutter their doors. Unemployment nationwide spiked. Jenson himself felt the effects of the depression as he struggled to improve his family finances while he was away for weeks. To offset his personal expenses, he attempted to collect on past-due accounts from his publications as he traveled but found little success, and his meager monthly stipend from the Historian's Office failed to cover all of his traveling expenses. In the remote stake of San Juan, he was reduced to soliciting donations from the local members for his return trip. He did the same in San Luis in southern Colorado.[22]

The tenuous financing of Jenson's historical tours underscored the grassroots nature of his effort to gather records on behalf of the Historian's Office. The project was makeshift, but it represented the best efforts of a church still emerging from an era of persecution and of a Historian's Office just beginning to emphasize the need for better record keeping. From tattered, aging, and incomplete records, and from the memories of Latter-day Saint pioneers, Jenson began to build an impressive archival record of the early Latter-day Saint movement. His field notes, often scrawled quickly on scraps of paper, symbolized the diligent efforts of a solo, wayfaring historian, capturing history from the road before it vanished.

In 1894, Jenson at last completed his circuit of the North American stakes of the church. In spring, he toured church units in Arizona, New Mexico, California, and the Latter-day Saint colonies in northern Mexico.[23] That summer and early fall, Jenson remained home, focusing on the church units in the Salt Lake Stake. In October, he departed for his tour of the Canadian ecclesiastical units, primarily in the Province of Alberta.[24] He spent the next week or so visiting the outlying settlements in the area before returning to Utah, via the Latter-day Saint settlements in Montana and Idaho.[25] His travels that year encompassed 9,030 miles.[26]

As a traveling historian, Jenson arguably saw the church from a vantage point unlike that of anyone else in his day, including General Authorities. His later histories based on his travel notes were replete with dates, geographic descriptions, statistics, and chronological details sketching the development of far-off Latter-day Saint settlements. Forty thousand miles took him to "almost every locality and tract of Country which is prominently connected with the history of the Church." Jenson became the crucial intermediary between local memory and the institutional preservation of the church's nineteenth-century expansion across the North American frontier. "I find that a thorough reform in record keeping throughout the Stakes of Zion is necessary," he reported to Richards in April 1895. "The public Church records is kept in a very imperfect manner; hundreds of the old records kept in older Wards years ago have been lost entirely, and others are found in the hands of private individuals and parties who have no right to them whatever." Jenson "made an extraordinary effort" to encourage leaders and members to more consistently make and preserve records, giving them instructions on "what ought to be written and what might be left unwritten."[27] What should be written haunted Jenson and fueled his efforts to expand and preserve Latter-day Saint records.

Into the Silence at Mountain Meadows

In the middle of Jenson's tour of the stakes of Zion, he was called into the Church President's Office and given an unsettling and challenging mission. Thirty-five years after the Mountain Meadows Massacre, church leaders felt impelled to gather facts to reconstruct the painful narrative. That horrific tragedy, masterminded and executed by Latter-day Saint militiamen with the assistance of recruited Paiute Native Americans, left 120 unarmed Arkansas emigrants—men, women, and children—dead in September 1857.[28] In the aftermath, those with memories of the event largely buried them, choosing to share them mainly off the record within a network of trusted church members or not at all.

Federal investigators attempted to gather information in the years after the massacre, and newspapers outside of Utah reported the events, but with few reliable details. Gilded Age literature on the Latter-day Saints was predictably unkind to President Brigham Young, who they suspected gave sanction to the massacre.[29] To their accounts was added the recollection of John D. Lee, one of the principal leaders of the massacre, in a posthumously published life sketch that implicated Young in ordering the massacre.[30]

Church leaders intended to push back on the existing literature by gathering more firsthand accounts and reminiscences. John Q. Cannon, the son of First Presidency counselor George Q. Cannon, who had been scouring for sources on the massacre to include in a new multivolume *History of Utah* (1892) written by Orson F. Whitney, found "that there is some information procurable," if the "right steps" were taken to "secure it."[31] After meeting with his son, John, and Orson F. Whitney, George Q. Cannon concluded that the "information which had not been published" about the massacre was in "danger of . . . passing out of reach by the death of parties who now knew something about that affair."[32] Jenson, whose proclivity for travel during the first year of his tour to the stakes of Zion had won him the trust of church authorities, was assigned the job of collecting the expiring memories of the massacre. Jenson, however, was a foreign-born outsider to southern Utah and its culture. Anticipating that he might be met with hesitancy and perhaps hostility, the First Presidency issued a letter of recommendation to credential him for the trip.

The recommendation stated that Jenson was acting as the First Presidency's appointed agent and that Latter-day Saints should cooperate with his official investigation. The First Presidency hoped to acquire the facts in case the church one day decided to correct the public record: "We are anxious to learn all that we can upon this subject, not necessarily for publication, but that the Church may have the details in its possession for the vindication of innocent parties, and that the world may know, when the time comes, the true facts connected with it."[33]

Armed with a list of questions, Jenson departed Salt Lake City and traveled south. He toured Parowan, Cedar City, and other Latter-day Saint villages in southern Utah, where he "interviewed a number of the old veterans who freely gave [him] the desired information."[34] His initial traveling companion was Ellot Willden, a participant in the massacre who held significant and untapped information on the tragedy. Jenson probed Willden for details, but he was not forthcoming at first. His information, however, could be purchased at a price. Willden knew that any information he furnished would potentially be included in Whitney's *History of Utah*, a for-profit venture backed in part by publishers George Q. Cannon & Sons. Jenson telegraphed Willden's terms to Abraham H. Cannon—fifty dollars and a complete set of Whitney's *History of Utah* when it was finished, worth approximately another thirty dollars.[35] Cannon, however, rejected the proposal by telegram the next day. Afraid that he might miss out on crucial information, Jenson issued a promissory note to pay Willden "if neither the Church or Cannon and sons would."[36] Eventually, after receiving confirmation that Willden had provided Jenson with promised information, church leaders agreed to assume Jenson's promissory note, issuing Willden a check for fifty dollars.[37]

The material from Willden complemented the other eyewitness accounts Jenson was able to acquire. His trip uncovered greater details on the week leading up to the massacre and on the planning of the massacre itself. His findings, however, did little to exonerate the involvement of local Latter-day Saint leaders and militiamen or to provide material that could be used to soften existing narratives of the massacre. The statements and reports in Jenson's notes, for example, told of the Parowan Stake leaders directly authorizing the massacre, Cedar City leaders surveilling the emigrant company in the lead-up to the massacre, and Latter-day Saint participants slaughtering emigrants who ventured away from the main encampment.[38] As Jenson returned to southern Utah on church history business over the ensuring decades, he would continue to add to his collection of notes about the massacre.[39]

Privately, Jenson lamented about the trip: "It has been an unpleasant business. The information that I received made me suffer mentally and deprived me of my sleep at nights; and I felt tired and fatigued, both mentally and physically when I returned home." Jenson shared his findings with the First Presidency.[40] However, to the public he described: "As to the information I obtained I can only say this, that while some white people were implicated in the Mountain Meadows Massacre, besides the Indians, I learned nothing that in any shape or form could connect the General Authorities of the Church with the affair."[41]

Jenson's authorized investigation of the massacre ultimately intersected with the politics of historical memory. He now carried the weight of the transgressions of his religion, of a people who had perpetrated a tragedy. After he listened to the memories about Mountain Meadows, the fact that dozens of Latter-day Saints had been active participants in the massacre became incontrovertible to Jenson. But retelling what he learned in southern Utah was a more complicated task. Into the twentieth century, Latter-day Saints largely vacillated between remembering and forgetting, often deferring to an impulse to defend their church by placing most of the blame for the massacre with the Paiute. Jenson was not immune to this trend. When he had an opportunity to write about the massacre for his *Encyclopedic History of the Church* (1941), he included one sentence on the origins of the massacre: "The Mountain Meadows are particularly noted from the tragedy which was enacted there in September, 1857, when a number of emigrants en route from Arkansas to California were murdered by Indians, assisted by a few whites."[42] No doubt Jenson remembered what he recovered in southern Utah in 1892, but he showed restraint when recounting the story to the American public, perhaps not wishing to fully publicize sensitive historical details that might provoke the disappointment of church leaders, as he did with his list of Joseph Smith's plural wives a few years earlier. Jenson, instead, relished in his role as an investigative historian for the First Presidency, a position that required trust and put him on the scene of past and present historical events.

A Mission to the 1893 Chicago World's Fair

The 1893 Chicago World's Fair, an American cultural celebration commemorating the four-hundredth anniversary of Christopher Columbus's "discovery" of the New World, marked the dramatic reengagement of the church with the outside world after decades of relative isolation in the Great Basin valleys of the American West.[43] Desiring to showcase the best of the United States to the rest of the world, national and state leaders invited their fellow citizens to imagine ways of exhibiting the best of Americana, including its cultural contributions, agricultural achievements, social successes, and religious realizations.[44] Like other Americans who heard this clarion call, many Latter-day Saints in Utah recognized that the upcoming events in Chicago would offer new opportunities for self-representation and a chance to contest their public image.

The Columbian Exposition marked the beginning of formal public relations for the church. The church began adopting a new strategy—public education instead of private evangelization alone; for the first time Latter-day Saints sought to be understood (not necessarily joined) by outsiders. Limited in the past to mainly the printed word, church leaders embraced the opportunity in Chicago to increase interpersonal contacts and tell the Latter-day Saints' own story in person to the outside world.

In preparation for these summer activities, the Utah Board of Lady Managers, an interdenominational commission based in Salt Lake City, determined to write a religious history of Utah for fairgoers in Chicago: *World's Fair Ecclesiastical History of Utah* (1893).[45] Church Historian Franklin D. Richards assigned Jenson the task of writing the chapter on the Latter-day Saint experience in Utah.[46] The book reads like a typical compilation of turn-of-the-century denominational histories, with chapters on the Roman Catholics and Episcopalians as well as the Presbyterian, Methodist, Baptist, and Unitarian denominations; on the Central Christian Church, Utah Sunday School Association, the Utah Christian Endeavor Work, and the LDS Church; and on Judaism. But the volume also reveals the power structure of denominations in nineteenth-century Utah: half of the book is devoted to Jenson's essay, "An Epitome of the History of the Church of Jesus Christ of Latter-day Saints."[47] The book was featured prominently in the Utah Building at the Columbian Exposition.

Over seven thousand Latter-day Saints in Utah journeyed to the Chicago World's Fair in the summer of 1893 to view the church's contributions to the exposition. While many traveled as tourists, other church members actively participated in reshaping their church's public image. At the fair, hundreds of congregants helped create, manage, and staff their territory's impressive exhibit in the Utah Building.

That summer Jenson had planned to continue his historical labors by gathering information in the stakes and wards in Arizona and Colorado. But in late August, the Church Historian invited him to postpone that trip in order to travel instead to the world's fair, gathering Latter-day Saint history along the way.[48] In his written acceptance of this new assignment, Jenson penned a letter to Richards with an update of his past year of accomplishments gathering records for the Historian's Office. He also requested a formal letter of missionary appointment from the First Presidency and a formal priesthood blessing from the Church Historian to set him apart for the mission.[49] Richards obliged his employee and consecrated him as an official church representative in Chicago. According to Jenson, the Church Historian promised "a successful trip and a safe return, and that the way should be opened up for me to obtain the desired information."[50] The First Presidency also wanted their traveling historian to be an on-scene reporter of contemporary church developments. The church was slowly pivoting toward American and Protestant respectability. As one familiar with the arc of Latter-day Saint history, Jenson was capable of contextualizing events related to this transformation for the Utah readers. He departed Utah for the Midwest days later as a correspondent for the *Deseret News*.

Jenson took about a week and a half total to visit each church history site and gather materials on his railroad journey to the Columbian Exposition. He traveled on the Union Pacific route to reach Independence, Missouri, which had been designated as Zion by Joseph Smith in 1831. There he met with members of the RLDS and the Hedrickites, both Restoration movements with strong feelings against the Saints in Utah. He then traveled north to Richmond, Missouri, where he met David J. Whitmer and his nephew George Schweich, who showed Jenson the manuscript history of John Whitmer in their possession, a privilege Jenson had been denied on his 1888 tour. He spent most of a day reading Whitmer's approximately hundred-page record of the early events of the church and planned to return to Richmond to make a handwritten copy after visiting the world's fair.[51]

Jenson arrived in Chicago on September 8 and went directly to the Utah Building on the Columbian Exposition fairgrounds. The following day, he attended the festivities surrounding "Utah Day" at the fair with hundreds of other Latter-day Saints and Utahns. He spent the next week touring the multitude of exhibits. For example, he joined B. H. Roberts in listening to papers delivered at the World's Parliament of Religions, just days before its organizers would rescind their official invitation for Latter-day Saint representation in the main

Columbus Hall.[52] After two weeks of wandering the fairgrounds, Jenson was exhausted: "I was getting very tired and fatigued both physically and mentally, and felt that I was full; I could not contain any more this time."[53]

Finally, on September 24, Jenson departed from Chicago's "White City" fairgrounds by a train bound for Richmond, Missouri, where he reunited with George Schweich and the John Whitmer manuscript history.[54] Now familiar with the manuscript's contents, Jenson intended to make a copy. He immediately began creating and verifying a transcription of the record in Schweich's store with his help.[55]

Jenson made his transcription on the back of loose leaves from one of his *Historical Record* volumes and from office letterhead donated by Schweich. Later, in an introduction to his transcription, Jenson recorded his methodology for copying the record. "I spent several days doing this labor and was very careful to copy verbatim every thing which the record contained," Jenson wrote, "except certain revelations, letters and documents which are already contained in the history of Joseph Smith." Jenson was careful to note the binding style and cover of the book as well as its size. He even measured the length and width of the original volume and included the measurements with his transcription. "The writing is that of an ordinary hand, without any pretense of advance penmanship," Jenson noted in his introduction. He also felt at liberty to correct the text at times. "The spelling and punctuation are bad; in copying I have corrected orthographical errors and introduced some punctuation, but have not altered the construction of sentences in any degree whatever." The few exceptions were instances when he supplied words, which he inserted in brackets, that were missing from the text or when clearly wrong dates had been given, in which case Jenson inserted the correct dates and underlined them.[56] The text as transcribed by Jenson and used at the Historian's Office was thus a hybrid of Whitmer's work and Jenson's own historical insertions.

Having secured a copy of the elusive Whitmer record, Jenson traveled around the area to gather additional church history materials, stopping at St. Joseph, Missouri, where he had started his pioneer overland journey in 1866; Lamoni, Iowa, where he had met Joseph Smith III; Garden Grove, Iowa, where the early Latter-day Saint pioneers had founded a settlement after their expulsion from Nauvoo, Illinois, in 1846; Mount Pisgah, Iowa, where about 150 Latter-day Saint pioneers were buried in a cemetery; and Council Bluffs, Iowa, where many of the early church members had camped before continuing on to the Salt Lake Valley. With his mission complete, Jenson boarded a train for Utah.

After five weeks away, Jenson returned to Utah on October 6, 1893, just in time for the church's general conference meetings. When general conference ended, Jenson met with Franklin D. Richards and showed him the copy of John Whitmer's history. Richards asked Jenson to make two typescript copies of the record, which he did over the next two weeks with the help of another clerk in the Historian's Office.[57] Jenson again had proven his worth on the road. His quick 4,200-mile trip netted not only a first-person account of the church's presence at the world's fair but also another day-to-day log of his trip through the "waste places of Zion." And it culminated with his recovery of the contents of the Whitmer record, a significant addition to the Historian's Office's collection of manuscript histories written by the church's official historians. There was no question at this point that Jenson's model of traveling to gather documents and record and preserve history was bearing significant and enduring fruit.

A Home for Document Preservation in Mill Creek

Back at home, Jenson for a time turned his focus from gathering historical records to preserving them. He had learned the power of the church's record holdings. Beyond simply telling an institutional story, the records of the Historian's Office were a means of public defense, a source base for church-sponsored publications, and a reference library for institutional doctrinal and policy questions. Jenson had been a firsthand witness to the disarray of the Historian's Office during the prior decade of federal incursions into Utah Territory. Documents had been moved, shuffled, and scattered. As he attempted to create and standardize local record keeping through his tours, he also hoped to adjust how the resulting documents were stored and preserved. If successful, his role in preserving church history would elevate his station from itinerant ambassador of the Historian's Office to one who controlled much of the institutional documentary record. Such a role would grant Jenson significant power over how the Latter-day Saint past was remembered and used.

Part of his plan for preserving and storing records involved his Rosenborg Villa, which had begun construction in the summer of 1892. He purchased a plot of land in Mill Creek, an emerging suburb of Salt Lake City.[58] After engaging contractors, masons, trench diggers, lumber suppliers, and so forth, Jenson ceremoniously placed the southwest cornerstone for his future home, mirroring the cornerstone ceremonies of sacred Latter-day Saint structures.[59] By that September, he needed a loan to help him complete the construction of the home. He intended to use a fireproof vault in the home to "preserve safely the valuable papers that are accumulating," which he "long considered exposed to danger" in his current home. He wrote to Church Historian Richards to see if he might use his connections in the Utah banking industry to help him secure a special low-interest loan from one of the local banks, given that his new structure would be used to archive church history records.[60] By mid-November 1892, construction was far enough along that he could begin moving his historical books and papers from his downtown home to his new villa.[61]

Late that fall, from the study of his new "country home," he wrote again to Richards expressing how pleased he was with his new dwelling, which he named after "the renowned castle" in Copenhagen, Denmark. The Renaissance-era Danish castle held "a peculiar charm for me ever since I was a little boy," wrote Jenson, and he drew parallels between the castle and his new home: "While the Danish Rosenborg preserves relics pertaining to one of the small political powers of the earth, my Rosenborg will preserve historical documents and books descriptive of the founding and growth of that grand power and Kingdom which is destined finally to fill the whole earth." His new study carried advantages for modern document preservation that the aging Historian's Office did not. Jenson described it as being large and secure; an "absolutely fireproof" room was separated from the rest of the building by a cement ceiling; and the two windows and the door will be protected by tight-fitting iron shutters." Jenson invited Richards to come and visit and "dedicate" his study by priesthood authority once it was finished.[62]

Jenson moved his family to Rosenborg Villa from their home in Salt Lake City's Seventeenth Ward in the cold days of December 1892. Only two rooms were finished besides Jenson's office, which left many of their personal belongings divided between the two homes. "The frost was quite severe, and the house damp and cold" during their first night. He wrote in his journal: "God grant that our lives may be preserved, and that we may prosper in our new home."[63]

Any prospering, however, was delayed for a season. The following March, Jenson moved his personal printing office from his Salt Lake City home to the Rosenborg Villa to reunite his publishing enterprise with his historical materials and to prepare his downtown home to rent. But reliable renters were tough to find, which denied Jenson the steady income he needed to repay his new loan and to finish off the new property.[64] In addition, Jenson's church history tours took him away from his Rosenborg Villa and his family for weeks—sometimes months—at a time. He was gone almost as much as he was home, leaving his wives and children impoverished in the relative isolation of Mill Creek. While the countryside provided Jenson with much desired solitude to write and read Latter-day Saint history, it cut off his family from their social networks and church community. He lamented the fact that to make his villa functional, he "had to deny the family some of the very comforts of life."[65]

The villa represented more than just an attempt by Jenson to create a safe space for historical documents. The Howell family—Emma, Bertha, and Fanny—immigrated to Utah Territory with few social connections to speak of and had labored to achieve any social capital they now possessed. Emma, through her work as a lady's maid to a wealthy "lady of culture," had spent time prior to her emigration traveling the popular destinations of England, sampling the elite culture of Victorian society.[66] She imported her acquired tastes to Utah Territory and sought some semblance of her old world in her new home. Jenson's aspirations as a principled man of literature and history pointed to at least a middle-class existence if not better for her family, and she soon installed her Victorian ideals within the Jenson home. Emma and Bertha were both regular patrons of the local theater, and Jenson and Emma frequently hosted large social events in their home, using a table they had specially built in the East to seat at least thirty people, a vestige of high-class British society.

The rigid mores of Victorian culture carried other costs. Emma and Bertha had spent the better part of seven years working out the internal dynamics of their plural family before moving to the villa. Both had fallen into familiar roles. Emma took control of the daily movements of the family; as a trained lady's maid she was accustomed to inserting herself into the logistics of the household. Her younger sister Bertha attended to the household chores and childrearing. Nonetheless, the spheres were not perfectly separated, and tensions arose. The unintended victims were often the late Mary's children, Andrew Alexander, Parley, Minerva, and Eleonore, who were forced to adjust to new stepmothers in the home. The rigid discipline imposed by Emma and Bertha did not appeal to Mary's children, especially Andrew Alexander, who was well into his teenage years. He recalled, "My Father is the best and smartest man on Earth to day but he does not know half what goes on in his own house."[67] Andrew Alexander resented Emma's seeming preferential treatment of her own children, Harold and Eva. He also felt like a misfit in the family when, for example, he was barred from attending a party in his father's honor where President Wilford Woodruff and other General Authorities would be in attendance.[68] The internal dynamics of merging plural families under one roof proved complicated.

At the same time, the Jenson family was keeping up appearances. The ill-fated Rosenborg Villa perhaps demonstrated that the young family was reaching too fast for respect and higher status. The mounting debt and social dislocation proved too much for the family. In January 1894, Jenson's discontented wives and children promised that if he would move them all back into the city, "they would be content with city life for the rest of their days."[69] He relented, as he was beginning to resent the time and expense it took him to commute back and forth between the countryside and his work in the city.

A week after moving his family back to their home in the Seventeenth Ward, Jenson offered his now vacated Rosenborg Villa to the Church Historian to archive some of the material housed at the Historian's Office.[70] Richards had visited the home to examine the repository the previous June and was pleased with both the accommodations and the way Jenson had arranged his documents.[71] Jenson anticipated that through his own gathering efforts, and once the material that had been removed during the federal raids was all returned, the Historian's Office would soon be crowded for space. He hoped Richards would see the logic behind keeping at least the "duplicate matter, both written and printed," at his villa in case the main collections at the Historian's Office were ever damaged. The remote repository would potentially grant Jenson (and his family) stewardship over church documents beyond the ones he gathered in his travels.[72]

Richards kindly declined Jenson's offer because he knew the church would soon build an additional repository to address the lack of space at the Historian's Office.[73] He and the First Presidency had been working to find a secure alternative that matched the preservation standards of Jenson's villa, and the recently completed Temple Annex, started in 1892 and adjacent to the Salt Lake Temple, soon became the new overflow repository for Historian's Office collections.[74] Shelves were placed in a room in the annex, which was fire and water proofed as best as possible.[75] By June 12, Richards commented that the completed annex space "begins to afford Relief to my mind as a place of Safety for the Records Books & Documents of the Church." The First Presidency apparently also were "glad of it." The records "hidden during the Raid on the Church during the 1880s & that went underground suddenly all in one night" were now safely housed in the annex.[76]

With little prospect of the church taking an interest in his villa, Jenson requested space to work at the Historian's Office, which would allow him to more easily access resources as he prepared his manuscript histories. Richards eventually granted the request.[77] Jenson's repository at Rosenborg was over before it really began, and he left only a handful of select documents behind when his work shifted to the Historian's Office. What had started as an anticipated blessing to his family and his career had devolved into a social, financial, and, eventually, legal problem.

Shortly after Richards rejected his offer to lease the home for archival space, Jenson reached a tentative agreement with fellow Danish immigrant Soren P. Neve to exchange properties—his villa for Neve's property in Provo. Jenson signed a contract though he discovered that Neve still owed $2,000 on the Provo property, which left the deeds in escrow until the outstanding debt was paid.[78] Neve's firm went bankrupt, however, and his creditors began to circle his assets. The formal deed record in Provo was still in Neve's name, but he believed the deal was final and had started to occupy the Mill Creek property.[79]

By July 1894, the dispute had grown bitter. With a lien still on the Neve property, Jenson possessed no tangible asset in exchange for his villa. Appeals to ecclesiastical authorities failed to resolve the matter, and the case ended up in the Third District Court.[80] In the meantime, the villa had become a battleground between the Neves and Jensons. Attempts to come to a satisfactory solution broke down when Neve's wife, Emma, removed Jenson's press and type, cherished from his days working on *Morgenstjernen*, from the premises and scattered it "on the road from Rosenborg to Salt Lake City."[81]

Jenson felt overwhelming personal pain from his failed archival venture. He had decided to build the villa in part out of a zealous motivation to secure his documents and those of the church. His overconfidence and rash decision-making, however, resulted in great personal stress and financial loss. And in a suggestive postlude to his battle over his villa, Franklin D. Richards came to Jenson's Seventeenth Ward home (rather than his villa, as originally planned) to dedicate his modest second-story accommodations for his historical records.[82]

Jenson was soon called to go on a historical tour of the church's missions abroad, and he spent his final evening in Utah with his wife Bertha at his beloved Rosenborg Villa. While there, they were unexpectedly confronted by an upset Emma Neve, who verbally assaulted Jenson. She angrily pushed her way into Jenson's study and declared her intention to remain there. According to Jenson, he then "took her by the shoulders and put her out" of the room.[83] The next day, a deputy notified Jenson that assault charges had been brought against him by Emma Neve. Jenson was ultimately fined five dollars plus court fees for using "a little more force than necessary in ejecting the woman."[84] He later reflected on recent events and felt "somewhat sad and thoughtful" by the burden that his Rosenborg Villa and the Neve affair had placed upon his family. Though the perfect repository eluded him, what he would find among the scattered church records around the world recommitted him to document preservation and the systematization of church record keeping.

Touring the Stakes of Zion outside of North America

Amid his real-estate battle with Neve, Jenson continued his assigned tours through the church's stakes and units in North America. Though his personal finances were in no state to support additional trips, he sent a letter to First Presidency counselor Joseph F. Smith, hoping to broaden the scope of his travels. He intended to replicate his domestic labors abroad.[85] Although Latter-day Saint leaders would not create the first church stake outside of mainland North America until 1935,[86] there were nine non–North American church missions and numerous branches that needed to improve their record keeping.[87] In November 1894, Jenson was summoned to meet with another counselor in the First Presidency to discuss his proposed global historical work. "Had a conversation with Pres. Geo. Q. Cannon who was in favor of having me visit the respective missionary fields for Church history purposes," Jenson recorded, "and it was suggested that I start immediately after the April conference next year."[88]

Jenson was increasingly eager to document the young global church from beyond the comforts of the Historian's Office and beyond North America. As an immigrant, he was perhaps more aware than many of his US-born associates at church headquarters that the traditional North American narrative of the church needed to be broadened and nuanced to encompass a variety of perspectives and histories. By heritage, aptitude, and interest, Jenson was tailor-made to jumpstart the transition of church record keeping from a provincial endeavor to a global one.

The General Authorities had been impressed by Jenson's North American labors. According to President Cannon, Jenson had "labored with great diligence in collecting information for historical purposes . . . and has proved himself to be a very useful man in this kind of work."[89] Jenson's proposal and its timing also seemed right to church leaders at the close of the nineteenth century. After sixty-five years of persecution and decades of exile in the US West, the church was emerging from the shadows of plural marriage, theocracy, and isolationism and was adopting a new identity as it began to join the American mainstream and global Christianity. Up to that point, the initiatives and activities of the Historian's Office had largely been focused on chronicling the histories of Joseph Smith, Brigham Young, and the Latter-day Saint colonization of the Great Basin kingdom.[90] The evolution and growth of the church necessitated an expanded scope and a more comprehensive focus in gathering and writing history at the Historian's Office. Jenson would be at the vanguard of this transformation.

Despite their initial endorsement of Jenson's proposed global tour, the First Presidency suggested Jenson delay his departure by one month so he could be home for the birth of his child and to at least temporarily resolve the Neve legal affair.[91] On April 8, Emma gave birth to Jenson's seventh child (his fourth son), whom they named Harold Howell.[92] Concerned that Jenson was not paying the proper attention to his convalescing wife and their newborn son, the Church Historian encouraged his ambitious employee to curtail his history-gathering activities outside of Salt Lake City until his new departure date in May.[93]

In the April general conference, Jenson's record-keeping initiatives finally received their due. Franklin D. Richards spoke of Jenson's diligent efforts to reform church record keeping: "We have had brother Jenson visiting from ward to ward, from stake to stake, from mission to mission, gathering up the early history of the founding of the settlements in Utah and the surrounding territories. He has been with you, learned of your condition, and has gathered up what information he could get necessary for a faithful history of all the stakes of Zion." Richards then reprised Jenson's sentiments about the inadequate state of most local ecclesiastical records. In addition, he called for better family record keeping: "It is time that these brethren who are bald and gray with age were instituting this order of things in their households that they, as the heads of their families, their tribes or their generation, may establish a history that shall go down to the generations after them."[94] Richards's passionate call for better record keeping meant that Jenson's reforms were taking root and climbing the list of institutional priorities.

Beginning on May 2, Jenson enjoyed a series of good-bye gatherings with his family and fellow Saints. That evening, the First Presidency, members of the Quorum of the Twelve, and other local church leaders and members, assembled at the Jenson home in downtown Salt Lake City for a farewell party. Before eating dinner, the presiding brethren examined Jenson's collection of history books and papers and were most impressed. Then he was set apart for his global mission by President Cannon. According to Jenson, he was told he would travel safely on "railways, steamers, schooners, canoes, on the backs of animals and even on foot, while visiting the different nations of the earth to obtain the historical information for which [he] would be searching." Importantly, he was "blessed with the power of speech," that his "words in public and in private should reach the hearts of the honest." The blessing also promised that the trip would yield "valuable information to be used in the future history of the Church."[95]

During his last full day in Utah for the next two years, Jenson wrapped up his professional affairs at the Historian's Office and bid farewell to the First Presidency. They presented him with his official elder's license, which authorized Jenson "to collect information by the examination of records, etc., essential or desirable for the writing and preservation of the correct history of the various missions of the Church."[96] Later that day, Franklin D. Richards also supplied Jenson with a letter of introduction to all of the mission, conference, and branch presidents of the church. According to Richards's letter, Jenson was also visiting the units as an officer of the Genealogical Society of Utah, recently created in 1894, tasked with gathering ordinance and family history information, and as such should be afforded respect and cooperation.[97]

Finally, that evening on May 11 Jenson bid farewell to his family. "I called the family into the library, where I united with them in earnest prayer," he noted. He then gave priesthood blessings to his two wives, children, and in-laws. "In blessing and praying with the family we were all melted to tears and the spirit of God was with us." At 5:20 p.m. his train pulled out of the Union Pacific Railroad depot in Salt Lake City.[98]

Creating a Global Historical Record

From the deep-water Canadian port of Vancouver, Jenson crossed the Pacific Ocean by steamer and arrived in the Honolulu harbor. He remained in Hawai'i for two months, touring the branches and districts of the Hawaiian Mission. Jenson next boarded a steamer heading to Suva, Fiji, although the islands of Melanesia hosted no Latter-day Saint congregations or missionary outposts. After the Fijian islands, he toured the Samoan Mission, which at the time comprised the island nations of Samoa and Tonga. Next on his itinerary was New Zealand, where in a matter of weeks Jenson came to love the Maori Latter-day

Saints and their devotion to the gospel. From New Zealand, he traveled east to the Society Islands and French Polynesia, the region of the church's earliest venture into the Pacific world, in 1844. He stayed there for nearly two months. Next, he went to Australia, where he met with the members and missionaries of the Australasian Mission. Jenson then made his way to the Middle East via the Indian Ocean. After stopping in Cairo and Jerusalem, he made a circular tour of Europe, collecting Latter-day Saint historical data from England, Denmark, Norway, Sweden, Germany, Switzerland, the Netherlands, Wales, Ireland, and Scotland. Jenson did not return to Utah until June 1897, after a twenty-five-month circumnavigation of the world.[99]

His tour coincided with a rise in global tourism. Advances in transportation, including the development and expansion of steamships and railways, facilitated greater movement between far-flung global attractions in the latter half of the nineteenth century. Travel writers helped foster a popular culture of leisure and travel by extensively documenting their adventures and observations abroad for US and European audiences. Jenson had already tried his hand at this genre of writing by reporting to the *Deseret News* on his travels to church historic sites in 1888 and on his recent tour through Latter-day Saint settlements in North America.

Jenson similarly kept meticulous records during his global adventures. Before leaving Utah, he arranged to have the editors of the *Deseret News* serialize his travelogue letters, just as it had during his 1888 tour of the church's historic sites.[100] Travelogues in general sold at quick rates, and Jenson's writings were no exception. His first letter, written on May 13, 1895, from Portland, Oregon, was published two weeks later on June 1 under the series title "Jenson's Travels."[101] Over the next year, Jenson drafted regular letters chronicling his adventures.[102]

Jenson concluded his serialized travelogue by expressing hope that his two years abroad on behalf of the Historian's Office would lay the foundation for future historical studies of the global church. "During my mission," he wrote, "I circumnavigated the globe, traveled about 60,000 miles, preached the Gospel on land and on sea, whenever I had the opportunity, and gathered a great deal of historical information, which I trust will prove beneficial and interesting when it is prepared hereafter and incorporated in the history of the Church of Jesus Christ of Latter-day Saints of the Nineteenth century."[103]

When Jenson departed on his trip, he became part journalist, part ethnographer, part diplomat, and part historian. As he traveled and wrote, he considered his audience: English-speaking Latter-day Saints in Utah who, with the exception of a few missionaries, would never see the places he visited. His travel chronicles reveal both how he imagined the places he visited and how he wanted Latter-day Saints to imagine the places he visited. Jenson resourcefully relied on interviews with church members, missionaries, leaders, former members, other religionists, nonreligious locals, government officials, librarians, museum curators, newspaper editors, site docents, and anyone else whose ear he could bend. He often worked about sixteen hours a day gathering historical information and documents to take back to Utah.

As a journalist, Jenson furnished his readers with extensive, often romanticized, commentary about the geography and landscape, as well as the politics and demographics, of the nations that hosted him.[104] Jenson also witnessed the sprawling colonial empire of Great Britain in the South Pacific and recorded the resulting imperial and Christian influences that inflected the local culture. Jenson was hardly a critic of British rule—as an Anglo-Danish American, he remarked frequently on the civilizing influence colonial rule had on native peoples. Often he deferred to published government reports and handbooks on the nature and customs of the native people he visited.[105] To these published accounts, Jenson liberally added his own observations. After surveying the sugar cane fields and the colonial labor system in Fiji, for example, Jenson observed, "There are three classes of colored laborers, viz., Fijians, Polynesians, and coolies. White men rarely work in the field; they are mostly employed as overseers, mechanics, mill hands."[106] "Well, taking everything into consideration," Jenson concluded, "I cannot say that I admire contract labor. The question naturally arises, what are these people but slaves during . . . their indenture? Their bodies are certainly not their own during that length of time."[107]

Like most travel writers, Jenson had a tendency to exoticize local traditions, making them more interesting for his domestic audience. From Jenson's perspective, many of the scenes he witnessed proved curious and foreign.[108] For example, upon reaching Fiji, Jenson recorded that his first impression was "rather . . . unfavorable," which informed his first strained interaction with the local people in Fiji: "While strolling along in the neighborhood of the graveyard, I suddenly came upon a small party of natives armed with long, sharp-bladed knives. For a moment all the horrors of cannibalism rushed to my mind; but as they simply smiled and shook their heads as I addressed them in English and made no move toward seizing me, I soon breathed more freely and also discovered that their long knives were intended for cutting grass instead of human beings."[109]

Stories of Jenson's personal interactions were also flavored with commentary on the diets, housing, labor, and administration of native communities across the South Pacific.[110] In New Zealand, Jenson failed to give a traditional Maori greeting known as the *hongi* and instead opted for a handshake with village elders. Fearful he had offended, Jenson "made a public confession before conference was through, and in the absence of a better excuse I tried to make them believe that I was a bashful young man who feared that I would be laughed at if I shouldn't do it just right."[111] Jenson hazarded the local customs of many of the cultures he entered and then sketched them out for his Utah readers to imagine and appreciate.

As he mingled with foreign dignitaries and local village elders, Jenson also served as a global ambassador for the church. His visit, especially in the South Pacific, disrupted the day-to-day flow of local villages and attracted significant local attention. Some were familiar already with the resident Latter-day Saint missionaries, who attempted to integrate into the local culture as best as possible. Jenson, however, was clearly an outsider and one who came to observe and document their lives and histories. At every opportunity, Jenson sought an audience with kings and prominent native rulers in an attempt to demystify the church and to promote formal proselytizing efforts. In Fiji, he met the royal family, showing them images of Salt Lake City and discussing his extensive travels. To another chief, Jenson displayed a picture of the Salt Lake Temple and described how Latter-day Saints represented "Christianity in its primeval purity and preached the gospel exactly the same as it had been preached by Christ and his Apostles in ancient days."[112] Jenson repeated the presentation for King George Tupou II, king of Tonga, and briefly discussed Latter-day Saint views with King Malietoa of Samoa.[113] Representing the church and the Latter-day Saints to foreign cultures was a challenging and rewarding task, and it offered Jenson the chance to not only record and document church history abroad but also proselytize.

His main task on his world tour, however, remained to gather documents and to train missionaries and mission secretaries on proper record-keeping practices. Readers in Utah were rewarded by Jenson's diligent efforts in combing extant mission records. For example, his letters to the *Deseret News* detailed the history and growth of the church in New Zealand.[114] As he traveled among the branches of the church there, he wrote brief descriptions of their development.[115] The scope and detail of these histories were remarkable for one writing on the road, and they formed the raw product of what became the extensive manuscript histories on the church's global branches and missions.

Jenson uncovered several problems among the collections of disorganized mission records. When he wrote of the Australasian Mission during his visit to New Zealand, he found "that no accounts of the labors of the early missionaries have been preserved" and "the record, which is known as the mission history, has been well kept since that date."[116] When ecclesiastical records were sparse or inadequate, Jenson attempted to hunt down any records kept by local church members and missionaries. In Samoa, he met with Samuela Manoa, who with Kimo Belio were the first missionaries sent from Hawai'i to proselytize in Samoa. Manoa maintained a missionary journal and "could give accurate information about his labors and those of his fellow laborer, who now rests beneath the sod of Tutuila."[117] Occasionally, Jenson also ran into translation challenges.[118] While perusing branch records in New Zealand, for instance, he "experienced great difficulties in keeping track of Maori names. The natives of New Zealand are in the habit of changing their names repeatedly in the course of a lifetime; and thus we often find that a native has been baptized in one [name], ordained to some office in the priesthood in another, and perhaps set apart to preside over a branch in still another name." Jenson further wrote, "I have used my utmost influence against this practice. . . . Such a practice would almost destroy the value of records for historical purposes."[119] Responsibility for reform fell upon branch leaders and mission secretaries, who were to take the general principles Jenson expounded in their meetings and apply them going forward.

Taken collectively, Jenson's reports for the *Deseret News* provided a panoramic view of the globalizing church. He recorded details on the day-to-day lives of South Pacific missionaries, the worship practices of native members, and the challenges confronting the still undeveloped church as many converts gathered to the Great Basin. In Samoa, Jenson found the missionaries stationed in eleven branches with three elders located at mission headquarters in Fagali'i. The missionaries survived based on the kindness and hospitality of the locals who gave them regular food and lodging as they traveled. Jenson reported that "when at their regular stations, the elders make their home in the respective meeting-houses, which are generally partitioned off into two rooms, the smaller of which is occupied by the elders as a private apartment and the larger one reserved for meeting purposes."[120] In New Zealand, he found the mission similarly organized.[121] Latter-day Saints were accustomed to printed missionary reports from far-off lands, but Jenson's letters were uniquely comprehensive and systematic in how they animated Latter-day Saint proselytizing abroad with historical and cultural context.

While readers were gripped by Jenson's reports home, his own family began to suffer the toll of his absence. His wife Emma decided to join him unexpectedly in Europe in July 1896. She waited for nearly a month in Liverpool for word from Jenson about his location and that he was indeed doing well. Finally, she received correspondence from him in Egypt and surprised him upon his arrival in England. The meeting indeed proved a shock to Emma, since Jenson's travels had caused his appearance to change significantly. While he took pride in his hardiness and preparedness for the rigors of travel, Emma found Jenson looking "dreadfully worn and thin, also shabby."[122] For approximately a month, she became his traveling companion and assisted him with his historical labors before returning home. As he prepared to say good-bye to Emma on the deck of a ship docked near Copenhagen, Jenson found his wife "in tears on the ship, she having become uneasy because of my long absence."[123] The presence of Emma likely stirred Jenson's desire to follow her home as he wrote to the First Presidency and the Quorum of the Twelve to see if he should continue his labors or postpone them for a time to return to his family. Church Historian Richards and the First Presidency, eager to see Jenson's reforms instituted in every mission, advised that he stay until his task was completed.[124] Jenson heeded their advice and remained until the following May (1897).

Over twenty-five months Jenson had traveled over sixty-five thousand miles.[125] The legacy of his world tour, however, was not simply the vast territory through which he traveled, but in what his travels symbolized for a church preparing to better care for its members outside of North America. By describing the small communities of Latter-day Saints overseas to his Utah audience, Jenson placed disparate communities in dialogue. He introduced his readers to the future of their faith tradition, even if his accounts were sometimes romanticized or simplified.

In many ways, his travels illuminated the modernization and transformation of a globalizing world. And more simply, Jenson enjoyed the celebrity of touring the church's missions as an official representative of presiding Latter-day Saint leaders. Back at headquarters, he was an overworked and underappreciated clerk in the Historian's Office. But abroad, he mingled with heads of states and gave directives to mission presidents, branch presidents, and local church members. Feasts and meetings were held in his honor; away from church headquarters, his voice was amplified and his influence made visible. For two years, he was a historian on the peripheries of church expansion and, as one reporter in New Zealand titled him, "an observant traveller, an up to date man of the world, and an earnest worker for the faith he professes."[126]

An Assessment of Global Church Record Keeping

Arriving back in Utah on June 4, 1897, more than two years after his departure, Jenson was greeted by his wives and children.[127] Latter-day Saints were eager to hear about Jenson's church history mission, and over the next several weeks he became something of a celebrity in the Salt Lake Valley. He shared tales of his world tour from the pulpit in the Salt Lake Tabernacle[128] and recapped his tour for the Church Historian, copying the First Presidency on his letter.[129] Through diligent gathering and synthesizing, Jenson was confident he had acquired "the foundation and outline for histories of nearly every" overseas church unit. Apart from his travel reports, however, there was little material ready for public consumption. "To bring all this into readable shape will necessarily require years of patient toil and labor," Jenson wrote to Richards.[130] Jenson had thus given himself years of more work that only he could perform.

In addition, Jenson advocated for a "thorough reformation in regard to record keeping" throughout the church.[131] He had already initiated the framework for such a reformation by offering suggestions on better record-keeping practices in the church's branches, wards, stakes, and missions. He had also shipped home over a hundred crates with books and documents for storage at the Historian's Office. But these documents held little value without the interpretive work of the historian or an archival space to make them accessible to Historian's Office staff. Modernization would come, and Jenson would get increasingly eager to see his own vision for the future of the Historian's Office implemented. For now, his world tour was a reminder of how linked Latter-day Saint identity was to its own historical sensibility. The Latter-day Saint faith had been born out of American culture, but through the addition of other foreign historical accounts and new documents, Jenson expanded Latter-day Saint memory beyond its traditional home to new, global environs, suggesting a future where global Latter-day Saint history was tantamount with church history and a crucial component of the institution's identity.[132]

5 Assistant Church Historian

Away from the bustle of the steamship and the clack of the railcar, Andrew Jenson felt less at ease. His two-year world tour, though challenging, gave the restless employee of the Historian's Office a sense of purpose and importance. His extensive travels, unprecedented among the Latter-day Saints, had enlivened him and equipped him with captivating tales that made him a novelty back in the Salt Lake Valley. On his trip Jenson had sought not only documents and experiences but also higher status among his fellow record keepers. To his disappointment, however, the incredible work he had performed over the last several years did not immediately improve his professional fortunes at home.

While he was abroad, the small Historian's Office staff had expanded with the appointment of Charles W. Penrose in February 1896 as a second Assistant Church Historian, to work under Apostle and Church Historian Franklin D. Richards.[1] John Jaques had already been serving as an Assistant Church Historian since 1889.[2] A gifted orator and politician, Penrose was a relative newcomer to the church history scene. He was an editor and writer for the *Deseret News* and most recently the *Salt Lake Herald*, but outside of that work he had accomplished little to further the historical interests of the church, and the choice to appoint him instead of Jenson seemed at worst overtly preferential, and at best an embarrassing oversight of Jenson's growing historical credentials. Penrose was offered a full salary, a luxury Jenson had not been given yet.[3]

Though Richards reassured Jenson in the summer of 1897 that the First Presidency was considering appointing him as another Assistant Church Historian, by that September the call still had not come.[4] Jenson mulled over Penrose's appointment, and for a moment, he was uncertain he had a future at the Historian's Office: "Before speaking to Bro Richards I had decided to quit working for the Church unless there is a change in the policy pursued toward me. I have been the lack[e]y of the Historian's Office for many years, in one sense; and have perhaps done more historical work then all the rest put together; and still I have never been sustained as one of the [assistant] historians of the Church, while Penrose was sustained at once when he was appointed to work there. I certainly don't consider that just or right."[5]

Jenson's anxieties about his future at the Historian's Office were made worse by the earlier Soren P. Neve legal affair, which remained unresolved even after his two-year absence around the world.[6] The civil proceedings came to a close in late September and resulted in the forfeiture of Jenson's Rosenborg Villa to satisfy the Neves and a number of other creditors.[7] Resulting in over $15,000 in expenses and lost assets, the case plunged Jenson into temporary financial straits.[8] But with the Neve matter nearing a conclusion, Jenson again turned to sorting out his professional future. Despite his frustration with the delay of the promised appointment, Jenson hoped church leaders would finally put his name forward in the upcoming October general conference to be sustained as an additional Assistant Church Historian.

Called before the First Presidency

Jenson attended general conference on October 5, 1897, when the names of the General Authorities and general officers of the church were read to the congregation for their sustaining vote. He listened intently as Franklin D. Richards was announced as Church Historian, with John Jaques and Charles W. Penrose as Assistant Church Historians. Jenson's name was not presented. Jenson was disappointed; he believed that it was "Geo. Q. Cannon who interposed," preventing him from receiving the appointment.[9] The reasons behind President Cannon's seeming objection were a mystery to Jenson but one he intended to solve.

On October 19, Jenson met with the First Presidency and Church Historian to discuss his unmet expectations. Jenson wrote in his journal, "I explained my feelings and talked freely about my labors for the Church, and how I had felt myself slighted when Charles W. Penrose was taken into the Historian's Office . . ., when I who had labored so earnestly for years and who then was performing a very trying foreign mission in the interest of Church history had been ignored." Cannon then unexpectedly "expressed . . . personal satisfaction" with Jenson's past historical work and believed that, if not for Jenson, "important matters pertaining to Church history would have been lost forever." Both Woodruff and Richards agreed, and Cannon explained further that the "apparent slight" was due to an oversight. He then recommended to his fellow First Presidency members that Jenson be appointed as an additional Assistant Church Historian to Richards from that moment forward. Woodruff seconded his motion, and Jenson was sustained by all in the room to his new ecclesiastical position.[10]

Though it was not the public validation Jenson had sought earlier at general conference, he "returned home rejoicing" following his meeting with the First

Presidency. He recorded: "Ever since August, 1896, when I first saw the appointment of a second assistant [Penrose] to Bro. Richards, I have at times felt very bad, and have wondered what I had done to displease the Presidency. Now, after the matter has been explained I am perfectly satisfied, and will endeavor to renew my efforts, and work more diligently than ever to make my life's labor as a Church historian a success." Jenson would be publicly sustained as an Assistant Church Historian at the next general conference, on April 10, 1898.[11]

After the Call

Jenson's role within the Historian's Office remained largely unchanged by his appointment as Assistant Church Historian, as did his interactions with the general church membership. If anyone understood the vague boundaries that shaped the role of Assistant Church Historian, it was Woodruff and Richards—both had occupied the office in the past. Richards succeeded Woodruff in 1884 after Woodruff was promoted to the office of Church Historian.[12] Richards followed again in Woodruff's footsteps and was elevated to Church Historian when Woodruff became the church president in 1889.[13] For Jenson, who was well versed in the historical development of his new role, the developing pattern of an Assistant Church Historian progressing to the position of Church Historian occupied his mind. But both Jaques and Penrose were senior to him in their ongoing tenure as Assistant Church Historians. If Jenson hoped to one day direct the Historian's Office, he felt he needed to increase his standing soon.

Short of giving definition and status to his work, Jenson's new position came with more anxieties and frustrations. To be sure, he appreciated the job security; unlike some other compensated callings in the church, the role of Assistant Church Historian carried no fixed term, and the job, which came with a regular paycheck, was expected to last indefinitely. The stability was welcomed, even though the advancement did not result in an immediate salary increase for Jenson.[14] It was not these arrangements that distressed Jenson, but rather the lack of ecclesiastical authority and influence that he had hoped would come with the position.

Traditionally with most church offices and callings, the selected individual would be "set apart" by a priesthood authority through the laying on of hands and a spoken blessing. Neither the Church Historian nor his Assistant Church Historians were regularly set apart by church leaders after they were called and sustained, which left the parameters of their authority undefined and unofficial.[15] Jenson was close enough to his superiors in the First Presidency, Quorum of the Twelve, and First Council of Seventy to voice his concerns, but because church administration did not always share those concerns, his publications and projects, for the most part, remained his alone.

Fund-Raising for a New Historian's Office

Jenson set up a temporary office in the Salt Lake Temple Annex because the outdated Historian's Office was nearly at capacity with records and staffers. Beyond its space limitations, the Historian's Office was in a critical state. As part of his duties at the office, Jenson assessed the church's record holdings and commented to his ecclesiastical leaders on their poor condition. Many of the church's historical collections and books were housed in "unsafe places," according to Jenson, and needed rehousing in a "fire-proof building," where they could be "properly arranged for perusal." The basement proved susceptible to mildew and excessive dust and even hosted a few vermin. As a result, the books and newspapers stored there were "fast decaying." Jenson's investigation turned up "disorder . . . everywhere."[16]

The adobe structure of the Historian's Office was now showing damage and decay from external elements.[17] The over forty-year-old building was inadequate for the church's growing historical enterprise, and thus, Jenson's call for better quarters, however self-interested, was well justified. But Jenson also knew getting approval for a new building could be difficult given the church's current dismal financial holdings and poor accounting measures. With debts exceeding $2 million, church leaders were hardly in a position to authorize construction of a modern Historian's Office.[18]

Determined to find a solution, Jenson wrote a letter in April 1898 to Richards that included a fund-raising proposal: "My 'Church Chronology' which has been proven to be a popular and valuable work of reference to the Saints, has been out of print for several years and the issuing of a second and revised edition with dates brought down to the present time has been suggested by many students of Church History." Jenson believed that popular demand for his *Church Chronology* (1886), which outlined the major events in church history, might prove profitable to the church if it agreed to sell it.[19] "I therefore propose to make the Church a present of all my rights to said work," Jenson continued, "which represents years of patient labor." Jenson suggested that at least twenty-five thousand copies be printed as a second edition, with all profits earmarked for the construction of a new Historian's Office. Jenson intended to sell his second edition of *Church Chronology* for around one dollar per copy, which he calculated would yield a profit of at least $10,000 for the office's construction.[20] One month after his initial proposal to Richards, he was informed by the Church Historian that the First Presidency and Quorum of the Twelve had approved his proposal.[21]

Jenson immediately set about revising and updating his chronology through 1898. He added several pieces of introductory material, such as a lengthy section on the history of the church's General Authority positions, including the ecclesiastical offices of Church Historian and Assistant Church Historian. He also authored an essay on the priesthood and provided an exhaustive list of General Authorities called since the organization of the church, alongside their respective priesthood "line of authority." The list was designed to help male church members ordained to the priesthood lineally trace their authority back to the Prophet Joseph Smith.[22] Jenson hoped this introductory material would make the volume immensely valuable to the average Latter-day Saint, who otherwise might not show interest.[23]

In July, the First Presidency announced their endorsement of *Church Chronology* to the public in a *Deseret News* feature. "We trust that the Latter-day Saints will manifest a general interest in this enterprise both by furnishing the required data and by patronizing the work after it is published," they wrote. They promised that any profits would be used to construct a new Historian's office.[24] The work was largely Jenson's alone to complete, though Richards did appoint a committee, which included himself and Assistant Church Historians Jaques and Penrose, as well as clerk A. Milton Musser, to proofread and approve the manuscript.[25]

Jenson intended to market the *Church Chronology* extensively at the upcoming October conference. He laid out his promotional strategy to Richards (at his request) two weeks before the start of the conference: "I think it would be a good plan to make public mention of the work, and the object of its publication at the next general conference of the Church, and afterwards in all the quarterly stake conferences that will be held between Oct. 1898, and Jan. 1899, and that during these three months every household of Saints throughout the entire land be visited and orders taken for the book which then can be delivered at once when ready from the press in January, 1899." Jenson also suggested that the work be pushed by "ward teachers," who made regular visits to appointed families within their ecclesiastical wards. Jenson was counting on local members sympathizing with the publication's noble cause. "When the cramped condition of the Historian's Office and the unsafe condition of the most valuable Church records are made plain to the Saints," he wrote to Richards, "I am satisfied that all faithful members of the Church will consider it their special duty to do something in aid of our undertaking."[26] Jenson asked permission to visit the various quarterly stake conferences personally in order to further advertise their mission.[27]

The financial risk of this endeavor to Jenson personally was sizable. He had already assumed a loan of over $500 to cover the initial printing costs at the Deseret News office, and more funding would be necessary before the presswork was done. He feared that without sufficient advertising at general conference (and the subsequent sale of orders), more private debt would be necessary to see the project through. He suggested the First Presidency write a circular, "setting forth the object of the work and what is desired of the people . . . and which also can be presented as a leaflet for universal circulation among the Saints."[28]

His marketing plan was ambitious. Prior building projects relied on the generosity of local members and tithing funds, but for Jenson, who had so far earned a modest living through subscription-based publishing, the proposal seemed achievable. Richards put Jenson's suggestions in motion and furnished him with a detailed circular from the First Presidency, lauding his work of reference as being "of great value to all Saints, and especially to students of Church history."[29] Armed with approximately seven hundred printed copies of the circular, Jenson set about canvassing the special priesthood meeting of general conference held in the Assembly Hall on Saturday, October 8, 1898.[30] The initial response appeared favorable, and Jenson remained confident that his campaign would be successful.

In the late nineteenth century, most Latter-day Saints' primary point of interaction with the church was in local wards and stakes. As a result, ecclesiastical power, in the experience of church members, was localized in ward and stake leaders. Bishops and stake presidents served undefined terms and often remained in their positions, barring apostasy or significant illness, until death. These long-standing leaders knew personally the residents that lived within their church jurisdiction and were often the most trusted individuals in a community. Their positions gave them significant sway in local civic, political, economic, and ecclesiastical matters. They ruled on civic disputes, collected tithes, and counseled with members.[31] Jenson knew that if he could deploy the authority and gain the endorsement of the bishops and stake presidents successfully, he would bring in the necessary profits to build a new Historian's Office.

In November 1898, Jenson sent out promotional circulars to ward and stake leaders throughout the Intermountain West. The endorsement letters—one from Richards, a second from the First Presidency, and a final from Jenson—praised the value of Jenson's compilation and explained the number of subscriptions needed to meet their goal: "It is necessary to obtain the patronage of the Saints to the extent of, at least, one subscriber for every ten members (children included)." Total church membership had just surpassed 250,000 in the last year, and Jenson and Richards calculated from statistical reports the total number of members in each ward and stake that received the circulars and assigned each a subscription quota.[32] Based on these quotas, the Historian's Office bound an allotment of books for each ward, even if the ward had not forwarded on any subscribers. Ward leaders who had delayed sending in their orders were encouraged to pick up their allocation at the October 1899 general conference and to bring with them payment.[33]

However, response from ward and stake leaders was unenthusiastic. That, plus publication delays, made the First Presidency hesitant to assume complete control of the *Chronology* as originally planned. At a meeting in February 1899 with Lorenzo Snow, the new church president, and First Presidency counselor George Q. Cannon, Jenson was "advised to keep the work as [his] own property . . . and not to transfer all [his] rights as author and owner to the Church."[34] Cannon was apparently concerned about the church placing too much faith and "obligations to any man in the way proposed."[35] Cannon's personal reluctance was understandable. His printing company, George Q. Cannon & Sons, had spent the better part of the last decade attempting to rescue the multivolume *History of Utah* (1892–1904), authored by Orson F. Whitney, from financial ruin.[36] The cash-strapped Utah economy and the church's own financial struggles persisted, limiting the church's ability to assume any additional financial risks. Jenson would not officially sign over his rights to the second edition of the *Chronology* to Lorenzo Snow, as president and trustee-in-trust of the church, until December 1899, when Jenson had finally acquired some proceeds from the book's sale and had placed them into a Historian's Office building fund. He transferred his work to the church for the sum of one dollar.[37]

Like Whitney's *History of Utah*, subscriptions to the *Chronology* trickled in slowly. Jenson's *Chronology* was a full five months behind its initial schedule as he waited for responses to his circulars. When the book finally came off the press in March 1899, Jenson felt "relieved of a burden which has almost crushed me in the ground. Never in my life have I been subject to such a mental strain; and at times I have felt as if I could not possibly stand it. I have often worked till long past midnight. God grant that the chronology, which has cost so much labor and anxiety, may prove of great use to the Saints, be well received by them and the financial outcome be of such a nature that a new Historians Office may be the result."[38]

Unfortunately, Jenson's *Chronology* became one of the first major disappointments of his young career as Assistant Church Historian. By June 1899 he had finished sending circulars to every bishop in the church. He issued reminders to ecclesiastical leaders to forward on subscribers in September 1899.[39] A month later, he spoke at general conference, making an appeal on behalf of the *Chronology*. His committed efforts bore little fruit. Discouraged, he went to the First Presidency for counsel and received another letter from them to share with local leaders recommending the publication for purchase.[40] Despite his best intentions and hard work, Jenson had overestimated the interest of local ecclesiastical leaders in serving as pseudo-agents for the Historian's Office. With a host of other responsibilities, many failed to give the circulars any serious thought. Some even resented how stridently the *Chronology* was being pushed on them. Though Jenson encouraged church members with little interest in his *Chronology* to directly donate to the Historian's Office building fund, he was met with no great success.[41] By the close of 1900, only $1,647 had been transferred to the building fund. The total would barely surpass $2,000 four years later.[42] Jenson would eventually receive partial reimbursement for the loan he took out to front publishing costs. But the project was expected to be profitable only if wards, stakes, and missions purchased their quota of books, and many did not. Among those that did, some were unsure of what to do with multiple copies of the *Church Chronology* and asked church headquarters to reassume custodianship of the surplus books.[43]

With little fund-raising assistance from the sale of the *Chronology*, the First Presidency searched for alternatives to resolve the deteriorating physical conditions at the Historian's Office. Jenson's proposal to build an entire wing onto a new administration building was tabled and, instead, renovations were conducted on the old Historian's Office.[44] The changes addressed two pressing issues: the need for office space and the need for a modern, secure place to store records. On the main floor, between the residence space and the rooms of the Historian's Office, a new room was enclosed for Jenson to use as a private office. In addition, a new roof, door, and shutters—all made of iron—were added to the exterior building to decrease the possibility of a devastating fire.[45] The upgrades were completed by the fall of 1900, and Jenson moved into his new office with a renewed enthusiasm for his work.[46]

Financial and Record-Keeping Reforms

Jenson's vision of a new Historian's Office building fell short for the time being, and he directed his attention to another ambitious modernization project—overhauling the church's record-keeping practices. His past decade of travels to the stakes and missions of the church had turned up a troubling pattern of neglect and carelessness in creating and preserving institutional records in the wards, stakes, and missions. After he returned from his world tour in 1897, he submitted a report to the Church Historian that captured the unorganized state of the church's records: "I would earnestly recommend a thorough reformation in regard to record-keeping. There is a lack of system and uniformity throughout the Church in the recording of ordinance work and in the making of minutes, rolls, statistical reports, financial reports, etc. Each mission, Stake and Ward seem to have its own peculiar system or no system at all; and until regular forms and blanks are furnished from headquarters for use throughout the entire Church, this irregularity must necessarily continue."[47]

Jenson's observations and recommendations, while accurate, failed to gain traction until December 1899, when Apostle Rudger Clawson brought the matter to the attention of the First Presidency and the Quorum of the Twelve.[48] Clawson had discovered the sad state of record keeping after being tasked with improving the church's financial stability through a large-scale effort to reform and modernize its financial accounting.[49] Clawson bleakly concluded that the church "was surely upon the verge of bankruptcy," with debts exceeding $2 million.[50] In the process of making the church fully solvent again, Clawson reviewed extensively the church's financial books, which contained a complex puzzle of active, inactive, and incomplete accounts. The apostle's assessment of the state of the record books employed by the church harmonized generally with Jenson's long-standing complaints. The entries in existing record books were incomplete, and the work required to recover pertinent information was tedious and frustrating.

Church leaders mulled over Clawson's and Jenson's complaints about the poor state of local ecclesiastical records and resolved to create a new committee to implement record-keeping reforms. The Committee on Records included both Jenson and Clawson, and its first task was to explore the feasibility of instituting a churchwide "record day," or "a day appointed (preferably the Sabbath day) when the presidency of the stake would visit the ward and spend the forenoon in inspecting the records—first, the records of the ward proper, then the records of each organization and of each quorum of the priesthood."[51] Over the next year, the committee refined their proposal and eventually determined that a "record day" would be most effective if it were held in association with ward conferences, where stake leaders, who would be attending the conferences anyway, could train congregants on proper record-keeping procedures.[52]

In March 1901, the Committee on Records sent an official circular to all stake and mission presidents and ward bishops. Some "secretaries and recorders," the committee declared, "have been careless and indifferent in discharging their duties, in consequence of which much ordinance work and many transactions of great importance have not been properly recorded and preserved." By "proper inspection and auditing" of the records, "no historian, clerk or recorder who is now in office . . . will neglect the sacred trust imposed upon him of making true and complete records."[53]

Local record-keeping reforms, like those advocated by Jenson, also served a more obvious and immediate benefit to church headquarters. In March 1900, Clawson reported to the First Presidency that "there were some 10,000 members of the church living in different Stakes and throughout the country, without recommends" that showed they had been members in good standing in their previous wards or branches.[54] The resulting confusion in membership record books made tithing nearly impossible to track, since members could theoretically move between wards without paying tithing. The chaotic state of local membership records came as a shock to the First Presidency.[55] "This evil is widespread," the First Presidency warned, "through indifference or neglect, or from some other cause, there are numerous members of the Church 'floating' around and living in various wards, but with no standing on the records." Church leaders urged a swift resolution to the membership-record crisis. All Latter-day Saints needed to "be identified with the organization of the Church."[56]

The Committee on Records thus set out to create new record-keeping tools to facilitate reform. At the committee's first meeting, Jenson, who had already circulated new forms on his tours of the wards, stakes, and missions of the church, "exhibited some forms that he had drawn up suggestive of simplifying and perfecting Ward records or records of members, records of blessings, ordinations, etc."[57] By March, Jenson and the committee had finalized their recommendation. Since many of the old forms were out of print, they elected to distribute freshly printed, bound books containing forms that would assist the church in keeping track of not only its members but also significant ecclesiastical information, such as members' ordinances. In the new account books, ward clerks could record "the names, genealogies etc of the members, ordinations to the Priesthood etc." In addition, clerks could issue a "certificate of standing" to members who were moving "from one ward to another" and a stand-alone form for temple recommends, which granted worthy members access to Latter-day Saint temples.[58] These new forms apparently were almost entirely derived from Jenson's earlier creations.[59] The new books and forms were ready to be distributed early the following year.

Though implementing these reforms was painstakingly slow, the Committee on Records continued to emphasize streamlined protocols for local record keeping. In October 1901, the committee directed that any historical records kept at the local level should be combined into one historical record book that was separate from the membership record book. The membership record was described as "a Genealogical Book" divided into three parts—a record of baptisms, a record of priesthood ordination, and a record of children blessed in the church after birth but not yet baptized. The historical book was a "General Minute Book, or history, containing minutes of general Ward meetings." Bishops were responsible for overseeing both of these record books.[60] In addition, ward priesthood quorums were to maintain "a record of members (genealogical book) and a minute book." All auxiliary organizations, such as the Relief Society, were to keep a general minute book.[61] Only "one general record book" was to be kept at the stake and mission level.[62] The church's missions were asked to send in annual historical reports, including detailed proselytizing statistics, to the Historian's Office.

The success of the reforms recommended by the Committee on Records was largely contingent on the cooperation of local leaders and the competency of ward and stake clerks. With this in mind, the committee instituted a formal procedure, at the suggestion of President Smith, for bishops to render an account to their stake presidents. The reporting structure was imperfect, but it was another mechanism for ensuring that local records met Historian's Office standards and Jenson's approval as he traveled to gather histories from wards, stakes, and missions. By 1902 many of the wards and stakes, especially those in Utah, had adopted the new forms, and changes would continue to be made to local membership forms and statistical reports throughout Jenson's time as Assistant Church Historian.[63]

Selecting a New Church Historian

Building renovations and policy reforms were not the only changes afoot at the Historian's Office at the turn of the twentieth century. In December 1899, Church Historian Franklin D. Richards passed away after battling the effects of a stroke.[64] Questions began to swirl about his successor. Precedent, though not official policy, created some expectations in the minds of close observers. Since the formal establishment of the Historian's Office in the Great Basin, the Church Historian served in the highest leadership circles of the church, either in the Quorum of the Twelve or in the First Presidency, both apostolic roles. Moreover, since the passing of Church Historian Orson Pratt in 1889, the succeeding Church Historian had always been appointed to the office after serving as Assistant Church Historian.

Since Franklin D. Richards had assumed control of the Historian's Office in April 1889, however, the number of Assistant Church Historians who were not General Authorities had multiplied—John Jaques (also serving since 1889), Charles W. Penrose (since 1896 until 1899), Jenson (since 1897), and Orson F. Whitney (since 1898).[65] None of these men had been serving as members of the First Council of Seventy, Quorum of the Twelve, or First Presidency. Since no Assistant Church Historian had higher ecclesiastical authority than another, choosing a successor became complicated.

With the Assistant Church Historians left to manage the day-to-day affairs of the Historian's Office, the First Presidency set about determining who would follow Richards. The possibility of being called as Church Historian weighed heavily on Jenson, at least privately. Rumors in the Latter-day Saint community whispered his name as a potential replacement. Over the past decade, however, Jenson had received an agonizing tutorial in how church leadership was conferred. While he still trusted that his ecclesiastical superiors sought to discern God's will through inspiration before making leadership assignments, he had also perceived a pattern of preferential treatment given to the direct descendants of church leaders or their closest friends. The church's presiding quorums were filled with members of the church's first families, and while there were certainly exceptions, the dynastic lines of some General Authorities disheartened the Danish immigrant.[66] Jenson was not a descendent of prominent church leaders, past or present. It made sense for General Authorities to select new leaders from among their family and social circles—people they knew and trusted—but Jenson constantly worried, as he would later write, that "true merit" would be disregarded in favor of the "close relatives or special friends" of General Authorities, to his detriment.[67]

His fears had been stoked recently with the unexpected appointment of Orson F. Whitney as Assistant Church Historian after Charles W. Penrose returned to manage the *Deseret News* in 1899.[68] Whitney's familial roots in the church ran deep. His grandfather was Newel K. Whitney, who had served as bishop of the church at Kirtland, Ohio. Orson's father, Horace K. Whitney, had married Helen Mar Whitney Kimball, the daughter of Heber C. Kimball, an original member of the Quorum of the Twelve and later a counselor in the First Presidency. Helen was also a plural wife of Joseph Smith.[69] Latter-day Saint leaders held high hopes for Orson F. Whitney given his heritage, but he had some unconventional beliefs and so far had yet to meet expectations.[70] Whitney, however, was a gifted orator, writer, and politician whose potential value to the church was evident. He was also a committed bishop, presiding over the Eighteenth Ward in Salt Lake City, and benefitted from a close friendship with Apostle Lorenzo Snow.[71] His literary contributions up to this point included a biography of his grandfather, *Life of Heber C. Kimball* (1888), and a commissioned multivolume *History of Utah* (1892–1904). Despite the money earned from his literary works, Whitney still had a number of financial struggles.[72]

With the vacancy at the Historian's Office, Whitney spotted a fresh opportunity to find steady work. His friend Snow, now church president since September 1898, had already intimated that he would "do what he could" to improve Whitney's situation. In November 1899, Whitney went to Snow's office to ask for a position as Assistant Church Historian. While en route to see Snow, Whitney ran into the son of Church Historian Franklin D. Richards, Franklin S. Richards, who told Whitney that he had already "strongly urged his father to use his influence" to get Whitney the appointment. Whitney's subsequent meeting with Snow yielded good news. The Church Historian had already recommended to Snow that Whitney be made an Assistant Church Historian, despite the fact he had never worked in the Historian's Office as a clerk or in any other position. Snow of course approved of the decision, but Whitney expressed some concern that others in the First Presidency, especially George Q. Cannon, would have reservations about the appointment. Snow reassured him: "Well, it don't matter what he thinks of it. We'll fix it up for you."[73] Whitney began his work in the Historian's Office in January 1899.[74] Whitney's appointment undoubtedly irritated Jenson, who had waited years for a similar appointment.

In the interregnum following Richards's death, the obvious frontrunners for the Church Historian position were Assistant Church Historians Jaques, Jenson, and newcomer Whitney. In June 1900, the frail and elderly Jaques passed away, leaving Jenson and Whitney, as well as clerk A. Milton Musser, to shoulder the work of the Historian's Office.[75] Jenson was now the senior historian, and the First Presidency seriously considered him for the role of Church Historian. But rumors of Jenson's potential appointment stirred resistance from those inside and outside the Historian's Office. Fellow employee Martin S. Lindsay questioned Jenson's aspirations and demeaned his character in a letter to the First Presidency:

> Jenson early nurtured the ambition to become the Church Historian. . . . I heard him once, when speaking of his probable promotion to be Historian, "Time will tell." He said this in a prophetic tone of voice. . . .
>
> It is well know[n] that Jenson is possessed of a very violent temper, which, coupled with a quarrelsome and overbearing disposition, has often brought himself and others in trouble. . . .
>
> Jenson's egotistical, inquisitive and fault-finding spirit has long since disgusted every employee in the office, and I dare say that not one of them would voluntarily work under him, or even in the same room with him.[76]

Soren P. Neve, still upset with Jenson over their past real estate deal, also gave his opinion on the quality of Jenson's historical work. Referencing the *Church Chronology*, he wrote to the First Presidency: "While the book contains many references to its author and compiler, whose works and movements are paraded as events of great importance, it is silent regarding men far more worthy and much more prominent than himself. . . . In his index he refers to Andrew Jenson fifteen times and to the Prophet Joseph Smith 12 times."[77]

Neve's and Lindsay's disparaging remarks about Jenson understandably gave the First Presidency pause. Fearful that appointing Jenson as Church Historian would cause an irreparable division at the Historian's Office, President Snow and his counselors searched for an alternative candidate. In late July 1900, they selected Apostle Anthon H. Lund as Church Historian.[78] Lund was personable, well liked, and judicious, and though he lacked the practical training of past Church Historians, the former European Mission president was a skilled diplomat who could cool the simmering divisions in the Historian's Office.[79] Lund, as a friend of Jenson's and a fellow Scandinavian, was also best suited to soothe any of Jenson's sore feelings and could check his combative temperament. Concerned that Jenson might again feel cheated of a longed-for promotion, the First Presidency instructed Lund to "take hold gradually and try to reconcile the parties."[80]

The news, while disappointing, did not come as a surprise to Jenson. The day after Lund's meeting with the First Presidency, President Cannon announced the decision to the staff. Jenson wrote in his journal, "Pres. Geo. Q. Cannon came over to the H. O. accompanied by Apostle Anthon H. Lund, whom he introduced as our new chief, he having been appointed Church Historian the day before. I learned of this appointment last night. This was not at all unexpected to me. I had favored the appointment of either F. M. Lyman or A. H. Lund as the only two members of the quorum of the Twelve who had historical ability. Since the days of the Prophet Joseph one of the twelve Apostles has always been chief historian."[81]

Struggling for Support

With the succession issue finally settled, Jenson moved forward with his projects, but he continued to be burdened by the failed sale of his *Chronology* and frustrated by general affairs at the Historian's Office. He also started to doubt that his ecclesiastical leaders supported or appreciated his work, which began to darken his outlook on the future. Over a year had passed since Richards's death, and the presiding brethren had not formally recognized him as an Assistant Church Historian at the last general conference in October 1900, when Lund was first sustained as Church Historian.[82] The formal sustaining process was a marker of institutional prestige and a mechanism for gauging public support for his position. It placed Jenson in proximity to a limited circle of General Authorities and signaled that his new role was set apart from his prior work as a clerk in the Historian's Office. But since his last sustaining, he began to wonder if he had lost favor among church leaders. He watched, for example, at the October 1901 general conference as the other general officers in the church were sustained in quick succession. President Joseph F. Smith presented only the name of "Church Historian and general Church recorder," Anthon H. Lund, on that occasion, omitting the traditional sustaining of Assistant Church Historians in general conferences.[83]

Around this time, Jenson began to put in motion plans to launch his own private historical research firm: the Andrew Jenson History Company.[84] With church authorities unwilling to assume ownership over future editions of his *Church Chronology* or the first volume of his *Latter-day Saint Biographical Encyclopedia* (1901), Jenson intended to unify his publications under one chartered corporation.[85] The move was as symbolic as it was practical. Jenson always believed his publications were his foremost contribution to the church, and if his leaders were unwilling to officially sanction his works, they would bear his name instead and he would continue to earn a living as an independent historian.

Jenson, despite feeling unsupported by his leaders, felt obligated and empowered to closely manage the day-to-day affairs of the Historian's Office, especially when Lund was away. Others, however, were not eager for Jenson to be in charge. For example, as B. H. Roberts began work on his *History of the Church* (1902–12), he tussled with Jenson over gaining access to the Historian's Office holdings. According to Jenson, Roberts was "occupying a room in the basement of the office, doing some extra work in connection with the history of Joseph Smith" and "came to the library door and said: 'I want to get a book.' 'All right,' I answered, 'what book do you want?' He answered: 'Well, I want to get a book, I don't have to tell you what book I want every time.' In reply, I said, 'yes, you have. I have to keep track of the books that go out of the library.' 'All right,' he retorted, and went away angry." Jenson's initial attempt at keeping watch over the library's holdings clearly failed to impress Roberts. Jenson continued: "Last Thursday I had occasion to use a book that he had and when I took it . . . away, I remarked 'you can have it again whenever you need.' 'Of course I can,' he said sneeringly." Roberts later took all the volumes of the Nauvoo church periodical, the *Times and Seasons*, out of the library without notifying Jenson and failed to return them in a timely manner. "Bro. Roberts is an 'officious fellow,'" Jenson concluded, "and seems to think he can run the Historian's Office. He has only been here a few weeks."[86]

The mental strain on Jenson during this period was nearly unbearable. "For some time past I have felt a combination of influences at work to crush and discourage me," he confided in his journal, "and I felt that I needed to seek comfort from the Lord on the mountains, where I could be all alone and undisturbed. I laid before my Creator the feelings of my heart most openly and sincerely, and then waited for his inspiration."[87] Jenson's place of seclusion was Ensign Peak, the popular hiking destination on the northern end of the Salt Lake Valley, in the foothills overlooking the city. The peak was renowned in Latter-day Saint culture. Brigham Young reportedly saw it in a vision in the Nauvoo Temple while seeking for revelation on how to lead the church after Joseph Smith's death. In his vision, the peak was a geographical marker meant to help Young identify where he was to lead the Latter-day Saint pioneers. When Young first glimpsed the Salt Lake Valley on July 24, 1847, the sight of Ensign Peak confirmed to him the decision to settle the Saints there.[88] Steeped in historical and revelatory significance, the peak seemed an appropriate place for Jenson to search his soul.

The response Jenson received in answer to his prayer came in the form of personal revelation, which he recorded while on the mountainside in August 1901. The revelation repeated a phrase oft-used in both the New Testament and the Doctrine and Covenants that marked Christ's disciples and faithful followers.[89] "My Son, be of good cheer," Jenson was told. "Thy prayers are heard and shall be answered upon thy head with the blessings thou so earnestly desire. The Lord has not rejected thee; but he has permitted thee to pass through trials and afflictions in order to try thy faith and thy integrity. But if thou wilt do what thou understandest to be right hereafter the Lord will forgive thee thy past sins and prosper thou in thy labors henceforth, and grant thee the righteous desires of thy heart." Jenson's greatest anxieties were also addressed: "Thou hast not lost thy position in the Church as a Historian; the zeal and integrity in that capacity is known to God, and is pleasing in his sight; and it is God who has inspired thee to do the work which thou has done. But thou has been too ambitious and has cared too much for the opinion of men; and this is the main cause of thy present disappointment. But don't get discouraged. God loves thee, and thou art not rejected. Be patient yet a little while, and all will be well." The personal inspiration also addressed Jenson's sometimes vindictive spirit: "Forgive thy enemies. . . . Let them alone bear thy losses like a man of God, and that which has been taken from thee shall be given thee in blessings in a hundred fold." He was also reassured that his career as an Assistant Church Historian was not coming to a close but that, if he watched his behavior "hour by hour and day by day," his "future days" would "be happy and useful" and his career would "be successful throughout."[90]

Jenson's mountainside revelation resembled other divine directives of strength and comfort received by Latter-day Saint leaders, like the one received by the prophet Joseph Smith while he was imprisoned in Liberty, Missouri, in 1839. Smith reported he was told on that occasion, "My son, peace be unto thy soul; thine adversity and thine afflictions shall be but a small moment; And then, if thou endure it well, God shall exalt thee on high; thou shalt triumph over all thy foes."[91] Jenson too was comforted and felt assured that his enemies would be overcome. Jenson likely saw historical continuity and significance in this private scripture. He "remained on the mountain till after sundown" and then "returned home fully determined to take a new stand and obey the words of inspiration."[92]

Eight months later, at the April 1902 general conference, Jenson was unusually absent from the Sunday morning session. He chose to spend the morning alone at the Historian's Office in fasting and prayer. While reflecting on his current situation, he reached for a copy of the Doctrine and Covenants on a nearby bookshelf and "turned at once to the 98th section and read from [verses] 23 to 32 inclusive." The selection—part of a revelation to early Latter-day Saints who were experiencing persecutions in Jackson County, Missouri—instructed on how to bear oppression from enemies.[93] "This passage was so strikingly fitting to the subject matter of my prayer, at least to part of it," Jenson remarked, "that I at once was impressed to write to a man, that I consider my only enemy in the world and who is perhaps now upon his death bed." Though not explicitly mentioned, the recipient of Jenson's letter was Soren P. Neve, who was battling stomach cancer and would die three days later, on April 9, 1905.[94] The letter no longer exists, but in the wake of his recent revelatory experience on Ensign Peak, Jenson was likely hoping to put an end to their long-standing feud.

Following this prayerful seclusion at the Historian's Office, Jenson returned to the Tabernacle on Temple Square to take in the final session of general conference. When he heard his name read as Assistant Church Historian and put forth for a sustaining vote, he was both relieved and overjoyed. Church Historian Lund was also sustained, as were fellow Assistant Church Historians Whitney, Musser, and B. H. Roberts. "This I consider right and just," Jenson wrote in his journal. "Since bro. Lund was appointed Church historian in 1900 no assistant historians have been sustained. This was according to the plan of the late President Lorenzo Snow, but was not in harmony with the feelings of Bro. Joseph F. Smith, who considered, as I now understand, that I, who was the only one of Bro. Richards' assistants left, was treated unjustly." Now feeling comforted and supported by his leaders, Jenson decided to not let his private history venture distract him from his role as Assistant Church Historian. "If there had not been a change," he wrote, "I should have withdrawn from the Historian's Office, having already commenced a private business . . . but now, after being acknowledged and sustained in the position I think I am entitled to, I shall once more throw my whole soul into the work at the Historian's Office."[95] While the Andrew Jenson History Company continued, it functioned only to help fund the printing of his independent publications, like future editions of the *Latter-day Saint Biographical Encyclopedia.* His full-time focus remained on his work at the Historian's Office.

Jenson's renewed sustaining as an Assistant Church Historian signaled a new beginning for him at the Historian's Office. In his short tenure thus far, he had already agitated for significant change, inflamed divisions at the Historian's Office, struggled to acquire support for his publications, and nearly quit. For now, however, with his calling clearly distinguished from a general clerkship or lower-level ecclesiastical position, Jenson relished being a formal officer of the church (although not a General Authority). By remaining inside the ranks of church employment, he felt he could implement impactful change and also receive greater opportunities to serve on behalf of the church. And when those assignments came, Jenson welcomed the opportunity to step out of his routine and circle of influence at the Historian's Office to represent the church more broadly.

6 Elder and Emissary

Early in 1900, the Latter-day Saint Scandinavian community looked forward to an upcoming jubilee, held to commemorate Apostle Erastus Snow's arrival in Copenhagen in June 1850 to introduce the gospel. The proposed celebration had been announced in the Scandinavian meeting of the October 1899 general conference by Apostle Anthon H. Lund.[1] Andrew Jenson's heritage and deep connections to Utah's Scandinavian communities made him a natural choice to sit on the planning committee.[2]

In the months leading up to the event, Jenson was hard at work compiling biographies for the planned jubilee book.[3] The resulting souvenir album was impressive. The keepsake opened with a concise narrative history of the Scandinavian Mission, followed by details on the church's entrance into Denmark, Sweden, and Norway. A comprehensive list of the missionaries who served in Scandinavia each year through 1900 was also included. The volume concluded with over 350 concise biographies of Scandinavian Latter-day Saints, including illustrated portraits.[4] Jenson's traditional subscription-based model was used to fund the project, but as opposed to his experience with *Church Chronology*, he found great success this time. The album turned a profit, and the proceeds went to support a building fund for chapels in Copenhagen and Stockholm.[5]

The four-day event launched on June 14, 1900, in the Assembly Hall on Temple Square. Nine members of the Quorum of the Twelve were on the stand alongside prominent members of Utah's Scandinavian community. Elder Francis M. Lyman, speaking on behalf of the apostles, highlighted Jenson in his account of Scandinavian contributions to the Latter-day Saint community: "From your ranks there has sprung a man who is doing more than any other in preserving the records of the church."[6] The main events of the commemoration included a concert in the Salt Lake Tabernacle, a missionary reunion, a trip to the pleasure grounds of Saltair and Lagoon, and a meeting led by Scandinavian women.[7]

Jenson's opportunity to speak came on Friday morning, when to a capacity crowd he recounted the history of Scandinavians in Utah for a full hour. He described the challenges and stigmas they experienced during early assimilation: "At that time the Saints in Utah knew little of the Scandinavians and were inclined to look upon these emigrants as a half civilized people. Today they were recognized as one of the great factors in Utah. Positions of honor and trust in ecclesiastical, civil and political life, had been given to representatives of the Scandinavians here."[8] The sentiments offered by others at the event generally echoed Jenson's remarks. With the Salt Lake Tabernacle draped in the cultural trappings of Denmark, Norway, and Sweden, the celebration suggested a comfortable marriage between Scandinavians and the Latter-day Saint faith.

But the jubilee also symbolized a pervasive tension caused by the pressures of assimilation in Utah's Scandinavian community at the turn of the century—a tension that highlighted the community's distinctiveness and also portended its changing future. For much of their first fifty years in Utah, Scandinavian converts congregated in their own communities, held separate local and general meetings in their native languages, and hosted their own cultural celebrations. Despite committed efforts to retain their cultural distinctiveness, Scandinavian immigrants linguistically assimilated at much higher rates in Utah than they did in other communities across the United States. Among second-generation Danish immigrants, for example, only 23 percent retained their mother tongue in comparison with a national rate of 31.2 percent. The rate was even more striking among immigrants from Norway and Sweden. About 17 percent of second-generation Norwegians and 24 percent of second-generation Swedes retained their mother tongue in Utah (compared to 52 percent and 43.7 percent, respectively, nationwide).[9]

While threads of Scandinavian exceptionalism colored the jubilee celebration, church leaders consistently emphasized the ultimate goal of integration and assimilation for Utah's Scandinavians. Apostle Brigham Young Jr. remarked in the Tabernacle at a Sunday afternoon session of the jubilee that "it was a peculiar fact . . . that in other localities of our country the nationality of immigrants can easily be determined many years after their arrival in the country; but when foreigners come to Zion and mingle with the people here in the valleys of the mountains the identity of their nationality is soon lost." Indeed, President George Q. Cannon, at the same session, "approved of the celebration being held" but "as a general rule . . . did not approve of encouraging national feelings."[10] Latter-day Saint leaders envisioned a blending of the races and a people united under the cause of the gospel. Their vision was largely fulfilled as the second generation of

Danish, Norwegian, and Swedish church members quickly assimilated into the general Latter-day Saint populace, cementing lasting Latter-day Saint ancestral ties to northern Europe while erasing most of the population's unique cultural markers.

With convert immigration to Utah slowing, the jubilee refocused the state's Scandinavian community back on their homeland. As converts gathered to Utah over the last half-century, the number of Latter-day Saint congregations in Denmark, Norway, and Sweden had been greatly reduced, and church leaders now hoped to buttress and reinvest in a population that was once a significant source of new members for the church. At the final day of the jubilee, a fund to build new meetinghouses and mission offices in Copenhagen and Stockholm was announced. The Scandinavian community intended to raise from their own personal funds $20,000 to reinvest in the Scandinavian Mission.[11] As converts remained in their homelands, they needed more visible and material support from church headquarters to subsist as a minority religious movement. Over the next decade, Jenson would become increasingly important to this renewed institutional effort in Scandinavia.

Scandinavian Assignments at Home and Abroad

Through his past Danish-language periodicals, Jenson had served as a prominent voice in Utah's Danish community. However, his time spent on English-language publications and his around-the-world tour had created a brief interlude when he was less visible in local Scandinavian communities. That changed in 1898 when the First Presidency asked Jenson to take over editing the Danish Norwegian newspaper *Bikuben*, which remained one of the church's few institutional avenues for communicating with Utah's Danish and Norwegian church members in their own language. *Bikuben* was the same paper he had unsuccessfully attempted to manage with business partners two decades before. Now with an extensive knowledge of subscription-based publishing and a wide-ranging network of connections in Utah's printing industry, Jenson faced with confidence the daunting task of reclaiming the indebted newspaper.

Jenson was tipped off by one of the paper's proprietors that "certain parties" were purposefully mismanaging the paper in order to "fleece the church." According to Jenson, the paper owed $7,000 to the *Deseret News* for printing expenses and another $900 for unpaid wages. The church had already invested $2,500 to keep the paper afloat, but *Bikuben*'s managers still petitioned the First Presidency for a weekly stipend.[12] Though committed to his new assignment, Jenson lamented the difficulty of his new role as editor of the struggling paper: "I would rather have gone on another foreign mission than to have accepted of this appointment; but I have accepted of it as a call from the highest authority in the Church and as a matter of duty, as I have accepted of so many appointments before."[13]

As he did with his other publications, Jenson set out on a tour around Utah, soliciting subscribers and donations from Scandinavian church members and collecting on unpaid subscriptions. "This paper has been from its very beginning a church organ for the Latter-day Saints," Jenson announced in the pages of the February 1898 issue of *Bikuben*. And in the future, he continued optimistically, "it will work for the spreading of the principles of the Gospel of Jesus Christ; it will work for a better social spirit among mankind; it will work for the interest of brotherly love and unselfishness."[14]

Through Jenson's dedication to improving the paper's fortunes, he had nearly paid off all the paper's debt and turned a profit by the end of 1899.[15] In the process, he angered the paper's former proprietors, Charles V. Anderson and Janne M. Sjodahl, whom he dismissed from the staff for their prior mismanagement.[16] Both men were prominent Swedes in Utah; Sjodahl still presided over Salt Lake City's Scandinavian meeting, and their departure created a rift between *Bikuben* and some Scandinavians in Salt Lake City.[17] Jenson, however, was less concerned about the bitter feelings of his Scandinavian brethren and more concerned with accomplishing the task assigned him by the First Presidency. His heavy-handed approach in steering *Bikuben* aright, as well as the demands of managing his other publications, left little time for deference or preferential treatment.

Occasionally he became overzealous and critical as he attempted to recruit and collect from subscribers. In a petty slander case in February 1900—a case that Jenson won easily—he was forced to defend his poor choice of words to fellow Dane Claus P. Madsen, said in a heated dispute over Madsen's lack of support for *Bikuben*. According to one newspaper report, Madsen told Jenson he was taking a "foreign" Scandinavian paper instead of *Bikuben* after having had a bad experience with the latter paper's previous editors. In response Jenson stridently exclaimed: "You steal from the brethren and feed the devil: you steal from everywhere."[18] Jenson did not deny the statement and explained that he was simply "quoting Brigham Young who used the same expression while speaking upon the subject of home industry and advising the Saints to keep their money at home."[19]

Interethnic battles aside, Jenson proved to be of immense value to the First Presidency in his literary work. He worked quickly and could be counted on, even when the assignment was undesirable. After reversing *Bikuben*'s course, Jenson asked the First Presidency for a release from his assignment so he could focus on his publications and the "stacks of historical notes on hand—the accumulation and results of my travels in all the stakes of Zion and missionary fields of the Church."[20] The release, however, never came, and his work for *Bikuben* continued even as he performed his duties at the Historian's Office.

Despite Jenson's already long list of responsibilities, the First Presidency had more in mind for their Assistant Church Historian. The Scandinavian jubilee indicated that church leaders understood the far-reaching potential of Utah's Scandinavian community when combined with the contributions of church members still residing in Scandinavia. And now that a new mission home was to be built in Copenhagen, thanks to the funds raised in the jubilee, the time also seemed right to further the church's investment in other missionary work, including improving the Danish church literature. Since December 1900, Jenson and Church Historian Anthon H. Lund had spent countless hours together preparing a new Danish edition of the Book of Mormon.[21]

The new edition revised extensively the dated edition done by Jenson while on his second mission to Denmark in 1881.[22] Only a day into their revisions, Lund recorded in his journal that they had found "many changes needed."[23] Though Jenson reverenced the first edition produced by Apostle Erastus Snow and Peter O. Hansen and had been "somewhat reluctant in making changes in 1880–81," he now felt confident to "take greater liberties" than he had before.[24] The result was a volume "printed with large type on good paper and furnished with an elaborate and plain index."[25] The approved changes would alter how Danes would interact with the scripture. The design catered to family study rather than just to proselytizing, enabling Danish church members to improve their literacy of the church's foundational text. Additionally, the new edition gave Danish Latter-day Saints and prospective converts renewed access to the Book of Mormon after a fire at the mission home a few years prior burned the mission's remaining stock of scripture.

On April 16, 1902, Lund instructed Jenson to prepare for a mission to Denmark, his third formal mission to his homeland, to publish their new translation.[26] This important assignment seemed welcomed. The simultaneous work of running *Bikuben*, publishing *Church Chronology* (1899) and *Latter-day Saint Biographical Encyclopedia* (1901), and supervising work at the Historian's Office had tested Jenson's usual tireless spirit. This special literary assignment would give him time to recover and reset.[27]

Jenson departed Salt Lake City on May 14 and arrived in Copenhagen on May 31, 1902.[28] He was joined on his mission by Christian D. Fjeldsted, who was already serving a mission in Denmark at the time. Fjeldsted was an early Danish convert and a member of the First Seven Presidents of the Seventy (and the one selected over Jenson to fill a vacancy in the Presidents of the Seventy in 1884).[29] Shortly after arriving in Copenhagen, Jenson rented out a room for his manuscript work and sought out an agreement with a publisher. The print shop of F. E. Bording, which had performed the presswork for the first edition of the Danish Book of Mormon and other Latter-day Saint works, agreed to publish the new edition of the Book of Mormon at an approximate cost of 3,000 kroner ($750) for three thousand copies.[30] By mid-November, Jenson finished reviewing proofs, and the volume was fully in the hands of the press. On Jenson's fifty-second birthday, December 11, Scandinavian Mission President Anthon L. Skanchy presented Jenson with a "beautifully bound copy" of the new Danish Book of Mormon. Jenson declared his work "undoubtedly the best printed and most carefully prepared book ever published in the Scandinavian mission."[31]

Apart from his work on the new Danish Book of Mormon, Jenson participated in the dedication of a new mission home, which the jubilee had raised funds for, in Copenhagen. Fjeldsted was tasked with securing land for the building. A plot in the heart of Copenhagen was purchased in September 1901, and the new building was constructed and ready to be dedicated by July 4, 1902. Five hundred Latter-day Saints from throughout the mission gathered for the dedication ceremony on July 4, and Jenson gave the concluding address. In his remarks, he referred to the new mission home as "a token of friendship on the part of the many Scandinavian Saints in the West who, some of them, many years ago, left the lands of their birth and were now located among God's people in the Rocky Mountains of America."[32] The financial offerings from the Scandinavian community in Utah evidenced the lack of centralization in church building projects, since the funds were appropriated not from the budget of church headquarters but from localized donations. The fund-raising also marked a sizable reinvestment in church infrastructure in international locations. Another new meetinghouse was dedicated in Christiania (now Oslo), Norway, only a year later, and planning was underway for one in Stockholm, Sweden.[33]

Unexpected Challenges

The excitement associated with a new meetinghouse and a new translation of the Book of Mormon was overshadowed by what would be one of the most painful experiences of Jenson's life. Since late 1900, Jenson's son Andrew Alexander Jenson had been serving as a missionary in the Scandinavian Mission. Jenson anticipated a happy reunion with his son while he was in Denmark. However, their meeting in late June 1902 brought the unwelcome news that his son, serving in Norway's Bergen Conference, had committed adultery with local member Thora Olsen, and she was now pregnant. The confession from Andrew Alexander caused Jenson a "shock that will never be forgotten as long as life lasts."[34]

As a married man, Andrew Alexander's indiscretion was grounds for excommunication, and he was called before a church disciplinary council at mission headquarters. Several church leaders, as well as Jenson, attended the meeting. According to Jenson, "Remarks were made with much sympathy and feeling and all testified that the young Elder who had transgressed had been one of the most zealous and faithful Elders in the mission." Many "expressed a great desire to forgive the erring man." When Lyman eventually invited Jenson to speak, the usually stolid Dane "broke down." Jenson, however, knew that there was "only one thing to do, and that was to excommunicate the transgressor." Regarding this excruciating ordeal, he remarked in his journal: "O what a terrible ordeal this was. To raise your hand to sever anybody from the Church is a hard task in all cases . . . but for a man to raise his hand for this purpose against his own flesh and blood is a trial that can best be imagined by those who have passed through a similar experience." Jenson then reflected that, fifteen years earlier, he had had to bury Andrew Alexander's mother. "Would to God," Jenson remarked, "that I had done the same in his case rather than to live to see him severed from the Church."[35] Andrew Alexander, however, still felt supported by his disappointed father for a time. Though his relationship with Jenson had been significantly strained since the death of Mary with the presence of both Emma and Bertha in the household, Andrew Alexander remarked before his departure home that he was "pleased to be in [Jenson's] company." During a few days of sightseeing he had never been "treated . . . better" by his father.[36]

Andrew Alexander's adulterous relationship and his excommunication created significant complications in his domestic life, and he would struggle to regain respectability and earn a livelihood for the rest of his life. Thora Olsen eventually immigrated to the United States, and Andrew Alexander illegally married her in Chicago on their way to the Salt Lake Valley. When Andrew Alexander returned home to his first wife, Mary Elizabeth Crane, he apparently kept his new illicit marriage secret from her, though she was aware of his excommunication for adultery.[37] While Andrew Jenson was still on his mission, Thora moved into his Eleventh Ward property in Salt Lake City to have the baby (who was born on September 14, 1902).[38] Jenson may not have known the details of his son's dual marriages initially; contact between son and father was sparse in the years after Andrew Alexander's return.[39] His first marriage continued for three more years, and Mary bore two more children, even as he maintained his illegal second marriage to Thora.[40] Andrew Alexander and Mary legally divorced by 1905.[41] Jenson periodically supported Andrew, Thora, and their children financially over the next two decades.[42]

Despite family adversity early in his mission, Jenson pressed forward and received other assignments outside of his literary work. Before his return to America, the First Presidency instructed Jenson to travel throughout the Scandinavian and neighboring missions to gather historical information and documents. President Skanchy, however, devised a different mission for Jenson and sent a letter to church headquarters asking for approval. Aware of Jenson's reputation as a fund-raiser among the Scandinavian Saints, Skanchy hoped Jenson could return home directly to commence raising money in Utah's Scandinavian communities for the proposed meetinghouse in Stockholm.[43] Jenson was enthusiastic about the plan and while awaiting the First Presidency's response, he traveled to Liverpool to correct inconsistencies in the mission's annual report and to meet his wife Bertha, who was arriving from America to accompany him around Europe and on his return trip home.[44] On December 23, Jenson received a telegraph from Skanchy informing him that he was to continue his original mission and visit Norway before returning home, according to the First Presidency's wishes.[45]

To fulfill his earlier commission, Jenson traveled with Bertha, after some sightseeing in Liverpool and London, to the headquarters of the Netherlands Mission at Rotterdam. After a few days of historical work, the two continued their journey and headed to the headquarters of the German Mission in Berlin to cull the records there. By the end of January 1903, Jenson and Bertha had returned to Copenhagen for more sightseeing. They then headed northwest to Jutland. Along the way they stopped at a Seventh-day Adventist estate where Jenson was invited to give a lecture on Latter-day Saint history. The Adventists, another homegrown American religion, kindly took Jenson and Bertha on a carriage ride through the country, allowing Jenson to visit his birthplace. Their trip then continued across the sea, through Sweden, and northward to Christiania, Norway, where Jenson spent an entire month gathering historical data from mission records. During his time in Norway, he made a quick trip to Stockholm to survey the proposed site for the new meetinghouse. Jenson and Bertha then returned to Liverpool, where Jenson prepared a shipment of historical records to send back to the Historian's Office and joined an immigrating company of seventy-six Latter-day Saints, whom he was assigned to lead to Salt Lake Valley. They then set sail for the United States, reaching its eastern shore on March 29.[46]

Continuing Scandinavian Support at Home

On April 6, 1903, three days later after arriving in the Salt Lake Valley, the First Presidency invited Jenson to report on his mission at the closing session of general conference. Jenson took the stand in the Salt Lake Tabernacle and emphatically declared God's interest in all people, including the Scandinavian Saints: "We rejoice in the fact that the Lord is pouring out His Spirit upon His people in those lands, and I am a living witness and want to bear testimony to the fact that I know God is no respector of persons. It does not make any difference where we are born, nor the language we speak. The Lord can be found upon the islands of the sea, upon the continent of Europe, and the continents of Africa and Asia . . . as well as upon this land of America."[47] Jenson's testimony was a reminder to the Latter-day Saints gathered in Utah that the Saints scattered in the peripheries of Europe were equally worthy of God's blessings and required the support of those comfortably at home in the center stakes of Zion.

Unbeknownst to Jenson at the time, his remarks foreshadowed the focus of his upcoming tour around Utah's Scandinavian communities, which was to generate financial support for the church on Scandinavian soil. This short fund-raising mission, as originally imagined by Mission President Anthon L. Skanchy, took another year before it began. Jenson's relentless approach in soliciting donations had irritated some local church members before and at times made him something of a last resort for church leaders. But his trustworthiness and work ethic also made him a valuable resource for sorting out and accomplishing church business. And with donations for the Stockholm meetinghouse fund well below building expenses, the First Presidency again employed Jenson as their fund-raising agent. The First Presidency called the assignment to raise funds a "mission," and Jenson responded immediately to the call.[48]

Three days later, on January 30, 1904, Jenson set out for the Scandinavian settlements in Sevier, Sanpete, and Utah Counties with Swedish church member (and bishop) Carl A. Ek. Prior notice was given to the stake presidents and bishops in the area that the two were coming, and meetings were scheduled. In Jenson's first two weeks of fund-raising, he gathered $300, with more money pledged.[49] A day after arriving home, the pair repeated the process in Latter-day Saint Scandinavian communities in northern Utah and southern Idaho with similar success. Jenson was now very accustomed to representing the church in diverse financial and ecclesiastical settings. Shortly after arriving home from his fund-raising mission, his expertise was called upon again and tested as the church found itself embroiled in a national public-relations crisis over plural marriage.

The Reed Smoot Hearings

Upon returning home from his tour of the Scandinavian settlements in Utah on February 25, 1904, Jenson learned from church leaders that he had been summoned, along with President Joseph F. Smith, Apostles Francis M. Lyman and Hyrum M. Smith, and others, to testify at the congressional hearings currently underway in Washington, DC, on whether Apostle Reed Smoot should remain in the US Senate.[50] In 1903, Smoot, a Republican, was elected to the Senate by the Utah legislature. The news of his victory at the polls provoked outrage from many corners, especially the nation's Protestants, who maintained that Smoot's prominence in the church hierarchy was an obvious conflict of interest, rendering him incapable of fairly serving the interests of the American people. The protests resulted in a hearing before the Senate Committee on Privileges and Elections.[51] Jenson, a Republican himself, recorded in his journal shortly before leaving for the nation's capital: "None of us have any idea as to the nature of the questions that will be propounded to us, only we surmise that the Church will be on trial rather than Bro. Smoot." Jenson anticipated a "close examination as to the doctrines of Christ or the Church" and suspected he had been subpoenaed with prominent church leaders because of his closeness to Latter-day Saint records, including "perhaps those in which [plural] marriages are supposed to be recorded."[52]

The travelers arrived in Washington, DC, on March 1, and President Smith and Apostles Lyman and Smith took lodging at the Raleigh Hotel on Pennsylvania Avenue, while Jenson and the remainder of the party found rooms a few blocks away. The Raleigh Hotel became the improvised headquarters for the church delegation. For the next few days, the attorneys briefed Jenson and the others on their upcoming testimony.[53] Jenson, however, intended to "follow [his] own council" unless he was "advised by Pres. Smith."[54]

The proceedings, which took place from Wednesday, March 2, until March 7, 1904, were crowded into a relatively small room at the Capitol building, but reporters and onlookers flocked to Capitol Hill to catch a glimpse of the scene. Jenson's subpoena had placed him at the center of a nationwide political spectacle. His biographical sketch and photographs, along with those of the other church leaders, were splashed across newspapers around the country. Through these hearings, the American people were hoping to get a rare inside look at the church and its people.

From the opening of the hearings, Jenson observed the committee's interrogation of President Smith. "He was subjected to a most trying ordeal," Jenson reported, "and seemed somewhat confused in giving some of his answers."[55] The committee asked President Smith questions to uncover the truth about his plural-marriage practices, particularly those that occurred after the 1890 Manifesto, which prohibited future plural marriages in the church. Jenson watched as Smith recounted his polygamous arrangement with five wives and "said that 11 children had been born to him by these wives since the manifesto," proof that unlawful cohabitation (or residing with more than one spouse) had occurred.[56] Smith was resolute, almost defiant, in defense of his current family structure and in his unwillingness to abandon spouses or children from pre-Manifesto marriages, which he felt were lawful. Yet, he also asserted that church leaders had not sanctioned or performed a plural marriage after the Manifesto. It was this point of post-Manifesto polygamous marriages that Smith and subsequent Latter-day Saint witnesses attempted to carefully navigate in their testimonies. None wished to perjure themselves, since indeed, such marriages had taken place and many leaders continued to cohabitate with their wives. But Smith expertly modeled the Latter-day Saint delegation's position: even if post-Manifesto polygamous marriages had occurred, the church as an institution neither solemnized nor sanctioned these marriages.[57]

While Smith had been calm and confident during his testimony, Francis M. Lyman was decidedly less so. And Jenson, anxious to testify, made a poor quiet observer. On Tuesday, March 8, he watched apprehensively as Lyman stumbled during his testimony. The committee pinned Lyman in a corner on questions of his persistent cohabitation with his two plural wives. Lyman confessed he violated the law in continuing to cohabitate with both of his wives. Though the 1887 Edmunds-Tucker Act prohibited unlawful cohabitation, most General Authorities continued to live with their plural wives. Subsequent statements by church leaders made clear that obedience to current church law included no unlawful cohabitation, and church leaders also signed an amnesty pledge that they would obey current anti-bigamy laws if past violations were pardoned, which US president Benjamin Harrison did in 1893.[58]

Since then, however, little had changed in the living arrangements of many Latter-day Saint polygamists, and confusion abounded as to current church policy on cohabitating with polygamist spouses (Jenson continued to live with both of his wives without any discernible conflict over doing so). Lyman's testimony brought this confusion to bear on the proceedings. His admission that he knowingly lived in defiance of the law and current church revelation was headline worthy.

Jenson and the other church leaders, who too were cohabitating polygamists, showed visible signs of frustration during Lyman's testimony.[59] None wanted to jeopardize their family arrangements back home or trivialize the importance of divine revelation. Jenson fancied himself an expert communicator and lamented that he was not the one offering a defense of plural marriage. "He seemed to get confused," Jenson wrote in his journal, speaking of Lyman, "and his answers, at least some of them, humiliated me very much, especially his answers or endeavors to explain revelation."[60] The headlines back home agreed. The *Salt Lake Herald* on March 9 printed "Apostle Lyman Injures Case of Senator Smoot," with the subheading "His Testimony Regarded as More Damaging Than That of Church President."[61] In the evening, Jenson took a walk around "the streets of Washington annoyed in [his] mind over the nature of the testimony given by Bro. Lyman."[62] He spent a restless night in his hotel rehearsing the potential fallout from the day's events.

The next day, Wednesday, March 9, President Smith was again called to the stand for a brief interrogation and then officially discharged by the congressional committee. Jenson was then sworn in. The committee's line of questioning centered on his authorship of the *Church Chronology* and *Latter-day Saint Biographical Encyclopedia*, which members of the committee had combed as an introduction to Smoot and the Latter-day Saints in general.[63] Jenson denied that the *Church Chronology* was an official work of the church and claimed it as his "own work." Though the church had legal claim to the printed volumes and its profits (which Jenson did not disclose in his testimony), he asserted he remained solely responsible for the book's contents, a distinction he underscored by pointing out a few errors in the book. He also testified that, with Church Historian Lund frequently away on church business, he was the de facto leader of the Historian's Office.[64] He only occupied the stand for a few minutes before being dismissed.

On March 10, Jenson was again called to the stand and spent the better part of the morning being cross-examined by the committee. He explained in further detail how he had compiled the biography on Smoot for the *Latter-day Saint Biographical Encyclopedia*. Then he entered into a long discussion on the relationship between local ecclesiastical leaders and General Authorities. "As to moral conduct," Jenson related to the committee, "there is no officer of the church, no matter how high, the president not excepted, who is not amenable to the bishops and the teachers. As an officer he is responsible to them."[65] His testimony pushed back on the prevailing narrative that the church hierarchy had an authoritative grip on its membership. Instead, Jenson described a decentralized church that allowed its members the freedom to act how they wished in local affairs, including in politics. He also described the predominance of Latter-day Saints in counties throughout Utah and promised to furnish the committee with a list of local bishops and stake presidents who could be subpoenaed as witnesses.[66]

There was nothing new or confidential about the information Jenson revealed in his testimony, but he did speak candidly about certain matters, and many outsiders curious about the distant religion in the West felt Jenson's testimony pulled back the curtain on the Utah-based church. Headlines across the country announced that the inner "machinery" of the Latter-day Saint church had been unmasked by its own Assistant Church Historian. Others alluded to "Mormon secrets" told in great detail by one who knew.[67] Jenson, indeed, had announced that pre-Manifesto polygamists were essentially beyond the law, since the Latter-day Saint majority in Utah was unlikely to seek indictments for cohabitating polygamists. Jenson's testimony likewise cast President Smith as being essentially immune to any legal prosecution concerning his polygamous family arrangement, given Utah's predominantly Latter-day Saint population. While Jenson certainly never intended to characterize Utah as a lawless frontier, many newspapers used Jenson's conclusions to paint Utah as a rogue and dangerously sovereign state.

Jenson's involvement in the Reed Smoot hearings reaffirmed the important role the Historian's Office played in the making and recording of church history. His proximity to potentially illuminating and damaging records made Jenson a star witness to current and past church affairs. And though he lamented that his position lacked formal ecclesiastical authority, he still retained a measure of informal power as the steward of the church's historical records and therefore its institutional memory. His unique role gave him the ability to speak to the systematic operations of a church attracting nationwide attention at a level most others could not. Jenson reveled in the elevated stature two weeks in Washington had given him. He gave an exclusive interview to the *New York World* on Latter-day Saint missionary work, which resulted in a full-page feature on the hearings. On the evening of his discharge, he wrote that the *Washington (DC) Times* "had pictures of Pres. Joseph F. Smith and myself, side by side, together with a short article under the caption 'Two prominent members in the Smoot Investigation.'"[68] For a couple of weeks in March 1904, Jenson was not simply a record keeper for his fellow church members, but a prominent Latter-day Saint before the American public.

Family Life in the Jenson Household

If Jenson's polygamous household (and Latter-day Saint plural marriages more broadly) attracted the curiosity of national journalists and inquiring legislators, his actual daily lifestyle matched his congressional testimony—his marriage arrangement appeared ordinary within the state of Utah. Without fear of reprisal, Jenson publicly celebrated his wedding anniversaries with both Bertha and Emma, and frequent social gatherings at the family home just blocks from church headquarters allowed many in the Salt Lake City community to witness the plural family firsthand. He was also seen on evenings traveling to and from the local theater with either Bertha or Emma. He rarely traveled large distances with both of his wives, perhaps to prevent attracting attention but also out of practicality. Someone needed to remain home to tend to the children and household. Though Jenson's plural family carried few public consequences within the safety of the Salt Lake Valley, there were private consequences made worse by his frequent absences on church business.

Emma and Bertha both endured Jenson's 1895–97 world tour well. They split the household duties, except for when Emma met Jenson in Europe. They reared the children together. The missed holidays and birthdays perhaps filled them with the most longing for a complete household again. But Jenson's frequent absences after his world tour eventually exposed some of the challenges ahead for the sisters, who generally took pride in keeping an organized and disciplined household. Parley, Eleonore, and Minerva, all children from Jenson's late first wife Mary, increasingly expressed their independence as they moved into their teenage years and took less kindly to domestic chores or instructions from their stepmothers. They also interacted poorly with Emma's younger children, Eva and Harold. The chasm only widened with time until Jenson saw fit to alleviate the situation by moving Parley, Eleonore, and Minerva to his Eleventh Ward property to live rent-free with Andrew and Thora.[69] Even Jenson strategically avoided his home office before this transition so as to not disrupt his work with regular family squabbles.

Emma Howell Jenson and Andrew Jenson, circa 1909. Courtesy Church History Library.

The contention was not just confined to the children. In September 1900, the relationship between Emma and Bertha reached a boiling point and Bertha moved out of the family home for a time, first to Manti with her mother and then to her own separate apartment.[70] Jenson offered few written comments on his domestic situation, but he did encourage both Emma and Bertha to keep home journals, which they did sporadically and concisely within Jenson's own journals. Both women charted different paths within the household and not all appeared equal, which perhaps led to some resentment between the sisters. Emma managed the housekeeping and finances while Bertha cooked. Emma routinely made improvements to the home and scheduled repairs if Jenson was away.[71] United as tough disciplinarians who expected much of their stepchildren, the sisters nonetheless sometimes diverged over resources and conditions in the household. Emma frequently fretted about money and also worried over Jenson's affection for her.[72] Bertha found more time and freedom to assist Jenson with his historical work and also cultivated a vocation outside the home as a birth nurse. When Bertha and Jenson traveled together, Emma struggled to cook, clean, care for the children and her aging mother, as well as host frequent guests and boarders.[73] Scandinavian Latter-day Saints visiting Salt Lake City regularly stopped at the Jenson home for meals and lodging. Emma found comfort in these Scandinavian connections and through families like the Widtsoes and Lunds, who checked in on the household regularly. Still, she battled reoccurring bouts of debilitating pain and also spells of anxiety and exhaustion.[74] Her mental and physical health slowly declined as she advanced in years, which confined her even more to home.

Bertha, however, also navigated her own painful struggles. She watched with envy as Emma bore and raised children with Jenson. Despite blessings and prayers for a resolution to her battle with infertility, Bertha remained childless. While she, by virtue of her presence in the Jenson household, still participated in child-rearing duties, the lack of her own progeny shifted some of her focus from household to career and church duties. She became one of Jenson's primary assistants in his historical work, helping to compile, copy, or index ecclesiastical histories and other record-keeping projects. The work allowed her to join with Jenson in some of his travels, easing the loneliness she felt when he left on business. Eventually, in October 1906, Jenson and Bertha (who had returned to living in the Jenson home) made the decision to adopt a ten-month-old baby boy, Leo, from Logan, Utah, making Jenson a father again at age fifty-five and giving Bertha (age forty) a child of her own for the first time.[75] The youngest Jenson children, Harold and Eva, were ages eleven and sixteen, respectively, in 1906, so the adoption of Leo placed a child in the Jenson household for years to come, affording Bertha one of the greatest joys of her life.

Emma and Bertha, however, did not simply confine themselves to domestic duties while Jenson traveled. If the difficulties of managing a polygamous household caused fatigue and frequent challenges, both sisters contributed meaningfully in political and civic endeavors. Utah boasted a long history of female activism inspired in part by the cooperative work Latter-day Saint women performed within polygamous households and from their gathering outside the home in their own Relief Society organizations. Emma's Utah peers regarded her as a committed supporter of the women's suffrage movement. As a member of the Seventeenth Ward Relief Society, she also sought out and served the poor. Additionally, she served as treasurer and secretary of the Utah Women's Press Club, organized in 1891 to foster women's literary ventures, journalism, and discussions on current events.[76] The club's founders included the wives of General Authorities and prominent and influential women in the Utah community like Emmeline B. Wells, Lula Greene Richards, Susa Young Gates, and Ruth May Fox. The club supported the *Woman's Exponent*, a periodical published by and for Latter-day Saint women, to which Emma contributed articles.[77] In addition to honing her literary talents, the press club afforded Emma sociality with other women in her community. Those bonds carried over to more casual and frequent social gatherings within the Jenson home. Emma and Bertha came to Salt Lake City as immigrants of little means, but they slowly built a network of friends and associates that placed them at the center of elite society in Salt Lake City.

A Fourth Mission to Denmark

A few months after Jenson returned home from Washington, DC, another mission call to Denmark was on the horizon. By mid-June 1904, Jenson and President Anthon H. Lund had completed their revised translation of *Joseph Smiths levnetsløb* (History of Joseph Smith), which they had been working on since at least October 1903.[78] Jenson's career had come full circle as he worked again on the historical project that had helped launch his career as a Latter-day Saint historian in 1878. This time he envisioned a more precise translation that would assist missionaries in Scandinavia in combatting current sentiments against Latter-day Saints. Jenson, along with Lund and fellow Assistant Church Historians B. H. Roberts and Orson F. Whitney, also sat on an appointed committee to read through and suggest revisions to Roberts's *History of the Church*, which was published across seven volumes and soon became the popular version of Smith's history.[79] Jenson's modest Danish translation, which ended with the martyrdom of Joseph and Hyrum Smith in 1844, would be produced alongside Roberts's work, but decidedly in its shadow.

Perhaps inspired by (or envious of) Roberts's recent undertaking, Jenson intended to quietly cement his legacy by bringing revised translations of the church's sacred texts to Scandinavian Latter-day Saints and prospective converts. However, most of Jenson's scriptural translations were greeted with little fanfare or acclaim. He would later work on new Danish translations of the Latter-day Saint hymnbook, published in 1906, and the Pearl of Great Price, published in 1909 while he served as mission president in Denmark.[80] In his first decade as Assistant Church Historian, Jenson translated most of the church's major scriptural works into Danish.

With the translation work of *Joseph Smiths levnetsløb* completed, Jenson anticipated a mission call to oversee its publication in Denmark. The call came, and he was set apart for his mission on August 26 and set out for Denmark the next day. Before departing Salt Lake City, Jenson had brashly petitioned church leaders to allow him to temporarily preside over the Scandinavian Mission, anticipating the end of President Skanchy's three-year tenure. President Lund politely refused his offer.[81] On his way east, Jenson went with his wife Emma to St. Louis to view the Louisiana Purchase Exposition (also known as the St. Louis World's Fair) and examine the Utah exhibits.[82] He then traveled alone to

Copenhagen, where he arrived by September 21; by October 4, he had arranged with the staff at F. E. Bording's to print four thousand copies of the *Levnetsløb*.[83] Jenson also arrived in time to attend the dedication of the Stockholm mission home, for which he had been instrumental in raising funds.[84] By the end of December 1904, only three months after he left on his special mission, the presswork was completed.[85]

After publishing the *Levnetsløb*, Jenson put aside his work at the mission office in Copenhagen for an extensive mission tour. His travels reaffirmed his intention to use the new Danish edition of Joseph Smith's history to combat false information circulating about the Latter-day Saints. In early December, Jenson attempted to get an audience with the king of Denmark to ascertain his feeling toward the Latter-day Saints. Despite the positive endorsement of his faith by some Danish officials, Jenson learned "the king was no friend of the Mormons," and he was denied a meeting.[86] As Jenson investigated further, he learned that the Danish government, troubled by press reports on the Reed Smoot hearings, was considering expelling US Latter-day Saint missionaries from the country. The American diplomat to Denmark defended the Utah-based church, asserting to government officials that Latter-day Saints from the United States were in fact "American citizens and worthy of protection." But the minister of justice, the king, and other government officials still favored expulsion. Jenson reassured the US diplomat that "no plural marriages had been solemnized since 1890 with the sanction of the Church."[87] While Jenson received the diplomat's goodwill, he understood that lecturers opposed to the church and unfavorable press reports were generating significant animosity toward missionaries and local Latter-day Saints. He hoped his *Levnetsløb* would make significant inroads in combatting the false reports in his beloved Denmark.

Jenson's tour around Denmark put him in the path of agitated Lutheran ministers set on disrupting Latter-day Saint missionary work. During Jenson's visit, for example, a local Lutheran priest challenged missionaries serving near Nibe, a town on the northern Jutland peninsula, to a formal debate. The missionaries invited Jenson to anchor the side of the Latter-day Saints. Terms and arrangements for the debate were agreed upon and signed by both parties. The discussion pitted Jenson against Lutheran pastor H. O. Frimodt-Møller, who had gained local notoriety for publishing and preaching against the Latter-day Saints. On January 13, 1905, Jenson and a group of missionaries entered a crowded hall, filled with twelve hundred onlookers, at a local hotel. "The whole town of Nibe," wrote Jenson, seemed to be "in a state of excitement over the advertised discussion." Frimodt-Møller spoke for fifty minutes, ten minutes short of his allotted time. Then for a full hour Jenson refuted "point after point what the pastor had said." Jenson declared his defense successful and headed south for the city of Aarhus the next morning.[88]

Frimodt-Møller was apparently incensed that he had been forced to debate the knowledgeable Jenson instead of an inexperienced missionary. Resolved to no longer "dance to 'Mormon' music," Frimodt-Møller returned to his parish at Aarhus, Jenson's next destination, intent on fully exposing the claims of Jenson and the Latter-day Saint missionaries on his own terms.[89] He attended two Latter-day Saint meetings the next Sunday, provoking a response from Jenson: "I alluded once to the vilifier who . . . had stated that the fruits of 'Mormonism' were murder, adultery and perjury, and prophesied in the name of Jesus Christ that if that man persist[ed] in lying about the people of God the Lord would slay him." Jenson's extemporaneous prophecy apparently angered Frimodt-Møller, who took the stand after Jenson to announce his planned lecture against the Latter-day Saints for the next week.[90]

Feeling he had already gained a victory over the Lutheran priest, Jenson had intended to ignore the lecture, but, at the insistence of the missionaries in Aarhus, he agreed to attend. Frimodt-Møller's lecture, which turned into an event held over the course of two evenings (January 19 and 20), attracted a crowd of two thousand each evening. On the first evening, the Lutheran priest railed against Jenson for an hour. Jenson responded to the accusations, offering a defense of "the Prophet of God and the religion of the Savior with courage and spirit in the face of such an immense opposition." Jenson felt he was encircled by adversaries and that "abuse and vilifications and warnings" abounded.

The next evening, however, a different atmosphere prevailed as Jenson witnessed Latter-day Saints and missionaries crowd the hall. By this debate, both Jenson and the Lutheran clergy present were quite familiar with the other's arguments. Jenson recalled: "Under the influence of the spirit of God I spoke as I seldom have spoken before in defence of truth and the work of God. . . . I soon learned that I had many friends in the congregation." After Jenson's opening statements, a series of Lutheran clergymen, Frimodt-Møller included, responded, and the debate now pitted the solitary Jenson against the city's prominent Lutheran authorities. "It was almost the opportunity of my life," Jenson reflected in his journal.[91] In his passionate defense of the church, Jenson had made himself something of a local celebrity in Aarhus. After the debate, an impromptu party broke out at the local Latter-day-Saint meetinghouse, celebrating the defeat of Frimodt-Møller, who had been a menace to the church at Aarhus for months.[92] The exuberant gathering of missionaries and Latter-day Saints pushed late into the evening on Jenson's final night in Denmark.

Jenson departed the next day, and, not wishing to waste a return trip through Europe, he stopped over in Germany and Switzerland to peruse and gather historical records. He did the same in England, New York, Milwaukee, and Kansas City.[93] While in Switzerland, he visited Hugh J. Cannon, the Swiss German Mission president, for a week in Zurich. Cannon and Jenson met daily, discussing the affairs of the mission and taking long walks around the scenic parts of the city. Cannon admired Jenson's zeal but admitted that when it was time for Jenson to head to England, "it was a relief to see him go." Cannon's observation of Jenson was a characterization that followed Jenson many places he traveled. "He is a jewel in his line," Cannon wrote, "that of gathering data for Church history, but he is very tiresome. . . . I admire his perseverance, but I don't think I should ever choose him as a bosom companion. If I did, he would certainly be an 'acquired taste.'"[94] Though Jenson's intensity and drive both inspired and tired those around him, those qualities were central to his successful defense and work on behalf of the church.

As for Jenson, though he enjoyed meeting people and appreciated his loyal friends, his sense of importance was garnered not through popularity but through obvious displays of respect and formal markers of authority and status. He was a wandering historian who in almost all cases privileged his historical and literary works above public admiration. Yet, after a series of important missions, Jenson returned to daily life at the Historian's Office and resumed a position that sometimes failed to bring the sense of exhilaration and obvious standing he had recently experienced in Europe.

Jenson would have to wait a few more years for another opportunity to elevate his status through church service. For the time being, he resumed his travels throughout the stakes of Zion to collect and preserve Latter-day Saint history. At the same time, his homeland continued to be set aflame by anti-LDS sentiments and nationalist fervor. Given Jenson's extensive missionary and literary experience, he seemed poised to take charge of missionary work in Scandinavia during this era of renewed animosity and change. Church leaders eventually issued Jenson a formal assignment in 1908 to preside over the Danish-Norwegian Mission. The calling transformed him into a minister and ecclesiastical leader tasked with a far different work than what he had performed from the Historian's Office.

7 Scandinavian Mission President

Over the first decade of the twentieth century, Jenson spent a third of his time away from home and the Historian's Office in Utah on special missions to his Danish homeland. Jenson's credentials in missionary work were well earned, but, to his disappointment, from spring 1905 until the fall of 1908, he performed his labors at church headquarters without a trip of any significant duration. Challenges at the Historian's Office were also testing his fortitude. For example, Jenson was irritated by a romantic courtship that had developed between Joseph Fielding Smith, the widowed Assistant Church Historian, and unmarried staff member Ethel Reynolds. Feeling that the budding relationship was becoming a distraction, he went to Church Historian Anthon H. Lund's home to vent his frustrations.[1] Along with his concerns over personnel issues, Jenson also suspected that someone was secretly taking documents from the office, only to return them days later.[2] Circumstances at home were also strained. In October, Jenson's twenty-three-year-old daughter, Eleonore, was preparing for a trip abroad to study music in Germany. Jenson opposed the trip but could not stop it.[3] He was afraid that if his daughter left the spiritual protection of Zion and entered the "world," she would lose her commitment to the church. Weighed down by these challenges, Jenson felt his professional work had become "onerous" and he needed a change.[4]

His friend and supervisor Lund finally reassured him that a change of scenery might be coming. While at the Historian's Office one day in October 1908, Lund tipped Jenson off about a forthcoming mission call. Their conversation avoided specifics about the timing of the call or the duties and destination involved, but the news offered Jenson hope.[5] It also, however, stirred his usual insecurities. What of the challenges still afoot at the Historian's Office? And certainly his family still required his assistance at home. On the night before Eleonore's departure, he laid awake most of the night "thinking of the future."[6]

Jenson had to wait two more restless months before official word of his call finally came. On December 9, two days before his fifty-eighth birthday, he received a letter from the First Presidency, then composed of Joseph F. Smith, John R. Winder, and Anthon H. Lund. "You are hereby appointed to succeed [President Sören Rasmussen] in the watchcare and presidency" of the Scandinavian Mission (now officially the Danish-Norwegian Mission), the letter read.[7] In this new undertaking, the First Presidency delegated to Jenson the "full power to regulate everything connected with the Mission."[8] Though Jenson would be the presiding ecclesiastical leader in his homeland, the mission fell under the jurisdiction of the president of the European Mission, who simultaneously served as president of the British Mission and coordinated missionary work for all missions in Europe.[9] Jenson reported regularly to his superiors, Mission Presidents Charles W. Penrose (who presided until 1910) and Rudger Clawson (who presided 1910–13), as well as the First Presidency and Quorum of the Twelve in Salt Lake City.

On January 12, 1909, President Joseph F. Smith set Jenson apart for his mission.[10] Jenson spent the next week attending farewell gatherings, visiting family, and wrapping up his work at the Historian's Office. On the evening of January 18, approximately fifty of Jenson's closest friends and family gathered at the train depot in Salt Lake City to bid him farewell. Jenson turned over his Historian's Office keys to Lund just prior to boarding the train. He said good-bye to Bertha and his children Eva, Harold, and Leo one more time before departing for Ogden. Emma accompanied him to Ogden.[11] From Ogden, Jenson boarded a Union Pacific train, bound for the East Coast, alone.[12]

Initial Assessment of Missionary Work in Scandinavia

The new mission call did little to dampen Jenson's exuberance for Latter-day Saint history. As his train moved across the flattened plains toward the populous East, he made stops to gather information on the early church. He visited Independence, Missouri—which Joseph Smith had designated as Zion and where many of the early Saints had gathered before being violently expelled.[13] While traveling toward New York, his rail route passed through Ohio, which prompted a stop at the Kirtland Temple, another jewel of the early church.[14] He also stopped at another early Latter-day Saint settlement in Canandaigua Township, New York. While there, he arose early on a chilly morning in late January, anxious to inquire at the county clerk's office about historical documents on the Latter-day Saints. Jenson soon found, however, that old prejudices prevailed. The clerk asserted that Joseph Smith was a fraud and denied Jenson access to the records.[15]

Jenson's pursuit of church history en route to Scandinavia soon left him weak and exhausted. He left Canandaigua and traveled a short distance out of town to the Hill Cumorah, the site where Joseph Smith had received the Book of Mormon golden plates from an angel in 1827. He climbed the hill in "a blinding snow storm." Jenson enjoyed standing where pivotal events of the Restoration had occurred but, plagued by a persistent cough and an empty stomach (he had not eaten a solid meal in nearly two days), his energy was clearly depleted.[16]

By the time Jenson reached the headquarters of the Eastern States Mission in New York City, he was in visibly poor health, which alarmed the office staff and prompted them to place the usually vigorous traveler on bed rest.[17] He appreciated the staff's generosity but refused to delay his journey across the Atlantic because of illness. Around noon on January 30, 1909, Jenson boarded the *Baltic*, bound for Liverpool, England, and bid a grateful farewell to his new friends in Manhattan.[18] By the time the ship reached Liverpool on February 8, Jenson had recovered. He arrived in Copenhagen by train on February 11, 1909, nearly a full month after he was set apart for his mission by President Smith.[19] The "tedious and unpleasant" nature of the trip had exacted a toll on Jenson. Nonetheless, with "the full-hearted reception" he received from the Saints, he felt "at home at once" for the first time in a month.[20]

The high-profile call to preside over the Danish-Norwegian Mission placed Jenson at the forefront of Latter-day Saint proselytizing in Europe. For over half a century, the church's missionary work abroad had predominantly targeted the Western Christian world, with substantial success.[21] Missionaries had made inroads in other countries, to be sure, but recent proselytizing efforts, such as those in Japan, had revealed the challenges of sharing the gospel with a foreign people whose culture and language differed from those of US and European Saints.[22] Missionaries called to serve in new mission fields often lacked the language skills or a fundamental grasp of the culture to successfully grow the church in these areas. And despite new efforts to establish missionary training courses in colleges in Utah, the training and education of prospective missionaries was still uneven.[23]

Though some of these problems surfaced in Scandinavia, the mission had been the vanguard of Latter-day Saint missionary work overseas, starting in 1850. It thus benefited from a long history of Latter-day Saint presence. Most of the nearly 170 missionaries called to proselyte under Jenson's supervision were from Utah. Over fifty years of emigration by Scandinavian converts to that state had resulted in a large pool of prospective missionaries with Scandinavian heritage.[24] Heeding their mission calls, second- and third-generation Scandinavian Latter-day Saints were returning to their ancestral homelands to seek converts and reconstruct kinship networks that had been partially severed when their parents or grandparents emigrated. At their core, these missionaries identified primarily as Latter-day Saints, but their shared ethnic heritage with the Scandinavian people could in theory boost proselytizing efforts in Denmark and Norway.

Results for returning missionaries in the past, however, had been mixed, in part because of the ambiguous status of the church as a Christian faith in Scandinavia. These religious concerns sometimes overshadowed the shared ethnic ties. In the eyes of native Scandinavians, missionaries returning to the home of their ancestors were first and foremost American.[25] Their cultural roots were unmistakable to twentieth-century Danes and Norwegians who opposed Latter-day Saint proselytizing on both religious and nationalist grounds. Cultural and religious aversions to the religion seeped into the realm of law and politics in both Denmark and Norway, where, even with constitutional protections for religious liberty, missionaries were occasionally barred from openly proselytizing.

Despite these challenges, Jenson was optimistic that the situation between Latter-day Saints and the Danes and Norwegians had improved since his prior missions. He wrote to Apostle Charles W. Penrose that the Saints in Copenhagen were enjoying "a privilege which [they] did not enjoy in this country when I was here on my former missions. A number of other liberal laws granting more equal rights to the inhabitants of Denmark have recently been passed by the 'Rigsdag' and received Royal sanction." The Danish Saints were now holding meetings without "any interference on the part of the Lutheran clergy." One Danish Latter-day Saint even belonged to the Rigsdag, the Danish parliament, and had recently succeeded in helping pass a bill that allowed "dissenters" from the state church to bury their dead according to their own religious preferences. As Jenson presided over a funeral for a deceased Latter-day Saint in Copenhagen, he sat in awe at the progress that had been made in just the last decade.[26] His initial observation that the relationship between native Scandinavians and their Latter-day Saint neighbors was improving was certainly correct, but the legitimacy of the Latter-day Saint faith as a Christian religion was still decidedly unsettled.

Touring the Mission

Immediately after arriving in Copenhagen, Jenson began acquainting himself with the affairs of the Danish-Norwegian Mission. He was quite familiar with the geographic area he now presided over. Close to 140 missionaries at any given time were scattered across Denmark and Norway in six conferences (three in Denmark and three in Norway). Jenson launched a quick tour of the conferences to acquaint himself with the current missionaries and affairs. Back in Utah, the chain of ecclesiastical authority was well established: ward bishops, when necessary, counseled with stake presidents and the high council, who would then take more complex or serious matters to the General Authorities in Salt Lake City. But abroad, the mission president was the main point of contact for issues that arose in the church's scattered branches. Jenson's administrative style was informed by his historical work and his personality—he was going to perform his duties while traveling. Such a tour would be challenging since the Danish and Norwegian church members were widely dispersed across thirty-nine branches, but Jenson preferred the circuit lifestyle to the confines of the mission home.[27]

His initial tour of the conferences lasted only a week, but it gave him a stable assessment of the needs of the mission and confirmed his belief that changes to the missionary work were necessary.[28] His first report to his leaders in England was sober. Writing to Penrose after his return to Copenhagen, Jenson complained that a good number of his missionaries were "entirely incapable of doing efficient missionary work." Most intended to perform their duties faithfully but lacked the training or stamina to be effective. Jenson also felt church leaders in Salt Lake City were targeting the wrong demographic to serve in his mission—most were too old, and those of Scandinavian descent were given too much preference. "I think it is a mistake to send out middle aged men over here to learn the language of the country even if they happen to be born of Scandinavian parents," he continued to Penrose. Jenson's report tallied that out of 135 elders, including himself, forty were over forty-five years old. "Where physical exertions to any considerable extent" were necessary, maintained Jenson, older missionaries were sidelined "a great deal of their time in their rented rooms." His "youthful Elders" had difficulties learning a new language, but the "older men" could "neither travel as they aught to nor speak the language." The result was a body of elders unprepared to take on the challenges that awaited them in the Danish-Norwegian Mission. In addition, the mission contained a few poorly behaved missionaries who were ruining the work in some areas. Without significant changes, Jenson felt the mission might collapse and he would be left "Elder less in Scandinavia."[29] Jenson made repeated requests throughout his mission for more and better prepared missionaries, but the pool of missionaries prepared to take on the challenges of proselytizing in Scandinavia was shrinking fast.[30]

His vision for change, however, went further than raising the standard for service in Scandinavia. As he explained to the First Presidency, Jenson envisioned "a general revival" in the mission, a near return to the golden age of the 1850s and '60s, when missionary work flourished in Scandinavia. He surmised that the current crop of missionaries lacked faith that such a turnaround was achievable and believed "that the work of God had nearly run its course in these lands, and that only a little more remains to be done." Old preaching methods seemed tired and ineffective; Jenson imagined a wholesale change in the approach to proselytizing, one that would take the elders out of their "cottage meetings" in their "small hired halls" into larger meetings where they could deliver advertised, prepared lectures.[31]

While on his first, quick tour of the mission, Jenson experienced the success such large lectures might have. Missionaries widely advertised a gathering in Aalborg, which brought in a congregation of "respectable citizens," and Jenson, always eager to give a speech, delivered a sermon to them. "The spirit of God was poured out upon us," he reported, and the visitors expressed great "satisfaction with what they had heard."[32] Encouraged that perhaps similar town hall–style meetings could be held elsewhere without local agitators interfering, Jenson recommended advertising more lectures to "get the masses out." The lectures were to be held in capacious venues and cover general topics like "Utah and the Mormons." He sensed that Scandinavians possessed a general curiosity about the Latter-day Saints, which elders of the mission could draw on to assemble crowds and correct misinformation about Utah and its inhabitants.[33]

One month after a quick visit to his daughter Eleonore in Berlin, Jenson launched another, more extensive tour of the mission conferences. It would be the first formal tour of several that he would take as mission president. Each of his tours of the mission followed the same general pattern. His travels first took him northward from Copenhagen to the Aarhus Conference and then to the Aalborg Conference. He would then depart Aalborg for the coastal city of Frederikshavn, where he would sail for Sweden. From Sweden he would travel by rail across the border to Christiania (Oslo), Norway, before heading west to the Bergen Conference, on the Norwegian coast. He would then travel up the coast to the northernmost conference at Trondheim before returning to Christiania for the final conference meeting. At each location, Jenson would meet with the missionaries and church members at regularly held conferences. Conference proceedings generally spanned multiple sessions and could last up to a week. They usually convened on the weekends, with general sessions, for all church members, held in the evenings. Reports were heard from missionaries, mission leaders, local branch presidents, and the Sunday school leadership. In addition, special meetings for priesthood holders and the youth were often held, at which the mission president and other church leaders would speak. Jenson spent the time between sessions sightseeing or in the homes of local church members. In addition to the conferences, he was also sure to schedule public meetings where he could preach or give interesting reports on his around-the-world trip.[34] The entire tour generally took more than a month and was repeated each fall and spring.

The semiannual conferences held across the mission allowed Jenson to gather information on missionary activities and observe the spiritual health of local congregations. Occasionally he confronted circumstances that threatened the success of the mission, as he did on his first official visit to Christiania. Upon arriving in Europe, Jenson became aware of a troubling situation growing in Norway. A proposed bill targeting Latter-day Saint preaching was about to be introduced in the Storthing, the Norwegian parliament. The bill was grounded in widespread fears that missionaries were duping naive Norwegians to immigrate to Utah. Jenson was optimistic that the bill would fail, since he felt the Norwegians "were a liberty loving people."[35] Nonetheless, Jenson sought to actively effect change rather than wait for the parliament to act.

Following the Christiania conference, Jenson scheduled a meeting with officials at the US Consulate in Christiania. The conversation centered on missionary work "and the proposed legislation to stop our propaganda in Norway." US ambassador Herbert H. D. Peirce promised to lobby the state minister on the Latter-day Saints' behalf and to push for a meeting with the king. The meeting never materialized, but Jenson had shown he was willing to lobby American diplomats (and later, government officials) for the gospel cause.[36]

Jenson also welcomed speaking and traveling opportunities outside of the twice-yearly conference circuit. In July 1909, only six months into his tenure as mission president, he hosted Charles W. Penrose and Anthon H. Lund in Copenhagen. Penrose, as a member of the Quorum of the Twelve, and Lund, as second counselor in the First Presidency and Church Historian, stirred anticipation and excitement among local church members and missionaries, who rarely had occasion to interact with members of the church's highest presiding councils. The two visiting authorities decided to go on a tour of the mission with Jenson.[37] Lund and Penrose were accompanied on their transatlantic journey by members of Jenson's own immediate family, including his wife Emma and his daughter Eva. His daughter Eleonore also joined the group from Germany. For nearly a month Jenson balanced time with his family with mission business and touring with presiding leaders.

While visiting the less-frequented towns of rural Norway, Jenson decided to try out his proposed change to mission lectures by renting out a large hall and circulating advertisements for a lecture in the local newspaper. At Vardø, Penrose and Jenson convened a meeting in the village labor hall. The *Vardø-Posten* featured details of the lecture that morning, and the town's crier announced it throughout the day. The result was a curious crowd of around 250 people, who "listened with marked attention" to a discourse by Penrose, for which Jenson served as translator.[38] The program was so successful that Penrose and Jenson attempted another lecture a few nights later while at Narvik, a coastal town off the Ofotfjord. Two hundred people crammed into a Methodist hall to hear Penrose speak, and Jenson again deemed the meeting an overwhelming success.[39]

Lund and Penrose were not the only notable visitors to tour the Danish-Norwegian Mission during Jenson's tenure. Twice, Apostle Rudger Clawson, the new European Mission president, visited the mission.[40] And in 1910, President Joseph F. Smith became the first church president to visit Scandinavia. The Latter-day Saint prophet and his party toured through Scandinavia and notably attended the opening of the Universal Peace Congress in Stockholm, for which Jenson was a delegate.[41] The optimism brought on by visits from church leaders, however, was disrupted by a rise in agitation against the church and subsequent challenges for the Danish-Norwegian Mission.

Countering Opposition with Illustrated Lectures

The tranquil sectarian forces Jenson had observed when he first arrived in Scandinavia as mission president started to foment again in 1910, provoked by a transatlantic flow of headlines about the Latter-day Saints from the United States. Indeed, while antagonistic Lutheran clerics and officials in Denmark and Norway often generated their own attacks against the church, they also latched on to news wired over from the States. The contentious congressional hearings over the retention of Utah senator Reed Smoot in the US Senate had gripped Europe as they did the American public. Swirling accusations about the continuation of polygamy stirred salacious rumors about the church's leaders and gave rise to imaginative political cartoons and opinion pieces about Latter-day Saints and their fitness for citizenship. A fascination with plural marriage—shrouded in popular tales of illicit sex and secrecy—brought the Latter-day Saint story to the European commoner and gave opposition to the church new life.

Circulating stereotypes about church members were amplified by deep-seated social anxieties in Britain and elsewhere in Europe. Like those in the United States, many in Europe were wrestling with the implications of modernization and industrialization, including an upheaval of traditional moral, cultural, and political structures.[42] Some responded with calls for a retrenchment or a return to Victorian morality. For example, Winifred Graham launched a tireless crusade against Latter-day Saints in England in 1911, playing on the fears of conservative Christians by depicting Latter-day Saint men as a threat to traditional womanhood and virtue.[43] The campaign intended to stoke fears that sexually debauched Latter-day Saint patriarchs were hunting down European women, persuading them to immigrate to Utah, and enslaving them in their plural-marriage system.

Graham's campaign was indicative of the stereotypes missionaries were up against in Europe.[44] Caricatures of Latter-day Saint polygamists appeared in cartoons, editorials, and novels, where they were depicted as southern slaveholders, charismatic seducers, lecherous foreigners, and enslavers and kidnappers.[45] These images took on added potency in Great Britain and Scandinavia, where Latter-day Saint missionaries had experienced significant success since the mid-nineteenth century. To some in these areas, missionaries appeared to be recruiting future Latter-day Saint polygamist men and unsuspecting women from the working classes and importing them to the United States. The backdrop of polygamy—what some outsiders labeled "white Mormon slavery"—was not just the far-off American desert but Europe's own backyard, the site of Latter-day Saint convert strength and immigration.[46]

Caricatures of the Latter-day Saint people appeared outside of print as well. Intrigue over Latter-day Saints and their plural-marriage system made them an easy target for illustrated lecturers (who used projected images to make their arguments) looking to turn the curiosity of crowds into a quick buck.[47] Former Latter-day Saint William Jarman, destitute and in search of a profit, was one person who sought to launch a tell-all lecture tour in his European homeland that would lay bare the supposed sexual exploits and malicious doings of the Latter-day Saint people. Despite his past failures, in Britain in the 1890s, Jarman remade himself into an influential itinerant entertainer and respected town councilman, who eventually drew thousands of people to his lecturers for a penny a head.[48]

While magic-lantern shows were used to stoke sentiments against Latter-day Saints, they were also helpful mediums for the church's missionaries, who used them to assert a different image of their faith abroad and counter distorted images of Utah and its people.[49] In 1898, the British Mission received approval from the First Presidency to conduct an extended lecture tour around the United Kingdom "to peacefully combat the extraordinary ideas prevalent in the world, regarding the moral status of the Latter-day Saints as a people." The First Presidency selected notable academic and lecturer James E. Talmage to make the tour.[50] By July 1898, Talmage was lecturing to large crowds in halls throughout England, Ireland, and Scotland, using images of Utah and its people "vastly different," as one person in attendance remarked, "to Jarman's lecture."[51] Illustrated lectures spread beyond the borders of Great Britain to other missions in the late nineteenth century.

Shortly after arriving in Denmark in 1909, Jenson implored the First Presidency to allow him a greater stake in the day-to-day work of preaching the gospel. Inspired by illustrated lectures he had given during his 1902 mission and Talmage's earlier success with them, Jenson hoped he "could see a little daylight" and after "securing a good lamp and lantern slides . . . give illustrated lectures in the cities of Denmark and Norway."[52] Jenson reprised the subject again when Lund toured the mission in July 1909, and Lund agreed that Jenson's time might be best spent in the lecture hall instead of the mission office. The proposed illustrated-lecture tour would occur in conjunction with the twice-yearly mission conferences and would pit the energetic and emphatic Jenson against Scandinavia's most oppositional clerical and community forces. Jenson wrote to Lund a few weeks after his visit, asking him to "secure . . . all the lantern slides . . . appropriate for an illustrated lecture on the history of our people." In January 1910, the long-awaited lantern slides finally arrived, and Jenson set about making arrangements with conference presidents to secure large lecture halls for his illustrated tour.[53]

Anticipating the public nature of Jenson's lecture tour, Lund advised Jenson to be cautious about sharing too much of his own personal marital situation with the Danish public. Jenson hoped Bertha could come for a visit, similar to Emma's visit the previous summer. Lund told Jenson: "The [First] presidency talked it over and they consider it would be unwise to do it. Emma having been over and been in every conference in Scandinavia the Saints are not prepared to see another wife with you. They do not know the difference [between] Polygamy and lawful cohabitation and will be making conclusions that we are not honest in our public declarations. . . . It would handicap your usefulness."[54] Jenson's public lectures were intended to normalize the Latter-day Saint image before the Danish people, not complicate it.

After holding two lectures in Copenhagen to test the lantern and slides, Jenson was prepared to hit the road.[55] With missionary Lars Frederikson as his lantern operator, Jenson first traveled southward to the town of Næstved. About 175 people packed a local hotel to hear Jenson's lecture, which went off nearly as planned until a local Lutheran priest interrupted the proceedings. The priest

Andrew Jenson using a magic lantern while serving as Danish-Norwegian Mission president, October 1910. Courtesy Church History Library.

was well-known in the town for his disdain of the Latter-day Saints, and Jenson felt he "acted more like a saucy school boy or a mobocrat than a man of supposed culture." The crowd appeared to Jenson to be tired of the priest's act, but his disruptive behavior was still a sign of lingering tension between Lutherans and the Latter-day Saints.[56]

Jenson's initial illustrated-lecture tour lasted close to a month. He delivered fourteen lectures, mostly in towns outside of his traditional conference circuit. After only a few weeks, his tour had run up a debt, as donations at the door failed to offset advertising and venue expenses.[57] Jenson felt his lecture tour, despite some lantern-operating troubles and a few negative reviews from the press, was a triumph. As his lectures attracted more attention and became a regular feature of his conference tours, the traditional forces of opposition gave increased attention to Jenson and his work. In the village of Frederiksværk in September 1910, a district judge prohibited Jenson and his team from holding an illustrated lecture. With the hall already hired out, an enraged and somewhat belligerent Jenson demanded answers from a representative of the court and was informed the lecture was canceled because they were "'Mormons' and . . . taught immoral doctrines."[58] Further inquiry uncovered an alliance between the courts and the local Lutheran parish priest, who would need to give his "permission to hold a public lecture." After the local priest again objected, court officials sent Jenson away with an official refusal in writing. An incensed Jenson marveled at the prospect of being "outwitted and defeated by a Danish priest" despite honest intentions to "give an innocent lecture."[59]

At Nyborg, Jenson confronted a similar situation. This time, the town mayor, who also served as the chief of police—"a small, officious and bigotted man who could scarcely talk decent," according to Jenson—forbade him from showing images on account that he was "going to say and do something in favor of the 'Mormons.'"[60] Apparently local laws did not permit the mayor to ban the lecture entirely, but despite pleas from a local newspaper editor who invoked "religious liberty and the common rights of citizens and men," the mayor refused to relent. Jenson proceeded with the lecture anyway, without his images, to the great enjoyment of his audience, who by the end of the lecture had turned against the mayor's decision.

While local officials and Lutheran clergymen were the most committed opponents of Jenson's lecture tour, he also occasionally ran up against disruptive citizens who spread salacious gossip about the Latter-day Saints. At Assens, Denmark, a former visitor to Utah alleged he had witnessed old Latter-day Saint men pressing young Danish girls into marriage. A Danish girl "would be forced to marry" a Latter-day Saint man "even if he looked like a monkey," the Dane asserted. Jenson "called him a liar to his face," and, when the man failed to produce any plausible details of wrongdoing, the confrontation ended.[61] In November

1911, agitation in Gjentofte (now Gentofte) resulted in a similar situation: the village Lutheran priest and a wealthy merchant shouted down Jenson while he was lecturing. The obstinate Jenson refused to relent and continued with his lecture.[62] The week after the lecture, however, his opponents in Gjentofte held a meeting to preach against the Latter-day Saints. Johannes Thorsen, a Danish American Lutheran minister, spoke first at the meeting and was followed by the town's Lutheran priest. Though Jenson attended the meeting with his fellow missionaries and spoke out against the slander and rumors, after an exhausting evening he determined that "no good comes out of a discussion no matter how ably we may defend the cause, especially in a community when the great majority is against us."[63] They had already rented the local hotel hall for the next evening to give a lecture free of debate and interruption and to combat the significant opposition they were experiencing in Gjentofte. Their intentions, however, were thwarted by the owner of the hall, who refused to grant them access to the venue and was, according to Jenson, under the employ of the wealthy local merchant who had earlier spoken out against them.[64]

The grassroots tactics of the Scandinavian locals were augmented and encouraged by more formal anti-LDS efforts in Denmark and Norway. In 1911, Thorsen, described by Jenson as the mission's "arch-enemy," traveled around Denmark performing his own illustrated lectures to give a thorough "'unveiling' of Mormonism."[65] To counter his influence, Jenson attempted to schedule illustrated lectures in the wake of Thorsen's tour; according to mission secretary, Joseph K. Nicholes, it was "in [Thorsen's] footsteps" that "the greatest interest" was found among the people.[66] Thorsen's attacks, however, were soon intensified with the arrival of Utah native Hans P. Freece, who had initially gone to Great Britain to actively lobby for legislative action against the church.

The Persecutions of Hans P. Freece

Freece was known to Latter-day Saints inside and outside of Denmark. He hailed originally from Scipio, Utah, near Scandinavian settlements in Sevier and Sanpete Counties. The child of a polygamous marriage, Freece likely inherited much of his disdain for the Latter-day Saint faith from his father, who had been excommunicated by the church.[67] Freece's first significant exposé of the Latter-day Saints—*Letters of an Apostate Mormon to His Son*—was published in 1908 while he was in New York training to become a lawyer.[68] His career as a lecturer against the church took off while he was in New York, and he eventually agreed to represent the Interdenominational Council of Women for Christian and Patriotic Service overseas in combatting the proselytizing efforts of Latter-day Saint missionaries.[69] Freece was particularly seeking evidence that missionaries were enticing the young eligible women of Great Britain to head to Zion and unite in plural marriage. According to the *New York Times*, Freece's "War on Mormons" netted evidence that "325 American Latter-day Saints engaged in inducing young women to emigrate to Utah." In addition, Freece claimed to have signed affidavits from "parents whose daughters had been enticed to emigrate."[70]

Freece's repeated accusations of Latter-day Saint kidnappers roaming the British countryside and cityscapes attracted the attention of government leaders, prompting an investigation. Though Home Secretary Winston Churchill found no grounds to move against the church with legislation, church opponents and dissidents continued to lobby the British citizenry to revolt against the Latter-day Saint visitors.[71] Freece, while disappointed with Churchill's decision, felt satisfied that his efforts had significantly derailed missionary efforts in the country and had already set his sights set on another captive audience for his campaign.[72] His Danish homeland seemed ripe for an uprising against the Latter-day Saints.

Freece's campaign hoped to arouse Danish sympathy in two ways—by aligning with the interests of the Danish Folkekirken, and by appealing to the shared ethnic heritage of all Danes. According to Freece and his allies, Latter-day Saint immigration and the persistence of the plural-marriage system threatened the traditional culture and ethnic identity of Danes everywhere.

Movements within the Lutheran Church of Denmark had already shown interest in rescuing their compatriots lost to the Latter-day Saint sect. The "Utah-Missionens Udvalg" (Utah Mission Committee) and the Church Association for the Inner Mission in Denmark (Indre Mission) both worked to reclaim Danes in Utah and fight against the Latter-day Saint church.[73] Freece felt a kinship with both organizations because they appeared united in an effort to rescue "the Danish girls from the grip of the Mormon octopus."[74]

Freece provoked the Danish religious establishment into action but again failed to compel government authorities to act decisively against Jenson's missionary enterprise. The minister of justice, Frits Bülow, and the minister of church and state apparently listened attentively to Freece's objections but were hesitant to enter a conflict that seemed better waged on US soil. In the estimation of Bülow, Freece had "no message for the Danish people."[75] The previous December, after the incident in Nyborg, Jenson too had lobbied Bülow and received a similar diplomatic and noncommittal response—he had refused to give Jenson carte blanche to lecture across Denmark but instead encouraged him to apply for permission from each municipality.[76]

The dialogue between the church and the government was open, however, and Jenson soon felt he had found a sympathetic ally in Bülow when he met with him in person in January 1911. According to Jenson, Bülow, "a tall fine looking man and very bright and intelligent," promised to investigate any instance where the religious liberties of the Saints were being violated.[77] Jenson called upon the minister only a month later when a missionary was denied the opportunity of giving Jenson's illustrated presentation in Næstved. Jenson's letter appealed to the minister to protect free speech and religious liberty and dismissed fears that the lectures were thinly veiled Latter-day Saint "propaganda." Jenson represented himself as a "Danish-American Journalist" and friend of the Danish people who was merely offering up "information about Utah and its inhabitants."[78] The mostly warm response Jenson received from government officials moved Freece's battle against the Latter-day Saints to the local level, where the antagonistic Dane's 1911 campaign was waged on two fronts—in the press and in local halls across the country.

After returning from a trip to northern Norway, Jenson had only a morning and afternoon to prepare for a showdown that would pit him and two of his fellow missionaries against three local Lutheran priests and three others, including Thorsen and Freece. The supposed purpose of the meeting was to test the authenticity of documents on the Latter-day Saints that Freece claimed to possess. In reality, the "Great Anti-Mormon Meeting," as Jenson titled it, was a public hearing on the fitness of the Latter-day Saint faith for Danish society. Over one thousand people, including many local Saints and missionaries, crowded the Konsert-Palais in downtown Copenhagen. Freece's main source text "was the official report of the Smoot investigation affair in Washington, D.C., by which he wanted to show up Prest. Joseph F. Smith and Francis M. Lyman as criminals."[79] Jenson's personal life came under attack as Thorsen retold the details of the mission president's plural family. The trio of missionaries—Jenson, Oluf J. Andersen, and Anthon J. T. Sorensen—received no opportunity to speak in the main meeting. Instead, at a more private gathering the same day, with much of the press still in attendance, the missionaries countered the accusations made in the main session. "The Lord was with us and gave us words to say," Jenson wrote after the meeting. "We were able to down our opponents so much so that nearly the entire body of newspaper men who were present became our friends and took sides with us something hitherto unheard of in the history of 'Mormonism' in Denmark."[80]

When Jenson woke the next morning, his initial impression that the missionaries had won over the local press proved correct. The headline in *Politiken*, the respected Copenhagen daily, declared the meeting a "failure." "Mr. Freece will do well if he packs his valise as soon as possible and returns to America," the newspaper continued, "where the soil is no doubt more fertile for his agitation."[81] But the battle with Freece and Thorsen was not over. Jenson wanted to be sure that Freece was stopped for good.

According to a report in Freece's *How Mormons Recruit Abroad*, the intrepid mission president took the fight to the courts. As Freece was giving his last lecture in Denmark, he was served with papers informing him that a lawsuit for slander had been filed against him on "behalf of Joseph F. Smith and the

Mormon Church." Jenson had filed the suit against Freece, Thorsen, and a local Danish clergyman in the city of Silkeborg, the residence of Thorsen. Jenson may have intended to gain a favorable judgment by default, anticipating that Freece and company were already scheduled to leave the country and would fail to appear for the summons.[82] Freece, however, hired legal counsel, and the suit was tied up in the courts for the remainder of the year. In addition, Freece's lawyer countersued Jenson for libel, based on an article about Freece in the July 15 issue of the *Skandinaviens Stjerne.* "We don't fear the consequence of this," Jenson reported home to the First Presidency in November 1911.[83] Jenson felt the "case [was] . . . clear" and that the courts would rule in the church's favor.[84]

To the Land of Fire and Ice

On the heels of his victory over Freece, a confident Jenson welcomed new challenges and turned his sights on Iceland, then still formally a part of Denmark. Despite select visits from missionaries since a year after the founding of the Scandinavian Mission, no mission president had ever visited that Nordic island, and the insatiable traveler aimed to be the first.[85] Iceland had once been a promising mission field, but only a pair of missionaries remained in the region, and Jenson was aware that the elders were struggling. With permission from the First Presidency to take his lecture slides with him, Jenson planned to make a lecture tour in select towns in Iceland over the summer of 1911.[86] In early July, Jenson wrote ahead to Elder Jacob B. Johnson, stationed in Iceland, to prepare for his visit.[87]

Jenson's traveling companion was Elder Alma L. Petersen of the Aarhus Conference.[88] In August the pair sailed from Copenhagen to Reykjavik. Jenson and his companion spent most of their first week in Iceland exploring the sites on horseback. They returned to Reykjavik on August 18 to prepare for a scheduled illustrated lecture. The crowd at the opening lecture in Iceland was sparse, despite significant efforts to advertise around the community.[89] Jenson's second lecture the next evening brought in more locals, but the total attendance over the two days barely surpassed one hundred, a small fraction of the crowd he usually received elsewhere in the mission.[90]

Audiences may have been deterred by articles against the church that had been printed in the nation's newspapers, which had received word of Jenson's trip ahead of time. "The Mormon missionaries paint a bright picture of Utah in every detail, so that those who are ignorant think that there is some kind of earthly paradise there," an editorial in the local newspaper read, "but when they arrive there the many evils amaze them. . . . The Missionaries intend to have 5–10 wives each." The writer repeated the same themes that sustained the anti-LDS campaign throughout the rest of Europe.[91]

Though Jenson was disappointed by the tepid response to his lectures, he expressed optimism about Iceland's potential. "If we had a couple of efficient and zealous missionaries there, we would be able to make Iceland a good field for our missionary operations," he wrote to the First Presidency, encouraging them to look among Utah's Icelanders, who had largely settled in Spanish Fork, Utah, for worthy elders who could move missionary work along in their homeland.[92] To Clawson, Jenson was a little more forthright: "unless we can find a couple of young and able Elders to send to Iceland—men that have courage and a little means—we shall never make a success of the Icelandic Mission."[93] Nonetheless, upon returning to the mission office in Copenhagen, Jenson reported that "I have great hopes concerning the future, I believe the majority of the inhabitants of Iceland, have more or less, the blood of Israel flowing in their viens [*sic*], and consequently are entitled to the blessing of the Gospel."[94] Jenson, however, failed to reset missionary work in Iceland during his tenure as mission president. The First Presidency ended missionary work in the area in 1914, on the eve of World War I.[95]

A Victim of the Mormons

The calm that followed Copenhagen's "Great Anti-Mormon Meeting" in June was punctuated by a resurgence of vitriol against the Latter-day Saints in the fall of 1911. The Danish company Nordisk Films was one of the first organizations to harness the power of motion picture to warn people "against the deception of Mormonism."[96] The company premiered an hour-long feature, *Mormonens Offer* (*A Victim of the Mormons*) in Copenhagen in October 1911 to great acclaim, and the silent film was quickly planned for release in England and the United States. The dramatic film—inspired by images from the lectures of Freece, Thorsen, and others—featured a celebrity cast and brought to life Danish fears that Latter-day Saint missionaries were kidnapping and enslaving Danish women. The plot followed the attempt of a "Mormon priest" to lure a young and attractive Danish woman to Utah as his plural wife. Entranced by the Latter-day Saint preacher's artfulness, the woman agrees, and the Latter-day Saint man drugs, gags, and disguises his new wife-to-be to elude police. He eventually takes her to Utah, which proves a tragic disappointment to the young woman as she is secreted away with only her new husband's first wife to offer consolation. In true cinematic climax, the film closes with a gun battle between the woman's Danish rescuers and the polygamist villain, who is fatally shot by his own gun.[97]

The effect of *A Victim of the Mormons* was far-reaching. Prior to the advent of the motion picture, opposition to the Latter-day Saints was confined, apart from a few popular theatrical productions, to oral and print media. Olsen's silent film, however, pushed the boundaries of the anti-LDS imagination beyond the standard fare of drawings, paintings, and lecture slides to moving images intended to re-create reality for audiences. *A Victim of the Mormons* focused the audience's gaze upon scenes that could allegedly unfold in any town across Denmark.

The corresponding sixteen-page pamphlet for *A Victim of the Mormons*, replete with picture stills, read more like a traditional tract against the Latter-day Saints and was calculated to elevate ticket sales by highlighting the alluring yet dangerous traits of the American sect. The film was introduced as "a drama about love and sectarian fanaticism" and was intended to disarm virulent Latter-day Saint propaganda afoot in Europe. The pamphlet argued that the filmmakers' chief antagonists were the Latter-day Saint missionaries who enticed Europe's more susceptible individuals, especially women, to "go over to the sect's teachings and emigrate to the New Zion."[98] The paternalistic handbills marketed the film as a tool to "open the eyes of the gentler sex who are unluckily too easily gulled by the oily tongue of the deceiver." At last, the pamphlet extolled, Europe possessed a "drama which . . . should do more to counteract the growth of Mormonism in this country than all the preaching against it, even by the most noted clerics."[99]

A Victim of the Mormons elevated the campaign against the church in Denmark by injecting its message into popular culture. No longer was the crusade for social reform best suited for local Lutheran clerics and professional lecturers—it was one befitting all good Danish citizens. As the nation secularized, Lutheranism faded as the premier cultural identity for Danes, and the Latter-day Saint faith became a threat, not just to religion but to traditional Danish identity and respectability. *A Victim of the Mormons* was not inherently Lutheran, nor was it overtly theological or religious. Instead, the film—by connecting Latter-day Saints to forced emigration and "white slavery"—was deployed to shore up Danish allegiance to cultural and national values.[100] As Jenson had learned in his travels around the mission, the Lutheran clergy would not go quietly, but the Latter-day Saint message was seen as a social, political, and moral danger, not just a religious one.

A month after the film's release, Jenson noted to the First Presidency that "in some places, especially in the smaller towns, it has exasperated the people and created a bitter feeling against us for although the fabrication is as absurd as it is false, yet many of the ignorant people believe it is based on facts."[101] In Trondheim, missionaries witnessed the bitter feelings firsthand when a mob gathered outside the church's meetinghouse during Sunday services, vandalized a missionary apartment, and assaulted a local church member and his friend. Joseph Nicholes alleged to the *Deseret News* that *A Victim of the Mormons* inspired the mob action.[102] Jenson lobbied local Danish authorities to stop the film from showing but was greatly disappointed when police officers refused to shut down the debut showings at Aarhus after concluding the film contained nothing "obscene" to pose a direct threat to the public.[103]

Yet, as 1912 began, the campaign against the church that had surged throughout 1911 was finally on the wane in Scandinavia, and Jenson felt confident his mission had weathered the attacks relatively well. The dual cases with Freece were still stalled in the courts, and on February 9, 1912, Jenson made one of his final appearances in the courtroom before he was released as mission president.[104] Confident the cases were moving in his favor, Jenson prepared to return home before they were resolved.

In February 1912, word reached Jenson that the First Presidency had appointed his successor, Martin Christophersen.[105] Christophersen arrived in Copenhagen on March 31, and by May Jenson finished arranging the affairs of the mission for his departure and turned management over to Christophersen. He gave a farewell address in Copenhagen on May 15, and a celebration was held for him

Andrew Jenson (left) with Martin Christophersen, Copenhagen, 1912. Courtesy Church History Library.

that evening; the staff at mission headquarters, where Jenson had made his home over the last three years, along with the entire Copenhagen branch gathered to bid him farewell. "Bouquet after bouquet was fastened upon me and given into my hands," Jenson wrote in his journal, "and the good wishes and loving words uttered in my behalf melted my heart and brought tears to my eyes again and again."[106]

The address he gave that evening reflected on the ties that still bound him to his homeland and composed his dual identity as both a Latter-day Saint and a Scandinavian: "Though my home for the past 46 years has been in far-away America, I still feel that I am one of the sons of the North, and my heart continues to beat warmly for the Old Country and its welfare. I know the Scandinavian people better than any other folk in the world and I love them as I love my own flesh and blood."[107] Throughout Jenson's presidency, his identity as a true native Scandinavian was consistently called into question by his own people—he was a Latter-day Saint, a polygamist, and an American, which in some minds erased any claim to his Danish heritage. Yet, Jenson still felt a connection to his homeland, which sustained his service in Scandinavia and moved him deeply at his departure.

Around the World a Second Time

Jenson's return trip would not be a restful experience. The Assistant Church Historian was determined to again circumnavigate the globe, just as he had during his westward global fact-finding mission between 1895 and 1897. Now, fifteen years later, Jenson hoped to return home to Utah in the opposite direction, traveling eastward across Sweden and Finland and then to Russia by steamer. He would then traverse the sprawling Russian Empire by railroad and sail to Japan and Hawai'i before arriving in San Francisco. This ambitious itinerary would allow him to experience areas that were new to him and the church, particularly parts of eastern Europe and northern Asia. It would also mean more than doubling the distance of his return trip home. His extensive journey was noteworthy among church leadership at the time. Not a single member of the past or present Quorum of the Twelve had ever enjoyed this kind of travel opportunity.

Jenson was joined by Peter Christian Rasmussen, a missionary who had been laboring in the Aarhus Conference.[108] The two men traveled from Denmark to Sweden and then on to Russia. On May 20, the two travelers cruised into Russian waters near the head of the Gulf of Finland.[109] They disembarked at St. Petersburg, the country's westernmost city. After showing their passports to Russian customs officials, they checked into their hotel and spent the next day and a half touring the sites of the city. Just days after their arrival in St.

Petersburg, Jenson and Rasmussen felt compelled to continue their journey east. They purchased their train and steamer tickets to get them all the way to Japan on the Trans-Siberian Railway.[110] They traveled by rail to Moscow, which was another revelation to the two Latter-day Saint tourists. As did most travelers, they made their way to the historic Kremlin in the heart of Moscow.[111] The duo also visited the Grand Kremlin Palace, where the tsar resided, and the Cathedral of Christ the Saviour, which Jenson described as "one of the most beautiful and costly buildings in the world."[112]

On the evening of May 24, Jenson and Rasmussen departed Moscow, and over the next twelve days, the two travelers rode in train carriages across the breadth of Russia, as well as parts of China and Manchuria. On June 5, Jenson and Rasmussen's train arrived at the train station at Vladivostok, Russia.[113] The next morning they made their way to the harbor to confirm their tickets to Japan on the Russian SS *Penza*. After a two-day crossing, Jenson and Rasmussen finally saw the mountainous western coastline of Japan as they steamed into Tsuruga Bay. They then traveled to the main railroad station, located a few miles from the seacoast. "This was the second time I rode in a jinrikisha (a two-wheeled cart propelled by human instead of horse flesh) and we found this way of locomotion at least interesting."[114] At the railroad station, they purchased their second-class tickets and then traveled by train eastward through mountainous country, passing Lake Biwa and the city of Maibara, where they changed to the Shimbashi Express train bound for Tokyo.

Like most first-time travelers to Japan, Jenson was impressed by his first sight of Mount Fuji, which rises over twelve thousand feet above sea level. He was likewise surprised by how dissimilar the Land of the Rising Sun was from eastern Europe and northern Asia. Jenson wrote: "It seemed as if we suddenly had been dumped into a new or different world. The clattering of wooden-bottomed slippers on the feet of the natives at the stations, and the . . . outcries of vendors of wares at the stations were deafening, and yet it was very amusing indeed to see these little Japs imitate the Anglo-Saxons in dress, manners and general deportment. Throughout these Japs that we met on that journey seemed extremely obliging and courteous, and quite a number of the men could speak English."[115] After years of living in occidental Scandinavia, Jenson encountered the novelty of the Orient.

When Jenson had conducted his earlier world tour, in the mid-1890s, he did not pass through Japan, since the church did not yet have a presence there. A few years later, in the summer of 1901, the church sent a small band of missionaries to Japan, and by the time Jenson and Rasmussen arrived in Tokyo in June 1912, missionaries had been evangelizing in Japan for eleven years.[116] The two visitors were picked up at the Shimbashi station in Tokyo by Mission President Elbert D. Thomas. Jenson and Rasmussen lodged in the Tokyo mission home over the next eight nights. On their first Sabbath morning in the non-Christian nation, Jenson and Rasmussen attended Sunday school services at the mission home. Unable to converse with the Japanese congregants, they "listened with interest to what was going on, though [they] could not understand the language used." That afternoon they each spoke in sacrament meeting, aided by missionary interpreters, and that evening they joined the missionaries at a public meeting attended by about thirty people. "In being introduced to the different members and friends after the meetings we noticed the awkwardness of some of the natives in shaking hands, a custom with which the Japanese do not seem to be acquainted. They simply bow to each other when they greet one another, and hardly ever touch each other," Jenson explained.[117] The two visitors came to appreciate how difficult it was to proselytize among the non-Western and non-Christian Japanese in comparison to Western Europeans.

With only a week before their departure to the Hawaiian Islands, Jenson and Rasmussen busied themselves with sightseeing and church history work in Tokyo. The Latter-day Saint group rode jinrikishas to the hills of Yokohama, where Apostle Heber J. Grant had dedicated Japan for the preaching of the gospel on September 1, 1901.[118] The men then strolled through the Bluff District, where foreigners traditionally lived, and enjoyed the view of Yokohama harbor below before returning to Tokyo.

After nine days in Japan, it was time for Jenson and Rasmussen to sail for the United States. On their final Sabbath, they said farewell and concluded their sightseeing; neither man would ever visit Japan again. As was his custom when traveling abroad, Jenson distributed his personal photo cards as a keepsake for the local Saints. Taking leave of the Sunday School children, Jenson and Rasmussen traveled with President Thomas by streetcar to the Tokyo foreigner quarter, where they stopped to see the Hotel Metropole, where Apostle Heber J. Grant and his first three missionaries had lived. The group then departed by train for Yokohama harbor to the south. After their arrival, they traveled by jinrikishas to the SS *Tenyo Maru*, bound for Honolulu, Hawai'i.[119]

As the two men neared Honolulu, Jenson sent a short telegram to President Samuel E. Woolley of the Hawaiian Mission, which read: "Please meet me at Honolulu Monday morning with mission records after 1895."[120] Seventeen years earlier, in 1895, Jenson had toured the Hawaiian Mission while on his first world tour of church history sites and congregations, gathered all of the records there, and sent them to the Historian's Office.[121] The purpose of the present Hawai'i trip was apparently to gather the records that had been created after Jenson's visit in 1895. After only one day on the islands, Jenson and Rasmussen, along with their fellow passengers, steamed out of Honolulu harbor and headed for San Francisco, 2,100 miles to the east.

By the first of July, less than a week after leaving the harbor of Honolulu, they sighted the California coastline and were escorted through the Golden Gate by a pilot boat. The following day Jenson received a telegram from Bertha and his son Harold and daughter Eva, who had traveled to the Bay Area for a family reunion. Their reunion in California was a much-needed reprieve for the family, who had suffered greatly in Jenson's absence over the last three years. Since his departure in 1909, Jenson had missed the death of his eighty-year-old mother-in-law, Fanny, who had lived with the family for years, as well as the serious illness of Harold, and the marriage of Jenson's son Parley. Jenson's absence for major life events had caused Bertha and Emma serious reflection and loneliness over the preceding three years. For example, on Christmas Eve immediately following the death of their mother in December 1909, Bertha wrote of the "sad and lonesome" feeling in the household as the family, though together, felt "entirely alone." Only Leo was interested in hanging a stocking to celebrate the holiday. Leo (age four), Harold (age fourteen), and Eva (age twenty) remained in the home then, but the increasing independence of the two oldest children and Fanny's death signaled a significant change in the natural seasons of life that left the Howell sisters melancholy.[122] Thus, the return of Jenson and the reunion of a portion of the family brought a reprieve to the loneliness. The family enjoyed the next few days touring the sights of San Francisco, Oakland, and Berkeley before departing by train for Los Angeles. While in Southern California, they spent some leisure time on Santa Catalina Island, toured Venice Beach, and socialized with President Joseph F. Smith and his wife and daughters—including Martha, who was being courted by Harold—in Ocean Park. They also met up with Apostle George Albert Smith and his family and other families from Utah vacationing in the beach towns of Southern California. True to form, Jenson also found time to peruse church mission records in Los Angeles.[123]

After enjoying two and a half weeks of California sunshine, the Jenson family left Los Angeles on a train bound for Utah. Two days later, on July 19, 1912, they arrived in Salt Lake City. Finally home, Jenson took pride in the fact that he was probably the first Latter-day Saint to ever travel around the world twice. He "greeted a number of former friends and associates in the street" as he traveled his normal route between his home and church headquarters. On the surface, not much had changed since his departure for Scandinavia in January 1909. Several new buildings had been constructed in his absence, including the Hotel Utah, which he called "magnificent," on the prominent corner of Main and South Temple Streets, and the Deseret Gymnasium, located on Main and North Temple.[124]

There had been some changes, however, at the Historian's Office in Jenson's absence, which distressed him. Church leaders had promoted A. William Lund, the son of Church Historian and First Presidency counselor Anthon H. Lund, to be an additional Assistant Church Historian at the April 1911 general conference.[125] In comparison to Jenson, William Lund had sparse credentials, other than having a prominent father. Distressed by seeming office politics and a cramped workspace, Jenson waited a week before returning to his office and then demanded that changes be made to his workstation. On July 30, he "commenced laboring again at the Historian's Office." As he explained in his journal, "I objected to going back into my old small illshaped room, and therefore my desk was placed in the southwest corner of the biggest room at the H.O. where the air and light was good."[126]

A Complicated Mission Legacy

It took a few months after Jenson returned home for his contributions on his recent and final extended mission to Denmark to be fully understood. When it came time to account for how he had fared against the forces in Denmark and Norway that opposed the church, the Danish American historian highlighted his illustrated-lecture tour as a buttress against the partisan forces hindering missionary work in Scandinavia. "I have traveled about 64,000 miles," Jenson reported to his superior Rudger Clawson, "and delivered nearly 1,000 public addresses, including a number of illustrated lectures on church history and affairs in Utah." This was all done, in Jenson's estimation, "in the midst of the most bitter opposition."[127]

Despite this opposition, Jenson felt the Scandinavian mission field had reclaimed a portion of its former glory under his leadership. He measured the fruits of his presidency in total baptisms (1,146) and books and tracts distributed (2,933,700). He had also personally delivered almost one thousand lectures.[128] The baptism totals under Jenson's presidency were better than that of his predecessors and on par with levels not consistently seen in the Scandinavian Mission since the 1890s. But the true impact of Jenson's three years in Denmark and Norway was far more complex than the statistics bore out. His presidency had been consumed by efforts to counter the public's negative perception of the church. And while Jenson felt that his leadership and the resiliency of the missionaries he supervised had subdued the anti-LDS forces that had taken root in Scandinavia during his presidency, issues that continued to linger in the mission after his departure suggested otherwise.

Problems in the mission continued to plague the presidency of Christophersen throughout 1912. One such challenge was the financial situation of the mission. Jenson's final report to the First Presidency contained an optimistic assessment about the mission's finances: "All is well with myself and the mission, and in making up our financial report today, we were pleased to note that the financial condition of the Mission was better than we expected, and Brother Christopherson will have no trouble in keeping the ship afloat financially."[129] Christophersen, however, spent the first months of his presidency anxious about the mission's financial future. In July, he wrote to the First Presidency, complaining: "At the time when Pres. Jenson turned over the Mission there was a total of Kr. 14,648.06 cash on hand in the office and in the bank. Practically all of this sum has now been paid out for Emigrants fares for emigrants who already had money on deposit, for contracted and past due printing bills, attorney's fees, and other various items. Now we have only a few Hundred Kroner left."[130] The situation was dire indeed—a comprehensive financial evaluation found that the mission's immediate liabilities totaled 11,014.06 kronor ($2,976.78). The problem apparently was exacerbated by an overstock of books and tracts in the conferences of the mission, something Jenson had periodically encouraged throughout his presidency.[131] The mission depended on orders of these printed materials from the various conferences as a source of revenue, but with the conferences awash in publications and short on cash, Christophersen saw no way to escape the current budget deficit without help from Salt Lake City. The First Presidency ultimately decided to forward payment to cover the mission debts.[132]

Of particular concern to Christophersen was Jenson's lawsuits, which continued to accumulate a sizable legal debt. Despite Jenson's previous optimism about the cases, new developments over the summer suggested that the two pending suits with Freece were turning against him. By the end of July, judgment was rendered in the case brought by Freece, and Jenson was ordered to pay out a significant sum in court costs. Christophersen fended off the police, who called on the mission office to collect the debt, long enough to write Jenson about how he would like to proceed. As Jenson mulled over an appeal, Christophersen was anxious to end the cases altogether.[133] Jenson's attorney advised Christophersen that "there was absolutely no chance for Jenson to win the case" in an appeal, and the mission president feared any obstinacy by Jenson might recirculate the cases in local headlines for months. Apparently one paper had already concluded, based on the legal proceedings, "Now we find no law against writing against the Mormons."[134] Such a sentiment could encourage more egregious slander. Jenson's hard-won victory in the press the previous years seemed all but erased, and his profile appeared in newspapers across Denmark throughout the fall, accompanied by accusations that the Danish American had fled the country to escape justice.[135] A win for Freece was a win for his message—the press turned their focus again to Latter-day Saint polygamy and emigration, and, according to Christophersen, Lutheran clergymen hatched their own "plan whereby they will wipe the 'Mormons' off the earth."[136] The Latter-day Saints were branded

"Kvinde Jægere" (woman hunters) by the press, and the courts "sustained that charge" with their ruling in Jenson's cases.[137] The campaign against crusaders opposing the church in Denmark, pioneered largely by Jenson, had backfired.

The longtime advocate for the Scandinavian community in Utah thus left behind a complicated legacy in his homeland, one that likely caused him internal turmoil. Throughout the three years of his mission—his first significant opportunity to preside as an ecclesiastical authority beyond his own congregation—Jenson had labored diligently, only to be met with mixed results. He received the most hurtful news about the fallout from his presidency well after he had returned to US soil. In a letter from his lawyer in Copenhagen, he was informed that he either had to pay the significant fine levied in the Freece case or face imprisonment if he ever returned to Denmark.[138] The sentence was suggestive of the cultural and ethnic tensions at work in Jenson's life and in the lives of Scandinavians who converted to the church, even in the twentieth century. As Jenson's time as mission president had attested, one still could not identify fully as a Latter-day Saint and remain a true Scandinavian in the eyes of the Danish people.

8 Modern Record Keeper

A steady stream of documents flowed into the Historian's Office when Andrew Jenson traveled. Since the creation of the Historian's Office, the institution stored only a fraction of the records created by the church and its members. Many of the historical records remained with families and in local wards, stakes, and missions. Thus, Jenson's frequent travels to gather, transcribe, and collate these documents generated a massive collection of notes and boxed documents, which he shipped home to add to the archives of the Historian's Office. Ever ambitious, Jenson dreamed of creating a comprehensive church history, one that documented not only important developments at church headquarters but also the growth of the church's widespread ecclesiastical units. "The labor of my life," he stated, was to take his notes, "written hurriedly, and frequently under difficulties," and with a staff of clerks write a full history of the church under his "personal supervision." In his mind, a complete history of the church included a comprehensive "general history" written from his notes of every ward, stake, and mission.[1]

Jenson hoped his project to fill out and complete the church's historical record would receive the formal approval and resources of the Historian's Office, including an expansion of the staff. "I made an estimate the other day, that if I worked incessantly on the history, as outlined, with one stenographer or typewriter to assist me, I might finish one year's history, in all its branches and segregations, in about six months," he wrote to the First Presidency in 1906. "This means 36 years of hard labor on my part to compile the contemplated history from 1830 to the close of 1900."[2]

Writing such a history would necessitate a shift in the priorities of the Historian's Office. Since Jenson had become an Assistant Church Historian in 1897, one of the primary focuses of the Historian's Office was to compile a daily log of institutional developments and news. Outside of this daily chronology and a few in-house indices of periodicals and records, the attention of Historian's Office employees centered on special projects, like B. H. Roberts's edited compilation *History of the Church* and occasionally Jenson's own publications.

Little changed after Jenson's request to the First Presidency. He was permitted to hire his own family members for clerical work at the Historian's Office (presumably because they would work well with him), but the office's current priorities continued. Jenson's recommendation that the office make better use of his gathered material did inspire a far-reaching and detailed scrapbook, titled "Journal History of the Church," which covered the church's organization in 1830 to the end of 1900.[3] Jenson began working on the "Journal History" in 1906, but his contemplated stake, ward, and mission histories remained sidelined.

To start the "Journal History," Jenson largely borrowed material directly from Roberts's first volume of *History of the Church*, published in 1902. According to Historian's Office rolls, he employed his daughter Minerva as his assistant, and the next year, in 1907, Lillian Cameron was hired to work on the scrapbook.[4] But the project moved in fits and starts as Jenson's frequent travels and personal projects hindered any steady progress on the "Journal History." Though he received some of the assistance he had requested, his travels, combined with a lack of approval and insufficient resources, meant that any larger-scale project like his envisioned general history would have to wait. Still, Jenson remained rooted in his belief in the universal need for comprehensive record keeping. From the increasingly cramped and dated confines of the Historian's Office, Jenson was driven by the global potential of the church, and he intended to stay ahead of its growth by advocating for best practices and a record-keeping infrastructure that could document the church's establishment worldwide, even if he had to go it alone. Over the span of six years after Jenson's return from Scandinavia, much would be made new—a new church office building, new modes of transportation, renewed attempts to improve record keeping, and a new church presidency. As he pushed for reform at church headquarters, Jenson soon learned that administrative modernization invariably left some behind as the torrents of change carried the church forward along new paths.

Expanding the Work of the Historian's Office

After returning from presiding over the Danish-Norwegian Mission in 1912, Jenson saw an opportunity to inaugurate a new era at the Historian's Office. He had been separated from his daily historical labors for three years, and with the distance came a renewed enthusiasm for recalibrating the office's priorities. He turned again to his longtime friend and supervisor Anthon H. Lund, whose time was split between his duties in the First Presidency and his role as Church

Historian. Jenson's new proposal differed very little from the one he had sent the First Presidency almost six years earlier, and Lund met Jenson's call for a transformation with hesitation. The counsel back to Jenson from the First Presidency would follow a similar line for the next decade: "I told him that I want him to get at the notes which he has gathered and have them translated, for none but him can do it."[5] By "translated," Lund meant transcribing Jenson's hastily written historical summaries into readable form. Most of Jenson's summaries had been quickly scrawled on poor-quality scraps of paper while he was on the road. They were of immense historical value, but only Jenson as the author could read and interpret them correctly. Before the First Presidency would consider placing a larger team of clerks at his disposal to prepare manuscript histories, Jenson needed to get his own historical work in order.

Without Lund's support, Jenson tabled his proposed systemization of Historian's Office projects for a time, but by March 1913 he decided to press Lund again for changes to the office's priorities. This time the Church Historian invited Jenson to put his recommendations on paper, which he did.[6] In the report—which displayed Jenson's intention to make his longtime manuscript projects the central work of the Historian's Office—he listed the "the work to be done in systematic order at the office": the "Journal History," which included "histories of the general quorums of priesthood, auxiliary organizations, church emigration, etc."; histories of every stake ("about eighty in number") and ward ("about eight hundred in number, counting those which exist no longer"); and histories of every mission of the church. By this point, Jenson had brought the "Journal History" up to 1852 and compiled manuscript histories of the British and Scandinavian missions. Through the effort of compiling the "Journal History," he analyzed and ordered his notes through the year 1852. He had also systematically combed through the other two thousand documents (up to 1852) that he had gathered on his travels, as well as the office's extensive periodical holdings, private journals, and correspondence. The procedures for drafting comprehensive manuscript histories as Jenson imagined were now established, but he needed more resources.

Inefficiencies apparently abounded at the Historian's Office, slowing the work. Jenson also observed divisions in the staff. The ecclesiastical business of Lund and Joseph Fielding Smith often took them away from their Historian's Office responsibilities, and B. H. Roberts often separated himself from the other Assistant Church Historians and retreated to another building while authoring a comprehensive Latter-day Saint history for the *Americana* magazine. A few of the clerks at the Historian's Office spent time working for the Genealogical Society of Utah. The remaining clerks indexed, clipped, and typed for the Historian's Office, working on assignments that included Jenson's own publications and projects.[7]

Jenson, however, was not left completely alone to accomplish his work. Behind the preparation of his histories, including a new edition of his *Church Chronology* (1914), were several female clerks who clipped newspapers, read and transcribed documents, and typed from dictation or from draft copies. Between the end of the Civil War and the start of the twentieth century, women flocked to clerical wage work, aided by technological advances in the typewriter.[8] The Historian's Office was no different. Since the 1870s, the Historian's Office relied on female clerks to help prepare manuscript histories. These women usually conformed to a strict set of social and cultural norms—they were most often young, unmarried, and childless. They rarely wrote about their work, but the archival holdings of the Historian's Office bear their imprint.[9] In the early twentieth century, longtime clerk Larinda Pratt Weihe marked papers for clipping for the new "Journal History."[10] The process gave Weihe a measure of intellectual control over the scope and breadth of the scrapbook history. In October 1913, as Jenson prepared ward and stake histories, Weihe worked on his *Chronology*, Bertha Emery typed, and Tamar Gunson and Paula Halvorsen clipped and scrapped from documents and newspapers, presumably for the "Journal History."[11] Jenson told Lund that the work of these women had been "a perfect revelation to me, and with more such workers we can accomplish something."[12]

With limited institutional resources, laboring at the Historian's Office also became something of a family affair. At times, Jenson was assisted with his personal publications by his son Parley as well as Emma, Bertha, and his daughters Minerva and Eva. Much of the Jenson family participated in late nights of bookkeeping, typesetting, proofreading, transcribing, and typing. Jenson also welcomed Minerva and Eva into the Historian's Office to type and perform other necessary tasks as clerks.[13] At the time of his request to Lund in 1913, Jenson's son Harold served as Jenson's immediate assistant.[14] Though giving his family members preferential treatment by hiring them was certainly a form of nepotism, which Jenson despised in others, the practice was not uncommon in the Historian's Office. Other Assistant Church Historians took a similar hiring approach.[15] Since Lund did not significantly expand the Historian's Office workforce in 1913, Jenson relied heavily on the diligent labor of a small staff of female clerks and his own family to move his projects forward.

Publications and Challenges

Despite repeated calls from Lund for him to get his notes in order, Jenson remained focused on his publishing projects and over the next seven years released a new edition of his *Church Chronology* (1914) and two new volumes of the *Latter-day Saint Biographical Encyclopedia* (1914, 1920). Jenson was an expert at repurposing and expanding previous historical projects. His *Biographical*

Encyclopedia, for instance, was created from an ongoing column of biographies of prominent church members published in his *Historical Record*. In 1888, he issued a supplement to the *Historical Record* titled "Biographical Encyclopedia," containing approximately three hundred biographies of Salt Lake City church leaders.[16] That initial work inspired a larger project of nearly seven hundred biographies—the *Latter-day Saint Biographical Encyclopedia* (1901)—which focused on the "prominent men and women in the Church of Jesus Christ of Latter-day Saints."[17] His expanded encyclopedia also drew on Orson F. Whitney's biographical work for the fourth volume of *History of Utah* (1904), which had largely been prepared by 1901.[18]

The first volume of Jenson's encyclopedia laid out the scope of his multivolume project. The handpicked list for his first volume included "General Authorities of the Church, Presidents of Stakes and their counselors, Presidents of Seventies, missionaries, Utah Pioneers of 1847, members of Zion's Camp and the Mormon Battalion, martyrs for the Gospel's sake, prisoners of conscience sake, and other historical and active men and women, both dead and alive, who have taken part in public affairs among the Latter-day Saints."[19] To those still living who met his criteria, Jenson mailed a circular and invited them to furnish a personal sketch. This enabled him to serve mostly as editor rather than author, though he still had to produce some original content for his series. Jenson at one point estimated that naive church members were paying scheming biographers in the range of $75 to $500 for poor-quality life sketches.[20] Instead, patrons of his *Biographical Encyclopedia* retained some authorial control over their sketches and could therefore feel confident in their quality and accuracy. For $5.00 ($2.50 up front and $2.50 at the time of delivery), patrons could have their sketch published and receive a copy of the volume.[21]

Similar to his *Church Chronology* (1899), Jenson hoped that wards and stakes, as well as church auxiliaries like the Sunday School and Mutual Improvement Association, would purchase the encyclopedia for their own libraries. Turning a profit on his subscription-based publications was always a challenge, and the *Latter-day Saint Biographical Encyclopedia* proved no different. With Jenson frequently away, his son Parley (age twenty-two in 1901) acted as his business manager. Parley and, later, Jenson's son-in-law Alvin E. Olson frequently pursued delinquent accounts. At times Jenson refused to publish sketches for those with unpaid accounts. This hard-line approach limited the scope of his first two volumes mainly to those who could afford to pay.[22] Efforts to collect on delinquent accounts or pledged funds, however, were often ineffective, which caused Jenson to devise promotions (including offering a copy of volume 1 instead of the delayed volume 2) to defray printing costs.[23]

The success of Jenson's publications stood at the mercy of the members of wards and stakes, and, as usual, he overcalculated consumer interest in his work.

He regularly sent letters to local leaders asking for their support in compiling and selling copies of the *Latter-day Saint Biographical Encyclopedia*.[24] He also petitioned the church to assume control of the *Latter-day Saint Biographical Encyclopedia* in August 1914, as he contemplated work on a third volume in the series. The church firmly declined but agreed to issue an endorsement of his work.[25] Repeated attempts to gift control of his series to the church in 1915 and 1916 also failed as he stared down a sizable printing debt on volume 2.[26] Jenson believed the economic benefit of his project was clear. He valued his collection of biographies at over $20,000 and claimed the collection spared Historian's Office staff from "days" of "hunting up the information which now is ready at hand."[27] After Jenson's repeated pleas for assistance, the First Presidency in January 1919 finally approved $1,000 to aid in volume 3's publication but reemphasized the individual nature of the project. Their financial support was offered in part to encourage Jenson to refocus on his primary role at the Historian's Office; the publication of the third volume was not to "interfere with or curtail" his work in placing into "readable form the notes taken . . . in [his] travels."[28] A complete edition of the third volume was not off the press until 1920, six years after the project started.[29]

The extra funding went toward publishing sketches of people who either could not afford to pay their account or who had died but were noteworthy enough to warrant inclusion in the edition.[30] Jenson was thrilled with the financial aid, interpreting it as a clear sign that his ecclesiastical leaders saw enormous value in his historical work. And despite the financial challenges related to his publishing ventures, Jenson's family finances remained relatively stable. His salary for his work at the Historian's Office rose to $2,405 a year by 1918. Jenson also maintained various real estate and stock investments from which he drew modest yearly gains.[31] The financial challenges related to the publication of the *Latter-day Saint Biographical Encyclopedia* were wholly confined to his private venture, the Andrew Jenson History Company, which oversaw the publication. His debts for volumes 1 and 2 nearly surpassed $2,000 in 1918, with hundreds of the 3,200 volumes still unsold.[32] The stress of publishing volume 3 ultimately forced Jenson to the "end of [his] rope" mentally and financially, and he verbally committed to the First Presidency that the third volume would be his last in the series and his farewell to publishing in general (a promise he later reneged on with the release of volume 4 in 1937).[33]

The series was a remarkable achievement in its scope and detail even if it was not fully appreciated at the time of its publication. Over the course of three volumes, Jenson published approximately three thousand biographical sketches documenting the lives of the most prominent General Authorities and church officers as well as the lay men and women of the church. The volumes were a testament to Jenson's untiring focus on gathering history from all corners of the church and his relentless pursuit of, as Apostle James E. Talmage noted in his recommendation of the third volume, "fact and data relating to the men and women who have labored so faithfully in their varied callings and diversified ways . . . to the development of the Church, and of the building up of this part of the Land of Zion."[34] Without regard to time or cost, Jenson pushed forward with his publications, confident their value would be realized long after he was gone.[35]

Other publications also fought for Jenson's attention. The same year he released volume 2 of his *Latter-day Saint Biographical Encyclopedia* (1914), he also published another edition of his *Church Chronology*. He backed off the lofty print run of his 1899 edition, which of the twenty-five thousand copies printed had sold only fifteen thousand. He repurposed the unsold ten thousand copies for the 1914 edition, adding supplements that extended the timeline to 1913. The new volume sold for two dollars apiece.[36] Prior to the sale of the first edition, Jenson had transferred the rights to the *Chronology* over to President Lorenzo Snow, the church's trustee-in-trust.[37] The First Presidency maintained its interest in the profits from Jenson's new edition and encouraged "presidents of stakes, bishops, of wards, superintendents of auxiliary societies, presidents of quorums and of missions and of other organizations throughout the Church" to purchase the volume.[38] As with his first edition, Jenson intended the profits to go to a new Historian's Office, now formally under development since 1913 with the construction of the new Church Office Building (later known as the Church Administration Building). He also hoped to recover, through accelerated sales and reimbursement from church coffers, the costs of typesetting, printing, and traveling to promote the work; he was often forced to front these expenses himself.[39]

Seven months after he received the first copies of the new *Chronology* from the printer, Jenson noted that the book "without being pushed sells very slowly."[40] He solicited the General Authorities for help, and they offered up another public endorsement of his work.[41] Jenson was accustomed to promoting his publications as he traveled to quarterly conferences throughout Utah. It appeared, however, that the general membership was growing weary of the push to buy copies of the *Chronology*. In March 1915, Apostle James E. Talmage received word that the "brethren in the Box Elder Stake were displeased because . . . Church Chronology was being pushed" too forcefully. Jenson's techniques used to advertise both his *Chronology* and the *Latter-day Saint Biographical Encyclopedia* had finally exhausted the patience of stake president Oleen N. Stohl. According to Stohl, the wards objected "to being agents to sell and buy books that are the personal property of one individual." To underscore his refusal to further promote the work, Stohl commented, "I have never undertaken any small thing, as I regard this, that has taken so much of my time, and been so annoying to me."[42] After Stohl's complaint, Talmage visited Jenson at the Historian's Office and encouraged him to tone down his campaign. Jenson, feeling Talmage's "faultfinding spirit" was unwarranted, wrote a letter to the First Presidency questioning the sustainability of his historical enterprise given the lack of support or interest.[43]

Hoping to assuage the wounded Jenson with a larger venue to advertise his publications, church leaders offered him a speaking slot at the upcoming special priesthood meeting in April 1915, held in association with the annual general conference, but Jenson felt the subject would be more authoritatively and effectively addressed by the First Presidency. At the priesthood meeting, Presidents Charles W. Penrose and Anthon H. Lund gave their hearty endorsement of the *Church Chronology* and *Latter-day Saint Biographical Encyclopedia*. They reminded the audience that Jenson contracted no monetary benefit from his work on the *Chronology* and celebrated his $3,000 donation of profits to the Historian's Office building fund.[44]

From the perspective of those outside the Historian's Office, the financing of Jenson's projects, including his travels, was always murky. He operated the Andrew Jenson History Company as a separate and private venture, but his day-to-day work showed little distance between his labor for the Historian's Office and his personal publications. The lack of distance created some confusion about the expenses Jenson incurred in the course of his work. For example, in August 1917, Jenson wrote a letter to the First Presidency requesting reimbursement for traveling expenses created by his multiple missions to Scandinavia and his regular travels gathering records for the Historian's Office from 1888 to 1905, a total that surpassed $3,000 by his calculation.[45] In the past, he had received multiple reimbursements for work he did on his *Church Chronology*, including compensation for travel associated with its promotion. His own family members—Parley, Minerva, Eva, and Bertha—who worked on the volume also received compensation.[46]

He perhaps had pushed too far in his appeal, however, which triggered a rare audit of his tithing receipts by David A. Smith, a member of the Presiding Bishopric. All faithful church members—by divine commandment—were expected to donate a tenth of their income to the church, but Jenson's deductions and reimbursements complicated matters. The Presiding Bishopric investigated and determined that, even if the proposed tithing credit was granted for Jenson's traveling expenses, he was still delinquent in his tithing by $1,400.[47] The report was shared with the First Presidency and prompted a detailed defense from Jenson, who was well prepared as a meticulous record keeper. He calculated that through 1917 he had been paid $44,784.05 in total salary for his historical work.[48] In addition, he received $3,255 in reimbursements for expenses incurred for recent travel, for work on the *Church Chronology*, or for other miscellaneous items.[49] Since 1888, Jenson's account books showed that he had accumulated over

$4,000 in traveling expenses alone between the years 1888 to 1905.[50] "I invariably paid for my own transportation except in one instance, in 1904, when I was sent back to Denmark to republish my history of the Prophet Joseph Smith in the Danish language," Jenson wrote to the First Presidency in May 1918. "Not one dollar was either asked for or furnished to me in any manner whatsoever as family expenses, aside from my regular allowance. . . . On the eight missions which I have filled for the Church I have, like other missionaries, borne my own expenses except in a few instances."[51]

According to an earlier inquiry into his tithing record, Jenson automatically deducted any uncompensated travel expenses from the tithing he owed and then paid the difference to the church. This method convoluted the tithing record for the church employee, whose regular stipend was known to church authorities. To clarify matters, from 1906 onward Jenson received annual reimbursements for expenses incurred while he was on church business, for which he did not pay tithing; he paid tithing on only his regular income.[52] The new approach, however, failed to resolve the sizable amount of expenses Jenson had not been reimbursed for before the change in payment method.

The new inquiry into his tithing record caused Jenson "serious reflection" about his value to the institution, since he viewed the financial burden he bore in the early years of his career as a noble sacrifice for the church's sake. For most of his early tenure at the Historian's Office, "including the years 1895–97," nearly 100 percent of his salary from the church, by his calculations, went to offset his traveling expenses. At that time, prior to his call as Assistant Church Historian, both Jenson and church leaders understood his regular stipend as compensation for both wages and extraneous work expenses. But after being appointed as Assistant Church Historian, Jenson's understanding had evolved, in part because he had received reimbursement on occasion for expenses incurred while on church business. And though his finances were stable, he still carried close to $3,000 in debt and surplus copies of the *Latter-day Saint Biographical Encyclopedia*.[53] The outstanding tithing credit that he felt was owed to him by the church—$3,285.15—was more than enough to cover his printing debt. But Jenson remained more concerned that he did not "go down into history as a man who has not paid a conscientious tithing."[54]

The inquiry into Jenson's tithing record caused Jenson to question his future relationship with church leadership: "If such a thing can happen now, when I think I can class all the members of the First Presidency as my close and personal friends, what may not happen when 'another Pharoah [*sic*] may arise who knows not Joseph.'"[55] Jenson eventually met with Presidents Penrose and Lund to sort out the affair and was assured that his tithing record "should be corrected in a manner that was right and should be satisfactory to [him]."[56] Nonetheless, Jenson was increasingly guarded about how a less supportive First Presidency in the future might impact his historical projects and personal finances.

Modernizing Historical Work

A wave of change swept over the church in the latter part of the nineteenth century and accelerated at a quicker pace post the plural-marriage Manifesto in 1890. The trappings of a theocracy in the Great Basin were shelved over time as Latter-day Saint economic cooperation, political uniformity, and state control yielded to a more formal embrace of American political, economic, and government structures. This era of assimilation, as many have called it, roughly coincided with a period of rapid change within the larger US nation, characterized by urbanization, industrialization, and unfettered capitalism. The church modernized in the twentieth century in ways that paralleled the quest for rational order, bureaucracy, and administrative control in US government and corporations.[57] What Jenson witnessed over the first four decades of the twentieth century was an expansion in church administration that placed the church presidency increasingly distant from the day-to-day operations of its auxiliaries. Such a move had a critical effect on Jenson, who frequently sought the ear of the First Presidency to validate his own work and to air grievances about the current functions of the Historian's Office. Complexity in the procedures and administrative structure at church headquarters grew subtly over time, but the church's development into a modern organization made Jenson anxious about his place within the expanding institution. He frequently searched for signs that his work had both a function and place at church headquarters.

As the sole field laborer at the Historian's Office, Jenson also sought to update his own method of work. Faithfully visiting and collecting records from every settlement of the Latter-day Saints remained a significant goal for him, but such a task seemed ambitious if not impractical as the church continued to grow. He, however, saw no other way to fill out his historical accounts of the stakes, wards, and missions of the church. Since such work required traveling to far-flung towns to interface with old Latter-day Saints and longtime settlers, modern transportation proved invaluable in helping him achieve his historical aims.

Accustomed to traveling first by foot and horse and buggy and then by train to his many domestic destinations, the advent of the automobile offered Jenson new mobility and revolutionized how he performed his duties. Despite fronting most of the expenses for his publishing projects, Jenson's salary for his work at the Historian's Office and his investments provided enough disposable income to purchase his own vehicle in April 1915. Moderately priced automobiles were commonplace during this period, and many Americans of modest means sacrificed hard-earned wages for the freedom that cars provided.[58] Jenson opted for a mid-level touring car from REO Motor Car for $1,000 and began taking driving lessons.[59]

When he made his first domestic tour of ecclesiastical units beginning in 1891, he did so slowly, by train and by team and buggy. For two months of that trip, from September to October 1891, Jenson visited the stakes and settlements in Wyoming and Idaho, traveling 599 of the 639 total miles by buggy.[60] He commenced a nearly identical trip in 1918, this time using his own car. His first trip included a visit to twenty-nine settlements, but on this occasion, over the span of two months, from June to July 1918, he reached "nearly all the [167] wards and branches of the Church in 14 Stakes of Zion" scattered throughout Idaho and Wyoming. He traveled "about 2750 miles" almost entirely by automobile.[61] The trip was not only a manifestation of the substantial growth of the church in Idaho and Wyoming but also an indication that advancements in transportation better equipped him to travel and collect historical details about the domestic settlements of the church.

Despite improved travel conditions, the schedule Jenson kept on the road was still arduous and ambitious. He was quite aware of how the general church membership occasionally perceived his travels. At general conference in 1926, he reflected: "Sometimes, when I visit some of the stakes of Zion in the interest of history, I am looked upon as a sort of Rip Van Winkle, or some ancient of days, who has been asleep for twenty years, or more, and it seems as if some people are actually annoyed by it." A lone wanderer, a solitary figure stuck in the past and out of touch with the present—these were the caricatures of Jenson that stemmed from his aggressive approach in hawking his publications and proclaiming the importance of the Historian's Office.[62]

In 1917, an opportunity came that would underscore for Latter-day Saints that Jenson served a vital function within the maturing church administration. In September, Church President Joseph F. Smith invited Jenson on an official automobile tour of Utah's southern settlements. The party included President Smith and his wife Mary, President Anthon H. Lund of the First Presidency, as well as President Heber J. Grant, who presided over the Quorum of the Twelve. Apostles Joseph Fielding Smith and Stephen L. Richards and their wives, Ethel and Irene, respectively, were also on the trip, as were members of the Presiding Bishopric Charles W. Nibley and David A. Smith and their wives, Julia and Emily. Clarissa Beesley, secretary of the Young Ladies' Mutual Improve Association, was also present. The group, including children, numbered twenty-nine.[63]

The festiveness of the occasion and the historic nature of the trip was not lost on any of the participants. Until his death in 1877, President Brigham Young had made regular visits to southern Utah during his presidency to preach to church members and inspect their settlements.[64] Though other church presidents continued the tradition, they had not traveled there as frequently in recent years, a realization that prompted President Smith to make the journey. Smith announced that his present journey had no stated purpose other than to make the church authorities visible to the members.[65]

Jenson was invited with Frank W. Otterstrom, a church reporter, to document the historic trip. Like his visits to quarterly conferences in stakes throughout the church, Jenson spoke multiple times and gathered historical details from southern Utah's residents after meetings were adjourned.[66] The trip proved successful on both fronts, and it also helped legitimize the Assistant Church Historian in the eyes of his fellow church members. Though he often rode in the last car (known as "the baggage car"), away from the rest of the party of dignitaries, Jenson's journey south was an opportunity to visit southern Utah in an official capacity and to be seen alongside the church's highest officers.[67] At each stop, the cars were swarmed by onlookers—children lined the streets, bands and choirs serenaded the travelers, and large feasts were prepared. Though Jenson had often relied on the generosity of church members on his previous tours, in neither his private ventures nor his work for the Historian's Office had such a festive welcome been afforded him as he traveled.[68]

A New Building for the Historian's Office

The widely reported automobile trip and other such opportunities signaled that the work of the Historian's Office had achieved more visibility. Though at general conferences Jenson often felt like the lone voice committed to fostering better record-keeping procedures, his leaders were increasingly exhibiting more institutional support for the work of the Historian's Office. For nearly two decades, Jenson pushed for new work accommodations, citing poor conditions in the current office located in a retrofitted pioneer home on South Temple Street. His initial proposal was tabled as the church attempted to get on more solid financial footing, but by 1913, discussion about a new Historian's Office was revived. President Lund finally acknowledged Jenson's requests for more space and resources. In a letter to Jenson in February 1913, he wrote "I am in hopes that we shall get the new Historian's Office built, and then we can get a larger force located so that they can be used to advantage. I believe this will be done in the near future. It certainly is a necessity."[69] Lund was already aware of discussions underway to erect a new office building for church administration in which the Historian's Office would be located.[70] And on April 26, church leaders announced their plans for the spacious, new Church Office Building.[71]

Lund effectively relayed the wishes of the Historian's Office staff to his ecclesiastical peers and communicated his own anxieties (and those shared by Jenson) about the state of record preservation to those supervising the construction of the new building on 47 East South Temple Street, across the street from the old Historian's Office.[72] At general conference in October 1917, after the building had been finished, Lund described his feelings about the new administration

Andrew Jenson at the cornerstone-laying ceremony for the Church Office Building located east of the Temple Block in Salt Lake City, May 19, 1915. Courtesy Church History Library.

Andrew Jenson with staff on the upper floor of the old Historian's Office, 1917. (Left to right) John Powell, A. William Lund, Larinda Pratt Weihe, Anthon H. Lund, Harold Jenson, Andrew Jenson, and Alvin Olson. Courtesy Church History Library.

building and Historian's Office: "I have often been anxious about the precious documents, letters and books that we have in the Historian's office. If we should have been unfortunate enough to have had a fire and to lose them we could never have restored the loss, and I am therefore happy now that we have these splendid collections of historical matters pertaining to the Church placed in a safe building."[73]

The entire fifth floor of the new fire- and flood-proof structure was devoted to "a stack room for records and files and as it entirely surrounds the light well there is ample light and ventilation." The building's designer, former church architect Joseph Don Carlos Young, was confident the upper floors would provide both the Historian's Office and the Genealogical Society of Utah "room ample to supply all their needs as a stack room for files and records."[74] The new principal location for the Historian's Office was on the third floor and provided the staff with a sizable and modern workspace. Two entire rooms were devoted to the Historian's Office library; the "main working room" spanned three rooms; in addition, staff had access to a supply room, which also served as office space for Assistant Church Historian A. William Lund. The Church Historian and the other Assistant Church Historians were given individual offices; Jenson occupied the southeast corner office.[75]

The new Historian's Office ended Jenson's long quest for an updated space; he had been pushing for it ever since he was sustained as Assistant Church Historian in 1898. In late February 1917, he moved into his new workplace. He spent the remainder of the day organizing his papers, and when the office staff had departed for the day, he "engaged in secret prayer opening my heart to my heavenly father." Jenson's feelings on this "memorable occasion" were offered up in gratitude for the progress of the church's historical work, but also in sober recognition of the challenges still in front of him.[76] Jenson was indeed thankful for a better preservation space for his life's work, but he also understood that the safe housing of records was only half of his job. Only a week after the move, his focus turned back to compiling a complete written record of church history: "Thus, I am now ready for active work better than ever, but it remains to be seen whether the work will continue to drag through lack of much needed help, or thro' the positions occupied by those who do not care whether the work progresses or not."[77] Providing a hint as to whom his simmering frustration was directed, Jenson followed this statement by mentioning regrets about his longtime friend and Church Historian: "Pres. [Anthon] Lund visits us very seldom indeed."[78]

His lament about President Lund suggested a lingering divide in the Historian's Office as it ushered in a new era. Certainly, Lund was instrumental in securing the Historian's Office a new home in the Church Office Building and frequently represented Jenson's complaints to the First Presidency. He was

Jenson's chief advocate and counselor and often calmed the tenacious Dane's frustrations with the bureaucratic sluggishness of church administration. When Jenson's ego was injured by a seeming injustice in his professional work, Lund was able to steady his friend's emotions. For example, on a trip to the Sanpete Stake in mid-March 1917, Jenson crossed Apostle James E. Talmage, his companion on the trip. "Bro. Talmage thinks 'he is it' and has no consideration of other peoples feelings apparently," Jenson wrote in his journal. The two had an argument on the return journey in which Jenson "spoke to Bro. Talmage about his treatment of [him] on this trip and on a former occasion." Talmage, his temper provoked, "utterly astonished" Jenson "with some very insulting remarks." When the train pulled into Salt Lake City, the now irate and hurt Jenson "hastened to Pres. Anthon H. Lund and reported the whole affair to him in detail." "I feel that I do not deserve such treatment from anyone and especially not from an Apostle," he complained.[79]

If anyone understood the sensitivities of working with one as passionate as Jenson, it was Lund, but Lund, at the behest of President Joseph F. Smith, had apparently drawn a line between himself and his Scandinavian friend. Lund continued to insist that Jenson compile his many travel notes into a readable format before placing more resources at his disposal or allowing him to pursue other projects. The First Presidency was so anxious that Jenson get his notes in order that they assigned Lund to check in periodically with Jenson and then report on his progress. Though the First Presidency promised to address the staffing shortage at the Historian's Office, no progress was made on that front throughout 1917.[80] And Jenson, who foresaw no end to his work, especially without more resources, saw Lund's absence in the day-to-day work of the office as a clear sign he was out of touch with the modern needs of the office.

By the close of 1917, Jenson had "prepared the history in part of many of the Stakes of Zion with all their Wards ready to be read to the old settlers for their approval."[81] This he would do in the ensuing years. For the time being, Jenson was coming to grips with the inequities he perceived surrounding his employment. The year before he wrote in his journal a sobering account of his employer: "it seems that many of those employed by the Church in different departments have only one ambition, namely, to draw their monthly salaries; they seem to have no conception as to returning equivalents to the Church in faithful labor." Jenson was working, by his estimation, twelve- to sixteen-hour days, and he was confident that with more employees "that would at least work 7 hours a day faithful and true, our work at the Historian's Office would have told a different story for past years."[82] But little changed over the next year, causing Jenson to predict that though "apparently not much more credit is given the diligent worker than the drones and parasites in the employ of the Church, there must come a day of just reckoning some time when the faithful shall receive their just dues." As for himself, Jenson believed he had "done a great deal of real hard historical work" and felt "quite satisfied with his labors."[83]

The situation was, however, less bleak than what he privately intimated. In an October 1917 general conference sermon, Lund publicly praised Jenson's record-keeping efforts: "Brother Andrew Jenson . . . is continually giving his mind to the work of collating and collecting data and facts concerning Church history. When he finds a new fact or a new date that he didn't know before, he feels as happy as the placer miner who finds a nugget of gold in the first pan that he washes out." He recommended the purchase of Jenson's *Church Chronology*, "a work that has cost immense labor" and "should be useful in every family."[84] Lund's public endorsement of Jenson's historical work gave him the approbation he longed for from his ecclesiastical leaders. But by this time, Jenson measured support for his historical work in more than public recommendations—something he had received periodically since he was an unaffiliated, private historian. He wanted the Historian's Office and his comprehensive ward, stake, and mission history project to work in tandem.

The Historian's Office had finally acquired modern facilities—a significant accomplishment that helped ensure its long-term survival and success—and its work was generally looked upon favorably by the presiding brethren. With the church on solid financial footing in the second decade of the twentieth century, institutional means to fund the work of the Historian's Office were more readily available than ever before, but they were often prioritized below other administrative projects.[85] As epitomized in his confrontation with the Presiding Bishopric over his tithing credit, Jenson often found it difficult to navigate the bureaucratic procedures and oversight endemic to an expanding institution. Persuading the General Authorities of the value of his projects and work amid a number of competing claims on the church's resources would remain a major hurdle for Jenson during the remainder of his long tenure at the Historian's Office.

It also became clear that as Jenson was winding up some of his long-term projects, he envisioned being somewhere other than the Historian's Office. Either because he was tiring of the bureaucracy at church headquarters or because he wanted to lend his talents where they were more appreciated, Jenson hoped that in the near future he could wrap up his "historical labors in behalf of others before I get to be an old man, so that I could have the privilege to make some little history for myself." He hinted in a letter to the First Presidency in January 1919 that he desired some formal call as a General Authority or as a worker "in other lines in the way of Church activities." "I have buried myself in old records and history until I sometimes feel that I have specialized too much in that line and have been too much confined to office work of late years," Jenson continued in his letter. "If my time, after I get my notes into shape . . . could be divided between office work and other outside Church duties, I believe my days would be lengthened out several years."[86]

Just several years earlier, Jenson had laid bare to the First Presidency the tenuous nature of his position. "I am frank to acknowledge to you that I have felt slighted on many occasions," he wrote to Joseph F. Smith in 1915. "I both am and am not one of the general authorities of the Church. I am just outside the circle. When the question is up for transportation—something that I need as much as any man in the Church—I am just outside the limit. If any invitations are issued for the General authorities to attend, I am again just where I am missed. If I attend any stake conference or any other important meeting, I am simply tolerated."[87] His ambiguous position as a church official left him feeling powerless before the people he was attempting to motivate toward better record-keeping practices.

Jenson, as a result, was finding a future in the Historian's Office less desirable. He cherished his close association with the First Presidency and frequently sought their guiding hand and approval for his projects, but such a luxury became less tenable as the church expanded and demands on church leaders increased. He pushed for updates to Historian's Office priorities but was also beset by the changes that surrounded him. His historical ambition was born in a past era of church administration in which he frequently had the ear of leaders Erastus Snow, Anthon H. Lund, or Franklin D. Richards. His close relationship with President Joseph F. Smith (through friendship and family ties) had also given him a steady ally in church leadership and cover to push for changes in his work. Church leaders had been accessible and responsive, if not always sympathetic, to his goals and requests. But Lund and Smith were both aging, which caused Jenson to ponder and forecast his future position within an expanding and changing bureaucracy. If his own plan for the Historian's Office was to be implemented or if he was to receive a new calling as a General Authority, the process needed to be set in motion by his closest ecclesiastical allies.

The Death of Joseph F. Smith

President Joseph F. Smith opened the October 1918 general conference with a brief address confirming what the public already knew: "I have been undergoing a siege of very serious illness for the last five months." During that period, he was intermittently bedridden and showed few signs of improvement leading up to the October churchwide gathering.[88] Jenson attended the session and, with the audience, greeted Smith's address with an impromptu rendition of "We Thank Thee, O God, for a Prophet," a popular Latter-day Saint hymn.[89]

Shorty after the conference, Jenson spent evenings at home reflecting on the prophet's life and drafting a biographical sketch for his friend and ecclesiastical leader. In a tribute published in the *Deseret News* to commemorate the anniversary of Smith's sustaining as Church President, Jenson reflected: "Prest. Joseph F. Smith is greatly beloved and though at this time he is ill, the hearts and prayers of the people are with him."[90]

Smith's extended illness occurred at a time when Utah and the rest of the nation confronted a deadly outbreak of influenza. While Smith's symptoms stemmed from a persistent lung problem, the Salt Lake City area braced for the spread of the influenza virus, implementing quarantines and restricting large public gatherings.[91] The outbreak reached Jenson's own family. His daughter Eva lingered on the verge of death for a week and her husband, Alvin, also became gravely ill from the virus.[92]

Even with the health restrictions in place, to celebrate the conclusion of the Great War on November 11, 1918, residents poured into Salt Lake City's streets with "their automobiles, tin cans, bells, tin pans and everything imaginable that could make a noise."[93] Jenson went to the Historian's Office to celebrate and "exchanged handshakes with Presidents Lund, Penrose and Grant" and the other staff members.[94]

The excitement of the week's events, however, was disrupted by the news on November 19 of President Smith's death due to complications from pneumonia.[95] The loss of Smith greatly affected Jenson; Smith had clerked in the Historian's Office early in his adulthood and seemed to appreciate Jenson's work there more than other General Authorities. Smith presided over the church during almost the entirety of Jenson's career as Assistant Church Historian. In addition, Smith had commissioned Jenson for a series of missions to Denmark—and made a historic visit to the country during Jenson's mission presidency—and supported his publications and historical work. The two were also connected through the marriage of Jenson's son Harold to Joseph F. Smith and Edna Lambson's daughter Martha Smith and thus had frequent occasion to mix at social events.

Smith's death marked the ending of a significant chapter in Jenson's own life. Heber J. Grant, Smith's successor, knew less about Jenson and less about the Historian's Office than the prior administration. As Jenson remembered the life of Smith, and pondered his own future, one institutional development stood out as a lasting symbol of the prophet's presidency: the new Church Office Building, a modern monument to "the stability, steadfastness, and fair dealing characteristic of Prest. Joseph F. Smith."[96] Jenson relished the physical placement of the Historian's Office within the concrete borders of church administration. For the Danish American historian, such a reminder that his record-keeping work belonged at the core of the church would sustain him in the ensuing decades.

9 Explorer of Latin America

"At the beginning of this another new year I feel, that something important is going to happen in the experience of my life," wrote Andrew Jenson on New Year's Day, 1921. "I am now seventy years old . . . and I have always said that when I reached that age there would be some change in my life's activities. I am not going to withdraw from work with the intention of spending the rest of my life in idleness, but I do not expect to rush through as if I had not a moment to spare." In contrast to past eras in Jenson's life, the historian was now "quite comfortable financially." Through returns on various property deals, stock and bond investments, and savings accounts, Jenson had at last amassed a comfortable living.[1] Now that he no longer had to worry about feeding his family, his persistence and motivation stemmed simply from a commitment to the historical work of the church. He also feared that if he relaxed, he might slip into irrelevance as his age advanced.

Jenson was anxious about possibly being put out to professional pasture or cheated of future promotions that he felt he deserved for his past three decades of labor in the Historian's Office. He continued: "I am not fearful of the Lord, but sometimes in my past experiences in life I have been forced to believe that some of my brethren above me in the priesthood have done me injustice and have side-tracked me when they should have encouraged me or smoothed my pathway. But . . . by God's help I mean to continue faithful to the end, whatsoever the future may have in store for me."[2] After recording this sentiment, however, events would transpire that would test Jenson's resolve to follow his ecclesiastical superiors and his willingness to swallow his professional pride and abandon his worldly ambitions.

On January 11 Jenson wrote the entire First Presidency—now Heber J. Grant, Church Historian Anthon H. Lund, and former Assistant Church Historian

Charles W. Penrose—giving them an overview of his progress and accomplishments. Since the death of President Joseph F. Smith, Jenson felt a widening divide between him and his senior ecclesiastical leaders, particularly President Grant. Without their clear blessing of his work, Jenson stated that he would prefer to serve a mission or retire to some other useful avocation. Since serving as mission president almost a decade ago, he had been "subject to a continuous 'grind' dealing with 'musty' records and books."[3] To keep his enthusiasm for his labors fresh, Jenson desired a temporary transition, and so he requested one.

As a sign that Jenson's fears of aging into insignificance were perhaps coming true, in January, the same month he wrote his letter to the First Presidency, he was replaced as the president of the Utah State Historical Society, which he had presided over since January 1917. His replacement was John A. Widtsoe, the president of the University of Utah, a fellow Scandinavian Latter-day Saint, and a future apostle. Apparently "a click of University professors manipulated the whole affair in their own interest," Jenson complained in his journal.[4] Jenson certainly possessed talent as a historian, but he was self-trained and had earned his credentials on the job. As the field professionalized, Jenson sat in tension with formal academics and intellectuals who showed less interest in his untrained, personal brand of history.

Within a week, Church Historian Lund with the rest of the First Presidency had devised a mission around North America for their workhorse historian. The contemplated trip would finish the global historical survey of the church that Jenson had begun decades ago.[5] Traveling again allowed Jenson to control his own itinerary and to visit areas in which he was seen as a prominent authority and representative of the church, a privilege he longed to have in Utah as well.[6] He also planned to make a trip to Mexico.[7] The tour would not only offer Jenson a needed break from the professional "grind" but also give the historian an opportunity to explore Central America.

Church History Mission to the US South and Mexico

On February 1, 1921, Jenson departed for his "special mission to the United States" to gather historical facts about church missions and regional church history.[8] His journey through the US South and central Mexico would last until mid-June of that year. Generally traveling by train, Jenson first rode the rails eastward through Colorado, Kansas, and Missouri, where he rendezvoused with Rey L. Pratt, president of the Mexican Mission and a grandson of Apostle Parley P. Pratt, who had evangelized in Chile in 1851.[9] From the Midwest, Jenson traveled southward into Texas, stopping over in the city of Kelsey, which had just been selected as a regional gathering place for Latter-day Saints in the Southern States Mission. Jenson finally made his way through Austin and San

Antonio, Texas, before reuniting with Pratt on February 26 at the El Paso train station, on the United States–Mexico border.

As Jenson had on his previous trips, he gathered documents everywhere he went and mailed them home to be used in preparing manuscript histories of the places he had traveled to. He visited local libraries and historical societies when his schedule and train timetables permitted. Whenever possible, he stayed in the guest bedrooms of mission homes or in the spare bedrooms of church members he met along the way to save money and to hear firsthand about their experiences as Latter-day Saints in the area. He also sent a number of letters back to the *Deseret News* detailing his travels, just as he had on earlier trips.[10] Before leaving Texas, Jenson mailed home all of the church history information he had gathered during the first month of his so-called sabbatical.

In the spring of 1921, Jenson found himself in El Paso with Pratt and a dozen missionaries for a historic moment: the reintroduction of Latter-day Saint missionary work in Mexico City and the surrounding regions.[11] When Latter-day Saints had initially settled the Great Basin in 1847, they were in Mexican territory, but that quickly changed with the conclusion of the Mexican-American War in 1848 and the ceding of territory to the United States. Missionaries did not reenter Mexico until after 1875, when church leaders sent seven missionaries to Mexico with translated selections of the Book of Mormon (*Trozos Selectos del Libro de Mormon*) to aid their proselytizing. Their principal goal was to search out and preach to the indigenous descendants of Book of Mormon peoples in Mexico, and the missionaries also located potential colonist sites for Latter-day Saint polygamists looking to escape prosecution in Utah.[12]

Latter-day Saint missionary work formally began in Mexico City in 1879, and missionaries established several branches in the capital city and served there until 1889. Proselytizing efforts in central Mexico then ceased for about a decade.[13] Federal raids on polygamists in Utah Territory diverted church leaders from focusing on missionary work in Mexico, though it led to streams of Latter-day Saint polygamists flowing southward out of the United States to resettle in Mexican territory. In 1901, missionary work resumed in Mexico only to be disrupted again by the Mexican Revolution (1910–17). Anglo missionaries in Mexico City and most members in the colonies were forced to abandon their homes in 1912. In the meantime, local Mexican members assumed leadership of the church's activities in the country.[14] By 1921, the revolution had been over for a few years and mission president Rey L. Pratt again hoped to send Anglo missionaries back across the border.[15]

Passports in hand, Jenson and Pratt and their missionaries soon crossed over the Rio Grande into Mexico and made their way to Ciudad Juárez, where they secured reservations for a train to Mexico City. They passed south through the major Mexican cities of Chihuahua, Durango, Zacatecas, Aguascalientes, and

Querétaro, observing the wartime ruins of the Mexican Revolution.[16] They arrived in Mexico City on March 4, having traveled over twelve hundred miles from El Paso. After Pratt and Jenson found lodging for the young missionaries, the two men made their way to the center of the Mexican capital, securing rooms in the downtown district at the Hotel Cosmos. Jenson was once again on-site for a historic moment in the development of the global church, but what he missed while he was away would arguably have a more immediate impact on his professional and personal life.

The Unexpected Death of the Church Historian

Comfortably settled in his Mexico City lodging, Jenson received a shocking telegram from his wife Emma, back in Salt Lake City. She informed him that President Anthon H. Lund (age seventy-six), Jenson's supervisor in the Historian's Office for over two decades, had passed away two days earlier, on March 2.[17] Jenson was stunned and saddened to learn of his longtime friend and mentor's death. He had sent a letter to Lund only a few days before updating the Church Historian on the historical fruits of his travels. Lund was the one who had called Jenson in January to serve this special mission to gather church history. It was Lund, a fellow Danish immigrant, who had championed so many of Jenson's projects and initiatives. From Emma's telegram, Jenson learned that Lund was to be buried the following Sunday in Utah, while Jenson would be traveling through Mexico, giving Jenson no chance to bid his dear friend a proper farewell.[18]

As Jenson continued to muse about the implications of Lund's passing and the unexpected possibilities for his own career, he poured out his mixed emotions in his journal. Would the closing of Lund's life be an opening for his own service as the next Church Historian and as a General Authority? "I wonder what effect Bro. Lund's death will have upon my own career or usefulness in the Church in the future! Will justice have sway and will God's will be done, or will merit be ignored and favoritism be displayed?"[19] Jenson was concerned that he would once again be passed over for this coveted post by someone with familial or ecclesiastical connections.

Overcome with conflicting emotions, Jenson nevertheless determined to leave his hotel room and see the sights around him in Mexico City.[20] Lund's death, however, had significantly disrupted Jenson's trip and prompted him to write "a short letter to Pres. Grant, asking him whether I should carry out the itinerary planned by Pres. Lund and myself, or come home as soon as possible."[21] If leadership of the Historian's Office were to transition, Jenson wanted to be home for it. Divided between a desire to fulfill his special mission and a hope to play a role in the leadership change, Jenson awaited a reply from Grant, hoping prophetic counsel would resolve his momentary emotional paralysis in Mexico.

Andrew Jenson in front of the San Pedro Mártir meetinghouse in Mexico City, 1921. Courtesy Church History Library.

Jenson and Pratt spent the next several days in Mexico City. That Sunday they held church meetings with the local branch and nearly one hundred Mexican Saints.[22] Church leaders had not yet summoned Jenson home to help eulogize Lund or to attend the graveside services. For Jenson, Grant's silence was deafening, suggesting that he had been forgotten now that he was away from headquarters. Nobody knew the current state of the Historian's Office or its future needs better than Jenson—he had been the de facto administrator of the office's holdings for years. Regardless, there was precedent for making administrative decisions in the Historian's Office in Jenson's absence. The First Presidency had called A. William Lund, for example, as an Assistant Church Historian in 1911 while Jenson was presiding over missionary work in Scandinavia.[23]

Despite his uneasiness about affairs back in Utah, Jenson found a renewed sense of importance in the situation unfolding before him. In an intimate setting with a dozen young missionaries in Mexico City, he gave parting wisdom to the gathered men before they scattered around the city to proselytize.[24] Outside of Salt Lake City, Jenson was viewed as an experienced church leader, traveler, and missionary whose value and experience were immediately recognized. The opportunity to train the first missionaries to serve in Mexico in over a decade brought Jenson temporary reprieve from his anxious thoughts about Lund's passing and the future leadership of the Historian's Office.

With the Mexican capital reopened to Latter-day Saint missionaries, Jenson bid farewell to Pratt and his young elders and departed from the capital city on March 9 by train, traveling to the port city of Veracruz on the Gulf of Mexico about 260 miles to the east. While in the vicinity of Veracruz, the farthest south he had ever been in Central America, and after visiting ancient Aztec and Olmec ruins, he prepared to head back to the United States.[25]

With his excursion into Mexico complete, Jenson sailed on the *Hollandia* about eight hundred miles across the Gulf of Mexico to New Orleans. The long stretch of misty saltwater in the gulf provided an occasion for contemplation: "In the evening I sat a long time on the deck alone with my thoughts," Jenson recorded. "Peculiar reflections passed through my mind with contemplation of my life's career, and before I knew of it I was reasoning and talking with myself and at last prayed in a subdued voice, laying my case before the Lord in humility and asking him to guide me aright and give me strength to bear whatsoever might be coming into my life. I am very anxious now to hear from home and get intelligence from the headquarters of the Church."[26] At the age of seventy, Jenson recognized this might be his last chance to formally lead the Historian's Office, and he wrestled with his lack of control over the situation.

The pattern of past appointments suggested that a current Assistant Church Historian would likely be promoted to the role of Church Historian. Jenson also knew, however, that ever since Apostle Willard Richards had been appointed as the first Church Historian in 1842 in Nauvoo, Illinois, all Church Historians had come from the Quorum of the Twelve. Several Assistant Church Historians had also been called to their positions after becoming an apostle, including Charles W. Penrose in 1904, Orson F. Whitney in 1906, and Joseph Fielding Smith in 1910. And B. H. Roberts, another one of Jenson's peers in the Historian's Office, had served as one of the Seven Presidents of the First Council of the Seventy since 1888. With no similar position in General Authority leadership, Jenson was feeling left behind.

After several days aboard the *Hollandia*, Jenson welcomed the sights of the Mississippi River Delta banks as the vessel steamed north to New Orleans, where he arrived on the evening of March 15 in dense fog. From the docks he made his way to the church's missionary lodging, where he met with four missionaries who helped him search the local library for newspapers relating to the Latter-day Saint migration through that city in the mid-nineteenth century.[27] He was also able to locate a recent issue of the *Deseret News* and read the account of Lund's passing and funeral. Jenson was also pleased to receive his first letter from home since leaving El Paso. But he was disappointed that there was still no communication from President Grant inviting him to return to Utah or encouraging him to continue his travels through the US South.

Lacking real-time guidance from church leaders, Jenson determined to follow his approved travel plan, which meant his absence from Utah would continue. From New Orleans, Jenson roughly followed the route of the Mississippi River north by railroad to Baton Rouge, Louisiana; Jackson, Mississippi; Memphis,

Tennessee; and Little Rock, Arkansas. He finally arrived in St. Louis, Missouri, on March 23. There he met with a half-dozen missionaries and was able to find lodging with a local Latter-day Saint family. Once he had made himself comfortable, Jenson traveled to the reading room in the downtown library to catch up on the national news. By this time, he had been absent from Utah for nearly two months.

A New Church Historian

While researching in the St. Louis Public Library, Jenson perused recent back issues of the *Deseret News*, eager to learn what had transpired in Utah in his absence. As he scanned through the issues, his eyes finally met a column in the March 17 issue that sent a shock through his system and confirmed his anxieties of the past few weeks. The report announced that Apostle Anthony W. Ivins had been called to replace Lund as a counselor in the First Presidency and that John A. Widtsoe had been appointed to fill Ivins's now vacant spot in the Quorum of the Twelve. Jenson approved of both callings, but he was devastated when he read that his fellow Assistant Church Historian, Apostle Joseph Fielding Smith, had been appointed as Church Historian. Smith had been selected along with Widtsoe at a council meeting of the First Presidency and Quorum of the Twelve on March 17.[28] In his mind, Jenson had already called himself to the position, but President Grant had chosen another.[29]

By most measures, the appointment of Apostle Smith as the next Church Historian made complete sense. He had worked in the Historian's Office as a clerk since 1901, following his early missionary service to Great Britain as a young man. Jenson had helped train the new clerk in the procedures of the Historian's Office. Smith's father, the late President Joseph F. Smith, had appointed him as one of the Assistant Church Historians in April 1906. Joseph Fielding's prophet-father had also called him to the apostleship in April 1910, at the age of thirty-three, making him the youngest member of the Quorum of the Twelve to be called in the twentieth century. Moreover, Smith had already published a great deal of church history and theology.[30] He was currently engaged in an ambitious project—writing a singular volume of church history that could be used as curriculum; the work would eventually be titled *Essentials in Church History* (1922). Young and engaging, Smith held many leadership traits that Jenson did not. Smith also showed more interest in producing consumable content for the church masses than in improving archival holdings or painstakingly compiling local and mission histories and chronologies—manuscripts that largely sat on shelves in the Historian's Office, unavailable to the general church membership. In many ways, Smith was the counterbalance to Jenson's brand of historical production. For most, the apostle was the natural choice to succeed

Lund, but Jenson continued to condescendingly view the late prophet's son as his neighbor boy, a subordinate clerk, a young staffer who was twenty-seven years his junior.

In his journal that night in St. Louis, Jenson poured out his frustration and anger. He noted the callings of Ivins and Widtsoe without emotion. But the third appointment—Smith as Church Historian—left him cold and confused:

> That latter appointment certainly seemed unjust to me who have labored faithfully these many years. . . . I have frequently wondered how much dignity and how much relationships and favoritism there is in some of these appointments. Why have I been sidetracked so repeatedly? Why this slight in the face of my known ability and activity in the historical field? . . . Way back in 1884 when my name was canvassed in connection with filling a vacancy in the First Council of Seventy, and I was sidetracked, the late Apostle Erastus Snow told me not to feel bad about it for the Lord had a better position reserved for me. . . . Yet, here I am, sidetracked once more, after a life-long struggle, during which I have given my best to Church work and have reserved nothing so far as I understand myself, for selfish motives. Is it wrong in the sight of the Lord for a man to expect reward or recognizance for real merit. Is there no such thing as appreciation when a man puts his whole soul into a work which is aimed at doing good and to benefit the cause of God and mankind generally.[31]

Jenson left the St. Louis library in a "solemn mood" and took a long walk along the banks of the Mississippi River, alone with his thoughts. He stopped by the post office to see if any mail was waiting for him, but there was no word from Utah. That evening he retired to his room and wrote letters to Emma and Bertha, along with missives to Joseph Fielding Smith and John A. Widtsoe.[32] In his letter to Bertha, he invited her to "come immediately to St. Louis" to join him on the rest of his itinerary as they had planned. He also hinted to his wife about "the possibility of [his] career as assistant Church historian being at an end." He knew that, at seventy years old, he was no longer a young man and would labor under Smith for the remainder of his career, a prospect that left him unsettled.[33]

Finally, on March 28, Jenson received word from church headquarters. Newly called First Presidency counselor Ivins, writing on behalf of President Grant who was then in California, "suggested that [Jenson] carry out [his] traveling program as outlined with Pres. Lund."[34] This instruction turned out to be a mixed blessing for Jenson. Though it made clear that his help was not required (or wanted) to manage the transition in the Historian's Office, it also gave him the needed distance to process his injured feelings. Bertha arrived on March 30 and brought more unhappy news from Utah. A cousin had been staying with the family in Jenson's absence and had infected those in the house with measles, and his son Andrew had run afoul of the law again by stealing sheep. "Both Emma and Bertha had had a very hard time of it since I left home and our house had been more like a hospital than a home," Jenson wrote in his journal.[35]

As was his custom, Jenson turned to the Latter-day Saint past for peace. "I was soon buried in historical labors in St. Louis."[36] He and Bertha spent the next several days together gathering church history materials in Missouri until they departed on April 6 and headed to Atlanta, Georgia, to the headquarters of the Southern States Mission. President Charles Callis accompanied the Jensons throughout the mission, visiting church congregations in Alabama, Florida, South Carolina, North Carolina, and Virginia. The party finally arrived in the nation's capital on April 28. In Washington they enjoyed an audience with President Warren G. Harding, thanks to an introduction from Utah senator Reed Smoot, and they toured the White House. Other highlights of their visit included a tour of the Library of Congress and a visit to George Washington's Mount Vernon.[37]

After touring the nation's capital, the Jensons visited the major cities of the Eastern States Mission, including Philadelphia and New York, where Jenson continued his historical research. They also toured church history sites. On their way back to Utah, the Jensons toured the Northern States Mission to gather church records, and they arrived in Salt Lake City on June 18, 1921. Jenson had been gone from the Historian's Office on his "special mission" for over four months.

Though the church history tour had allowed Jenson to mourn the loss of his imagined professional future in private, now that he was back in Utah, he steeled himself for some difficult conversations. "Having returned home, I am now prepared for whatever may happen," he wrote in his diary.[38] Jenson reached out to his colleague First Presidency counselor Charles W. Penrose, who was convalescing at home. Penrose and Jenson had known each other for several decades, and Jenson viewed him as a longtime friend, one of his few remaining connections in the church hierarchy.[39] Penrose gave Jenson a straight answer when asked why he had not been called as Church Historian. According to Jenson's retelling, Penrose "was almost too weak to speak, but he took great pains to explain to me how he felt in regard to the selection of the new historian, realizing full well that I was entitled to the position, but he begged of me to take it in good part, assuring me that everything would come out all right in the end. Pres. Grant only was responsible for the appointment." Jenson was frustrated but not surprised. Penrose's supposed deference to Grant in the decision, however, was not fully accurate. According to Grant's journal, both Ivins and Penrose expressed "favor" toward the selection of Joseph Fielding Smith as Church Historian as early as March 12.[40]

Regardless, this was not the first or last time that Jenson felt a lack of support from the church president. "For many years I have believed that Bro. Grant has not been interested in historical labors and consequently has not attached any importance to the work to which I have devoted almost my entire life," wrote Jenson. "I refrain from saying any more in writing at this time, but it remains to be seen or proven whether it is 'relation' or 'revelation' that has guided in this matter."[41] With no familial ties to those in the church hierarchy and as a hardworking Danish immigrant, Jenson believed he was self-made. Joseph Fielding Smith on the other hand, enjoyed every social and ecclesiastical advantage because of his lineage, and this, in Jenson's mind, had destroyed his own aspirations of being the Church Historian. As Jenson continued to be troubled by what he viewed as a trend of nepotism in General Authority appointments, he considered publicly opposing the selection of Smith: "I shall either have to grin, suffer and bear it, or come out in open rebellion against a policy that undoubtedly has caused thousands of people to sever their connection with the Church, namely, the ignoring of true merit and faithfulness and the elevating of mediocre men to high positions in the Church because they are somebody's sons or close relatives or special friends. . . . This is a hard pill for me to swallow."[42] The situation pointed Jenson toward a solution that he had contemplated numerous times in his career but had ultimately never executed—a complete exodus from church employment.

This weighty decision regarding his professional future ultimately placed Jenson on a collision course with Joseph Fielding Smith. On Sunday, June 26, Jenson spent the day at the Historian's Office "in prayer and meditation," preparing for "a long conversation with" Smith "in regard to Historian's Office matters," which was scheduled for the next day.[43] Through meeting with Smith, Jenson was likely attempting to get a sense of the direction Smith might take the Historian's Office and whether or not Jenson would be able to retain the freedom to work as he pleased. Smith was apparently conciliatory in hearing out Jenson's suggestions.

In a move of diplomacy, the July 1921 issue of the church magazine the *Improvement Era* featured a glowing article, written by James H. Anderson, on Jenson's accomplishments. The singularity of the Danish American historian's contributions to church history was noted in the title, "One Andrew Jenson." Anderson wrote: "Andrew Jenson's data and publications are history; they are as near accurate in statement of time, place and event, as human care and inquiry can make them. No man has done more—if any has done so much—in the cause of abundant and correct data for the Church records. He has traveled around the world, practically to every branch of the Church, in his duties as an Assistant Church Historian, and the same characteristic has attended all his efforts." The article continued, "It is not within the ability of man to measure now the full value of his contribution to this and the coming generations in the Church; but his example of aiming at accuracy in statements of history is one of the best that the youth of Zion can follow. It makes them feel safe, and gives to others confidence in their integrity, and purpose, and truthfulness."[44] Very pleased by the public praise, Jenson characterized Anderson's tribute as "one of the few bouquets which seldom come to a man more than once during a lifetime."[45]

Still, despite the public adulation, Jenson remained on the brink of departing from his life's work. The personal crisis he was mired in sharpened his assessment of his own legacy. Jenson sent a letter to the First Presidency to give them an overview of his accomplishments. If the new Church Historian was planning to implement a vision that conflicted with Jenson's, he was attempting to cut Smith off at the pass.

The letter appraised the state of record keeping around the globe and the state of the work of the Historian's Office, including the effort led by Jenson to compile a wide-ranging history of the church. Although the Committee on Records had attempted to reform and standardize record keeping in the early twentieth century, on his recent tour Jenson found that many of the conferences and branches he visited had "next to no records at all" preserving their history. "No general instructions seem to have been given in these missions regarding the proper keeping of records," reported Jenson, "and consequently each mission has its own system and has adopted methods according to the best judgment of the respective presidents and mission secretaries, without being in harmony with the plans adopted for church records generally." Given the ardent attempts at reform decades earlier, his findings were a disappointment. They also, however, highlighted his value to the church. Once again, he called for "a traveling historian to visit the different missionary fields . . . to give proper instructions in record keeping."[46]

As for what he had already accomplished, Jenson tallied 336 volumes of the Journal History, covering up to 1900; 67 volumes of stake and ward histories; 82 volumes of mission, conference, and branch histories; and 25 miscellaneous volumes. All of this work totaled 510 volumes of prepared manuscripts. Despite the magnitude of what Jenson had accomplished in organizing and creating these volumes, much was left to do. The extensive ground Jenson had covered across the globe and the records he had gathered along the way had created a backlog. Among the unassessed records were 1,300 hundred miscellaneous volumes, 50 letter books, 500,000 letters, 500 private journals, and 140 boxes of his own notes. In addition, according to Jenson's assessment, only he possessed the language skills necessary to handle the Scandinavian language material at the Historian's Office.

His lengthy recounting of the state of his work stemmed from his anxiety about the new leadership in the Historian's Office, which he confessed to the First Presidency. And his persistent angst was rooted ultimately in the fear that his life's work would be wasted. "I think elder Joseph Fielding Smith will endorse what I say, but whether he does so or not I feel that now is the proper time and place for me to speak and tell facts as they are," he wrote in his letter to the First Presidency. "I feel grieved," he confessed to the First Presidency, "to think that part of my life's labor should be thrown away so unnecessarily, and yet that is exactly what will happen, unless a thorough change is inaugurated at the Historian's Office."[47] The change Jenson advocated was not just the addition of a traveling historian and the appointment of a new records committee but also an expansion of the Historian's Office staff to give Jenson enough clerks to help him turn the raw historical material he had gathered in his travels into a comprehensive church history. He feared the entire system he had helped establish for record keeping globally and its historical returns was eroding unless significant attention was offered to it by the new Church Historian and the First Presidency, whom Jenson had yet to win as allies. Smith and the First Presidency saw things differently, however, and no immediate adjustments were made to the Historian's Office program in Smith's early tenure.

Jenson delivered a general conference address on Mexico and the Lamanites, a group of people in the Book of Mormon, that October, but despite his enthusiasm on the subject, that evening he went to bed disheartened. Within hours of retiring, however, he had a powerful spiritual impression. "Before going to sleep that night I felt somewhat depressed in my feelings. But in the night I had a remarkable dream, in which I thought I was climbing to a certain height, choosing a road, or a sort of cut-off, shorter than the one traveled generally; but just before reaching the top I was stopped, I thought, in a narrow stairway and could not extricate myself without calling upon friends for help," he described in his journal the following morning. "When I awoke the meaning of my dream came upon me like a flash to the effect that I had better remain in line, loyal and true as hitherto; if not, I might place myself in a position where I could not help myself." He concluded: "God is just, even if some of his representatives on earth are partial to their friends and unjust to others."[48] This dream helped him stay faithful to the church and its leaders and persist in his role at the Historian's Office.

An Advocate for Missionary Work in Latin America

Despite his frustrations with Grant's selection of Joseph Fielding Smith as Church Historian, Jenson had not forgotten his recent experiences in Mexico and the feelings they conjured about the ancient Book of Mormon peoples, whom Latter-day Saints believed were a branch of ancient Israelite lineage and the ancestors of present-day American Indians and peoples in Latin America. Latter-day Saints believed they had a divine mandate to share the gospel with the descendants of the Lamanites. On August 6, 1921, weeks after his special mission to the church's historic sites and missions and the Republic of Mexico,

Jenson visited a congregation at the Alpine Stake Tabernacle in American Fork, Utah, and "told of the future mission of the American Indian as referred to in the Book of Mormon."[49]

Furthermore, at the October 1921 general conference overflow meeting at the Assembly Hall in Salt Lake City, Jenson detailed his special mission to Mexico and added his voice to the already emerging conception that Central and South Americans were the modern-day Lamanites. He developed this view in part because of Book of Mormon prophecies that Lamanite descendants would be receptive to the gospel message; while early missionary efforts among the North American Indians had largely failed, the relatively recent Mexican mission, where he had just toured, was showing great promise. He related:

> The remnants of the House of Israel, now known as the North American Indians, have so far disappointed us to a certain extent. . . . We, therefore, cast a glance southward into old Mexico and through the great countries beyond—down through Central America and South America, where there are millions and millions of Lamanites. . . . I would further suggest that whenever the time comes that these Lamanites in the south shall embrace the gospel, there will be a sufficient number of them to fulfill every prediction contained in the Book of Mormon concerning the Lamanites.[50]

Jenson's predictive declarations at the October 1921 general conference launched his personal campaign to convince Latter-day Saint leaders to spread the gospel into what he and a growing number of others considered Book of Mormon lands in Central and South America.[51]

Jenson's speculation that Latin America was the location of ancient lands mentioned in the Book of Mormon was not new. Since the earliest years of the church, Latter-day Saints used scriptural passages, modern-day geography, and ancient American archaeology as a means to locate bygone Book of Mormon lands.[52] In the early twentieth century, some even organized expeditions to Central and South America to try to locate Book of Mormon places.[53] Both explorers and academics eventually created maps, which proposed various geographies within North, Central, and South America.[54]

During the October 1922 general conference, Jenson again addressed an overflow meeting outside the Salt Lake Tabernacle, speaking on the future of the Lamanites living in Latin America. His discourse repeated almost verbatim his statements from a year before.[55] The prospect of new converts to the south filled Jenson's imagination, and he felt an urgency to travel to South America to document the establishment of the church there. Informed by a biblical tradition, church record keeping included documentation of God's promises and their fulfillment; Jenson intended to record Book of Mormon prophecies as they were realized in Latin America.

A Latin American Expedition

By 1923 Jenson had long contemplated a trip to the capital cities of Latin America. His fascination with modern-day descendants of ancient Mesoamerica had continued to grow, stemming in part from his many years of studying the Book of Mormon, which he had been interested in since boyhood. He had read it over fifty times during his lifetime and revised its official Danish translation twice. The senior historian was thus well acquainted with the historical record of the ancient Nephites and Lamanites and believed that "to the Latter-day Saints it seems plain as daylight that some of" the ruins of Central and South America "are the remnant work of the ancient God-fearing and liberty-loving people called the Nephites."[56] Moreover, South America was one of the few continents that the Assistant Church Historian had never visited. The Latter-day Saint globetrotter looked forward to the chance to explore this terra incognita and add it to his map of world travels.

Jenson's longing to visit Latin America, coupled with his desire to compile historical information on early Latter-day Saints in California, culminated in a personal meeting and a written request to President Grant on January 5. His lengthy visit and letter included several offers and requests—to donate his large collection of books to the Historian's Office, to be refunded $10,000 from previous church history–related travels, and to take leave from his labors in Salt Lake City in order to enjoy a Central and South America trip.[57] After years of what he called "strenuous efforts" in gathering, compiling, and making inventory of the large collections of minute books, manuscripts, and other historic artifacts at the Historian's Office, Jenson found his "eyesight impaired and threatening to a degree of nervousness." He claimed he had never taken a vacation and believed that, to properly complete his life's work, he needed "to get a little change."[58] Jenson had already proposed at least two other expeditions in the last year—a mission call to Scandinavia and an automobile tour of the Mormon Trail—but all were declined in hopes that he would continue to put in order and analyze his personal notes and files so he could complete the manuscript histories of the church's ecclesiastical units.[59]

Once again, Jenson's desires and Grant's wishes were not aligned. Of Jenson's travel proposal, Grant journaled: "He is very anxious to make a trip to South America, also to South Africa. . . . I hardly think that it would be right for us to bear the expense of such a trip. Told him to put his desires in writing and I would submit them to the Brethren for consideration."[60] Grant, however, was simply placating his anxious historian. The First Presidency was not interested in using church funds to support Jenson's trips.

While awaiting a formal reply from Grant about his contemplated trip to Latin America, Jenson moved forward with his travel preparations. The following week he completed his medical evaluations, secured an updated passport, received letters of introduction, and created a tentative itinerary.[61] Thomas Phillips Page, his would-be travel companion, had already begun updating his passport for the trip southward on January 3, before Jenson had even proposed the trip to the First Presidency. Clearly the two men had been thinking about the pending trip for some time.

Page proved uniquely prepared to journey southward with Jenson. He was a fellow world traveler, amateur historian, and charter member of Jenson's Round the World Club in Salt Lake City.[62] Page, described as a hard-of-hearing, often stuttering, toupee-wearing "smart duck," had served a three-year church mission to Turkey from 1899 to 1901 and made a trip around the world from 1911 to 1912. In 1922, the year before he and Jenson traveled to Latin America, Page traveled along the west coast of Central America and crossed the Panama Canal on a pleasure trip to Cuba. Thus, Page was already familiar with a large part of the southward journey into Latin America.[63]

Nearly two weeks after his initial request and with still no formal reply from the First Presidency, Jenson again asked for approval through a January 16 letter to Grant, who had traveled to California several days earlier. Since the presiding quorums (the First Presidency and Quorum of the Twelve) were responsible for opening missionary work in foreign lands, they may have been reluctant to send Jenson southward, where he might attempt to do what could be seen as their apostolic duty. Jenson also expected to be reimbursed for the costs he would incur throughout Latin America, just as he had on similar trips, but Grant wondered if the proposed trip was worth the hefty expense.[64] Grant eventually signaled his displeasure by giving approval on January 18 for the Latin American expedition but asking Jenson to pay his own way.[65]

Later that same day, Apostles Melvin J. Ballard, John A. Widtsoe, and Church Historian Joseph Fielding Smith visited Jenson at his home to evaluate his personal library of books and manuscripts, which he had offered to the Historian's Office. Smith also informed Jenson that he could visit Latin America but "not as a regularly called missionary" or with church funding.[66] Though Jenson planned to (and ultimately did) compile historical information about Latter-day Saint pioneers in California and survey Latin America for prospective missionary work, the senior brethren determined the trip was more of a vacation. Page willingly covered much of the cost of the trip for both him and Jenson.[67]

The First Presidency's lack of enthusiasm for the trip was consistent with the decades-long general reticence of church leaders to open a mission field in Latin America. Nineteenth-century attempts to establish a church presence in South America had been largely unsuccessful.[68] Then in early October 1901, the Quorum of the Twelve recommended to the First Presidency that missionary work be opened in South America, but no immediate action was taken. A week later, Church President Lorenzo Snow passed away, and the issue remained unresolved.[69] In June 1902, then Apostle Heber J. Grant "remembered Pres. Snow's last instructions" and believed "that in the near future there would be openings for the gospel in South America."[70] Apostle John W. Taylor, in 1903, concurred with Grant that Snow's instructions should be fulfilled. Taylor felt that South America was "being neglected" and "believed that that country ought to be visited by an apostle."[71] No apostolic visit, however, was made during the presidency of Joseph F. Smith (1901–18). Thus, before Jenson's and Page's tour in 1923, commissioned Latter-day Saint travels to South America had been scarce.[72]

On Monday, January 22, as Jenson and Page bade farewell to their families, they arguably became the most prominent Latter-day Saints to embark on an expedition through Book of Mormon lands in the twentieth century. They began their trip by exploring historic sites of early Latter-day Saint pioneers in California. At times the duo split up—Page would make arrangements to sail southward while Jenson visited the state library in Sacramento to research the march of the Mormon Battalion and Latter-day Saint involvement in the California gold rush. After nine days in the Golden State, the two travelers boarded the *Colombia* and sailed for the Panama Canal.[73]

Along the way, the *Colombia* stopped at coastal towns in Mexico, Guatemala, El Salvador, and Nicaragua. As a routine, Jenson and Page would disembark at each port; gather geographic, economic, and demographic details of each country; record the information in letters to the *Deseret News*; and then send the letters to Utah to be read by the curious Latter-day Saint readership. In his persistent quest for ecclesiastical approval, Jenson wrote Grant while traveling to Guatemala to ask for permission to explore "the ruins from Ancient days . . . where many Book of Mormon students think the Nephi civilization flourished more than in any other part of the western world," but having heard nothing from Grant, Jenson and Page moved on to Panama "somewhat dissatisfied."[74] The two travelers stayed at the Panama Canal for about a week and half, waiting for a ship to South America.[75]

The two travelers left Panama—what they considered to be the "narrow neck of land" referenced in the Book of Mormon—on March 1 and sailed for South America. They became some of the first Latter-day Saints to set foot on South American soil in almost seventy years. After landing in Peru, the land of the Incas, they paid particular attention to the ruins of bygone civilizations.[76] From Peru, the duo traveled by rail to the republics of Bolivia, Chile, and Argentina.

Argentina in particular left a lasting impact on Jenson. He found the capital city, Buenos Aires, comparable to his native Copenhagen; they even found a colony of Danes living outside the city and stayed at the Hotel Scandinavia during their nine-day stopover. After receiving an invitation, Jenson delivered a lecture on Utah and the Latter-day Saints to a group of curious Danes. Though he would have liked to visit their homes and expound on the teachings of the Latter-day Saints, he felt it wise not to preach without permission from President Grant.[77] Jenson and Page continued their trip on April 12, passing through Uruguay, Brazil, and the West Indies on their lengthy journey home. In New York, while staying with his daughter Eleanore and her husband, George B. Reynolds, Jenson sent a telegram to Grant, asking for permission to complete his planned return trip over the Mormon Trail. Jenson hoped to purchase an automobile with church funds to survey the historical sites associated with the overland trek. Grant, perhaps tiring of Jenson's requests since he had already laid out the terms of Jenson's personal trip before his departure, sent him a reply by telegram: "No. Consider proposition waste of money and time. Welcome home."[78] Jenson arrived by train to Salt Lake City on May 10, 1923, after being gone over three and a half months.[79]

Traveling mostly by first-class steamer, ferry, and railcar, Jenson had journeyed over twenty-three thousand miles through Mexico, Guatemala, El Salvador, Nicaragua, Panama, Peru, Bolivia, Chile, Argentina, Uruguay, and Brazil.[80] Upon his return, he quickly arranged "the documents pertaining to Church history" that he had gathered on his trip to add to the Historian's Office.[81] Beyond expanding the institutional archive, Jenson's self-funded expedition—which came at a personal cost of $1,240—was rejuvenating for the aging historian and a moment of personal reprieve. Jenson expressed in his journal that he now "felt much better physically" than he had before he left.[82] He later commented that his "trip to South America stands out as one of the most interesting experiences of my life. It may be considered the only vacation I ever had since I commenced my historical labors for the Church and even that trip was more of a mission than a vacation."[83] For some, the arduous journey would look nothing like a leisure trip, but for an experienced traveler like Jenson, the voyage had been comfortable and returned his mind and soul to steady footing. It also brought Jenson distinction once again in the Salt Lake Valley.[84] His exotic trip was captured in thirty-eight published letters to the *Deseret News* and was retold to audiences throughout Utah upon his return.[85]

Both Jenson and Page immediately began publicizing their adventurous exploration. Three days following their return, Jenson addressed a congregation at the Granite Stake Tabernacle about his recent travels. He spoke again at the Salt Lake Tabernacle two weeks later, correlating the ruins, relics, and artifacts he saw in Latin America to the architecture, wars, and tools of the Nephites, Lamanites, and Jaredites in the Book of Mormon.[86]

Though Jenson was not the first to champion these widely held ideas about Book of Mormon geography, he was the most recent Latter-day Saint to do so, and as Assistant Church Historian, he lent major weight to such theories with his first-person observations. Between May and November 1923, Jenson spoke about his trip no fewer than fifteen times at venues throughout Utah. Page also lectured at several events.[87] Repeatedly the duo described Latin America as the primary location of Book of Mormon civilizations and declared that the countries of Central and South America seemed ready for missionary work. They would encourage young men "to learn Spanish, so they can go on missions to South America."[88] Jenson had returned from Latin America with a distinct impression that the gospel should be spread south of Mexico.

On July 11, Jenson presented a report to the First Presidency on his expedition.[89] Jenson highlighted the demographics, languages, and religions of the areas, and though Catholicism was by far the dominant religion in Latin America, Jenson emphasized that the inhabitants of Latin America currently enjoyed "perfect religious liberty" and would "welcome messengers who could declare unto them the true gospel of Jesus Christ."[90] Jenson concluded his spirited presentation to the First Presidency with a direct recommendation to spread the gospel into Central and South America. "Knowing, as I do, that the Lord has commanded the Latter-day Saints to preach the gospel to every nation, kindred, tongue, and people," he wrote, "I deem it my duty or privilege to draw the attention of the First Presidency of the Church to conditions in these different countries as I found them in my travels."[91] The First Presidency listened carefully to the Assistant Church Historian's recommendations and thanked him for his findings, but for the time being they did not move forward on his proposal. While Jenson's 1923 report did not immediately result in the dispatch of Latter-day Saint missionaries southward, it did demystify the demographics and geography of South America for Grant and the general Latter-day Saint audience, stoking new excitement over the prospect of finding and converting the descendants of Book of Mormon peoples.

The Opening of Missionary Work in Latin America

Two and a half years had passed since Jenson had written his strongly worded letter to the First Presidency about the importance of his role and contributions as Assistant Church Historian.[92] He had recently learned that only Ivins had read his 1921 report and failed to place it in the hands of the entire First Presidency. Jenson had taken his report back from Ivins and waited, wishing to choose a time when it would have a full hearing before his ecclesiastical leaders. Now, in his February 1924 meeting to present on his South American travels, he had the First Presidency's full attention, and he issued an ultimatum: his future at the Historian's Office "would depend upon their action" on his 1921 letter, which asked for clear signs of administrative support in the form of more staff and resources. Grant diplomatically dismissed Penrose and Ivins from the room to be alone with Jenson. The two men visited for over an hour, causing the church president to miss his dinner appointment while he attempted to "pacify" Jenson's feelings.[93] But nearly six months later, Jenson was pleasantly surprised: "My check for my past month's labor I found it read $225.00 instead of $200.00 as heretofore. This raise came unasked for on my part, so I suppose Pres. Grant thinks I deserve it."[94] A bit more money, rather than a new ecclesiastical title, would have to suffice in the latter years of his life.

By the beginning of 1925, Jenson seemed to be more at peace with his lot in life. In his seventy-fourth year, he wrote in his diary, "The dreams of my youth have become realities of life in a different way to what I had expected, and the period of building air-castles has, so far as I am concerned, passed away forever."[95] And though his professional status remained stagnant, the effects of his tour of Latin America began to bear fruit.

Unbeknownst to Jenson, on September 3, 1925, President Grant declared to church leaders that he was now determined to open missionary work in Latin America.[96] Over the past eighteen months, Jenson's formal report of his travels to Latin America had seemingly turned the minds of the senior brethren to the lands and peoples of the ancient Olmec, Aztec, Mayan, and Incan civilizations. His practical description of the demographic, cultural, and religious conditions of the countries he visited no doubt softened any hesitancy on the part of church leaders to place missionaries in South America.

On October 4, 1925, another semiannual general conference of the church began. Grant opened the conference with comments on missionary work and announced the opening of a new mission in South America, though the newspapers had already reported on the decision. The Latter-day Saint prophet then made a plea for more missionaries from the wards and branches of the church.[97]

Days later Jenson was invited to attend a special missionary meeting in the Presiding Bishop's Building, along with other church leaders and general officers. Jenson, a promoter of Latin American missionary work, noted with pride in his diary that evening: "A short program was rendered and Melvin J. Ballard, Rulon S. Wells and Ray L. Pratt, who are called to open up a mission in South America each spoke a few words," and then Jenson was asked to speak. If the audience did not already know of Jenson's involvement in the historic moment, his addresses made it clear.[98] "Addressing myself to President Grant," Jenson wrote of the occasion, he announced "that two years ago I had paved the way for these three brethren, on my visit to South America, and that I then delivered the first address ever given by a Mormon Elder in Buenos Aires." Jenson also publicly volunteered to be a fourth missionary, joining the three missionaries who had already been called to Argentina. Grant, however, politely declined his offer.[99]

The aging but seemingly ageless historian never enjoyed being sidelined for historic moments. Yet, his life-changing experience in the Mexican Mission and in Latin America underscored a theme that reappeared frequently in his life: making history proved more difficult than writing or gathering it. As the church administration moved forward with plans to proselytize in Latin America, Jenson's trip slipped into the background, becoming a footnote to the church's long history of searching out and converting possible Book of Mormon peoples. And while in successive decades church leaders would repeatedly celebrate the swift growth of the church in Latin America, it was Jenson who offered a decisive voice to the swelling aspirations of white Latter-day Saints to find and convert Lamanite descendants. It was Jenson who recounted the demographic, cultural, and geographic landscape for church leaders, producing records that read like a travel book and stoking imaginations about a maturing church to the south. As a traveling historian, Jenson wrote and documented for the future, but his pathbreaking efforts brought poor returns in the present. His explorations prepared new gospel frontiers for the church, but the role of avant-garde explorer was lonely work.

10 Public Commemorator

The pageantry and patriotism surrounding the One Hundredth Annual General Conference of the Church of Jesus Christ of Latter-day Saints in April 1930 epitomized the church's graduation into America's legitimate religious marketplace from the perspective of the American public. In the nineteenth century, Protestant Americans feared that, in large settlements of Latter-day Saints, church leaders were dangerously combining religious and civil authority. But by 1930, with many of the religion's most distinctive features, particularly plural marriage, relegated to the past, the success of Latter-day Saints in the Rocky Mountains was celebrated by the national press.[1] Joseph Smith's movement was now a century old, yet it operated as a newly baptized Americanized faith. As a longtime Assistant Church Historian, Andrew Jenson had witnessed and documented the transition.

The press printed inflated figures of how many were expected to gather for the celebration on historic Temple Square—estimates ranged from fifty thousand to over one hundred thousand.[2] Latter-day Saint leaders anticipated the large crowds and circulated memos to local congregations encouraging church members to hold celebrations where they were instead of convening on Temple Square.[3] Still, the Latter-day Saint masses came, prompting some concern that the influx of visitors would exceed the capacity of local hotels.[4]

For the centennial celebration, a dramatized pageant was written and performed nightly. Titled *Message of the Ages* and involving fifteen hundred participants (including Jenson, who acted in the role of Old Testament prophet Jeremiah), the production retold the story of the founding narrative of the church and reenacted the events of the Restoration.[5] As the play wound toward its final act, the curtains opened to reveal a tableau of "The Coming of the Nations," with actors in native garb surrounded by an array of flags from foreign countries. In this scene, the church dramatized an imagined worldwide Latter-day Saint community.[6] At the centennial celebration, Latter-day Saints reflected on their church's founding, but the commemorative event was also informed by present and future possibilities. The diverse and international tableau that played out before a captive audience in the *Message of the Ages* was a symbol of the church's global aspirations.

The simplified and ritualized narrative of church history was similar to the one Jenson had reinforced throughout his career at the Historian's Office.[7] Jenson also consistently pointed toward a globalizing, diverse church, whose history needed to be recorded and shared. On the morning of April 9, 1930, Jenson spoke in the Salt Lake Tabernacle on Temple Square to a capacity crowd. Nearly eighty years old, Jenson had been anticipating the church's centennial for years. He was overcome with emotion when he stood to speak: "I have hoped and prayed that I might live long enough in mortality to be present when The Church of Jesus Christ of Latter-day Saints should be one hundred years old."[8] Given the commemorative occasion, his discourse moved away from his usual conference themes—that of record keeping and church history—and instead reflected on his legacy as a career ecclesiastical historian.

In his sermon, Jenson charted his path to his current position as Assistant Church Historian, which was unexpected but formative. He took pride in his homegrown talent and his perseverance in the face of challenges. "I came to this land when I was fifteen years of age," he recounted. "From the time I was first able to read I became a student of Church history, and as a boy I read extracts from the history of the Prophet Joseph Smith . . . and have been a student of Church history from that time until the present." After arriving in Utah Territory, Jenson discovered he had much to learn. He had been forced to learn the English language and "the customs and habits of a new country." "The Lord, however, was with [him]," and he "took hold of the task and did the best [he] could under the circumstances."[9]

After rehearsing his past, Jenson moved to the topic of his historical work. In his public self-reflection, Jenson outlined a strong legacy that was twofold: his greatest contribution to Latter-day Saint historical memory came first through his persistent travels and second through his many publications. "It has been my privilege," he said, "to be a field man, gathering historical data, most of my life, and in going into all parts of the world, to follow in the tracks of missionaries who were laborers in the vineyard before me, to find out what they had done, gather up historical threads, and weave them into history." His travels, more than the mere experiences of an aged historian, produced a material legacy, one that could be held in the hands of anyone who visited the Historian's Office: "from my field notes I have written and compiled some six hundred manuscript volumes containing Church history in general, and histories of our missions and stakes, with their subdivisions, in detail, and also histories of the different auxiliary organizations of the Church, both at home and abroad."[10]

From Manuscripts to Monuments

His final general conference sermon underscored a reality the almost octogenarian faced. Not only had he documented Latter-day Saint history for decades, but he also was among the dwindling pioneer generation, a living example of an eroding Latter-day Saint past. Each passing year brought more anniversaries of the church's formative years and growth, which the church could more comfortably celebrate from its secure position within American culture. As Jenson aged, he worked to etch his life's work into public memorials and monuments, symbolizing the historical sensibility that he hoped would continue to inform his religion.

The centennial celebrations occurred at a time when Latter-day Saint leaders were returning their attention to the church's historic sites. In the last thirty years, leaders had purchased historic sites in New York, Missouri, Illinois, and Vermont and had begun to install monuments and markers to celebrate the church's historical heritage.[11] Across the United States, the period from 1890 to the beginning of World War II was an impressive period of monument building. During this era, economic and social transformation and turmoil inspired the erection of a scattering of monuments to reassert cohesive national values and to instill civic pride.[12] Similarly, the Latter-day Saints' commemorations and monuments were created to reassert their own distinctive identity and to celebrate the miracles in their past for a new audience during a period of unprecedented institutional change. These monuments similarly ensured that Utah's dying pioneer generation would be remembered as colonizers of the American West and as pillars in the increasingly romanticized story within American culture of US westward expansion.[13] In building monuments and commemorating the church's history, the past, present, and future all converged into a physical form.[14]

Jenson's own quest to build monuments and memorialize church history was motivated as much out of personal interest as it was out of a public one. As the most productive documenter of the Latter-day Saint past, he maintained a stake in historical preservation, including the creation of monuments and the messages they conveyed to the public. The memorialization of the Latter-day Saint past was in many ways also the preservation of his life's work, in which he endeavored to endow his own people with an appreciation of their heritage. Jenson's literary work had, in a sense, always attempted to memorialize his historical subjects to prevent them from being forgotten. But in an era of public historical commemoration, Jenson also discovered that monuments could be as effective a purveyor of public memory as manuscripts, bringing into dimensional form the subjects of his chronologies, manuscripts, and biographies.

In the 1920s, Jenson began participating in the dedication of monuments in earnest, as he worked on documenting the route of the 1847 pioneers. He traveled frequently along the trail and wrote articles that brought publicity to the

Latter-day Saint pioneer experience. Jenson was thus in demand as a speaker at pioneer commemorations. In 1924, for example, the Woodruff Stake in Wyoming invited him to participate in the dedication of a monument to the pioneers. The nine-foot cobblestone monument, topped by a beehive, was originally located approximately twelve miles southeast of Evanston, Wyoming, on a hill overlooking Bear River Valley, at the site where Brigham Young and his vanguard pioneers passed on July 1847.[15] Jenson spoke at the afternoon dedicatory session and felt satisfied that he had witnessed the dedication of the "first monument erected on the pioneer trail in honor of the Utah Pioneers of 1847."[16] More such monuments, however, were planned. As reported by the *New York World*, Jenson intended to locate the Mormon Trail using diaries and maps and then construct "small stone monuments" with the assistance of church members or "the citizens of the towns and villages . . . marking the trail for all time."[17]

In the summer of 1927, Jenson attended the dedication of a monument honoring Captain John W. Gunnison and members of his US government surveying team who were murdered by Pahvant Indians in October 1853.[18] Jenson was the featured speaker at the dedication, and to a crowd of around two thousand, he recounted his attempts to commemorate the lives lost at the massacre site near the Sevier River south of Delta, Utah. He had visited the site in 1888 and created a makeshift marker, and he returned years later in 1923 with the promise of constructing a more permanent monument. With the help of the American Legion and the Daughters of Utah Pioneers, Jenson had fulfilled his promise. His talk honored Gunnison as a friend of Brigham Young, placing the Latter-day Saints alongside federal surveyors as the builders of the American West. Such a narrative favored Latter-day Saints, casting them as flagbearers of American expansion and commemorating a history (albeit a selective one) of friendly relationships with US officials.[19]

Just a month later, Jenson attended the dedication of a monument erected by the Summit Stake in Utah in honor of the Latter-day Saint pioneers who passed near Castle Rock in Echo Canyon in July 1847. The granite monument was similar in construction to the one placed near Evanston, with the iconic beehive gracing the top of a granite shaft. The proceedings were held at the same hour the vanguard pioneer company crossed where the Lincoln Highway was later constructed. Apostle George F. Richards gave the dedicatory prayer, and Jenson retold the events surrounding the original pioneer passage.[20]

At the dedication of pioneer monuments, Jenson was often asked to recount, from sources kept at the Historian's Office, the experiences of Latter-day Saint pioneers and settlers. These speaking opportunities for Jenson allowed the Historian's Office to be involved in public and local history ventures. In 1930, President Herbert Hoover announced a nationwide centennial to "commemorate the lives and the deeds of the heroic pioneers who won and held the West."[21] In response to this announcement, the Oregon Trail Memorial Association, the Boy Scouts of America, and other organizations began sponsoring local events to commemorate the Covered Wagon Centennial—one hundred years since the first wagon train set off along the Oregon Trail.[22] Church leaders formed an automobile caravan to attend one of the local commemorations at Independence Rock, Wyoming, and invited Andrew Jenson and B. H. Roberts to be tour guides, while Apostle George Albert Smith presided over the party of ninety-three. As the group traveled along the Mormon Trail, Roberts and Jenson favored the party with detailed scenes of the travels of the first company of Latter-day Saint pioneers. They reached Independence Rock before the July 4 festivities. During the celebratory ceremony, George Albert Smith, B. H. Roberts, Ruth May Fox (president of the church's young women organization), and Jenson were seated on the platform "among the guests of honor." The ceremony, sponsored by the Oregon Trail Memorial Association, mentioned the Latter-day Saint pioneers only in passing, however, and other groups dedicated and placed markers at Independence Rock. "It seemed that all groups entitled to recognition had been properly recognized except the 'Mormons,' who formed probably the largest body of emigrants and who undoubtedly had more of its members pass the rock in early days than any other group," the *Improvement Era* reported. Undeterred,

George Albert Smith, Andrew Jenson, and others at the *This Is the Place* monument in Salt Lake City, July 2, 1930, en route to Independence Rock, Wyoming. Courtesy Church History Library.

Smith selected a site on the rock to place a marker honoring the Latter-day Saint pioneers as soon as one could be created.[23]

The Latter-day Saint caravan participated in the remaining commemorative events before turning back to Utah. At Devil's Gate, five miles west of Independence Rock, they witnessed the placement and dedication of two markers, one to the female pioneers who traveled the trail, and one to the unknown pioneers who perished on the trail. The *Deseret News* reflected on the significance of the commemorative events the Latter-day Saint caravan participated in as they prepared to return home: "Here were gathered, pioneers, descendants of those who had passed on, historians, state, county, city and government officials, all interested in the important movement now gaining impetus rapidly." The Covered Wagon Centennial at Independence Rock displayed "evidences . . . that it had kindled new fires of loyalty to the noble people who gave everything that the west might be conquered and made ready as a place where home could be established."[24] The outcome was precisely what Jenson had pushed for in his historical work. The increased awareness of the pioneer experience memorialized Latter-day Saints as empire builders, conquerors of the desert, and primary actors in the quintessential American frontier experience.

Jenson also now had a fellow advocate for trail preservation in George Albert Smith. Smith created the Utah Pioneer Trails and Landmarks Association and served as the organization's president, helping to erect over one hundred monuments in the ensuing years.[25] In June 1931, with Jenson as tour guide, Smith and a company of Latter-day Saints made a repeat trip on the Mormon Trail to Wyoming to place their contemplated marker at Independence Rock. On this occasion, President Heber J. Grant eventually joined the party and presided and spoke at the dedication proceedings. The caravan also placed a temporary marker at Martin's Cove to honor the Martin Handcart Company.[26]

The flurry of monuments along the pioneer trail culminated in the twenty-third and "last" monument placed along the trail on July 23, 1933, in conjunction with the "Pioneer Day" celebration that would kick off the next day.[27] At a ceremony in Pioneer Park, in downtown Salt Lake City, Jenson graced the stand with numerous dignitaries, including George Albert Smith, as the stone monument with a bronze inset was dedicated. Though Jenson also spoke at the proceedings, it was Utah governor Henry H. Blood who explained to the audience the purpose and symbolism behind the efforts of Jenson, Smith, and others in memorializing the pioneer experience. According to Blood, the pioneers were "dreamers who worked, and workers who prayed." "They brought with them and implanted in this country the highest of American ideals," he continued.[28] In the commemorative event, the Latter-day Saint pioneers were celebrated not as exiles and refugees from a hostile American nation (which is how they had pictured themselves in the nineteenth century), but as banner bearers of American virtues and civic values.

Much had changed since Jenson had made his own pioneer trek in 1866, but he believed he was the beneficiary of an elusive "American Dream." From pioneer immigrant to frontier wageworker to celebrated historian, Jenson was part of the legacy enshrined in the modern monuments to the pioneers, which informed his interest in seeing the trail preserved. The tense struggle for religious liberty and sovereignty in the church's original kingdom in the West now yielded to a simpler narrative, one appropriated from contemporary, romanticized tales of the American empire, westward expansion, and the rugged frontier. Latter-day Saints happily located themselves within that narrative and in so doing rejoined the traditional American story as if they had always been a part of it. As Jenson worked to reconstruct church members' trek West through his efforts to erect monuments, he was rebuilding the Latter-day Saint image before the American public, an image fashioned in the likeness of his own pioneer experience.

A Farewell to Denmark

Jenson's final opportunity to travel outside of North America came in early 1935, when he was eighty-four years old. Stewards of a park commonly known as Rebild National Park in Denmark sent a request to Governor Henry H. Blood for an authentic Latter-day Saint pioneer wagon to put on display in the park, to commemorate the enormous Scandinavian migration to Utah during the second half of the nineteenth century. Rebild Park, composed of nearly two hundred acres of preserved countryside, was donated to the Danish government in 1911 with the intention of creating a wilderness space for Danish Americans to commemorate US holidays. For this year's Independence Day celebration, organizers at Rebild Park intended to give the requested pioneer wagon center stage. Governor Blood passed on the invitation to the leaders of the Daughters of Utah Pioneers, who solicited Jenson's help in locating the requested wagon. As a Danish American immigrant, Jenson was all too happy to oblige. That spring he searched a number of Utah villages for such a wagon, which had been ubiquitous a generation earlier but now was almost impossible to locate. Jenson finally found several decrepit wagons on a farm in Cache Valley, Utah, and from those scraps, he determined to piece a wagon together, commissioning new parts that could not be refurbished.[29]

By the end of April 1935, the reconstructed pioneer wagon was ready to be shipped overseas, and Jenson suggested that one of the pioneer immigrants who had been among the first Danes to trek across the plains in 1853 accompany the wagon to Denmark for its official presentation to the government there.

But none of the surviving pioneers from that journey—which had occurred eight decades earlier—were physically able to make the trip. Governor Blood subsequently appointed Jenson to accompany the pioneer wagon to his native Denmark, where he had not been since 1912. At that time, Jenson left behind a contested legacy in Denmark, one marred by his status as both a naturalized American and a Latter-day Saint leader. But now, over two decades later, a more secularized Danish state had become less hostile toward religious minorities. The country even commemorated the scores of Danes who left Denmark in the nineteenth century, not as defectors from their national heritage but as a critical part of a Danish intercontinental legacy.

Jenson made sure his travel papers were in order to guarantee his safe travel to and from Denmark. By the time Jenson, along with his wife Bertha and daughter Eva, sailed from the Hoboken harbor in New Jersey on May 22, 1935, he had proudly gathered a number of written endorsements and letters of recommendation and introduction, including ones from Governor Blood; George H. Dern, the US Secretary of War and the former governor of Utah; and William H. King, a US senator from Utah.[30] The impressive collection of professional recommendations was evidence of the reach of Jenson's personal network late in his life and also of how interested US dignitaries were in the commemorative festivities in Denmark.

The wagon was freighted down to Temple Square, where it was displayed for a few days. Jenson also met with President Heber J. Grant, who, as Jenson recorded, "congratulated me upon my appointment by the Governor and assured me of his full-hearted approval of my going and expressed his perfect satisfaction with what I as a most diligent worker for the Church had done throughout my life. He said he had always liked workers and busy men."[31] The next day, Jenson received a priesthood blessing from the church president: "I rejoice in the knowledge you possess regarding the travels from the Missouri River to the Salt Lake Valley—perhaps as great, if not greater, than any other man in the Church who is now alive. . . . We bless you, dear Brother Jenson, for your untiring labors as a historian in the Church, working early and late, and with energy and a firm determination in your heart to accomplish all that it is possible for you to accomplish for the good of the people in preserving the history of the people."[32] Shortly thereafter, the refurbished pioneer wagon was shipped across the Atlantic to Denmark.

When Jenson disembarked at Copenhagen in early June, he was briefly taken aback by the scene before him. Thousands of Danish citizens greeted the ship, a sea of Danish and US flags waving prominently on the shore. Jenson reported to the *Deseret News* that such a display evidenced "the good feeling that exists between the United States and the sons and daughters of the North."[33] The welcome party's attention turned specifically to the Utah guests as the mayor of Copenhagen, eagerly anticipating the wagon's arrival, personally singled out the Utah party among the hundreds of others on the ship. The mayor spoke on board the ship, along with a representative of the Rebild National Park Board, and the audience greeted Jenson with a hearty ovation.

Jenson's usual stoic demeanor melted before the unsolicited praise from his fellow countrymen and strangers. According to the local press, he was reduced to tears. The moment brought back a flood of painful memories from his past missions when he had frequently lobbied local officials, often to no avail, to support Latter-day Saint causes. Now he was apparently welcome again in the land of his youth. When he regained his composure, he thanked the mayor of Copenhagen for the kind greeting and proceeded to give the history of Danish immigration to the United States. Danish newspapers similarly lauded the Utah delegation and took interest in the pioneer story Jenson retold to the audience.[34]

On July 4, the same day Independence Day festivities were being celebrated in the United States, a crowd of at least ten thousand gathered to Rebild Park on a rainy afternoon to see the wagon, which arrived at the park behind a pair of oxen and teamsters in authentic pioneer garb.[35] The audience was captivated by the American pioneer relic. During the proceedings, Jenson sat in a prominent position, near the Danish prime minister, Thorvald Stauning, and the US ambassador to Denmark, Ruth Bryan Owen.[36] One would have expected Jenson to downplay the Latter-day Saint gathering in his address, given past negative tropes about missionary work in the country; instead, Jenson celebrated the efforts of Latter-day Saint missionaries in precipitating a massive Scandinavian outmigration to the United States in the nineteenth century. His address was broadcast by a national radio network in the United States.[37]

Through both modern communication technology and the Danish American historian's remarks, the United States and Denmark were linked. Through the act of memorializing and commemorating, public history was revised. The transnational story of Latter-day Saint religious migration—previously viewed as a betrayal of authentic Danishness—was now a legitimate part of the Danish national heritage. When Jenson returned from his trip to Europe in August 1935, he noted this shift in attitude among the Danes in his journal. "In all the experiences of my life I have never had so much honor shown me, and have never been in the newspaper lime-light so much before," he recorded with some awe. "How different the situation 24 years ago," serving as mission president in Scandinavia, "when I was subject to severe attacks on the part of the Lutheran clergy and others and was scorned by newspaper men repeatedly because of my preaching the principles of the restored gospel."[38]

Long haunted by the cold and antagonistic reception he had last received in his homeland, Jenson's final trip to Denmark reconciled the forced estrangement of his two identities. His Danishness and Americanness could be celebrated together as a worthy heritage, and his Latter-day Saint affiliation stirred fewer anxieties from his Lutheran counterparts. Copenhagen's *Social-Demokraten* newspaper lauded Jenson as one of the foremost historians of the Latter-day Saint tradition. The paper in Aalborg reprinted Jenson's "beautiful tale" of Latter-day Saint immigration, which he had retold at the Rebild festivities.[39] And at the center of the press's coverage of the Independence Day commemoration was the refurbished pioneer wagon. The wagon, once a part of Jenson's exodus from his native land, now marked his return.

The Round the World Club

The series of commemorative events Jenson participated in across the United States and Europe was the latest episode in a lifetime spent traveling to recover the histories of peoples, places, and events central to the restored gospel. A century before Jenson presented his 1930 general conference sermon, the founding prophet, Joseph Smith, dictated a revelation to John Whitmer, the church's official record keeper. In this revelation, the Church Historian was directed to "travel many times from place to place, and from church to church, that he may the more easily obtain knowledge." The church's appointed record keeper was not to be an armchair historian, merely summarizing reports as they came across his desk at the Historian's Office but an active leader, traveling both close to home and to the peripheries of the church to collect, preserve, and share Latter-day Saint history. Whitmer was further directed to fulfill his office by "preaching and expounding, writing, copying, selecting, and obtaining all things which shall be for the good of the church, and for the rising generations that shall grow up on the land of Zion."[40] Subsequent Church Historians, Assistant Church Historians, and their staffs sought to obey this commandment to travel churchwide and fulfill their record-keeping responsibilities.[41] But it was Jenson—more so than any of his peers, superiors, or subordinates in the Historian's Office, before or since his tenure—who fulfilled this scriptural mandate with the greatest zeal and results.

Within a year of returning from his stint as president of the Scandinavian Mission, Jenson had gathered with several friends at his home to discuss the possibility of creating a local organization for returned missionaries and other Latter-day Saints who had traveled around the world, crossing all of the longitudinal lines in one direction.[42] On the evening of May 15, 1913, Jenson visited with Elbert D. and Edna H. Thomas, David P. Howells, Frederick E. Barker, Heber C. Cutler, Thomas P. Page, and Ezra T. Stevenson. All eight friends were living in Salt Lake City and were seasoned tourists who had traveled around the globe.[43] In landlocked and parochial Utah, these world travelers looked to print, speak about, and forge a community around their experiences abroad.[44]

Jenson and his likeminded Latter-day Saint travelers were not alone in their desire to commemorate their personal circumnavigations of the globe. In the early twentieth century, a number of adventure gatherings and groups were formed in America. Possibly the best known was the Explorers Club in New York City. In May 1904, fifty celebrated explorers and travelers met at the Aldine Association and determined to form an association of their own to "unite explorers in the bonds of good fellowship and to promote the work of exploration." Members would gather regularly to regale each other with exotic tales of adventure, to share common traveling routes and pitfalls, and to listen to calls for fundraising to support proposed explorations. At the height of the explorer's era, as travel became easier and more affordable, disparate parties were often brought together by their shared experience of globetrotting.[45]

The Latter-day Saint travelers in Utah were inspired by the spread of groups dedicated to exploring the world and sharing their experiences with others. The Utah group determined to form their own Round the World Club.[46] At the first club meeting, the group nominated and elected Andrew Jenson as its president, David P. Howells as recording secretary, and Elbert D. Thomas as corresponding secretary. These three men became the inaugural executive committee. The club decided that a regular annual meeting would be held on the third Monday of each year, but additional meetings could be called when deemed appropriate by the executive committee.[47]

On May 16, 1913, the club members drafted bylaws to govern their organization. According to the bylaws, "the object of the association shall be the educational and social advancement of the members and the binding together more firmly the common interest of those missionaries who have made a complete trip around the world." Membership would be open to any Latter-day Saint who had "made a complete circuit of the globe." This hard-to-meet requirement added an air of exclusivity to the club. Eventually, however, restrictions were loosened, and numerous others who had traveled abroad were allowed to attend meetings.[48]

Over the next two decades, the Round the World Club met several times a year and rehearsed stories of global adventures. The group went through fits and starts, occasionally waning into inactivity before reviving regular meetings once again.[49] According to records that Jenson faithfully archived at the Historian's Office, he, at the age of eighty-four, attended the club's final meeting in February 1935.[50]

Whether at home or abroad, Jenson liked nothing more than to display and discuss his "collection of relics and souvenirs gathered on his extensive journeys," his son Harold Jenson reminisced. "Thirteen times he has crossed the Atlantic and four times the Pacific Ocean. He is a millionaire in miles of travel."[51] Jenson's travels were now badges of honor that he wore proudly, his relics of a lifetime of work and activity outside the borders of Zion. But more than vestiges of the exotic adventures of an anxious wanderer, Jenson's travels marked the efforts of an unofficial Latter-day Saint diplomat to not only document the church's engagement in foreign lands but to also help position its future.

Donation of the Andrew Jenson Library

Toward the end of his long career, Jenson became increasingly concerned about the preservation of his personal archive of church-related manuscripts, pamphlets, and books. He sought to protect his records and memorialize his career by finding a permanent home for his collection. Before leaving for Central and South America in the spring of 1923, he reached out to the First Presidency to see if an arrangement could be made with the church to safeguard his unique assemblage. He met with Presidents Heber J. Grant and Anthony W. Ivins and proposed donating his personal library to the church if the First Presidency would guarantee the creation of an internal "Andrew Jenson Collection" within the Historian's Office main library. "All I asked in return was the return of the means I had expended as traveling expenses during the earlier years of my connection with the Historian's Office, but not for myself, but to have it expended for making shelves for my books and binding the books not already bound," Jenson recorded. The move was somewhat symbolic for Jenson, who felt he had often been "sidetracked" by church leaders and hoped to finally showcase the massive fruits of his labors.[52] President Grant and his counselor patiently listened to Jenson's long-standing complaints and asked him to put his proposed donation in writing for the entire First Presidency and Quorum of the Twelve to consider. Church leaders evaluated his collection, but Jenson departed days later for Latin America with no formal donation agreement in place and without transferring his collection into church custody.

Feeling rebuffed, Jenson let four years pass before he again tried to secure the legacy of his library. At that time, the collection was still housed in a fireproof room in his downtown home and formed a sizable part of his estate. With no clear legal entity assigned to manage it, Jenson recognized that the library was liable to prompt an interfamily dispute at his death. Perhaps as a preemptive legal move, Jenson did what he had done in the past when the church declined to assume ownership over his publications; he revived the defunct Andrew Jenson History Company in 1927 and issued capital stock, appointing his own family members as officers to preserve his library.[53] The decision was likely meant to give family members clear custody of and instructions concerning his valuable collection prior to the division of his estate. Chief among those was the direction to keep his collection intact following his death. The move, however, also set in motion a process that ended with the First Presidency and Church Historian Joseph Fielding Smith accepting Jenson's donation terms a few years later.

By late February 1929, construction had begun on Jenson's memorial library, which would be housed within the church's larger library. "The steel arrived from the East intended for fencing in the southwest corner of the Historian's Office Library to receive the documents and books that I intend to deposit there for the benefit of the Church after my departure," Jenson noted in his journal.[54] By mid-March, his archival area was ready.[55] During March he moved his books from his home library in the Seventeenth Ward to their new home.[56] Finally, on March 30, he was able to secure his personal collection within the steel-enclosed space.[57] By July 1929, he had moved over all of his personal manuscripts, books, and indexes from his personal library to the Historian's Office.[58] His personal library and manuscript collection, priced by Jenson at $25,000 (about $358,000 in 2018) was no trivial matter. It formed about 20 percent of his entire estate.

With a dedicated space inside the Historian's Office, Jenson felt his legacy would be visually apparent to anyone who entered. At his advanced age, Jenson had the freedom to move about and to choose his projects, and he took few orders from the Church Historian or any other staff member at the Historian's Office. Such liberty he felt was owed him based on his seniority and accomplishments. But even though Jenson maintained strong opinions on Historian's Office matters, the ultimate decision-making, policy implementation, and overall direction of the church's historical enterprise rested with the Church Historian. Jenson continued to bristle over this hierarchical relationship to Church Historian Joseph Fielding Smith. Smith had been Jenson's former clerk and then fellow Assistant Church Historian, but since 1921, he had been Jenson's work supervisor. Whereas Jenson had admired and generally submitted to the directives of Church Historians Wilford Woodruff, Franklin D. Richards, and Anthon H. Lund, he struggled to sustain Smith in the same way. Simmering conflicts boiled over by mid-November 1929. "Worked at the Historian's Office and was insulted by Joseph F. Smith jun., in answer to a most proper question which I put to him," he recorded in his journal. "In the most angry tone he told me that he did not have to answer any questions, or to ask me for any thing. He is one of the most conceited fellows I ever had to do with, and the most inconsiderate, inappreciative and insulting individual that I was ever compelled to take orders from."[59]

With his pride wounded, Jenson left the Historian's Office in a huff and tried to meet with President Grant about his treatment by Smith. But since the prophet was out of town, Jenson instead vented to First Presidency counselor Anthony W. Ivins. "For eight long years I have had to take that man's insults and have felt from the beginning that it surely, sooner or later, would come to a break between us," Jenson confided in his journal. "It seems that the more faithful I work in the interests of the Church, the less pleased he is, and to think that such a man is an Apostle and the Historian of the Church; he has neither ability nor interest in Church history and the selection of such a man to hold escalated positions in the Church causes a thinking man to wonder to what extent the Church authorities are led by inspiration in selecting men to office."[60] But two days after the incident, according to Jenson, the Historian's Office colleagues attempted to reconcile or at least agreed to endure each other: "In the morning Bro. Smith came to me and apologized for speaking to me the way he did last Saturday. He said he felt sorry for what he had said in anger. Under the attitude I could only say in return: 'That settles the matter' and we shook hands."[61] The stare-down between Jenson and Smith exemplified the ongoing tension between these two noted authorities on church history and doctrine. Both felt they had managerial claim on the Historian's Office holdings, Jenson because of his past practice and experience and Smith because of his ecclesiastical appointment. Neither party was willing to defer to the other.

Storing his life's work at the Historian's Office in memoriam put Jenson's legacy at the forefront of public discussion and likely emboldened him. When the *Deseret News* printed a photograph of Jenson with his collection, Utah senator William H. King wrote to him, praising the historian as "one of the effective workers in the great Cause." "Your historical and other writings," he continued, "stand out as a most remarkable achievement and are of incalculable value to the entire membership of the Church."[62] Jenson's life's work and the development of the church were inextricable in his eyes and in the eyes of his supporters. Thus, it was fitting that, as the church's centennial celebration drew near in early 1930, Jenson finalized his major philanthropic gift to the Historian's Office. In a late January letter to President Grant, he wrote:

> It is with much pleasure that I welcome the time now arrived to carry out my long cherished intention, of which you are already informed, to formally present my private library to the Church. The collection I have made in the course of fifty years comprises about two thousand bound volumes, about three thousand titled pamphlets and above fifteen thousand manuscript biographies. . . . I appreciate the adequate and generous provision made to preserve the collection as a distinctive entity of the Historian's Office Library. . . . This consideration enhances my satisfaction and pleasure in tendering all of the above as a free gift to the Church which I now do and I hope it will be received with equal satisfaction and pleasure by you and the Church Historian.[63]

The following day, Grant responded to Jenson's generous gift with a letter of his own. He accepted "for the Church this generous and noble gift." Grant also hoped Jenson would feel permanent "satisfaction and comfort in the provision made to recognize and honor [him] for [his] faithfulness and diligence and unbounded industry in accumulating this library."[64] Jenson formally presented his library to the First Presidency that afternoon.[65]

The next month Jenson made some final improvements to his new space. He described:

> Under the direction of Elder Junius F. Wells, the iron or sheet iron partitions separating my private library from the general Historian's Office library, have just been decorated with gold ornaments, and the following words painted in gold letters above the door:
>
> The Andrew Jenson Library
> Presented to the Church
> A.D. 1930

Wells also placed "a life-size photograph" of Jenson near the partition.[66] The display satisfied Jenson, and he felt that his employer had adequately honored his contributions to the collection and preservation of church history. For the historian who agitated for years for a proper appointment, a proper office, and a proper building in which to perform his historical labors, his name was now etched in gold lettering at the Historian's Office—his record-keeping legacy sat for a time at the center place of church history.[67]

The Andrew Jenson Memorial Hall

Back in 1882, Jenson had moved his family from a Scandinavian immigrant community in Utah Valley north to Salt Lake City to further his career as a writer and historian. Their residence, at 154 North 200 West in the Seventeenth Ward (one of the original nineteen ecclesiastical units in Utah), was a few blocks northwest of historic Temple Square. In the spring of 1932, two years after donating his library to the Historian's Office, Jenson formally gathered his wives, Emma and Bertha, as well as his children Harold, Parley, Eva, and Leo. With the family, wrote Jenson, "I deliberated freely on matters pertaining to the building of a Memorial Hall and also in regard to what I had done for my children and what I intended to do in the future. We practically agreed upon forming a corporation for educational, historical and other purposes and electing five trustees to take care of the corporation after my departure to the Great Beyond. It is to be a corporation for non-profit purposes."[68] Again, Jenson hoped to preempt a family battle over his estate by depositing some of his saved funds into a corporate trust to maintain and exhibit the artifacts he gathered in his travels for interested Salt Lakers to peruse.

His envisioned memorial hall was to be a two-story brick building, built onto the rear of his existing home. After agreeing with his family to build the hall, "we commenced ordering materials," Jenson wrote, "which were brought upon

The Andrew Jenson family, 1932. Courtesy Church History Library.

the ground and during the month of April the masons who had commenced their work on April 1st, nearly finished their job. I built with the best material obtainable, solid and substantial, so that the building might stand for a thousand years."[69] As described by one friend, the memorial hall's main floor, complete with glass-faced showcases, functioned as a small museum "containing a valuable collection of exhibits gathered during his extensive travels," and the second story contained "a lecture hall with a seating capacity of 100 persons, furnished with modern folding chairs."[70] While the memorial hall was being constructed, Jenson drafted and filed the articles of incorporation for the Andrew Jenson Memorial Association with the Salt Lake County clerk's office and the office of the secretary of state of Utah.[71] According to the articles, the funds and property used to maintain the memorial hall would remain a part of the association until it became defunct, at which point it would automatically be deeded to the church, a safeguard in case his children later decided to dissolve the association and claim the assets. On May 10, carpenters fastened a sign over the entrance to his new brick building with raised letters reading "Andrew Jenson Memorial Hall."[72]

The construction of his memorial hall, together with improvements to his summer cottage, continued through the summer of 1932. Jenson chose the forty-seventh birthday of his daughter Eleonore, August 18, to host his first social gathering in his new brick building.[73] On October 1, he "commenced to draw the outline of a large map of the United States on the north wall of the lecture room in the Memorial Building."[74] He spent the next several weeks also framing and hanging special pictures on the walls, adding to his relics and building up a new personal library in the hall.

Finally, on December 10, 1932, Jenson opened the memorial hall to the Salt Lake public. He hosted a four-hour tour of the facility, allowing visitors to view his relics, see the lecture room, and take in the hangings and photographs that graced some of the walls. He estimated the entire display was worth about $5,000, a sizable sum in the middle of the Great Depression. Observers took note of the expense Jenson was incurring to construct a space for his legacy: "Some people, including some of my own children, are criticizing me because of the outlay, thinking the means spent for the building of the edifice should have been left for them to inherit and spend, but I feel that I have under the circumstances done the right thing."[75]

A day after his public opening, Jenson hosted a dedication ceremony for his memorial hall, on his eighty-second birthday. During the formal program, a number of invited dignitaries paid tribute to Jenson. Kate C. Snow, president of the Daughters of Utah Pioneers, gave a fitting tribute to the historian, astutely aware of the purpose for the hall: "People who live as Bro. Jenson has lived never die. He will live in this beautiful building and its relics and books; but long after this building has crumbled, he will live in the valuable books he has written, and the histories he has compiled. Future generations will profoundly thank him and call him blessed." After more speeches and songs, Nephi L. Morris formally dedicated the memorial hall. "It may be added that all the speakers were most profuse in their praise of my life's labor and said many things that are generally reserved for a man's funeral ceremonies," Jenson recorded privately.[76] This first gathering began a series of regular events and lectures at his memorial hall, including those hosted by other historically minded groups like the Daughters of Utah Pioneers, who would use his auditorium.[77]

A Pioneer in New Fields

In January 1938, Jenson and his wife Bertha spent a month in Southern California, where the Junipero Serra Museum expressed interest in building a monument dedicated to the Mormon Battalion, which had passed through the region in 1847. Although a monument was apparently never erected at that museum, the trip prompted Jenson to consider creating a revised history of the Mormon Battalion, which had been organized in 1846 to serve in the Mexican-American War. After returning to Utah, Jenson spent the next several months researching the members of the Mormon Battalion, and in June 1938 he took a train to Council Bluffs, Iowa, to begin a long historical journey. He traveled by car and bus, following the historical route of the battalion through Iowa, Kansas, New Mexico, Arizona, Mexico, and California, and then took the train back to Salt Lake—a journey of five thousand miles at the age of eighty-seven.[78]

Jenson's work on the battalion was prescient. Momentum soon built for a permanent monument commemorating the end of the battalion's trek in San Diego. With the help of the Daughters of Utah Pioneers, five branches of the church in San Diego gathered enough funds to construct the monument. Eventually, the Arts Division of the Works Progress Administration took notice of the project and offered to provide some labor for the monument. The monument, described as a "huge billboard in stone," displayed "eight life-size figures in colors, typical of the marching men of the Battalion."[79]

In late January 1940, Jenson traveled with Church President Heber J. Grant and Apostle George Albert Smith to California for the dedication of the Mormon Battalion monument in Old Town, San Diego, an event attended by five thousand onlookers.[80] Jenson opened the dedicatory program at Presidio Park with an address on the history of the Mormon Battalion. The featured and concluding speaker was President Grant, who framed the battalion march as evidence of the patriotism of the Latter-day Saints. "Once disfranchised and expropriated from their property," Grant declared, "our long misunderstood people today are becoming known as loyal, God-fearing patriotic citizens who believe absolutely in the final destiny of this glorious nation."[81]

A civic monument to the Latter-day Saints was now located outside the Great Basin, and the dedicatory proceedings were attended jointly by US military and government leaders and the Latter-day Saint prophet. Similar to the 1930 centennial celebration, the underlying message of this event was that Latter-day Saints now fit comfortably into the American union as faithful citizens and as ambassadors and conquerors of the US West. To nineteenth-century Americans, Latter-day Saint involvement in the founding and expansion of the American empire in the vast West would seem odd, even paradoxical, since many then considered Latter-day Saints to exist outside of American culture, but at the outbreak of World War II, celebrating the Latter-day Saint military force that had staked and defended the nation's claim on the frontier seemed obvious, even welcome. Jenson had witnessed the passage of the Latter-day Saints into the American body politic as one of the movement's most visible historians and narrators of the Latter-day Saint experience. And now his past articulations of the church's sizable influence on the development of the American nation were finally being enshrined in stone.

11 Twilight Church Historian

Mortality caught up to the Jenson family in April 1937. Emma Howell, whose health had been slowly failing due to the lingering effects of a stroke she experienced over a decade earlier, passed away, forcing Jenson to bury a spouse for a second time in Salt Lake City. Saddened but relieved that, at the age of seventy-five, his wife's pain had ended, Jenson spent the next few days making funeral preparations. In her husband's frequent absences, Emma had forged a female social support network and created a strong legacy of civic service. Her funeral served as a celebration of that legacy. Jenson's colleagues at the Historian's Office Joseph Fielding Smith and A. William Lund spoke at her funeral, as did other prominent Latter-day Saint leaders, including George Albert Smith, David O. McKay, and John A. Widtsoe.[1] The stream of dignitaries who attended Emma's funeral encouraged and comforted Jenson.

In Emma's final days, Jenson had been working feverishly to finish the fourth and final volume of his *Latter-day Saint Biographical Encyclopedia*. Late in his career, Jenson still hoped to monetize his works and recoup the costs incurred from publishing them, but his utmost concern was the availability and influence of his publications. He wanted his writings to enter the consciousness of Latter-day Saints and to be the definitive reference works on the church's past. When his *Biographical Encyclopedia* came off the press around the time of the April 1937 general conference, he sent a complimentary copy to President Grant to be placed on his office desk. According to Jenson's own perceptions, Grant had always been reserved in his approval of Jenson's accomplishments and the work of the Historian's Office generally. But the church president quickly penned a note after flipping through the fresh volume. "Thanks for sending me your book," he wrote to Jenson. "I appreciate your untiring energy early and late and hope the Encyclopedia will be a financial success. I want you to know that I consider you one of the hardest working men that I have ever been acquainted with."[2]

The personal note was high praise from the tireless church president. Grant looked to Jenson as a premier example of hard work, dedication, and zeal. Jenson was entering his twilight years, and though he was eventually grounded by his advancing age, his historical productivity showed few signs of flagging.

The Quest for Permanence

Jenson believed that his publications would grant him a kind of immortality. He often vocalized to his fellow Latter-day Saints the sentiments recorded in the preface to his *Encyclopedic History of the Church*: "While my labors have been a labor of love throughout, I have, however, one selfish thought in mind: *I desire to live after I am dead*."[3] Only through the recording of testimonies, thoughts, and actions could one survive completely in the minds of the next generation, Jenson believed. Personal record keeping "will serve a better purpose to perpetuate your memory than a costly stone monument," he told an audience at general conference in 1917.[4]

For the great gatherer of documents, however, records were a means to an end. They carried inherent value, to be sure, and Jenson advocated throughout his career for better conditions at the Historian's Office that would prolong the life of documents. But more importantly in Jenson's mind was that when a record passed through a historian, that person could interpret and synthesize its contents and mold it into an accessible format. Jenson ultimately valued the information gained from documents above the documents themselves. Thus, most of his career was spent compiling manuscript histories, scrapbooks, and reference volumes from boxes and crates of gathered documents. When he advocated for more resources at the Historian's Office, he was not in search for simply more space, but for more typists and clerks to clip and compile.

Similar to other historical societies in the United States, Jenson intended to preserve valuable historical materials through reproduction (usually through transcription), publication, and dissemination as far and wide as possible.[5] "There are yet 43 Stakes, nearly 500 wards, some 200 conferences and more than a thousand branches of the Church to finish for the 19th Century. There are the Scandinavian Mission history and the Pioneer history to be finished. There are more than a thousand written records that I have gathered from the missions, perhaps 500 private journals and tens of thousands of letters to be read and culled from, so that the cream or gist from them may be introduced into history before the historical work assigned to me can be completed," he reported to Joseph Fielding Smith in 1926. Jenson knew he was aging quickly and felt he "should be entitled to ease up a little, and could perhaps be used to direct the labors of others," and if not, he felt he "should be permitted to take leave of the Historian's Office for ever."[6]

Though he was committed to perpetuating copies of his work and promoting better record keeping, Jenson was more prohibitive in controlling access to the actual archive. He was fearful of scheming "historians" roving throughout Utah, offering to write personal histories at exorbitant rates.[7] Furthermore, he was protective of the historical spoils that could be gained from the documents at the Historian's Office. He hoped that what he gathered could be used for the benefit of the church, but only under his direction. For example, after his 1895 trip to Hawai'i to gather documents, Jenson had compiled an extensive manuscript history of the Hawaiian Mission.[8] Jenson continued to work on the history, and by 1923, his work on the mission was housed in "three large quarto volumes of typewritten manuscript, well collected and assembled." When Francis Russell, tasked with writing a lengthy history of the Hawaiian Mission, came to the Historian's Office to inquire into its holdings on the mission, Jenson became territorial. He allegedly lashed out at Russell: "You fellows come in here and steal o[u]r 'T[h]under.' I haf spent $15,000 of my own money collecting historical data for the church and you can see that we naturally resent ever[y] Tom, Dick and Harry coming in here to make money from our labors. I made the trip to Honolulu in 1895 to get that material, and if you want to pay my fare there, I shall feel more like helping you."[9] Jenson's good intentions in bringing church history to the Latter-day Saint masses was checked by his own selfish desire to control historical production. In Jenson's mind, all could be historians in their own record-keeping sphere, but few could or should produce quality narratives about the church as an institution.

Jenson's protectiveness of the holdings in the Historian's Office was fueled by ego as well as a historical methodology inherited from nineteenth-century American culture. That period produced a general climate one historian described as "documania," characterized by the belief that history exists as objective truth that could be discovered through document hunting, which would bring concreteness and completeness to the historical record.[10] Though Jenson was like his predecessors and peers in his record-gathering and -keeping efforts, he was also at the vanguard of historical recovery within the church, discovering and rescuing documents around the world well before many of his ecclesiastical leaders shared the same urgency. Safeguarding the many documents and manuscripts he collected, however, took a backseat to the nitty-gritty of historical synthesis. Jenson placed great emphasis on the chronologizing and compiling of manuscript volumes and felt the true treasure of the Historian's Office was the finished product of his efforts, not the documents themselves.[11]

Jenson's methods conformed directly with the tradition employed by historical societies for over a century. Purveyors of this tradition hoped to "multiply copies" of their prized material by organizing (generally chronologically), binding, and then publishing it. When the American Historical Association was founded in 1895, however, its Historical Manuscript Commission discovered a troubling nationwide trend. Custodians of important historical manuscripts were "indifferent to the importance of making known their possessions" and "some of the societies evince[d] a desire to keep their documents from public knowledge until they themselves [could] publish them."[12] Such sentiments seem to have been held by Jenson. This attitude toward organizing and sharing documents was permissible because of the unique position Jenson occupied within the Historian's Office; many of the new raw historical materials had been gathered or transcribed by him and existed in a rough organizational state or in scrawled notes that only he could read. This gave him unmatched creative control over how historical information could be used or disseminated.[13]

Permanence, Jenson hoped, would characterize both the final physical state of his work—reproduced, published, and distributed—and the quality of his historical narrative—truthful, comprehensive, and complete. Jenson saw his efforts to gather and publish church history as akin to the larger project of the Restoration, commenced by the church's founding prophet, Joseph Smith.[14] In his hope to restore the church's history to a completed state, however, Jenson did not foresee modern trends in the historical profession. He hardly anticipated how pervasively professional historians would chip away at the notion of objectivity, and he could not predict the later postmodernist aversion to alleged historical truths and master narratives. Decades later, at a time when Jenson hoped his publishing projects would prove most valuable to a growing church, the historian's craft became contingent and relative to the historians who synthesized and drafted the history, challenging the enduring value and definitiveness of Jenson's work.

Unaware of these future changes, Jenson spent the final years of his life on this quest for historical permanence, without the impulse for monetary profit that characterized his early entrepreneurial work. Instead he hoped to leave behind a corpus that represented well his legacy and that of the church he sought to document. Although he continued to preach and write articles for a variety of venues, he focused his energy on four major publishing projects: *History of the Scandinavian Mission* (1927), *Day by Day with the Utah Pioneers* (1934), *Autobiography of Andrew Jenson* (1938), and *Encyclopedic History of the Church of Jesus Christ of Latter-day Saints* (1941).

History of the Scandinavian Mission

As a Danish American emigrant who had embraced the church while growing up in Denmark, Jenson was especially interested in his homeland's history.

The overarching story of the Scandinavian Mission was also his story, which differentiated the *History of the Scandinavian Mission* from the dozens of other mission histories he would draft during his lifetime. The volume was years in the making. He had been gathering material for and drafting sections of the volume since his first mission to Scandinavia (1873–75). Four years later, during his second mission in Scandinavia (1879–81), Jenson gathered even more materials from across the entire mission. When he returned to Utah, he continued to cull additional information related to Scandinavians and the church from past issues of the *Deseret News*, other Latter-day Saint periodicals, church records, and personal histories.

While working on these histories of the church in Scandinavia, he became friends with Apostle Erastus Snow and many of the other luminaries of the Scandinavian Mission. Moreover, he was able to use the resources and files at the Historian's Office to further the work. While he was in Scandinavia in 1897, during the close of his world tour, he shipped all of the historical records from the local missions, conferences, and branches in Scandinavia back to the Historian's Office for additional preservation and use.[15]

His compilation on the Scandinavian Mission eventually spanned eighteen manuscript volumes and covered nearly eight decades. This work provided the underlying documentation for *History of the Scandinavian Mission*, which begins with the events leading up to the inaugural mission to Denmark in 1850, by Apostle Erastus Snow (whose portrait graces the frontispiece of the book) and his intrepid missionary companions. In the book, Jenson framed both his record keeping of missionary work and Snow's proselytizing in Scandinavia as being foreordained and directed by God.[16] Chapters one through eighty-nine chronicle the major developments of the Scandinavian Mission (1850–1905), and the final chapters detail the Danish-Norwegian Mission (1905–20), Swedish Mission (1905–26), Danish Mission (1920–26), and Norwegian Mission (1920–26). Two appendices comprise biographical sketches of men and women as well as four pages of statistical information. A gatherer of raw data, Jenson listed in a table the number of mission conferences, branches, male missionaries, female missionaries, elders, priests, teachers, deacons, and lay members in the Scandinavian Mission. He also detailed the numbers of individuals who were baptized or excommunicated and who emigrated each year between 1850 and 1926.

In March 1927, after more than four decades of research and writing on Latter-day Saints in Scandinavia, Jenson presented his nearly completed book manuscript to the First Presidency and Quorum of the Twelve for their approval to publish it, which they granted. By this time, he had already collected about $1,300 in advanced sales from his subscriber base, thanks to the canvasing work of his sales agents.[17] Despite the promising start, however, a tough road to publication and distribution lay ahead for Jenson.

Over the next seven months, Jenson worked tirelessly to finalize his forthcoming *History of the Scandinavian Mission* in order to meet the promised Christmas delivery date. Not wanting to let his loyal subscribers down, he often worked weekdays until midnight during the final typesetting stages. He even resorted to working with his small team on the Sabbath to hit his looming deadline. "I am not in the habit of working on Sundays," he confessed, "but I considered ourselves justified in doing it on this occasion, as we were working in the interest of the Church."[18] Days after celebrating his seventy-seventh birthday, Jenson finished his final, tedious review of the nearly six hundred typeset pages before they were printed and bound by the Deseret News Press.[19] Finally, he received the first hundred printed copies of his *History of the Scandinavian Mission* from the Deseret News Press just days before his holiday deadline.[20] It was published in a traditional six-by-nine-inch format, bound in a forest green cloth cover, complete with golden lettering, and featured more than 350 photographs.

The print run was capped at two thousand copies, only three hundred of which were committed to subscribers by the time the book was off the press. The remaining copies were to be sold at a cost of five dollars each until binding and printing costs were recouped.[21] Jenson perhaps thought the book would sell well among Scandinavian church members. Appointed agents, however, struggled to gain new subscribers, and a year after the book was released, only 750 books had been sold. By agreement of the Scandinavian Mission History Committee, which oversaw the production and distribution of the book, Jenson was allowed to assume the debts of the venture and took the remaining books to sell himself and to offer as payment to advertisers.[22] Earlier in life, Jenson would have been distressed by the slow sale of his book, but he now held a more seasoned perspective. Confident in his contribution to future historical works, and more financially stable, Jenson harbored no regret or resentment for his fellow Latter-day Saints. Instead, Jenson and the committee jointly felt that "the Scandinavian Mission History . . . was a monument to all who had anything to do with it. . . . It was a book, it was said, in which the Scandinavians and their descendants in the Church for many, many years, would find instruction, encouragement and joy."[23]

Day by Day with the Utah Pioneers

Jenson's second book-length publication during his twilight years came less than a decade later, commissioned by an unexpected 1934 agreement with the *Salt Lake Tribune*. Decades earlier, the *Tribune* had publicly ridiculed Jenson in its pages, an episode he would not have forgotten.[24] He also had a long-standing relationship with the *Deseret News*, the *Tribune*'s competing newspaper, as a travel writer, columnist, and author. Moreover, the *Deseret News* was the established newspaper of the Latter-day Saints. Jenson's agreement with the *Salt Lake Tribune* transgressed cultural boundaries in a longtime war of words between the two papers. Jenson later commented on the agreement: "For several years the *Tribune* had been very friendly in its attitude to the Church, as compared with what was the case years ago and it was agreed that we would furnish the paper with some original information about the pioneers."[25]

To celebrate the fiftieth anniversary of the Latter-day Saint pioneers entering the Salt Lake Valley in July 1847, the *Salt Lake Tribune* had run a popular daily column titled "Fifty Years Ago Today" from April 5 to July 24, 1897. Nearly forty years later, the *Tribune* determined to update the articles and rerun the celebrated column to expand their readership in a market dominated by Latter-day Saints. To add legitimacy to the series, the paper reached out to Jenson, in his capacity as Assistant Church Historian, to refresh the content. "Now with the finding of more diaries and the accumulation of more detailed accounting, this chronological history has been brought to what is believed by authorities of the church to be an accurate picture," the *Tribune* editors noted, highlighting Jenson's recent contributions. "Each day's story will be that of the corresponding day 87 years ago."[26]

In early April 1934, Jenson began his serialized column, "Day by Day with the Utah Pioneers," to coincide with the daily, 111-day experience of the vanguard pioneer company, led by Brigham Young, traveling to the Salt Lake Valley, which they reached in July 1847.[27] Hoping to use the series as a marketing windfall, the *Tribune* published blank souvenir scrapbooks for its readers to paste the daily newspaper articles into. By May 8, Jenson had finished updating all 111 earlier articles.[28]

Church Historian Joseph Fielding Smith, however, appeared to be bothered by Jenson's use of Historian's Office time to publish with the church's rival newspaper. Jenson recorded in his journal: "I had words with Joseph F. Smith jun. about my historical labors, and we both got angry, but we later made up, so that good feelings could prevail."[29] The conflict between Jenson, Smith, and the *Deseret News* had been brewing well before Jenson's decision to publish with the *Tribune*. Jenson felt slighted largely because, despite the success of his extensive writings for the *Deseret News* over the years, he had never received a penny of compensation. By contrast, the *Tribune* offered him $500 for his revised account of the pioneers of 1847. Feeling "sidetracked" by the *News*, Jenson vowed to never write for that paper again.[30]

The success of Jenson's pioneer account was measurable. One estimate put the tally of new subscribers to the *Tribune* over the span of his serial column at nine thousand.[31] This estimate was most likely an embellishment, since the *Tribune*'s circulation actually experienced a small decline from 1930 to 1935.[32] Still, the series brought Jenson's historical writings to new audiences and was met with praise from the newspaper's readership of fifty thousand. The success of the series turned the *Deseret News* repentant, according to Jenson. Earlier that year, the *News* came under new leadership, and the new manager, Seventy Samuel O. Bennion, with Joseph Fielding Smith's encouragement, took a renewed interest in Jenson's historical and journalistic talents. The *News* reached out to Jenson, and though obviously gratified by the paper's change of heart, Jenson refused to give an immediate answer to its inquiry.[33] The following day, Smith and Bennion called on Jenson again and he agreed to write a series of articles for the *Deseret News* on the 1834 Zion's Camp.[34] Bennion called on Jenson several days later and asked him to write an additional series on the early Latter-day Saint pioneers in Utah until 1850. Jenson agreed, and the series was eventually titled "The Building of Utah and Her Neighbors."[35] His column on Zion's Camp was published as a weekly feature in the church section of the *Deseret News*, while at the same time his compilation on early territorial Utah ran daily.[36]

Jenson's columns underscored the fact that he played the role of public historian well. Beyond simply producing reference volumes at the Historian's Office, Jenson displayed again the journalism talents that had given him his start in publishing and in the field of history. Such a blurred distinction between journalism and history made the story of church history relevant to the contemporary Latter-day Saint experience.

Autobiography of Andrew Jenson

After six decades of faithfully chronicling the peoples, places, and events of the Restoration, Jenson sought to publish his own life story. During his entire adult life, Jenson wrote the histories of many Latter-day Saint men and women, and the shift to autobiographical writing seemed natural: "When I reached the age of three-score and ten, after having written thousands of biographies of other people, I began to think seriously about one for myself," he explained. "Having kept a daily journal since I was thirteen years old I had plenty of source material from which to cull the necessary data for a history of my own life."[37] Drawing on his voluminous journals, correspondence, and personal writings, Jenson was able to reach into his past and create a remarkably accurate and carefully constructed personal history.

As a historian-turned-autobiographer, Jenson admired the distinct genre of Latter-day Saint autobiographical writings. Apostle Parley P. Pratt's autobiography served as the classic model to aspire to. The autobiography was renowned in Latter-day Saint culture for its eloquent depiction of Pratt's spiritual odyssey, and Jenson considered it both faith promoting and inspirational.[38] Jenson aspired to also create an inspiring history of his life for his posterity. He stated clearly the intended audience for his new project. "I now feel that I ought to write a history of my life for the perusal of my posterity and lovers of history," Jenson wrote in his journal.[39]

Grounded in romanticism, modern autobiographies during Jenson's time read like epics or quests for self-knowledge and displayed some of the private vulnerability familiar to real life. Religious writers, however, carved their own niche within this autobiographical tradition. In writing his life's history, Pratt leaned on the popularity of a number of Puritan authors who had merged history and piety in their own autobiographies to inspire audiences with a providential narrative.[40] This form of autobiographical writing was rarely an exclusive tale of self-discovery and was often written with a particular audience in mind.

Jenson embraced but also transgressed the genre. Professional historians were slow to embrace autobiographical sources because of their potential for bias.[41] Jenson's autobiography, however, displayed characteristics of the historian's craft he had developed and polished throughout his career. When recounting an event, he frequently quoted directly from his journal or correspondence, deferring to his original memory rather than to current retrospection. He also rarely slipped into spiritual interludes and proselytizing. Jenson aimed for an honest, chronological retelling of his life, akin more to a biography than to a self-styled memoir. He did, however, hope that his autobiography would achieve the same legacy as Pratt's. The preface to Jenson's volume reads: "I sincerely hope that besides its value as a work of reference, [this book] may also prove a faith-promoting production, and impress the younger and rising generation with the solemn fact that success in life (be it of a spiritual or temporal nature) can be attained by hard labor and honest endeavor, coupled with wisdom, will-power and determination."[42]

Despite its close reliance on records from his life, Jenson's *Autobiography* was still recollective and revisionist. Jenson had narrated his development into a historian once in his journal and now told the story again. Each time his thoughts were refracted through contemporary experience and interests. By the time he produced his *Autobiography*, much of his internal wrestle with his own position in the Historian's Office and the church hierarchy had expired. That, plus the public nature of the book, may have been why Jenson gave less expression to his thoughts on the qualities and characteristics of General Authorities. Most of the internal dynamics of his plural family, financial difficulties, and personal ecclesiastical aspirations were also left out. His *Autobiography*, instead, reflected the thoughts of a seasoned church official. By 1935, Jenson had had time to identify and digest the most compelling components of his personal story and legacy: his world tours and his development from a Danish peasant-boy into a successful public historian. These elements receive the most coverage in his *Autobiography*. Harold Jenson, in an addendum to the autobiography, admired the literary merits of his father's writing. Jenson composed "a story" that "reads much like a Horatio Alger book," a "rags to riches" narrative foregrounded in the Restoration.[43] The autobiography was not far from the historical tradition Jenson was accustomed to, but his story was also simplified, compelling, and relatable.

The *Autobiography of Andrew Jenson* finally came off the press in December 1938, just three years before his death. The book covered nearly his entire life, beginning with his birth in Denmark in 1850 and concluding with personal events through the end of 1935—his eighty-fifth year. He divided the book into ninety-three chapters, spanning about 670 pages of double-columned text. The book is also richly illustrated with photos from his travels.[44]

Jenson's decision to publish his autobiography was not an attempt at profiting from his life story (the book sold for $3.50 and was advertised but not sold by subscription).[45] Nor was it a heavy-handed attempt to rewrite his own legacy detached from reality. At his core, Jenson believed all Latter-day Saints were under a divine commandment to keep a personal record. And for the Danish American, who frequently felt underappreciated, publishing his life's record was an opportunity to get the entirety of his accomplishments before the eyes of church leaders. Apostle George Albert Smith, in the autobiography's promotional literature, captured the essence of the Andrew Jenson "story": "His simple story reads like a fairy tale but records only the truth. His accomplishment should be an inspiration to every boy to do his best and to keep at it."[46] Someone who had spoken for so many Latter-day Saints in the past had finally spoken for himself. In selectively reconstructing his life, Jenson hoped to be remembered as one who, as a traveler serving the voiceless converts of the Restoration, served God and church first.

Encyclopedic History of the Church of Jesus Christ of Latter-day Saints

Jenson's final book publication during his twilight years was his *Encyclopedic History of the Church of Jesus Christ of Latter-day Saints* (1941), published just eight months before his death. His idea to create an encyclopedia-format history of the Latter-day Saints came to him as a stroke of inspiration decades earlier while he was documenting the church's missionary labors in Europe in 1883. While there, he had the idea "of an encyclopedia of the most important events, places, and men in the Church from the beginning."[47] The contemplated encyclopedia became a lifetime project as Jenson regularly compiled and then revised ward, stake, and mission histories. In 1922, Jenson imagined the creation of a "Latter-day Saint Geographical Encyclopedia" that would contain brief articles on most of the ecclesiastical units of the church.[48] His initial proposal, which included a trip around the stakes of Zion, was not approved by the First Presidency at the time.

As the 1930 centennial celebration of the founding of the church approached, Jenson dusted off the idea of a "Geographical Encyclopedia" to commemorate the "first century of the new Christian Era." By this point, he and his team in the Historian's Office had compiled 560 manuscript histories, which he could draw upon for this major project.[49] Originally, Jenson had intended to write two histories associated with the centennial. The first would be a general history of the church to compliment his encyclopedic history. A couple of years before the centennial, however, a committee of church leaders tasked B. H. Roberts, Jenson's Historian's Office associate, with transforming his long-standing series for the *Americana* magazine into a comprehensive church history.[50] Around the time the First Presidency and Roberts conceived of expanding his history, Jenson pitched his encyclopedic history to President Heber J. Grant and his counselors. "If I am entitled to any place in the literary world, I would naturally belong to the group engaged in writing works of reference," he wrote to the First Presidency.[51] Jenson, who felt overlooked when Roberts's six-volume *Comprehensive History of the Church of Jesus Christ of Latter-day Saints* was privileged by church leaders and released in 1930, hoped his church encyclopedia would be his major contribution to the growing list of authoritative histories written about the church and that he too could be classed as a definitive authority on church history.

By summer 1931, Jenson had nearly completed entries on all the wards and stakes of the church for his encyclopedia and had updated the respective manuscript histories up to 1930. He felt, however, that the information he had readied on the missions of the church was outdated, most of it having been gathered on his previous world tours. He took an audacious request to Joseph Fielding Smith: a third and final world tour by airplane to visit all of the missions of the church to update his manuscript histories.[52] Smith reluctantly took Jenson's request to the First Presidency but expressed his opinion forcefully on the matter. He had already given Jenson approval to travel to the stakes and wards of the church but felt his advancing age would make a trip around the world unadvisable. Furthermore, Smith expressed the opinion that the church's record-keeping infrastructure was sufficient to gather the needed historical material without a traveling historian, whose efforts Smith felt would be repetitive and wasteful. For several years already, the Historian's Office had been relying on ward and stake clerks to compile local church histories. The frequent requests by Jenson had put Smith in a personal bind. He told the First Presidency that he "tried to favor Brother Jenson and avoid any difficulties with him as far as possible, but about the only way to keep peace with him is to grant him all that he desires.

Yet there are some things at times that I feel it is my duty to oppose."[53] Grant and Ivins, trusting in the recommendation of their Church Historian, kindly let Jenson know that his proposed worldwide tour was not approved.

Disappointed but undeterred, Jenson's attention turned to finalizing his church encyclopedia for publication. "Such a Church Encyclopedia in the field," Jenson explained, "used side by side with *Church Chronology* and the three volumes of *Latter-day Saint Biographical Encyclopedia* already published, would, as works of reference . . . contribute very much towards answering all questions of importance pertaining to the history of the Church." He continued final preparations on his manuscript until spring 1932.[54] That spring, Jenson sent his final version to the First Presidency for approval,[55] but a decision from the First Presidency was slow and Jenson grew anxious. At last, a General Authority committee (following precedent for church publications) was appointed in July 1932 to determine whether or not to publish the encyclopedia.[56]

Jenson, however, was fearful that the mounting delays were quickly making his work outdated and less valuable. With no word by the October general conference, Jenson wrote to Joseph Fielding Smith, urging immediate action from the First Presidency on his manuscript.[57] Behind the scenes, the reading committee, along with the rest of the Quorum of the Twelve and First Presidency, were dealing with other pressing matters and had made little progress toward reaching a final decision.

In November, Joseph Fielding Smith left an excerpt of Jenson's manuscript on Apostle James E. Talmage's desk, seeking his recommendation. Talmage read the excerpt quickly and gave his opinion just three days after receiving the assignment. Confirming Jenson's own fears, Talmage told Smith, "Such compilation as this can never be up to date; in fact, this is already behind the times as in the naming of branches within wards, or independent branches, several of which have been organized into wards with the last few weeks." Though Talmage recognized that such a compilation represented the "arduous and protracted labor" of Jenson and would "prove of great convenience and intrinsic value for reference purposes," he questioned whether the book would be of any interest beyond "the few researchers who seek after data of the kind presented." His final recommendation to Smith was that the work was too impracticable and costly to be published. He suggested that the entire book be retyped on "good paper" to be preserved at the Historian's Office.[58] It seems that Talmage's negative recommendation swung the committee's decision. Shortly after receiving Talmage's reply, Smith notified Jenson of the decision, sanctioned by the First Presidency, to not publish the work.[59] Upon hearing from Smith, Jenson recorded in his journal that he "had expected the decision for some time."[60] Later, Jenson suspected that the First Presidency's refusal to publish his work stemmed from the "heavy expense" the church had incurred by publishing Roberts's six-volume, 3,400-page history in 1930.[61]

Finally, three years after his historical encyclopedia had been completed, Jenson entered into arrangements with Samuel O. Bennion, manager of the *Deseret News*, to begin serializing his encyclopedic history, with an agreement that the Deseret News Press would eventually publish the series as a single volume.[62] His 1934 series on the Latter-day Saint pioneer trail in the competing *Tribune* had proven his marketability as a newspaper contributor, and the *Deseret News* took a renewed interest in Jenson's work. "Histories of the L.D.S. Church have been written and published before," began the newspaper's full-page advertisement. "But this is the first comprehensive encyclopedia history of the Church which has ever been attempted." The ad called it "a stupendous work," an "amazing achievement," and "the life work of Andrew Jenson." "It will eclipse in scope and importance," the ad continued, "anything which he has heretofore published."[63] Totaling over thirteen hundred articles, "Encyclopedic History of the Church" ran daily from March 16, 1935, until March 1939.[64] The series provided the Intermountain West with a four-year immersion of the church's ecclesiastical history and brought to the masses an awareness of Jenson's painstaking efforts to compile manuscript histories of the scattered church units.

The serial publication of his life's work, however, did little to realize Jenson's ultimate desire to see his encyclopedic history of the church bound in print. In May 1939, he petitioned the First Presidency again to sponsor the manuscript's publication at an estimated printing cost of just over $2,000. He hoped to give the church both the copyright and the proceeds. Church leaders deferred to Joseph Fielding Smith's judgment, and a decision was delayed until the manuscript was fully polished. In September 1940, Jenson at last received approval from Grant to publish the manuscript.[65] In 1941, six years after the serialization of his church encyclopedia had begun, the Deseret News Press printed, in full at 976 pages, the *Encyclopedic History of the Church of Jesus Christ of Latter-day Saints*. The Corporation of the President of The Church of Jesus Christ of Latter-day Saints copyrighted the work, the first time any of Jenson's works (including the church-owned *Church Chronology*) had received such a benefit. As Assistant Church Historian, Jenson had longed for the day when the First Presidency would formally own his work, giving it their full sanction.

Sensing that his long life was winding down, Jenson reflected on his career as a Latter-day Saint historian in the preface to his *Encyclopedic History*: "A man who enjoys his work finds life sweet and pleasant and every moment of it gives him joy and satisfaction. . . . I have become convinced that historians, like poets, are born as such, and that this enables them to make their life's labor successful."[66] Jenson viewed his professional labors through a theological lens, casting his labors onto a cosmic backdrop of premortal choices and aptitudes—a perspective that he drew from unique Latter-day Saint doctrines. "In connection with the creating of an earth on which to place His offspring," Jenson explained, "God chose . . . noble spirits as leaders and rulers." According to Jenson's gloss of the scriptural text from the Pearl of Great Price (Abraham 3:22–23) and the Old Testament (Jeremiah 1:5), biblical prophets and ministers had been foreordained to fulfill their roles based on their premortal spiritual progression. Likewise, Jenson was "impressed with the thought that certain spirits were selected to come down and mingle with these leaders and rulers in mortality as poets and historians to record the work to be done by these great and noble ones."[67] The agitation and anxiety Jenson frequently experienced in his historical work often stemmed from this sense that his labor and calling had been given to him by God, a sense he hoped his colleagues and superiors would share.

The First Presidency sent out a circular to all stake presidents and bishops advising them to acquire a copy of Jenson's *Encyclopedic History* at a discounted price for their meetinghouse libraries.[68] The editors of the popular *Improvement Era* also highlighted Jenson's latest publication, calling it the "crowning achievement" of the Assistant Church Historian's career. The volume represented "many miles of travel, long hours of patient study, and the perusal of countless records, many of which are now no longer accessible." As his manuscript sources aged, so too did Jenson, and he recognized his *Encyclopedic History*—his magnum opus—as his final attempt to give permanence to the historical information he had spent years gathering. As a fitting symbol of the tenuousness of both mortal life and historical preservation, an hourglass was depicted on the title page of *Encyclopedic History*. The top of the hourglass was empty.[69]

Celebrating the Twilight Years

On December 11, 1935, the day of his eighty-fifth birthday, Jenson, with his family, took "an automobile ride in the morning to the foot of Ensign Peak, going as far as the machine could consistently climb." "From that point," Jenson wrote, "we climbed to the top of the peak so as to enjoy the magnificent view looking east, south and west."[70] Even at his old age, he could still manage to hike to the place where he had received so much personal direction and consolation throughout his career. As he gazed over the Salt Lake Valley, he may have recalled the personal revelation he received on that hilltop in the summer of 1901, which had kept him professionally engaged at the Historian's Office during a dark season of his life.[71] After a drive down from the Ensign Peak trailhead, he parked and entered the Historian's Office, where his "office force" surprised him "with kind greetings and good wishes and presented . . . a large bouquet of yellow pom pom chrysanthemums and a card containing the names of all the employees, including the Church Historian, Joseph Fielding Smith, and A. W[illia]m Lund, Assistant Church Historian."[72]

That evening, Jenson's daughter Eva hosted a formal birthday dinner at her residence. Despite his occasionally abrasive personality, Jenson enjoyed hosting extravagant social gatherings for family and friends. His home on Second West was the frequent site of holiday and birthday events. This particular gathering showcased Jenson's large and connected social circle in the Salt Lake City community. In attendance were members of the First Presidency and Quorum of the Twelve, along with their wives, and other close friends.

In addition to its festiveness, the evening served as a reminder that Jenson had outlived most of his contemporaries and childhood family members. He was surrounded by his surviving posterity. His father and mother, Christian Jensen Jacobsen (1826–98) and Kirsten Andersen (1821–1917) had both passed away decades before. Both of his brothers, Jens Christian (1849–1931) and Joseph Julius (1862–1933), had also each died a few years earlier. Jenson's first wife, Kirsten Marie "Mary" Pedersen (1859–87), had passed away after only twelve years of marriage.[73] Of their four children, Andrew Alexander (1876–1928) had already died, but Parley Peter (1878–1957), Mary Minerva (1885–1955), and Eleonore Elizabeth (1885–1977) were still living. Jenson's second (plural) wife, Emma Howell (1862–1937),[74] though disabled, was also in attendance that evening.[75] Of their three children, Alfred Howell (1888–89) had passed away as an infant, but Eva Howell (1889–1980) and Harold Howell (1895–1978) were at the birthday celebration. Jenson's third (plural) wife, Bertha Howell (1866–1945),[76] along with their one child, Leo Rulon (1905–57) were also in attendance.[77] Moreover, a number of Jenson's grandchildren were there to help with the dinner service and musical entertainment.

Mary K. Pye, Jenson's longtime secretary, took notes of the evening's proceedings that would later be inserted into Jenson's journal. At the celebration, Jenson was afforded time to publicly reflect on his life, and his mind settled on his choice to immigrate to America as a young boy, a decision he called "one of the most important actions of his life."[78] The stream of dignitaries that spoke after Jenson included David O. McKay (second counselor in the First Presidency), Apostle Rudger Clawson, US senator and Apostle Reed Smoot, and others. They reflected on Jenson's indefatigable work ethic and commitment to his faith and marveled at his transformation from a young Danish peasant to a writer and public historian. Reed Smoot offered the praises Jenson so frequently yearned for: "You have made your mark in the world, you have been specially qualified for the work you have been called to do. You will never die, your name will live when ours may be forgotten."[79]

Church Historian Joseph Fielding Smith described what it was like to grow up across the street from the Jenson family. "He could remember as a mere boy seeing Bro. Jenson pulling a little cart on which were type sets and other matters connected with his printing and publishing business," read the notes in Jenson's journal. "Bro. Smith endorsed the remarks of others in regard to his being an indefatigable worker and could not bear to see time wasted" and told a funny story from 1895, when Jenson was circumnavigating the globe: While traveling aboard a ship, he became frustrated when he attempted to petition the captain for a Sunday service. The captain consented, but they soon crossed the international date line, and Sunday became Monday. The captain refused to allow the service to be held. "Bro. Jenson had no peace of mind," Smith continued, "until he had made another journey, traveling around the world in an opposite direction" in 1912 and recovered the lost time.[80]

Jenson's eighty-fifth birthday celebration suggested that his legacy had been planted in the minds of his peers. He was celebrated by the church's highest leaders as a devoted Latter-day Saint with an unmatched work ethic who had done more than anyone else to recover and share church history.[81] The next day, the *Deseret News* featured a large photograph of the event with Jenson seated at the head of the table surrounded by loved ones and church leaders.[82] But it was the small, unassuming headline that perhaps provided the most fitting tribute: "Historian Works at Desk as Usual on 85th Birthday."[83]

Retirement did not suit the restless Dane. On the occasion of his ninetieth birthday, Jenson told the *Salt Lake Telegram*, "I am one of the men who does not believe in retiring. I intend to keep right on working as hard as I can. I would die if I didn't have something to do."[84] Little work, however, would get done on his ninetieth birthday. A large celebration took place that evening at the Lion House near Temple Square, the former residence of Brigham Young and his family. Between four hundred and five hundred well-wishers attended, including seven members of the Quorum of the Twelve. He also received eighty cards and letters offering congratulations on the commencement of his ninety-first year of life.

For members of his family at an exclusive dinner just prior to the reception, Jenson played a recording he had made that afternoon that provided a brief sketch of his life and his testimony.[85] "I have implicit faith in my Redeemer, Jesus Christ, the Son of God, and in the divine mission of the Prophet Joseph Smith. In all my ups and downs in life, I have stood unshaken on these points." As he reflected on the legacy he left behind to posterity, his thick and deep Danish accent broke and he choked back tears:

> Now children, grandchildren, and my posterity that I leave in mortality, and those yet unborn but still follow, will you cherish in your memory, that Danish boy who left his native land for the gospel's sake, immigrated to Zion to become and remain a true Latter-day Saint, a devoted Christian, and a loyal citizen to the best nation on earth. Borrowing this sentiment from one of our own poets, I appeal

Andrew Jenson with family and friends at what was likely his ninetieth birthday party (1940). Courtesy Church History Library.

> to you with my heart full of affection and eyes filled with tears in saying, Will you be true to the faith that your parents have cherished? Will you be true to the faith for which martyrs have perished? May God bless you, help you, and enable you to do even better and greater work than I and my wives have done. And with this hope in mind, I, as a servant of God, bearing the holy priesthood, bless you with a father's blessing, in the name of Jesus Christ, my Redeemer, amen.[86]

Following Jenson's heartfelt testimony, the family serenaded him with his favorite song, "Grandfather's Clock" (1874) by Henry Clay Work.[87] The song carried echoes of Jenson's own father, Christian, a clockmaker, whose beautiful grandfather clock was situated in the Andrew Jenson Memorial Hall.[88] The tune now also served as the theme song for the conclusion of Jenson's life, the heartbeat of Latter-day Saint record keeping.

A "Pen Stilled"

In the days following his birthday celebration, Jenson struggled to recover physically from the activity and excitement. "Was far from being well," he confessed in his journal.[89] He received a priesthood blessing from two apostles, and his health started to improve in time for the winter holidays.[90] The Jensons celebrated Christmas Eve in "Danish style," with a family meal and gift exchange. That night several inches of snow fell, providing Jenson with what would be his last white Christmas. As they celebrated the birth of the Prince of Peace in the safety of Salt Lake City, the Assistant Church Historian pondered the growing military conflict in his beloved Europe.[91] Like other Americans, Jenson was increasingly worried about what was becoming the Second World War, the Nazi rise to power in Germany, and the fate of the free world. He feared for the future of the "civilisation of the Christian world" and wondered if the Second Coming of Jesus Christ was fast approaching.[92]

In the early months of 1941, Jenson, though increasingly tired, worked feverishly to proofread his *Encyclopedic History of the Church*. According to A. William Lund, Jenson told him, "I have asked the Lord to give me strength that I may finish [the *Encyclopedic History*], and then I will be willing to pass on."[93] With the *Encyclopedic History* wrapped up by spring 1941, Jenson finally enjoyed a short break from his work, and his interests moved away from his publications. On March 12, 1941, he attended the speech of political activist and advocate for the deaf and blind Helen Keller in the Tabernacle in Salt Lake City. After the meeting, he was introduced to her as "the 'oldest man in Utah,' which was stretching the facts a little," he admitted; however, he was certain that, at ninety years old, he was the oldest person in the meeting and was frequently described in other introductions as the oldest living church official.[94]

He then took what he called "the first real vacation" of his life. For a month in May, he toured Arizona and Southern California with Bertha. Contrary to his prior trips, he did not attempt to gather records or write local histories during his travels. Instead, Jenson read for leisure and took in the sights. When he returned home, he told the *Salt Lake Tribune*, "I've started out on vacations before, but I've always ended up working harder away from the office than in it." "This time," he continued, "it was a genuine rest."[95]

His health, however, continued to fade. He worked intermittently at the Historian's Office throughout the summer and early fall, revising his own papers and stake histories. He attended the October general conference and continued to labor closely on Historian's Office matters with his daughter Eva. Late in October, he advised Joseph Fielding Smith on the "condition of [his] department of the H.O." and "endeavored to have . . . the work done in a more practical way."[96] Jenson's work, however, soon came to an abrupt halt. On November 15, his journal entry trails off with commentary on the Second World War, then raging in Europe.[97] He tasked his daughter Eva with finishing his journal. That afternoon he felt fatigued, so he left his office and returned home to rest for the weekend, planning to return to the Historian's Office the following Monday morning. He took a nap, then worked from home until supper. "While eating a bowl of hot bread and milk he turned deathly white and was seized with a severe chill"—a heart attack.[98]

According to Eva, during the next few days, Jenson was "rational" only intermittently, and on November 18, "during the early morning [he] tho[ugh]t he was talking to Pres. Heber J. Grant and bore a powerful testimony to the truthfulness of the Gospel, etc. He told Aunt Bertha he was going home today and when she told him he was at home he said he was going to a home far away from here." Apostles Charles A. Callis and John A. Widtsoe, along with A. William Lund, gave Jenson "a beautiful blessing but did not promise him life." After eating dinner, Jenson "commenced reaching out his hands as tho[ugh] he were picking some kind of fruit." He passed into a coma and died at 8:35 p.m., less than a month before his ninety-first birthday.[99]

The next day the *Salt Lake Tribune* issued the most fitting tribute to his life. Two words above a large photo of an aged Jenson read: "Pen Stilled."[100] News of his death reached as far east as the *New York Times*, which printed an obituary listing Jenson's many life achievements.[101] The First Presidency also issued a public statement: "In the passing of Brother Andrew Jenson the Church has lost one of its unique characters and one who has rendered a great service. His devotion to historical research was of the highest character. He never wearied in finding facts and making a record of them. He was a staunch Latter-day Saint. He loved the work. His constant thought was service. His testimony was perfect. The Gospel was his whole concern. The Church will miss him."[102]

In the days that followed, relatives and friends flooded the Jenson home, mourning the loss of their Danish American historian and sharing memories of his life. Repeatedly, those who publicly remembered Jenson talked of his vast corpus of publications and histories. A whole generation or two of church members had learned of their church's past from the pen of Andrew Jenson. Death had now ended the journey of the great traveler of the Restoration. His writings, however, continued to tell his story. They remain as monuments to his life's work, bearing quiet testimony that silence is never the true historian's fate.

Epilogue

On November 22, 1941, at 1:00 P.M., throngs of well-wishers crowded into the Assembly Hall on Temple Square to attend the funeral of Andrew Jenson. The service, planned with the assistance of the Presiding Bishopric, fittingly took place at the site Jenson had given numerous historical and general conference addresses. General authorities, local dignitaries, friends, and family were in attendance. The funeral for the longtime church employee was not unlike those given for the church's highest authorities, though Jenson was never formally designated a General Authority.[1] In the remarks spoken at the funeral, Jenson's sacrifice for the church and his devotion to the Historian's Office took center stage.

Over the course of five decades in the service of the church, Jenson had built a network of friends and acquaintances who understood his personality and aspirations. As is customary at funerals, none of Jenson's faults—his interpersonal challenges and unbridled ambition, displayed most frequently in his work for the Historian's Office—were sounded from the pulpit. Instead, Jenson's matchless personality and his singularity as a record keeper and a historian were appreciated and honored by his friends. Jenson lived on, Apostle David O. McKay remarked at the funeral, because "his personality persists beyond the grave." Through his faithful "indefatigable efforts," he gave the church an inheritance of "valuable information," which they would not have had otherwise. For that, according to McKay, Jenson "has gone to a great reward."[2]

Jenson's persistence stemmed from a loyalty to his calling as a historian. When others were reticent to defend the mission of the Historian's Office to church leaders, Jenson filled the silence. He believed he was engaged in a noble undertaking as a historian and understood that decisions made by the First Presidency and Quorum of the Twelve would have dramatic consequences for his overall record-keeping vision. Fighting for and achieving his vision of record keeping and document preservation sometimes required the sacrifice of personal charm and popularity. His passion often turned into zealousness, at the expense of human connection. As admitted by his peers, his lifestyle was one few would choose; his travel schedule was arduous, and his work was best done either in the silent confines of an office or on the road, often without steady companionship. To produce usable history required focus, attention to detail, and patience for repetitive tasks.

The tireless and well-traveled Jenson was a curiosity to the public. At home and away, he became a novelty, one to be admired (though not envied), which caused many to write off his personality quirks as unique to the man. In the public mind, Jenson's mission was inseparable from his distinctive persona, which perhaps tempered more than aided the effectiveness of his mission. His message often failed to capture the enthusiasm of his audience. Historical work and record keeping were easily left by the general membership to those who could tolerate it; few desired performing the clerical tasks as Jenson envisioned them.

But the loneliness of his daily work did not fully disconnect Jenson from the domestic and international communities he served. Through crossing countless national borders and meeting with Latter-day Saints in far-off settlements, Jenson built a lifetime of connections and friends. His home was a social hub in Salt Lake City, often through the efforts of his wives, who were active in community service and tolerant of his frequent absences.

Jenson's life was dedicated to collecting records and creating historical consciousness. He joined the Historian's Office staff at an unsettled time in the 1890s. Records were unaccounted for or unorganized, and the entire office was in need of a system to ensure the future usability of the records. Jenson imposed order and advocated for standardized record-keeping practices that could be taught to clerks in the church's branches, wards, stakes, and missions. The record-keeping reforms he inaugurated in the early twentieth century, while unevenly applied by local ecclesiastical units, moved the church toward a uniform system of record keeping that persisted throughout the twentieth century. His efforts cemented the importance of record books and historical reports, which led to volumes of data being recorded and sent to the Historian's Office that would not otherwise have been preserved.

In his efforts to improve the church's records, Jenson pled with the church membership to take record keeping and the preservation of history seriously. At the October 1926 general conference, Jenson urged the congregation to become "better posted in regard to the history of this Church, the most important organization of its kind that ever existed upon the face of the earth. We cannot sit still . . . quietly at the Historian's office and steer the great ship of Zion historically." He needed "the cooperation of the local authorities and the people generally." He warned the Latter-day Saints "against the destruction or the losing of records" and "the folly of looking upon record-books in the same light that a school boy looks upon his copy book—when it is written full it is of no further use."[3] In another general conference sermon, he quipped, "We want to make . . . all [Latter-day Saints] historians" by enlisting them to keep and preserve both personal and ecclesiastical records for the benefit of the church and its historians.[4]

The end goal of Jenson's advocacy for record keeping was a complete history of the church, though he cared less for interpretive history; instead he aimed to compile dates and facts chronologically into a comprehensive record of the church. In Jenson's travel-centric approach, both human memories and the physical records in wards, stakes, and missions of the church were paramount in the creation of an accurate and unparalleled historical record. In his final general conference sermon, in April 1930, Jenson shared his guiding philosophy of history: "History is made up mainly from the acts of men and women, and . . . those who become converts to the true gospel of Christ" are generally organized into branches, wards, stakes, and missions. A "true and detailed history of the Church as a whole" required telling the story of the church's ecclesiastical units and "a history of the settlements of the saints in their gathering places."[5] Until his death, Jenson believed that collecting and preserving global church history was best accomplished by a historian traveling to the church's ecclesiastical units.

Aware of Jesus Christ's great commission to take the gospel to "all nations, kindreds, tongues, and people,"[6] Jenson's historical vision moved beyond the domestic church. In his first general conference sermon after his appointment as an Assistant Church Historian, Jenson set forth his view on the gospel's global appeal: "I am a living witness and want to bear testimony to the fact that I know God is no respecter of persons. It does not make any difference where we are born, nor the language we speak. The Lord can be found upon the islands of the sea, upon the continent of Europe, and the continents of Africa and Asia, where I have had the privilege of visiting, as well as upon this land of America."[7] Jenson's thoughts on the global destiny of the church were not necessarily unique for the time. Numerous church leaders had assessed the state of the church abroad, its potential future in lands across the globe, and encouraged expanding proselytizing in countries where the church previously had little significant presence.[8] But Jenson made sure the church's historical apparatus matched the expanding vision for church growth. At a time when the church lacked the resources and ability to make a large-scale effort to preserve its global history, Jenson traveled over one million miles to ensure that the memories from the church's early global outposts were preserved. As he had domestically, he put in place a record-keeping infrastructure of formal record books and protocols that laid the historical groundwork for the church abroad.

In addition to documenting the global church, Jenson articulated its importance. He served as an unofficial spokesperson for converts abroad and immigrants to the Salt Lake Valley. At Jenson's funeral, Apostle John A. Widtsoe recounted his own first interaction with Latter-day Saint literature in Norway: Jenson's *Ungdommens Raadgiver* (Counselor of youth), a monthly periodical for young Danish Norwegian Latter-day Saints. Jenson "conceived the Kingdom of God to be a means of uniting all peoples under one banner—the Gospel Standard," Widtsoe recalled. "The reestablished Church was to him a melting pot for making from all nations the army of the Lord, bearing the message of righteousness to all the world and preparing the earth for the coming of the Lord Jesus Christ." Jenson's own status as an immigrant gave him "an understanding and sympathetic eye upon those who, caught by the Gospel net, were obliged to give up home, native land, and often the mother tongue, to enlist in the great army of the Lord." With that experience, in Widtsoe's estimation, Jenson "became a defender and helper to those who came from foreign lands to help build Zion in this favored land."[9] Thousands of Scandinavian Latter-day Saints learned the gospel and church history with the assistance of Jenson's Danish-language periodicals and scripture translations. He brought church history to a foreign-born audience. He spoke at Scandinavian meetings in Utah and articulated the needs of the Danish-Norwegian Mission to the First Presidency.

Jenson's hopes to foster better historical consciousness among the Saints—what he called a "general awakening" in regard to history and record keeping—never came to satisfactory fruition in his lifetime.[10] Church Historian and Apostle Joseph Fielding Smith lamented this at Jenson's funeral. Smith called Jenson's *Church Chronology* "one of the most important books . . . that we have, yet I suppose there are very few members of the Church who know anything about it." Despite its circulation among the wards, stakes, and missions of the church and its numerous reprints and updates, Smith felt the work had not been fully embraced by Latter-day Saints.[11] For the most part, Jenson's books had sold less than he hoped for in his lifetime, a disappointment he slowly accepted.

Yet, as he expressed in his *Encyclopedic History of the Church*, Jenson wanted to live on through his publications long after his death, anticipating their use by future researchers.[12] In the 1950s and '60s, the field of Latter-day Saint history professionalized. The newly established Mormon History Association welcomed a generation of professionally trained scholars who began to study the church from new angles. Jenson's publications and manuscripts provided reference support and details to fill in these histories. The Journal History he helped begin is still invaluable to researchers. Today Jenson's books are companions to the scholar, genealogist, and archivist seeking biographical details about lives that would not have reached the public eye otherwise. The footnotes of scholarly studies on the Latter-day Saints still reference Jenson's historical work. Jenson anticipated the erosion of historical memory for future generations and rescued, wrote, and compiled an archive's worth of historical documents for a new generation of historians to explore.

The current church archive at 15 East North Temple Street in Salt Lake City, Utah, formally called the Church History Library, is home to the record books Jenson helped create and preserve and most of his surviving historical work. Researchers still visit frequently to review material that Jenson compiled one hundred years before. His private library, as well as volumes he gathered for the Historian's Office, are scattered gems among the library's expansive collection. Jenson's familiar stamp, fixed on items he once owned, can be seen on countless volumes and manuscripts. His historical and travel notes, often recorded on paper scraps, and his gathering methods, done without fealty to modern archival practices, posed challenges to later church archivists who searched for provenance and order in the records he brought in to the Historian's Office. Nonetheless, the physical volume of Jenson's historical product is staggering, a reminder of his dedication and persistence. Kate B. Carter, of the Daughters of Utah Pioneers, predicted at Jenson's funeral that "As long as the paper of this time remains in existence, the words of Andrew Jenson shall go forth and proclaim the Gospel of Jesus Christ, for we and all those who are students of history scan his papers every day and they become a part of our lives."[13]

Less tangible, but no less important, are the ways in which Jenson shaped church history for the public. Jenson shared history with Latter-day Saints more than any other figure at the Historian's Office, or within the church hierarchy. While other published works, including Joseph Fielding Smith's *Essentials in Church History* (1922), were more widely read by Latter-day Saints and influential in creating a formal institutional narrative of church history, Jenson was an unparalleled ambassador of history to the Latter-day Saint public. The Saints dialogued with him at quarterly conferences in their wards and stakes and attended his public lectures on Temple Square. They corresponded with him regularly, offering him facts and documents while also asking historical questions they believed only he could answer. Jenson published and lectured regularly on a number of topics, including Joseph Smith, Latter-day Saint missionary work, and Utah's pioneers, ensuring that his perspective on formative church events would be known to his fellow church members. His hundreds of biographies in the multivolume *Latter-day Saint Biographical Encyclopedia* brought to light the lives of many lesser-known men and woman in the settlement of the US West. If the general church membership were slow to heed his calls for better record keeping or to read his publications, Jenson's voice was still one they knew and respected. His history was their institutional and cultural inheritance.

When Church Historian Franklin D. Richards set apart Jenson as "a historian in Zion" in 1891, the Apostle promised the young chronicler that "when, at some future day, the books should be opened to view, the importance of [his] labors should become apparent and the good work done by [him] should bring a blessing and a benefit to all Israel."[14] Jenson, however, could not wait for the promised day of professional and personal appreciation. He knew his life's tale should be shared. He told the story himself in his voluminous journal and published autobiography (which he sought to have distributed throughout the church). He numbered his miles (over one million), his historical sermons (over six thousand), his manuscript volumes (over 850), positioning his legacy as a devout record keeper and historian. But his legacy is not comfortably contained within the product of his labors. While building and documenting the church, he crossed borders few Latter-day Saints had crossed before. In speaking, he enlarged the historical memory of Latter-day Saints and shaped their perceptions of the church's past. And in writing and compiling, he saved historical details from permanent loss while inspiring the work of countless historians who followed him. His historical imagination spread far and wide.

In December 1937, Jenson commissioned a stone monument to be placed over his selected burial site in the Salt Lake City Cemetery.[15] On the stone obelisk, he had etched the following tribute: "Andrew Jenson, historian, missionary, and extensive traveler. . . . His loyalty to his adopted country, America, did not diminish his love for his native Denmark." On the other three sides of the obelisk, he had inscribed the names of his wives, Mary, Emma, and Bertha. A stone globe was fixed atop the obelisk into which was etched the route of his first around-the-world tour.[16] Jenson saw both the past and present differently from most of his fellow Latter-day Saints, a viewpoint gained from thousands of miles of travel in places few Latter-day Saints had visited. His widened perspective was the burden and blessing of the historian, who had spent much of his life in the sources of the past. The stone monument commemorates his distinctiveness as a restless pilgrim to far-off lands, where he served as an ambassador and visionary for the church and its history.

Notes

Abbreviations

AJC/CHL	Andrew Jenson Collection, ca. 1841–1942. MS 17956. CHL.
AJL	Andrew Jenson, Letterbook, 1884–89, 16–17, Andrew Jenson, Collection, ca. 1841–1941, CHL.
CHL	Church History Library, Church History Department, The Church of Jesus Christ of Latter-day Saints, Salt Lake City.
HOJ	Historical Department, Office Journal, 1844–2012, 102 vols., CR 100 1, CHL.
Jenson	Andrew Jenson
A. A. Jenson	Andrew Alexander Jenson
Jenson Journal	Andrew Jenson, Autobiography and Journals, ca. 1864–1941, MS 1230, CHL.
SMLC	Scandinavian Mission Letterpress Copybooks, 1858–1920, 21:342, CHL

Prologue

1. Jenson Journal, April 5, 1934; "Editor of L.D.S. Saga Flies over Pioneers' Trail," *Salt Lake Tribune*, July 25, 1934, 24. See also Jenson, *Day by Day*.

2. Jenson Journal, July 12, 1934.

3. "Editor of L.D.S. Saga Flies over Pioneers' Trail," 24; Jenson, *Autobiography*, 632.

4. "Editor of L.D.S. Saga."

5. "Danmark Kirkebøger." Reinwand, "Andrew Jenson." For consistency we refer to Jenson by his most common, anglicized name but will use the nonanglicized *Jensen* when referencing his parents and siblings.

6. A stake is comparable to a Catholic diocese. A mission is a geographical jurisdiction independent of stakes over which a mission president presides and directs the proselytizing work of assigned missionaries.

7. Plural marriage, the practice of a man marrying more than one wife, was participated in openly in Utah Territory since 1852, though it had been selectively introduced by Joseph Smith earlier. At the height of the practice, around 1860, half of men, women, and children in Utah lived in plural families. Cornwall, Courtwright, and Van Beek, "How Common the Principle?," 152; Daynes, *More Wives than One*, 101.

8. Alexander, *Mormonism in Transition*; Mauss, *Angel and the Beehive*; G. Larson, *"Americanization" of Utah.*

9. *Deseret News 2013 Church News Almanac*, 212.

10. The mandate is recorded in Doctrine and Covenants 21:1.

11. Walker, Whittaker, and Allen, *Mormon History*, 14–18.

12. Doctrine and Covenants 128:8.

13. Apostles generally belong to the Quorum of the Twelve Apostles, the second-highest presiding body of the church, just below the First Presidency (a body of three that includes the church president). The church president selects new apostles.

14. Jenson, *Autobiography*, iii.

15. Jenson, *Encyclopedic History*, iii–iv.

16. Ibid., iv; Heb. 11:4 (KJV).

17. *One Hundredth Annual Conference*, 151.

18. "Oxen Driver Will Fly," *Omaha Bee-News*, July 18, 1934.

Chapter 1. Danish American Emigrant

1. Jenson, *Autobiography*, 1.

2. Allen, *Danish but Not Lutheran*, 25.

3. Christian Jensen was born at Grønholt on April 30, 1826, and he died at Richfield, Utah, on August 12, 1898. Jenson, *Autobiography*, 2, 527.

4. Jenson, *Autobiography*, 1.

5. Kirsten Andersdatter was born on July 7, 1821, and she died at Pleasant Grove, Utah, on December 16, 1917. Jenson, *Autobiography*, 2, 527.

6. Jenson, *Autobiography*, 4.

7. Ibid., 2.

8. Ibid., 3.

9. Jenson's older brother, Jens Christian Jensen, was born at their grandmother's home in Torslev parish on January 21, 1849. Jenson's younger brother, Joseph Julius Jensen, was born on January 9, 1862. Jenson, *Autobiography*, 4.

10. Jenson, *Autobiography*, 4.

11. Allen, *Danish but Not Lutheran*, 4.

12. Ibid., 37–40.

13. Ibid., 5–11.

14. See Jenson, *History of the Scandinavian Mission*; and Mulder, *Homeward to Zion.*

15. The June Constitution declared that "citizens shall have the right to gather together in communities to worship God in the manner consistent with their convictions, as long as nothing is done that contravenes civic order and common morality." Allen, *Danish but Not Lutheran*, 55–56.

16. Allen, *Danish but Not Lutheran*, 56–58.

17. Ibid., 56–57.

18. Ibid., 23.
19. Ibid., 68.
20. See Mulder, *Homeward to Zion*, 34–36; Allen, *Danish but Not Lutheran*, 66.
21. Allen, *Danish but Not Lutheran*, 66.
22. Ibid., 25.
23. Anders Christensen to C. C. Rich, January 4, 1861, in *Millennial Star* (Liverpool) 23, no. 6 (February 9, 1861): 92–93; Mulder, *Homeward to Zion*, 103.
24. C. A. Madsen to George Q. Cannon, July 24, 1861, in *Millennial Star* 23, no. 33 (August 17, 1861): 525–26, original emphasis; Mulder, *Homeward to Zion*, 203.
25. Jenson, *Autobiography*, 4.
26. Scandinavian Mission Manuscript History, vol. 8, December 28, 1854. Intramission jurisdictions were organized by geographical area and called *conferences* (later districts), which were overseen by a president, who reported to the mission president. The three conferences in Denmark included Copenhagen to the east, Aarhus in the center, and Aalborg to the north. Norway was subdivided into Christiania (Oslo) to the south, Bergen to the west, and Trondheim to the north. Rasmussen, *Mormonism*, 255n65; Baugh, "Defending Mormonism," 507.
27. Vendsyssel Conference Manuscript History, July 29, 1855.
28. Vendsyssel Conference Manuscript History, March 5 and June 21, 1857.
29. Vendsyssel Conference Manuscript History, October 18, 1857; Jenson, *Autobiography*, 5.
30. Jenson, *Autobiography*, 5, 6.
31. Ibid., 6.
32. Ibid., 5–6.
33. Ibid., 7.
34. A. Christensen, "Minutes of a Conference Held at Tidemausholm, Denmark, August 25, 1861," *Millennial Star* 38, no. 23 (September 21, 1861): 604–5.
35. Mulder, *Homeward to Zion*, 54–55.
36. Allen, *Danish but Not Lutheran*, 197.
37. Jenson, *Autobiography*, 7.
38. Ibid., 8.
39. Ibid., 7.
40. Ibid., 9–10.
41. Ibid., 7, 8, 10. Jenson wrote practically daily in his journal until shortly before his death in 1941. Fifteen volumes of his journals in English (1864–1941) are housed at the Church History Library in Salt Lake City, Utah. Clues in these journals suggest that Jenson transcribed and summarized from another source to record his daily entries. The Andrew Jenson Collection in Brigham Young University's L. Tom Perry Special Collections has Jenson's early Danish journals. These may be the early source Jenson used to re-create a few volumes of his journals in English. See Jenson Journal; Andrew Jenson Collection, 1850–1935, L. Tom Perry Special Collections.
42. Jenson, *Autobiography*, 8.
43. "Synopsis of a Conference Meeting Held in Aalborg, September 7, 1862," *Millennial Star* 24, no. 42 (October 18, 1862): 659.
44. Brøndal, "Danes and Danish Americans," 1:325.

45. Jenson, *Autobiography*, 10.

46. Ibid., 11.

47. Allen, *Danish but Not Lutheran*, 13.

48. Brøndal, "Danes and Danish Americans," 1:323–24.

49. Jenson, *Autobiography*, 4.

50. Ibid., 7–8.

51. Jenson, *Autobiography*, 11.

52. Ibid., 11, 11–12.

53. Brøndal, "Danes and Danish Americans," 1:323–27.

54. Mulder, *Homeward to Zion*, 80.

55. Neilson and Waite, *Settling the Valley*; Mulder, *Homeward to Zion*, 80.

56. Mulder, *Homeward to Zion*, 80.

57. "Emigration," *Skandinaviens Stjerne* 2, no. 7 (January 1, 1853): 110–11; see also Mulder, *Homeward to Zion*, 157.

58. Allen, *Danish but Not Lutheran*, 200.

59. P. C. S. Kragskov to J. C. A. Weibye, April 15, 1860, in *Skandinaviens Stjerne* 9, no. 14 (August 15, 1860): 344–46; Mulder, *Homeward to Zion*, 85.

60. "Fifth General Epistle and Addenda, April 1851," in Neilson and Waite, *Settling the Valley*, 120–21; "Femte almindelige epistel," *Skandinaviens Stjerne* 1, no. 1 (October 1851): 5–11.

61. Richard E. Bennett, "Upper Room," 15–17.

62. Approximately half of the 46,497 Scandinavian converts to the Latter-day Saint church from 1850 to 1905 were Danish. Mulder, *Homeward to Zion*, 107; Allen, *Danish but Not Lutheran*, 67.

63. Jenson, *Autobiography*, 12.

64. Ibid., 12.

65. Mulder, *Homeward to Zion*, 146–47.

66. Jenson Journal, book A, 14; Jenson, *Autobiography*, 12.

67. Ibid., 12.

68. "An Epistle of the Twelve," *Millennial Star* 1, no. 12 (April 1841): 312; Woods, "Men in Motion."

69. Those who drew from the fund committed to repay their loan upon settlement, though many failed to do so. Woods, "Men in Motion," 202–13; Arrington, *Great Basin Kingdom*, 77–79; Mulder, *Homeward to Zion*, 142–45.

70. Mulder, *Homeward to Zion*, 166–69.

71. Jenson, *Autobiography*, 13.

72. Ibid., 13.

73. Ibid., 14.

74. Of the passengers aboard the *Kenilworth*, 583 were Danish, 23 were Norwegian, 73 were Swedish, and 5 were German. Jenson, *History of the Scandinavian Mission*, 191.

75. Jenson, *Autobiography*, 15.

76. Jenson Journal, June 3, 1866.

77. Jenson, *Autobiography*, 17.

78. Jenson Journal, July 15, 1866.

79. Jenson, *Autobiography*, 18.

80. Jenson, *History of the Scandinavian Mission*, 192–93; Jenson, *Autobiography*, 18–19.
81. Jenson, *Autobiography*, 19.
82. Ibid., 19.
83. Arrington, *Great Basin Kingdom*, 206–9; William G. Hartley, "Down-and-Back Wagon Trains"; Jenson, "Latter-day Saints Emigration."
84. Jenson Journal, July 30–31, 1866.
85. Ibid., August 9, 1866.
86. Jenson, *Autobiography*, 22–23.
87. Jenson Journal, August 24, 1866.
88. Ibid., September 19–21, 1866.
89. Ibid., August 29–September 4, 1866.
90. Ibid., October 7, 1866.
91. Ibid., October 7, 1866.
92. Mounting tensions in Sanpete and Sevier Counties between settlers and local Indians broke out into war in 1865. Peterson, *Utah's Black Hawk War*.
93. Jenson Journal, book A, 102.
94. For more on labor in the American West, see White, *It's Your Misfortune*, 270–97; and Schwantes, "Concept of the Wageworkers' Frontier."
95. Jenson, *Autobiography*, 27; Jenson Journal, book A, 106.
96. Ibid., June 8–July 11, 1868; Arrington, *Great Basin Kingdom*, 260–64.
97. Jenson Journal, July 13–September 24, 1868.
98. Ibid., November 15 and 30, 1868.
99. Ibid., book A, 151–52.
100. Ibid., book A, 153–57.
101. Ibid., book A, 159 and 116.
102. Ibid., book A, 161.
103. Ibid., book A, 192.
104. Ibid., book A, 193–231.
105. Ibid., book A, 245–86.
106. Ibid., book A, 287.
107. Neilson, "Nineteenth-Century Euro-American Mormon Missionary Model," 75–77; Hughes, "Profile of the Missionaries," 176–81.
108. "General Conference," *Deseret News*, April 16, 1873; Jenson Journal, book B, 7.
109. Jenson Journal, April 10, 1873. The endowment ceremony was instituted by Joseph Smith in Nauvoo, Illinois, in 1842. The Endowment House, completed on the northwest corner of the Temple Block in 1855, was a designated site for Latter-day Saint temple work until 1889, when it was razed. Buerger, "Development," 49–50; L. Brown, "Temple Pro Tempore."
110. Jenson Journal, book B, 8; "General Conference," *Deseret News*, May 7, 1873.
111. Mulder, *Homeward to Zion*, 57–62; Price, "Mormon Missionary," 91–92; Neilson, "Introduction."
112. Jenson, *Autobiography*, 68; Jenson Journal, book B, 35–37. The Aalborg Conference had been organized in 1852 and consisted of 686 members spread across three branches—Aalborg, Hjørring, and Frederikshavn.
113. Jenson, Journal, book B, 40–41, 41–42.

114. Ibid., book B, 41.

115. Ibid., book B, 88.

116. Ibid., book B, 39.

117. Ibid., October 11, 1874. Jenson found similar conditions elsewhere in the region surrounding Aalborg. Jenson Journal, book B, 70–71.

118. Jenson Journal, October 11, 1874.

119. Ibid., book B, 69–70.

120. Allen, *Danish but Not Lutheran*, 43–55.

121. Jenson Journal, November 3, 1873.

122. Later in the century, the Indre Mission would export its movement west to the United States and even gain a foothold in Utah, where it would be just as outspoken against the church and offer outreach to disillusioned Danish Latter-day Saints. Mulder, *Homeward to Zion*, 39, 91–92, 288; Allen, *Danish but Not Lutheran*, 49.

123. Jenson Journal, July 13, 1874.

124. During Jenson's first mission to Denmark, yearly convert baptism totals never rose above five hundred, as they routinely had in previous decades. Jenson, *History of the Scandinavian Mission*, [534].

125. C. G. Larsen to Andrew Jenson, May 31, 1875, in Jenson Journal, June 5, 1875.

126. Jenson Journal, June 22, 1875.

127. Jenson, *Autobiography*, 86–90.

Chapter 2. Entrepreneurial Chronicler

1. Jenson Journal, July 23, 1875.

2. Ibid.

3. Jenson Journal, book B, 245.

4. "Theocrats at Provo," *Salt Lake Tribune*, August 4, 1875; "Two Days Meetings at Provo," *Deseret News*, August 2, 1875.

5. Turner, *Brigham Young*, 397–401; Arrington, *Building the City of God*, 135–54.

6. Jenson Journal, August 22, 1875. Ritual rebaptisms were performed as a sign that Latter-day Saints were willing to obey the rules of the United Order and to invite special divine blessings. Arrington, *Building the City of God*, 171. Rebaptism was a common practice in Utah Territory as a means of signifying repentance and recommitment to the church.

7. Mary's father, Peder, converted to the church in Ephraim, Utah, while her mother, Else, joined in Denmark in 1873. Jenson Journal, book B, 249–50.

8. Jenson Journal, August 30, 1875.

9. Ibid., book B, 263.

10. Ibid., March 15, 1976.

11. Ibid., book B, 290.

12. Ibid., book B, 295.

13. Ibid., book B, 296, 298, 298.

14. Ibid., September 17, 1876.

15. Ibid., book B, 296. The *Skandinaviens Stjerne* ran a serialized column titled Joseph Smiths levnetslob (History of Joseph Smith) from August 1852 until February 1872,

translating Smith's history through May 1842. Joseph Smiths levnetslob, *Skandinaviens stjerne* 1, no. 11 (August 1852): 161–64; "Uddrag af Joseph Smiths levnetslob" [Extracts from the history of Joseph Smith], *Skandinaviens stjerne* 21, no. 10 (February 1872): 158–59; see also "Introduction to History"; "Joseph Smith's Historical Enterprise."

16. The inaugural issue of the *Juvenile Instructor* in January 1866 ran a biographical narrative sketch of Joseph Smith. The column ran until December 1870. "Joseph Smith, the Prophet," *Juvenile Instructor* 1, no. 1 (January 1, 1866): 1; "Joseph Smith, the Prophet," *Juvenile Instructor* 5, no. 26 (December 24, 1870): 202; "History of the Church," *Juvenile Instructor* 6, no. 1 (January 7, 1871): 6–7.

17. Daniel H. Wells to Andrew Jenson, December 7, 1876, in Jenson Journal, book B, 296–97.

18. Jenson Journal, book B, 297.

19. Ibid., book B, 395.

20. See A. Larson, *Erastus Snow*, 201–45; and Hemming, "Voice."

21. Erastus Snow to Andrew Jenson, January 16, 1877, in Jenson Journal, book B, 312.

22. On subscription sales during this period, see C. Smith, "Plea for New Appreciation," 213–14.

23. Jenson Journal, February 18, 1877.

24. Bitton, "Strange Ramblings," 9–10.

25. Jenson Journal, February 25, 1877.

26. Ibid., April 21, 1877.

27. Ibid., April 4 and August 12, 1877.

28. Ibid., March 25, 1877.

29. Jenson, *Autobiography*, 100.

30. Jenson Journal, February 4, 1877.

31. Andrew Jenson and Johan A. Bruun, "Address to the Scandinavian Saints," *Deseret News*, April 25, 1877.

32. Jenson Journal, February 24, 1877.

33. Walker, *Wayward Saints*, 232–40.

34. Jenson Journal, May 20 and September 9, 1877.

35. "The Scandinavian Element," *Deseret News*, July 7, 1886.

36. Henrichsen and Bailey, "No More Strangers," 32, 36; Jenson Journal, book B, 256.

37. Henrichsen and Bailey, "No More Strangers," 40–42.

38. Jenson Journal, November 19, 1876; Allen, "Parallel Promised Lands."

39. Mulder, *Homeward to Zion*, 250–55.

40. See Jenson Journal, May 19, 1879.

41. Ibid., May 20, 1879.

42. Jenson, "Scandinavian Latter-day Saint Literature," 190.

43. Jenson Journal, December 31, 1877.

44. Ibid., May 6, 1877.

45. Ibid., December 31, 1877.

46. Invoices, 1878–1881, *Levnetsløb*, folder 3, box 60, AJC/CHL.

47. Jenson Journal, May 20, 1879.

48. Mulder, *Homeward to Zion*, 260–61.

49. Jenson Journal, April 6, 1878; John Taylor to A. W. Winberg, Andrew Jenson, and Johan A. Bruun, April 10, 1878, in Jenson Journal, April 28, 1878.

50. Jenson Journal, May 30, 1878.

51. Ibid., May 30, 1878.

52. Ibid., July 1, 1878.

53. Ibid., July 1, 1878.

54. Ibid., November 26, 1881.

55. This arrangement mostly occurred after the church-owned *Deseret News* assumed greater control of *Bikuben*'s publication and finances in 1893. Jenson was a faithful executor of the First Presidency's wishes in regard to *Bikuben*, eventually serving multiple stints as the newspaper's editor and responding to the difficult task of making the paper solvent when it became a drain on Church resources. Andrew Jenson, "Church Periodicals," *Deseret News*, May 14, 1932.

56. Jenson, *History of the Scandinavian Mission*, 533; Allen, *Danish but Not Lutheran*, 83.

57. Jenson Journal, January 24, 1879.

58. Jenson, *Autobiography*, 110.

59. Jenson Journal, May 19, 1879.

60. Mary Jenson, Journal, November 7, 1880, in ibid., book C, 173.

61. Jenson Journal, June 11, 1879; Jenson, *History of the Scandinavian Mission*, 210.

62. Jenson, *History of the Scandinavian Mission*, 533.

63. Ibid., 534.

64. Jenson Journal, June 25, 1879.

65. Ibid., October 9, 1879.

66. Ibid., October 9, 1879.

67. Ibid., November 8, 10, and 11, 1881.

68. Ibid., October 9, 1879.

69. Ibid., October 9, 1879.

70. Jenson, *History of the Scandinavian Mission*, 237.

71. Jenson Journal, June 25, 1879.

72. Jenson wrote a full report on his labors in the Copenhagen branch for the *Millennial Star* in September 1879. See "Abstract of Correspondence," *Millennial Star* 41, no. 40 (October 6, 1879): 634–35.

73. Jenson Journal, November 16 and 20, 1879; Scandinavian Mission Manuscript History, vol. 11, November 20, 1879. Other branches in Denmark soon followed Copenhagen in organizing local relief societies. The Relief Society—which had been first organized in Nauvoo, Illinois, in 1842—was formally reestablished in Utah Territory in 1867. Derr et al., *First Fifty Years*, 235–37; "R.S. Reports," *Woman's Exponent* 9 (September 1, 1880): [53]. The aging Copenhagen branch of almost four hundred members could not support a Young Women's Mutual Improvement Association, which had also been organized in Utah Territory, so the adolescent women joined the adult women in attending Relief Society. "News from Denmark."

74. Jenson, *Autobiography*, 110.

75. Jenson Journal, December 15, 1879; January 6, 1880. By March 1880, *Ungdommens raadgiver* had around 1,200 subscribers. The paper featured mostly translations from other church periodicals but also contained correspondence from Danish Latter-day Saints and short, original articles "treating upon the duties of young Latter-day Saints." "Paper for the Young Saints."

76. *Bibelske henvisninger*. The first edition was a four-page tract by Canute Peterson, a missionary in Scandinavia from 1852 to 1855. Jenson updated and significantly added to Peterson's work. Scandinavian Mission Manuscript History, vol. 11, November 15, 1879; Jenson, "Scandinavian Latter-day Saint Literature," 184.

77. Wilhelmsen, a native Dane, had emigrated to Utah Territory in 1861. Jenson, *Latter-day Saint Biographical Encyclopedia*, 3:564–65.

78. Jenson Journal, February 18, 1880; Andrew Jenson, letter to the editor, March 20, 1880, *Deseret News*, April 28, 1880.

79. Jenson Journal, May 1 and 13, 1880.

80. Mulder, *Homeward to Zion*, 79.

81. Hansen, "How the Danish translation," 2–3, CHL.

82. Snow, *One Year in Scandinavia*, 7; Jenson, "Scandinavian Latter-day Saint Literature," 181; Jenson, *History of the Scandinavian Mission*, 25–26; Scandinavian Mission Manuscript History, vol. 8, January 5, May 22, 1851.

83. Scandinavian Mission Manuscript History, vol. 12, May 31, 1881.

84. Gutjahr, *Book of Mormon*, 91–96.

85. Scandinavian Mission Manuscript History, vol. 12, May 31, 1881.

86. Jenson Journal, January 15, April 1, and May 31, 1881; Jenson, "Scandinavian Latter-day Saint Literature," 181.

87. Scandinavian Mission Manuscript History, vol. 12, September 7, 1881.

88. Jenson Journal, July 31, 1881.

89. Ibid., August 1, 1881.

90. See Andrew Jenson to Annie Christina Wilhelmsen, August 1, 1881, in *Bear Lake (ID) Democrat*, August 1881.

91. "General Council Meeting," in Jenson Journal, August 8, 1881.

92. Jenson, *Latter-day Saint Biographical Encyclopedia*, 1:203; Jenson Journal, September 1, 1881.

93. Jenson Journal, September 7, 1881.

94. Ibid., November 5, 1881; Invoices, 1878–1881, *Levnetsløb*, folder 3, box 60, AJC/CHL.

95. Jenson Journal, November 12, 1881.

96. Ibid., November 16, 1881.

97. Ibid., November 18, 1881.

98. Ibid., November 30, 1881.

99. Ibid., December 12, 1881.

100. Ibid., book C, 286.

101. Andrew Jenson to John Taylor, October 12, 1881, folder 25, box 6, First Presidency (John Taylor) Correspondence.

102. Jenson Journal, November 25, 1881.

103. Ibid., September 27, 1881; G. Cannon, *Journal of George Q. Cannon*, September 27, 1881.

104. Erastus Snow to Andrew Jenson, December 11, 1881, in Jenson Journal, December 15, 1881.

105. Jenson Journal, January 16, 1882; "Morgenstjernen," *Deseret News*, January 17, 1882.

106. Jenson Journal, January 16, 1882; Jenson, *Autobiography*, 138.

107. Jenson Journal, March 15 and 17, 1882.

108. Ibid., February 11 and March 10, 1882.

109. Ibid., April 25, 1882.

110. Ibid., May 8, 1882.

111. Ibid., January 5, 12, and 14–15, 1882.

112. "A New Magazine," *Deseret News*, March 14, 1882; "Morgenstjernen," *Deseret News*, March 16, 1882; Jenson Journal, April 29, 1882.

113. Jenson, *Autobiography*, 131.

114. "A Good Periodical," *Deseret News*, June 21, 1882.

115. Erastus Snow, "To Scandinavians," *Deseret News*, October 18, 1882.

116. "A Successful Canvas," *Deseret News*, November 20, 1882; Jenson Journal, December 2, 1882.

117. Jenson Journal, August 2, 1882.

118. Ibid., book C, 359.

119. Ibid., August 10, 1879; Andrew Jenson to Erastus Snow, April 11, 1883, in ibid., April 11, 1883.

120. Erastus Snow to Andrew Jenson, April 17, 1883, in Jenson Journal, April 17, 1883.

121. K. Perkins, "Andrew Jenson," 58–60; Jenson Journal, November 18, 1883.

122. Andrew Jenson, "The Historical Record," *Historical Record* 5, nos. 9–12 (December 1886): 120.

123. Jenson, *Autobiography*, 134.

Chapter 3. Historian's Office Affiliate

1. Jenson, "Historian's Office."

2. Doctrine and Covenants 21:1. For information on the Latter-day Saint tradition of record keeping, see Walker, Whittaker, and Allen, *Mormon History*; Searle, "Early Mormon Historiography"; Turley and Harper, *Preserving the History*; M. Jensen, "There Shall Be a Record."

3. See Baugh, *Days Never to Be Forgotten*, 257–58; Doctrine and Covenants 47:1, 3; see also Doctrine and Covenants 69.

4. For more on Whitmer's personal background and tenure as Church Historian, see Westergren, *From Historian to Dissident*; S. Esplin, "History"; Davidson, Jensen, and Whittaker, *Histories*, 5–10.

5. These include George W. Robinson, John Corrill, Elias Higbee, Robert B. Thompson, and James Sloan, aided by clerks like William Clayton and James Mulholland. Adams

and Larson, "Study," 373; Searle, "Historians, Church." For a discussion on the development of the office(s) of Church Historian and Recorder, see Neilson, "Traveling and Standing Ministers," 30–32.

6. For more on Richards's personal background and tenure as Church Historian, see Bitton and Arrington, *Mormons and Their Historians*, 3–14.

7. Adams and Larson, "Study," 374–76; Jessee, "Writing of Joseph Smith's History."

8. For more on Smith's personal background and his tenure as Church Historian, see Bitton and Arrington, *Mormons and Their Historians*, 15–28.

9. An apostle remained in the office of Church Historian for about 130 years, until 1972, when Leonard J. Arrington, a professionally trained scholar and nonapostle, was appointed Church Historian. See Arrington, *Adventures*, 74–91; Prince, *Leonard Arrington*, 88, 152–54.

10. Historian's Office, Letterpress Copybooks, 1:106; Adams and Larson, "Study," 378.

11. On Smith's duties with Congress, see Adams and Larson, "Study," 378–79; Jenson, "Historian's Office," 62–63.

12. Jenson, "Historian's Office," 62–65; Historical Department, Journal History, September 15, 1856.

13. "Minutes of the Semi-annual Conference," *Deseret News*, October 15, 1856. See also Turley, "Assistant Church Historians."

14. Adams and Larson, "Study," 378–81.

15. Searle, "Church Historian," 590.

16. Adams and Larson, "Study," 388.

17. E. Perkins and Woodger, "Administration."

18. G. Larson, *"Americanization" of Utah*, 165–82; Richards Journal, October 21 and November 5, 1887; Adams and Larson, "Study," 386.

19. Jenson, *Latter-day Saint Biographical Encyclopedia*, 1:195; ibid., 2:727; ibid., 4:374.

20. The seven presidents, or First Council of the Seventy, was then composed of John Van Cott, Henry Harriman, Horace S. Eldredge, Jacob Gates, William W. Taylor, Abraham H. Cannon, and Seymour B. Young.

21. Roberts, "First Council"; Parrish, "Seventy."

22. On the Seven Presidents of the Seventy, see Doctrine and Covenants 107:93–98. Jenson was ordained to the office of Seventy on May 4, 1873. Jenson Journal, May 4, 1873.

23. Gardner, "General Authorities." While apostles continue to serve until their deaths, members of the Seventy began to be released at their seventieth birthdays starting in 1984, or sometimes earlier due to health challenges.

24. Jenson Journal, February 19, 1883.

25. Ibid., March 23, 1883.

26. Taylor, Cannon, and Smith, *To the Seventies*. For more detail on the structural reorganization of the seventies that these instructions initiated, see Hartley, "Seventies in the 1880s."

27. Hartley, "Seventies in the 1880s," 69–71.

28. See Jenson Journal, April 17, 1883.

29. Richards Journal, May 9, 1883; Woodruff Journals, May 8, 1883.

30. Wilford Woodruff and Horace S. Eldredge to John Taylor, George Q. Cannon, and Joseph F. Smith, June 30, 1883, folder 14, box 10, First Presidency (John Taylor) Correspondence; Richards Journal, June 30, 1883.

31. "Fifty-Fourth Annual Conference," *Deseret News*, April 9, 1884.

32. Jenson Journal, April 6, 1884.

33. Jenson, *Latter-day Saint Biographical Encyclopedia*, 1:198–99.

34. Jenson Journal, April 6, 1884. Ibid., April 10, 1884; March 23, 1921.

35. Andrew Jenson and C. A. F. Orlob, agreement, August 18, 1884, AJL.

36. For more on Thomassen, see *Scandinavian Jubilee Album*, 230; Mulder, *Homeward to Zion*, 262.

37. Mulder, *Homeward to Zion*, 262.

38. Jenson Journal, January 1, 1885.

39. Andrew Jenson to Erastus Snow, February 28, 1885, 29–31, AJL.

40. "Scandinavian Literature," *Deseret News*, December 3, 1884; Erastus Snow to Andrew Jenson, November 19, 1884, in Jenson, *Autobiography*, 136.

41. Jenson Journal, April 3 and 13, 1885; "Bikuben," *Deseret News*, April 16, 1885.

42. Andrew Jenson to Erastus Snow, March 27, 1885, 34, AJL.

43. Jenson Journal, August 11, 1884.

44. Ellsworth, "Hubert Howe Bancroft."

45. Jenson Journal, September 30 and November 20, 1884.

46. Ibid., November 20, 1884.

47. Andrew Jenson to Wilford Woodruff and Franklin D. Richards, August 22, 1884, 18, AJL.

48. Jenson Journal, book D, 107.

49. Jenson, *Autobiography*, 139; Jenson Journal, January 27, 1886. See also John Taylor to Andrew Jenson, May 13, 1886, folder 13, box 16, First Presidency (John Taylor) Correspondence.

50. Jenson Journal, book D, 160.

51. Ibid., December 2, 1885; Jenson, *Autobiography*, 139.

52. "Prospectus," *Deseret Evening News*, November 12, 1885; Jenson, *Encyclopedic History*, 339.

53. "Early Church History," *Historical Record* 5, no. 1 (January 1886): 1–13; "Miscellaneous," *Historical Record* 5, no. 2 (February 1886): 30–32.

54. "The Twelve Apostles" and "Miscellaneous," *Historical Record* 5, no. 3 (March 1886), 33–44, 48.

55. "Young Folks' Day," *Salt Lake Daily Herald*, August 14, 1884; "Orphans' Free Excursion," *Salt Lake Democrat*, August 26, 1885.

56. Jenson Journal, August 18, 1885.

57. The Latter-day Saint delegation led by John T. Caine presented the document directly to President Cleveland, who told the delegation he would ensure that the Edmunds Act was impartially enforced in the territory. G. Larson, *"Americanization" of Utah*, 126–27.

58. Jenson Journal, May 2, 1885.

59. Driggs, "Prosecutions Begin."

60. Hardy, *Solemn Covenant*, 39–60.

61. "Appendix to 1886," in Jenson Journal, 223.

62. Olsen, "Other Mother."

63. Jenson Journal, February 28, 1887.

64. Ibid., September 12 and 26; October 17, 21, 25, 26 and 31, 1886; "Appendix to 1886," 223.

65. "Appendix to 1886," 223.

66. Between 1886 and 1888, there were over nine hundred indictments from federal officials for unlawful cohabitation in Utah Territory. Gordon, *Mormon Question*, 157–58.

67. Jenson Journal, November 2, 1886. To signal her formal approval, Jenson asked Fanny to place Emma's hand in his "and give her to me in that formal way." "Appendix to 1886," 223–24.

68. See Doctrine and Covenants 132:65.

69. Jenson Journal, November 2, 1886.

70. Ibid., November 2, 1886.

71. U.K.H. [Andrew Jenson] to Emma Howell, November 9, 1886, folder 32, box 27, AJC/CHL.

72. [Andrew Jenson] to Emma Howell, November 29, 1886, folder 32, box 27, AJC/CHL.

73. Jenson Journal, November 30, 1886.

74. Ibid., December 8, 1886.

75. Ibid., December 8–9, 1886.

76. Ibid., December 10, 1886.

77. Ibid., January 3, 1887.

78. Ibid., January 3, 1887.

79. Ibid., January 3, 1887.

80. Ibid., January 4, 1887.

81. Ibid., January 26, February 6, June 1, 1887.

82. Ibid., February 6, 1887.

83. Ibid., February 28, 1887.

84. Ibid., May 15, 1887.

85. Ibid., March 3, 1887.

86. Ibid., March 6, 1887. Ibid., June 5, 1887.

87. Hardy, *Solemn Covenant*, 52.

88. "Utah's Statehood," *Deseret News*, June 29, 1887.

89. Jenson Journal, book E, 37–38; G. Cannon, *Journal*, July 7, 1887.

90. G. Larson, *"Americanization" of Utah*, 220–22.

91. Jenson Journal, June 14, 1887.

92. Hales, "Identifying Joseph Smith's Plural Wives," 158.

93. On Willes sealed to Smith, see Hales, *Joseph Smith's Polygamy*, 2:116.

94. Hales, *Joseph Smith's Polygamy*, 1:498–502.

95. Malissa Willes to Andrew Jenson, June 27, 1887, folder 16, box 49, AJC/CHL.

96. According to handwriting analysis done by Don Bradley and Brian C. Hales, Jenson recorded thirteen names on an initial list of Smith's plural wives and the remaining

names were written by Eliza R Snow. It seems likely that Snow wrote approximately ten to thirteen of the names on Jenson's list and crossed out three names. A duplicate name was also crossed out, reducing the total of confirmed names on the list to twenty-five. Andrew Jenson, "Joseph Smith's Plural Wives," ca. 1887, box 49, folder 16, AJC/CHL; Hales, "Identifying Joseph Smith's Plural Wives," 158; Hales, *Joseph Smith's Polygamy*, 1:267; see notes in folder 16, box 49, AJC/CHL; Malissa Willes to Andrew Jenson.

97. See notes in folder 16, box 49, AJC/CHL.

98. Hales claims that Jenson wrote his article, "Plural Marriage," for the *Historical Record* on February 28, 1887. However, Jenson was visiting Ogden with Emma on that date. He likely prepared the final version of his article in late June 1887. Hales, *Joseph Smith's Polygamy*, 1:267; Jenson Journal, June 27–29, 1887.

99. Previously, church leaders Joseph F. Smith, George A. Smith, and William Clayton had all created lists of Smith's wives, though they were not considered authoritative and they remained unpublished. Hales, "Identifying Joseph Smith's Plural Wives," 156–58.

100. Jenson, "Joseph Smith's Plural Wives," ca. 1887; Andrew Jenson, "The following named sisters . . . ," ca. 1887, folder 16, box 49, AJC/CHL; Jenson, "Plural Marriage"; see also folder 16, box 49, AJC/CHL.

101. Jenson, "Plural Marriage," 219.

102. Ibid., 233.

103. Wilford Woodruff to Andrew Jenson, August 6, 1887, quoted in K. Perkins, "Andrew Jenson," 74; see also Andrew Jenson to Wilford Woodruff and Quorum of Twelve Apostles, August 8, 1887, 65–68, AJL/CHL.

104. J.J.J., "Two Prophets' Widows: A Visit to the Relics of Joseph Smith and Brigham Young," *St. Louis Globe-Democrat*, August 18, 1887, 6.

105. Richards Journal, April 25, 1889.

106. Andrew Jenson to Wilford Woodruff, August 12, 1887, 69–70, AJL/CHL.

107. Jenson Journal, July 14–19, 1888.

108. Andrew Jenson to John Taylor, May 7, 1886, 44, AJL/CHL.

109. John Taylor to Andrew Jenson, May 13, 1886, folder 13, box 16, First Presidency (John Taylor) Correspondence.

110. E. Perkins and Woodger, "Administration."

111. Jenson Journal, February 8, 1886; Jenson, *Autobiography*, 140–41. For a full account of the escape from the Historian's Office, see Wilford Woodruff to John Taylor, February 8, 1886, folder 22 box 18, First Presidency (John Taylor) Correspondence.

112. Andrew Jenson to Franklin D. Richards, February 20, 1886, in Jenson Journal, February 20, 1886.

113. Andrew Jenson to John Taylor, October 28, 1886, 50–54, AJL/CHL.

114. Andrew Jenson to George Q. Cannon, January 20, 1887, 57, AJL/CHL.

115. John Taylor to Andrew Jenson, February 20, 1887, quoted in K. Perkins, "Study," 42.

116. Andrew Jenson to Wilford Woodruff and Quorum of Twelve Apostles, August 8, 1887, 65–68, AJL/CHL.

117. Wilford Woodruff to Andrew Jenson, March 16, 1888, in Jenson Journal, April 2, 1888; Richards Journal, March 16, 1888.

118. Jenson Journal, April 2, 1888.

119. Ibid., April 5, 1888.

120. Jenson spoke at the first session of general conference on April 5, 1888. Of the members of the First Presidency and Quorum of the Twelve, only Apostles Lorenzo Snow, Heber J. Grant, and John W. Taylor were present. "General Conference: Andrew Jenson," *Deseret News*, April 11, 1888. For more on Andrew Jenson's sermons at general conference, see Neilson and Marianno, *Voice in the Wilderness*.

121. "General Conference: Andrew Jenson," *Deseret News*, April 11, 1888.

122. Jenson Journal, September 4, 1888.

123. Ibid., September 4, 1888.

124. Ibid., September 5, 1888.

125. Ibid., September 6, 1888.

126. Doctrine and Covenants 57:1–3.

127. Doctrine and Covenants 101:16–18.

128. "Historical Landmarks," *Deseret News*, September 15, 1888.

129. "Nauvoo the Beautiful," *Deseret News*, October 14, 1888; "Scenes in Church History," *Deseret News*, October 27, 1888.

130. Stevenson Journal, September 12, 1888.

131. See Davidson, Jensen, and Whittaker, *Histories*, 3–110; Westergren, *From Historian to Dissident*; S. Esplin, "History," 50.

132. Jenson Journal, September 12, 1888.

133. Ibid., October 15, 1888.

134. Ibid., October 11, 1888.

135. Ibid., January 2, 6, 10, 11, 17, and 20; March 20, 23, and 24, 1889; Jenson, *Autobiography*, 185.

136. See, for example, Andrew Jenson, "The Eight Witnesses," *Historical Record* 7, nos. 8–10 (October 1888): 609–22.

137. Andrew Jenson, "Jackson County, Missouri"; "Clay County, Missouri"; "Haun's Mill Massacre," *Historical Record* 7, nos. 11–12 (December 1888): 625–84.

138. Andrew Jenson, "Caldwell County, Missouri"; "Daviess County, Missouri," *Historical Record* 8, no. 1 (January 1889): 685–732; Jenson, "Quincy"; "Hancock County, Illinois"; "Nauvoo"; Andrew Jenson, "The Battle of Nauvoo" and "The Nauvoo Temple," *Historical Record* 8, nos. 4–6 (June 1889): 845–73.

139. Andrew Jenson, "Church Encyclopaedia," *Historical Record* 8, nos. 9–12 (December 1889): 941–1011.

140. Jenson Journal, March 19, 1889.

141. Andrew Jenson to Wilford Woodruff, George Q. Cannon, and Joseph F. Smith, September 20, 1889, in Jenson Journal, September 21, 1889, emphasis in original.

142. Jenson Journal, December 3, 1889.

143. Ibid., December 31, 1889.

144. Franklin D. Richards and John Jaques to Wilford Woodruff, George Q. Cannon, and Joseph F. Smith, February 13, 1890, folder 23, box 1, First Presidency General Authorities Correspondence.

145. Richards and Jaques to Woodruff, Cannon, and Smith, February 13, 1890.

146. Ibid.

147. Ibid.

148. Wilford Woodruff to Andrew Jenson, February 15, 1890, in Jenson Journal, February 17, 1890.

149. Wilford Woodruff to Andrew Jenson, February 21, 1890, in Jenson Journal, March 5, 1889.

150. Jenson Journal, March 1, 1890.

151. Ibid., April 7 and June 23, 1890.

152. Ibid., April 14, 1890.

153. Andrew Jenson to Wilford Woodruff, George Q. Cannon, and Joseph F. Smith, June 23, 1890, in Jenson Journal, June 23, 1890.

154. Jenson, *Autobiography*, 189–90; Jenson Journal, March 11, 1889.

155. Andrew Jenson, "Publisher's Valedictory," *Historical Record* 9, nos. 7–12 (December 1890): 124.

156. Jenson Journal, February 9, 1891; G. Cannon, *Journal*, February 9, 1891.

157. Jenson Journal, February 9, 1891.

158. Ibid., March 9, 1891.

Chapter 4. Itinerant World Traveler

1. Jenson Journal, April 16, 1891. See Franklin D. Richards and John Jaques to Wilford Woodruff, George Q. Cannon, and Joseph F. Smith, February 13, 1890, folder 23, box 1, First Presidency General Authorities Correspondence.

2. Franklin D. Richards to Andrew Jenson, April 16, 1891, in Jenson Journal, April 16, 1891.

3. R. Jensen, "Ignored and Unknown Clues."

4. Doctrine and Covenants 21:1.

5. Firmage and Mangrum, *Zion in the Courts*, 252–54; G. Larson, *"Americanization" of Utah*, 213–16.

6. Jenson, *Autobiography*, 194.

7. Ibid., 194–95.

8. Ibid., 195.

9. Ibid., 195–96.

10. Ibid., 196.

11. Jenson Journal, May 15, 1892.

12. Andrew Jenson to First Presidency, May 23, 1892, in Jenson Journal, May 23, 1892.

13. Jenson, "History and Genealogy," *Salt Lake Herald*, February 9, 1895; "Instructions Given the Saints at Conference," *Provo Daily Enquirer*, July 18, 1893.

14. Jenson to First Presidency.

15. Jenson, "History and Genealogy."

16. Andrew Jenson, "Salt Lake Stake," *Deseret Evening News*, December 20, 1894.

17. Jenson to First Presidency.

18. Ibid.

19. Jenson Journal, December 31, 1892.

20. Andrew Jenson to Franklin D. Richards, August 24, 1893, in Jenson Journal, August 24, 1893.

21. Jenson Journal, December 15, 1893.

22. Ibid.

23. See Andrew Jenson to Franklin D. Richards, March 20, 1894, in Historian's Office, Correspondence Files.

24. Jenson, *Autobiography*, 225–26.

25. Jenson Journal, October 29, 1894.

26. Ibid., December 31, 1894.

27. Andrew Jenson to Franklin D. Richards, April 3, 1895, in Historian's Office, Correspondence Files.

28. See Walker, Turley, and Leonard, *Massacre at Mountain Meadows*.

29. T. Stenhouse, *Rocky Mountain Saints*, 424–58; F. Stenhouse, *"Tell it All,"* 324–39.

30. Lee, *Mormonism Unveiled*, 213–92.

31. G. Cannon, *Journal*, January 21, 1892; Turley and Walker, *Mountain Meadows Massacre*, 2–9.

32. G. Cannon, *Journal*, January 21, 1892.

33. Wilford Woodruff, George Q. Cannon, and Joseph F. Smith to "Whom It May Concern," January 21, 1892, in Jenson Journal, January 22, 1892.

34. Jenson, *Autobiography*, 198; Turley and Walker, *Mountain Meadows Massacre*, 12–40.

35. Ellot Willden to Wilford Woodruff, George Q. Cannon, and Joseph F. Smith, January 29, 1892, folder 27, box 6, First Presidency (Wilford Woodruff) General Correspondence Files; Jenson Journal, January 27, 1892; Turley and Walker, *Mountain Meadows Massacre*, 5.

36. Jenson Journal, January 28, 1892. Apparently, Abraham Cannon met with George Q. Cannon before declining the Willden deal: "He [Abraham] did not feel that he could afford to give $50., or that the matter would be worth that amount, and President Smith did not seem inclined to have it appropriated by the Church." G. Cannon, *Journal*, January 28, 1892.

37. George Reynolds to Andrew Jenson, June 8, 1892; George Reynolds to Ellott Willden, June 8, 1892, First Presidency, Letterpress Copybooks, 25:354; see also Willden to Woodruff, Cannon, and Smith, January 29, 1892.

38. Walker and Turley, "Andrew Jenson Collection," 9. See also Turley and Walker, *Mountain Meadows Massacre*.

39. Walker and Turley, "Andrew Jenson Collection," 32–33.

40. Jenson Journal, January 31, 1892. Ibid., January 23–February 3, 1892.

41. Jenson, *Autobiography*, 198.

42. Jenson, *Encyclopedic History*, 552.

43. See Neilson, *Exhibiting Mormonism*.

44. Bolotin and Laing, *World's Columbian Exposition*, 2–3.

45. Ibid.

46. Jenson Journal, February 27–28; March 1, 3, and 16, 1893.

47. Jenson, "Epitome of the History."

48. Jenson Journal, August 21, 1893.

49. Andrew Jenson to Franklin D. Richards, August 24, 1893, in Jenson Journal, August 24, 1893.

50. Jenson Journal, August 24, 1893.

51. Ibid., September 5, 1893. See S. Esplin, "History," 61–65.

52. See Neilson, *Exhibiting Mormonism*, 141–75.

53. Jenson Journal, September 23, 1893.

54. For the history of John Whitmer's manuscript—known as the "Book of John Whitmer"—including Jenson's transcription of the record, see S. Esplin, "History," 49–82.

55. Jenson, *Autobiography*, 209; Jenson Journal, September 25–27, 1893.

56. See Andrew Jenson, introduction to Whitmer, "Book," 1–3.

57. Jenson Journal, October 11–26, 1893; Richards Journal, October 11, 1893. The typescript copies are in folders 5–6, box 98, AJC/CHL, and in Whitmer, "Book."

58. Jenson Journal, June 27–28, 1892.

59. Ibid., September 13, 1892.

60. Andrew Jenson to Franklin D. Richards, September 3, 1892, in Jenson Journal, September 3, 1892. Richards at one point held a controlling interest in the Utah Loan and Trust Company, established in 1888. See Walker, "Heber J. Grant."

61. Jenson Journal, November 15–20, 1892.

62. Andrew Jenson to Franklin D. Richards, November 26, 1892, in Jenson Journal, November 26, 1892.

63. Jenson Journal, December 17, 1892.

64. Ibid., March 20 and October 28, 1893.

65. Ibid., January 1, 1894.

66. Ibid., book E, 13.

67. A. A. Jenson Journal, 20.

68. Ibid., 34.

69. Jenson Journal, January 5 and 7, 1894; Jenson, *Autobiography*, 215.

70. Andrew Jenson to Franklin D. Richards, January 13, 1894, in Historian's Office, Correspondence Files.

71. Jenson Journal, June 30, 1893.

72. Jenson to Richards, January 13, 1894.

73. Franklin D. Richards to Andrew Jenson, January 18, 1894, in Jenson Journal, January 23, 1894; Richards Journal, January 18, 1894.

74. Richards Journal, May 26, 1894.

75. Ibid., May 2 and June 12, 1894.

76. Ibid., June 12, 1894.

77. Andrew Jenson to Franklin D. Richards, June 7, 1894, Historian's Office, Correspondence Files.

78. Jenson Journal, February 3, 1894.

79. Ibid., May 25, 1894.

80. Ibid., July 23, 1894; Ibid., September 19, 1894.

81. Jenson Journal, September 21 and 24, 1894.

82. Ibid., May 2, 1895.

83. Ibid., May 10, 1895.

84. Ibid., May 11, 1895.

85. Ibid., November 13, 1895.

86. Hawai'i became the fiftieth state in the United States in 1959, although it had been an organized incorporated territory since 1898. The Auckland Stake in New Zealand, created in 1958, was the first non–North American (including Hawai'i) stake of the church.

87. These missions were the British Mission, the Society Islands Mission, the Scandinavian Mission, the Sandwich Islands Mission, the Australasian Mission, the Turkish Mission, the Swiss and German Mission, the Netherlands-Belgium Mission, and the Samoan Mission.

88. Jenson Journal, November 13, 1894.

89. G. Cannon, *Journal*, May 2, 1895.

90. Turley, "Gathering Latter-day Saint History," 148.

91. Jenson, *Autobiography*, 228.

92. Jenson Journal, April 8 and 11, 1895.

93. Richards Journal, April 12, 1895.

94. Jenson Journal, April 6, 1895; Franklin D. Richards, "Records of the Saints," *Deseret Weekly* (Salt Lake City), September 14, 1895.

95. Jenson Journal, May 2, 1895; Edward Stevenson, "Ready for a Long Journey," *Deseret Weekly*, May 11, 1895.

96. Wilford Woodruff, George Q. Cannon, and Joseph F. Smith to Andrew Jenson, missionary certificate, May 9, 1895, in Jenson Journal, May 10, 1895.

97. Franklin D. Richards to Andrew Jenson, May 11, 1895, in Jenson Journal, May 11, 1895.

98. Jenson Journal, May 11, 1895.

99. See Neilson and Moffat, *Tales from the World Tour.*

100. See Neilson, Bray, and Johnson, *Rediscovering the Sites.*

101. "Jenson's Travels," *Deseret Weekly*, June 1, 1895.

102. "Jenson's Travels," *Deseret Weekly*, February 19, 1898.

103. "Jenson's Travels," *Deseret Weekly*, February 19, 1898. He compiled, translated, and published his travelogues in Danish as Jenson, *Jorden rundt.*

104. See, for example, "Jenson's Travels," *Deseret Weekly*, November 2, 1895.

105. "Jenson's Travels," *Deseret Weekly*, November 2, 1895.

106. "Jenson's Travels," *Deseret Weekly*, November 16, 1895.

107. "Jenson's Travels," *Deseret Weekly*, November 30, 1895.

108. For more on Latter-day Saint missionary work in French Polynesia, see Hendrix-Komoto, "Playing the Whore."

109. "Jenson's Travels," *Deseret Weekly*, November 2, 1895; "Jenson's Travels," *Deseret Weekly*, November 9, 1895.

110. See, for example, "Jenson's Travels," *Deseret Weekly*, December 14, 1895.

111. "Jenson's Travels," *Deseret Weekly*, March 7, 1896.

112. "Jenson's Travels," *Deseret Weekly*, November 23, 1895.

113. "Jenson's Travels," *Deseret Weekly*, January 4 and February 8, 1896.

114. "Jenson's Travels," *Deseret Weekly*, February 29, 1896.

115. "Jenson's Travels," *Deseret Weekly*, March 7, 14, 28; April 11, 18; May 9, 23, 1896.

116. "Jenson's Travels," *Deseret Weekly*, February 29, 1896.

117. "Jenson's Travels," *Deseret Weekly*, February 1, 1896. On the early activities of Manoa and Belio, see McBride, "Mormon Beginnings in Samoa."

118. "Jenson's Travels," *Deseret Weekly*, March 28, 1896.

119. "Jenson's Travels," *Deseret Weekly*, March 7, 1896.

120. "Jenson's Travels," *Deseret Weekly*, January 11, 1896.

121. "Jenson's Travels," *Deseret Weekly*, April 4, 1896.

122. Emma Jenson, Journal, July 31, 1896, in Jenson Journal, book F, 586.

123. Jenson Journal, October 8, 1896.

124. George F. Gibbs to Andrew Jenson, October 12, 1896, in Jenson Journal, October 31, 1896.

125. "Elder Andrew Jenson Reports His Travels throughout the World," *Deseret Evening News*, June 28, 1897; Jenson, *Autobiography*, 386.

126. "Mormonism," *Wairarapa (New Zealand) Standard*, December 27, 1895, in Jenson, Scrapbook C, 1895–1900, December 27, 1895, AJC/CHL; K. Perkins, "Andrew Jenson," 158–59.

127. Jenson Journal, June 4, 1897.

128. Ibid., June 27, 1897. See "Sunday Services," *Deseret Weekly*, July 3, 1897.

129. Andrew Jenson to Franklin D. Richards, July 3, 1897, in Jenson Journal, July 3, 1897.

130. Jenson to Richards, July 3, 1897.

131. Ibid.

132. Reid L. Neilson, introduction to Neilson, *Global Mormonism*, xv.

Chapter 5. Assistant Church Historian

1. Penrose Journal, February 4, 1896, and April 6, 1896. Jenson congratulated Penrose on his appointment while he was traveling in Jerusalem in September 1896. Andrew Jenson to Franklin D. Richards, September 16, 1896, in Historian's Office, Correspondence Files.

2. Jenson, *Latter-day Saint Biographical Encyclopedia*, 1:254–61.

3. Penrose Journal, December 16, 1895; Bergera, "Commencement of Great Things," 27–28.

4. Jenson Journal, July 16, 1897.

5. Ibid., September 14, 1897.

6. Ibid., October 14, 1892, and November 12, 1897.

7. Jenson Journal, September 22, 1897.

8. Ibid., November 12, 1897, and January 7, 1898. Neve and Jenson reached a final settlement in February 1898. Jenson deeded his Mill Creek property, and the Neves agreed to refund Jenson the property taxes for 1894–96 and cover the court costs. Jenson Journal, December 1 and February 8, 1898.

9. Jenson Journal, October 5, 1897.

10. Ibid., October 19, 1897. Over the next several decades, Jenson served under the following Church Historians: Franklin D. Richards, Anthon H. Lund, and Joseph Fielding Smith. He also labored alongside the following Assistant Church Historians: John Jaques, Charles W. Penrose, Orson F. Whitney, A. Milton Musser, B. H. Roberts, Joseph Fielding Smith, A. William Lund, and Junius F. Wells.

11. Jenson Journal, October 19, 1897. Ibid., April 10, 1898.

12. Richards Journal, January 16, 1884.

13. "General Conference," *Deseret Weekly*, April 13, 1889; Richards Journal, April 5, 1889.

14. After his appointment to Assistant Church Historian, Jenson continued to collect a yearly salary of approximately $1,200. See Jenson Journal, book C, 205. His salary was commensurate with other Historian's Office salaries. See Franklin D. Richards and John Jaques to Wilford Woodruff, George Q. Cannon, and Joseph F. Smith, September 11, 1891, folder 23, box 1, First Presidency General Authorities Correspondence.

15. Charles W. Penrose was an exception. He was set apart as an Assistant Church Historian on February 4, 1896. Penrose Journal, February 4, 1896.

16. Andrew Jenson to Franklin D. Richards, April 13, 1898, in Jenson Journal, April 13, 1898. Jenson Journal, June 27 and 29, 1900; Jenson, *Autobiography*, 400.

17. Jenson, "Historian's Office."

18. Alexander, *Mormonism in Transition*, 5.

19. Jenson, *Church Chronology* (1886). Jenson issued his chronology piecemeal to subscribers. Volume 6 of the *Historical Record* contained Jenson's chronology for 1885–87. He also appended to volume nine supplements with his complete chronology through 1887.

20. Andrew Jenson to Franklin D. Richards, April 13, 1898, in Jenson Journal, April 13, 1898.

21. George F. Gibbs to Andrew Jenson, May 10, 1898, in Jenson Journal, May 10, 1898.

22. A priesthood holder's "line of authority" is a reverse chronological listing of men ordained to the priesthood.

23. Jenson, *Church Chronology* (1899), v–xxviii.

24. "Church Chronology," *Deseret News*, July 13, 1898.

25. Jenson, *Church Chronology* (1899), [iv].

26. Andrew Jenson to Franklin D. Richards, September 22, 1898, folder 90, box 30, AJC/CHL.

27. First Presidency, "Church Chronology," circular, ca. October 7, 1898, folder 1, box 60, AJC/CHL.

28. Jenson to Richards, September 22, 1898.

29. First Presidency, "Church Chronology," circular, ca. October 7, 1898; Jenson Journal, October 8, 1898.

30. Jenson Journal, October 8, 1898.

31. Alexander, *Mormonism in Transition*, 111–13.

32. Franklin D. Richards and Andrew Jenson to "Brother," circular, November 10, 1898, folder 1, box 103, AJC/CHL.

33. Andrew Jenson to "Bishop," circular, September 1, 1899, folder 1, box 60, AJC/CHL.

34. Jenson, Journal, February 26, 1899.

35. "Will Build Fireproof Building for the Mormon Church Records," *Salt Lake Herald*, October 24, 1901.

36. For more information on Whitney's *History of Utah*, see Horne, *Life of Orson F. Whitney*, 145–63.

37. Jenson Journal, December 7, 1899. Subscriptions to the *Church Chronology* were recorded as early as October 1898. Ledger of subscriptions for Church Chronology, 1899–1900, 126, folder 2, box 60, AJC/CHL.

38. Jenson Journal, March 5, 1899.

39. Jenson to "Bishop," circular, September 1, 1899.

40. Jenson Journal, October 7 and 18, 1899.

41. Andrew Jenson to "Brother," circular, March 20, 1900, box 60, folder 1, AJC.

42. Financial Ledger for Historian's Office, 1898–1905, 3–4, folder 6, box 60, AJC/CHL.

43. Jenson to "Brother," circular, March 20, 1900; Emma Kelly to Andrew Jenson, May 9, 1905, in Financial Ledger.

44. For a rendering of this plan, see Historian's Office Plans.

45. Jenson, "Historian's Office," 67; Historian's Office Plans; Notes about the History of the Church Historian's Office and Its Move to the Church Administration Building, 1917, folder 15, box 51, AJC/CHL.

46. Jenson, Journal, October 4, 1900.

47. Andrew Jenson to Franklin D. Richards, July 3, 1897, in Jenson Journal, July 3, 1897.

48. Clawson Diary, December 14, 1899.

49. Alexander, *Mormonism in Transition*, 99; Bell, "Windows of Heaven," 56.

50. Clawson, "Memoirs," 57; Clawson, "Reorganization of Financial System." The efforts of Snow, his successor Joseph F. Smith, and the auditing committee, along with an increase in tithing receipts, rescued the church from debt by the April 1907 general conference. Quinn, *Mormon Hierarchy*, 202.

51. Clawson Diary, May 2, 1901, and December 14, 1899.

52. Ibid., January 24, 1901; Historical Department, Journal History, January 24, 1901.

53. Lyman, Clawson, and Jenson to "Presidents of Stakes"; see also Committee on Records, "Record Keeping."

54. Historical Department, Journal History, March 14, 1900.

55. See Woodworth, "Mormonism and Education."

56. Joseph F. Smith, John R. Winder, and Anthon H. Lund to "Bishop," circular, November 13, 1902, Church Records Committee History.

57. Committee on Records, Minutes, January 19, 1900, Church Records Committee History.

58. Historical Department, Journal History, March 22, 1900.

59. Jenson Journal, March 22, 1900.

60. Rudger Clawson to William C. Parkinson, October 29, 1901, Church Records Committee History; Committee on Records, Minutes, October 26, 1901, Church Records Committee History.

61. Committee on Records, "Record Keeping."

62. Ibid. A former circular also advised the adoption of these two record books. See Lyman, Clawson, and Jenson, circular, March 13, 1901.

63. D. Smith, "Formal Reporting Systems."

64. "Apostle F. D. Richards Is Dead," *Ogden Standard*, December 9, 1899.

65. Turley, "Assistant Church Historians."

66. According to historian D. Michael Quinn, 51 percent (123) of the appointed General Authorities during the years 1832 to 1932 were "related as kin to one or more general authorities." Thirty-eight percent (47) of the new appointees were second cousins or closer in relationship. During the period 1900 to 1910, 64 percent of new General Authorities were related to a current General Authority. Quinn, *Mormon Hierarchy*, 166.

67. Jenson Journal, June 23, 1921.

68. Whitney Journals, 8:142–45.

69. Jenson, *Latter-day Saint Biographical Encyclopedia*, 1:258–59; Whitney, *Life of Heber C. Kimball*, 339.

70. See Horne, *Life of Orson F. Whitney*, 79–85, 109–129, 165–210.

71. Jenson, *Latter-day Saint Biographical Encyclopedia*, 3:793; Horne, *Life of Orson F. Whitney*, 97.

72. Horne, *Life of Orson F. Whitney*, 177–78, 193.

73. Whitney Journals, November 10, 1898, quoted in Horne, *Life of Orson F. Whitney*, 194.

74. *Seventy-Second Annual Conference*, 84.

75. Jenson, *Latter-day Saint Biographical Encyclopedia*, 1:256; Jenson Journal, June 1, 1900.

76. A. Lund Journals, July 25, 1900; Martin S. Lindsay to Lorenzo Snow and counselors, June 29, 1900, quoted in K. Perkins, "Andrew Jenson," 109–10.

77. Historical Department, Journal History, August 4, 1900.

78. Clawson Diary, July 25, 1900.

79. Hatch, *Danish Apostle*, xxxii–xxxiii.

80. Lund Journals, July 25, 1900.

81. Jenson Journal, July 26, 1900; Historical Department, Journal History, July 26, 1900.

82. Jenson was last sustained at the April 1900 general conference. *Seventieth Annual Conference*, 52; *Seventy-First Semi-annual Conference*, 42.

83. *Seventy-Second Semi-annual Conference*, 62–63.

84. Jenson Journal, November 21, 1901.

85. The Andrew Jenson History Company was officially incorporated in December 1901 with $10,000 in capital stock. See Jenson Journal, December 5, 1901.

86. Jenson Journal, August 3, 1901.

87. Ibid., August 11, 1901.

88. R. Esplin, "Place Prepared"; Walker, "Banner Is Unfurled"; Andrew Jenson, "Historian Gives Account of Ensign Peak," *Salt Lake Tribune*, August 1, 1931.

89. See Doctrine and Covenants 112:4; 78:18; 68:6; Acts 23:11; 27:22; and Matthew 14:27.

90. Jenson Journal, August 11, 1901.

91. Doctrine and Covenants 121:7–8.

92. Jenson Journal, August 11, 1901.

93. See Doctrine and Covenants 98.

94. Jenson Journal, April 6, 1902; "Died," *Salt Lake Herald*, April 10, 1902.

95. Jenson Journal, April 6, 1902.

Chapter 6. Elder and Emissary

1. Sjodahl, "Estimate."

2. "The Scandinavian Jubilee," *Deseret News*, April 12, 1900; Sjodahl, "Estimate."

3. Jenson Journal, May 16 and June 4, 1900.

4. *Scandinavian Jubilee Album*.

5. The album had four hundred subscribers, and an extra six hundred albums were on hand at the jubilee to sell to the public. Sjodahl, "Estimate," 755.

6. "Scandinavians Rejoice," *Salt Lake Tribune*, June 15, 1900, 5.

7. "Third Day of Jubilee: Women Took Charge of the Morning Gathering," *Salt Lake Tribune*, June 17, 1900; "Scandinavian Ladies Speak," *Deseret News*, June 16, 1900.

8. Jenson, Scrapbook C, June 15, 1900, AJC/CHL.

9. Henrichsen and Bailey, "No More Strangers," 32, 36.

10. "Close of the Jubilee: Scandinavians Conclude Their Celebration," *Salt Lake Tribune*, June 18, 1900.

11. Ibid.

12. Jenson Journal, January 22, 1898. Ibid., February 9 and 11, 1898.

13. Ibid., February 16, 1898.

14. Andrew Jenson, letter, February 16, 1898, in *Bikuben*, April 21, 1898; Andrew Jenson, "Greetings," folder 34, box 30, AJC/CHL.

15. Jenson Journal, February 16, 1900.

16. Ibid., May 4, 1898, and February 6, 1899. Jenson was later able to mend his relationship with Anderson, and he worked closely with Sjodahl on the Scandinavian jubilee. Jenson Journal, August 4–5, 1901.

17. Jenson Journal, August 12, 1899; Jenson, *Latter-day Saint Biographical Encyclopedia*, 3:714.

18. Jenson Journal, February 8 and 16, 1900; "Slander Suit Heard," *Salt Lake Herald*, February 8, 1900.

19. "Slander Suit Heard."

20. Jenson Journal, February 16, 1900.

21. A. Lund Journals, December 3, 1900.

22. "To Publish New Book of Mormon," *Deseret News*, May 12, 1902.

23. Lund Journals, December 4, 1900.

24. Jenson Journal, December 3, 1900.

25. Jenson, Scrapbook D, 1901–3, January 1903, AJC/CHL; "New Editions of the Book of Mormon," *Latter-day Saints' Millennial Star* 65, no. 3 (January 15, 1903): 41–42.

26. Jenson Journal, April 25, 1902.

27. Andrew Jenson to Francis M. Lyman, May 3, 1902, folder 62, box 30, AJC/CHL.

28. Jenson Journal, May 14 and 31, 1902.

29. Peter O. Hansen ordained Fjeldsted an elder in 1853, only a year after his conversion. Jenson, *Latter-day Saint Biographical Encyclopedia*, 1:203–4.

30. Jenson Journal, June 16, 1902.

31. Ibid., December 11, 1902.

32. "New Mission House in Copenhagen," *Deseret News*, July 26, 1902.

33. "Dedication Service of the Christiania Meeting-House," *Millennial Star* 65, no. 31 (July 30, 1903): 481–84; *Seventy-Third Annual Conference*, 23.

34. Jenson Journal, June 26, 1902.

35. Ibid., July 8, 1902.

36. A. A. Jenson Journal, July 13, 1902.

37. According to the journal of Andrew Alexander, Mary forgave him for his adulterous affair, shortly after his return from his mission. A. A. Jenson Journal, August 31, 1902.

38. Jenson Journal, October 15, 1902, and June 18, 1903. On numerous occasions, Jenson attempted to mediate a resolution between Andrew Alexander and Mary, his first wife. Though Andrew Alexander and Thora promised to separate, such a separation never occurred. Jenson Journal, May 14 and July 8, 1904.

39. Jenson Journal, December 28, 1903. Mary Alice was born in 1903, and Louis Crane was born in 1905.

40. Bertha Jenson, Journal, October 6, 1902, in Jenson Journal, book H, 300.

41. By September 1905, Andrew Alexander was living in Idaho with Thora and Mary had elected to sue for divorce. Jenson Journal, September 3, 1905.

42. Jenson Journal, March 29, 1916, and September 11, 1918.

43. Ibid., November 13, 1902.

44. Ibid., December 16, 1902.

45. Ibid., December 25 and 27, 1902.

46. Jenson, *Autobiography*, 417–23.

47. *Seventy-Third Annual Conference*, 69–70.

48. Jenson Journal, January 27, 1904.

49. Ibid., February 12, 1904.

50. The entire party traveling to Washington included Andrew Jenson, Joseph F. Smith, Hyrum M. Smith, Francis M. Lyman, Alma Merrill, Thomas H. Merrill, Charles E. Merrill, and Lorin Harmer. Jenson Journal, February 27, 1904.

51. Heath, introduction, xi–xx.

52. Jenson Journal, February 25, 1904.

53. Heath, introduction, xiii–xiv.

54. Jenson Journal, March 4, 1904.

55. Ibid., March 2, 1904.

56. Ibid., March 3, 1904.

57. Flake, *Politics of American Religious Identity*, 56–81.

58. Hardy, *Solemn Covenant*, 141–46; K. Cannon, "Beyond the Manifesto."

59. "Apostle Lyman Injures Case of Senator Smoot," *Salt Lake Herald*, March 9, 1904.

60. Jenson Journal, March 8, 1904.

61. "Apostle Lyman."

62. Jenson Journal, March 8, 1904.

63. *Proceedings*, 1:498–501.

64. Ibid., 1:499.

65. Ibid., 1:533.

66. Ibid., 1:522–27.

67. Jenson, Scrapbook E, 1904–5, March 10, 1904, AJC/CHL.

68. Jenson Journal, March 12, 1904; "Historian Jenson Describes Mormon 'Missionary Work,'" *World*, March 13, 1904, in Andrew Jenson, Scrapbook E, 1904–5, March 13, 1904, AJC/CHL.

69. Jenson Journal, May 13, 1905.

70. Ibid., September 2, 1900.

71. Emma Jenson, Journal, February 15, 1903, in Jenson Journal, Book H, 497.

72. Jenson Journal, December 13, 1918.

73. Emma Jenson, Journal, February 15, 1903, in Jenson Journal, Book H, 497.

74. Bertha Jenson, Journal, September 3, 1902, in Jenson Journal, Book H, 297.

75. Jenson Journal, October 18, 1906.

76. "Mrs. Snow for President," *Salt Lake Herald-Republican*, October 31, 1906; "Emma Jenson," *Deseret News*, April 15, 1937; "Rites Arranged for Mrs. Jenson," *Salt Lake Telegram*, April 13, 1937. For information on the history of the Utah Women's Press Club, see Sillito and Thatcher, "Sisterhood and Sociability."

77. Sillito and Thatcher, "Sisterhood and Sociability," 144–46; E. Jenson, "Christmas in Scandinavia."

78. Jenson Journal, October 16, 1903.

79. Ibid., July 3, 1901. "Introduction to History."

80. Jenson Journal, July 17, 1905; Jenson, *Latter-day Saint Biographical Encyclopedia*, 3:753.

81. Lund Journals, August 20 and 23, 1904. President Skanchy left for Utah on December 6, 1904. President Christian D. Fjeldsted was appointed in his stead, once again assuming a role Jenson felt should be his. Jenson Journal, December 6, 1904.

82. Jenson, *Autobiography*, 430.

83. Jenson Journal, September 21 and October 4, 1904.

84. "Stockholm Mission House," *Deseret News*, November 19, 1904; Jenson Journal, October 21–26, 1904.

85. Jenson Journal, December 20, 1904.

86. Ibid., December 12, 1904.

87. Ibid., December 12, 1904.

88. Ibid., 436–37.

89. Jenson Journal, January 14, 1905.

90. Ibid., January 15, 1905.

91. Ibid., January 19–20, 1905.

92. Frimodt-Møller compiled his main claims against the church in a pamphlet that he circulated around Denmark in 1905. See Frimodt-Møller, *Flyveblad mod Mormonismen*.

93. Jenson, *Autobiography*, 439–43.

94. H. Cannon Journal, February 10, 1905, folder 2, box 3.

Chapter 7. Scandinavian Mission President

1. Jenson Journal, September 17, 1908; Lund Journals, September 16, 1908; Joseph Fielding Smith married Ethel Reynolds in the Salt Lake Temple on November 2, 1908. Gibbons, *Joseph Fielding Smith*, 138–40.

2. Jenson Journal, September 17, 1908.

3. Ibid., October 14–15, 1908.

4. Ibid., October 13, 1908.

5. Ibid., October 13, 1908.

6. Ibid., October 15, 1908. Eleonore studied in Berlin until December 1909. Her talent as a singer eventually led her and her husband, George B. Reynolds, to move to New York, where she allegedly became less involved with the church. Jenson Journal, December 5–6, 1909; "Eleonor Reynolds."

7. Since its founding in 1850, the Scandinavian Mission comprised Denmark (which then included Iceland), Sweden, and Norway. Beginning in 1905, the Swedish Mission was created out of the Scandinavian Mission, which then was officially renamed the Danish-Norwegian Mission. Jenson, *History of the Scandinavian Mission*, 410–11.

8. Joseph F. Smith, John R. Winder, and Anthon H. Lund to Andrew Jenson, December 9, 1908, in Jenson Journal, December 9, 1908.

9. Jenson, *Encyclopedic History*, 237–38.

10. Jenson Journal, January 12, 1909.

11. Ibid., January 18, 1909; Jenson, *Autobiography*, 448; Jenson, *Latter-day Saint Biographical Encyclopedia*, 2:201.

12. It was common for mission presidents who were plurally married to invite one wife to serve with them in their assignment. With Jenson, it appears church leaders wanted to avoid drawing attention to his plural family while he presided over the mission.

13. Jenson visited the home of Mary W. Mason, the daughter of Abner F. Staples, who had allegedly persecuted the Latter-day Saints in Jackson County, Missouri, in July 1833. Jenson, Journal, January 21, 1909; see also Bishop Edward W. Partridge. "To His Excellency, Daniel Dunklin," *Evening and the Morning Star*, December 1833, 114–15.

14. Jenson Journal, January 25, 1909.

15. Ibid., January 27, 1909.

16. Ibid., January 27, 1909.

17. Ibid., January 28, 1909.

18. Ibid., January 31, 1909.

19. Ibid., February 11, 1909.

20. Ibid., February 11, 1909.

21. Neilson, "Nineteenth-Century Euro-American Mormon Missionary Model."

22. For information on the Japan Mission, see Neilson, *Early Mormon Missionary Activities*.

23. Alexander, *Mormonism in Transition*, 213–15; Cowan, "Called to Serve," 24–26.

24. Baugh, "Defending Mormonism," 507–9.

25. Mulder, *Homeward to Zion*, 56–64.

26. Andrew Jenson to Charles W. Penrose, February 26, 1909, in SMLC. For the volumes covering Jenson's mission presidency, see SMLC, vols. 21–23.

27. President Lund would later remark on the significance of Jenson's traveling approach: "I must say that of all the Mission Presidents Scandinavia has had, you have done the most traveling and preaching, and have beaten the record of us all." Anthon H. Lund to Andrew Jenson, March 28, 1911, in letterbook, 4:308, folder 1, box 2, A. Lund Papers.

28. Jenson Journal, March 1–7, 1909.

29. Andrew Jenson to Charles W. Penrose, March 9, 1909, in SMLC, 21:355.

30. Lund remarked to Jenson in October 1910. Anthon H. Lund to Andrew Jenson, October 25, 1910, in letterbook, 4:279, A. Lund Papers.

31. Andrew Jenson to Joseph F. Smith, John R. Winder, and Anthon H. Lund, March 12, 1909, in SMLC, 21:359–61.

32. Jenson Journal, March 7, 1909.

33. Jenson to Smith, Winder, and Lund, March 12, 1909.

34. See for example, Jenson Journal, October 25, 1910; Baugh, "Defending Mormonism," 513–14; Jenson, *Autobiography*, 455–58.

35. Andrew Jenson to Charles W. Penrose, February 26, 1909, SMLC, 21:342.

36. Jenson Journal, May 12, 1909. Just prior to leaving for home in 1912, Jenson sought a meeting with the Danish king, Frederick VIII, and was nearly granted the meeting before the king learned that Jenson was Mormon. Frederick VIII allegedly said he "would not give audience to a 'Mormon.'" Apparently, the king was also in poor health at the time. Jenson, *Autobiography*, 490.

37. Anthon H. Lund to Andrew Jenson, June 4, 1909, in letterbook, 4:176, A. Lund Papers. See also "President A. H. Lund Leaves Europe," *Deseret News*, June 5, 1909; "President A. H. Lund and Party at Aarhus, Denmark," *Deseret News*, August 7, 1909; and "President Lund Home from Trip," *Deseret News*, August 30, 1909.

38. Jenson Journal, July 23, 1909.

39. Ibid., July 26, 1909.

40. Ibid., June 28–July 19, 1910; June 7–23, 1911.

41. Andrew Jenson, "The Late Universal Peace Congress," *Deseret News*, August 25, 1910; Jenson Journal, August 1 and 4–6, 1910.

42. Thorp, "Mormon Peril," 70–72.

43. Thorp, "Winifred Graham," 107–10.

44. Ibid., 110. See also Bunker and Bitton, *Mormon Graphic Image*; Talbot, *Foreign Kingdom*, 83–104; Givens, *Viper on the Hearth*, 97–167.

45. Arrington and Haupt, "Intolerable Zion," 245–48; Shipps, "From Satyr to Saint," 53–54, 62–68.

46. Talbot, *Foreign Kingdom*, 136–41.

47. See Vermeir, "Magic of the Magic Lantern"; Pfragner, *Motion Picture*, 12–13, 226; S. Palmer, "Projecting the Gaze," 19, 25.

48. Howard, "William Jarman."

49. Rasmussen, *Mormonism*, 127–29.

50. "The Stereopticon Versus Prejudice," *Millennial Star* 60, no. 32 (August 11, 1898): 504.

51. "Lime-Light Views," *Millennial Star* 60, no. 32 (August 11, 1898): 510.

52. Andrew Jenson to Joseph F. Smith, John R. Winder, and Anthon H. Lund, March 12, 1909, in SMLC, 21:359–360; Jenson Journal, October 14 and December 9, 1902.

53. Andrew Jenson to I. A. Jensen, January 31, 1910, in SMLC, 21:615. The First Presidency sent close to sixty-three slides for Jenson to create his lecture. Jenson Journal, January 31, 1910.

54. Anthon H. Lund to Andrew Jenson, January 26, [1910], in letterbook, 4:228–29, A. Lund Papers.

55. Jenson Journal, February 2 and 9, 1910.

56. Ibid., February 10, 1910.

57. Ibid., March 2, 1910.
58. Ibid., September 14, 1910.
59. Ibid., September 14, 1910.
60. Ibid., November 18, 1910.
61. Ibid., November 23, 1910.
62. Ibid., November 17, 1911.
63. Ibid., November 23, 1911.
64. Ibid., November 24, 1911.
65. "Messages from the Mission"; Baugh, "Defending Mormonism," 527.
66. Joseph K. Nicholes to *Deseret News*, March 11, 1911, in SMLC, 22:341.
67. See Brackenridge, "Are You That Damned Presbyterian Devil?," 100.
68. *Light from the Home Paper*.
69. Thorp, "Mormon Peril," 75.
70. "War on Mormons Is Waged in Britain," *New York Times*, February 5, 1911, quoted in Baugh, "Defending Mormonism," 539n35.
71. Parshall, "Winston Churchill"; Peggy Fletcher Stack, "Churchill—Yes, That Churchill—Investigated Mormon Missionaries to See If They Were Just Shopping for Wives," *Salt Lake Tribune*, June 20, 2016, http://archive.sltrib.com/article.php?id=4028652&itype=CMSID. For more on Freece's campaign in England, see Clawson, "Memoirs," 417–48, CHL.
72. Stewart-Freece and Freece, *How Mormons Recruit Abroad*, 19. Jenson retained a copy of Freece's pamphlet for his personal library, now kept in the Church History Library.
73. See Vig, *Danske i Amerika*, 148–50; Stewart-Freece and Freece, *How Mormons Recruit Abroad*, 21; Mulder, *Homeward to Zion*, 287–88.
74. Stewart-Freece and Freece, *How Mormons Recruit Abroad*, 22.
75. Ibid., 23.
76. Jenson Journal, December 31, 1910; Jenson, *Autobiography*, 476.
77. Jenson Journal, January 18, 1911.
78. Jenson, *Autobiography*, 478.
79. Jenson Journal, June 21, 1911.
80. Ibid., June 21, 1911.
81. "Anti-Mormonernes store møde igaar blev en fiasko" [Big anti-Mormon meeting yesterday a failure], *Politiken* (Copenhagen), June 22, 1911; Joseph K. Nicholes, "Danish Conference," *Deseret News*, July 15, 1911; Baugh, "Defending Mormonism," 528.
82. Stewart-Freece and Freece, *How Mormons Recruit Abroad*, 25–26.
83. Andrew Jenson to Joseph F. Smith and Anthon H. Lund, November 20, 1911, in SMLC, 22:879–80; *Light from the Home Paper*; Jenson, *Autobiography*, 489; "Hans P. Freece," *Skandinaviens Stjerne* 14, no. 60 (July 15, 1911): 216–19. See also Jenson Journal, July 15, 1911.
84. Andrew Jenson to Joseph F. Smith and counselors, October 5, 1911, in SMLC, 22:795.
85. For more on the church in Iceland, see Iceland Mission History, folder 21, box 40; and Woods, *Fire on Ice*.

86. Andrew Jenson to Joseph F. Smith and counselors, February 23, 1911, in SMLC, 22:310–11; see also Woods, "Andrew Jenson's Illustrated Journey."

87. Andrew Jenson to Jacob B. Johnson, July 1, 1911, in SMLC, 22:590.

88. A native of Huntsville, Utah, Petersen arrived in the Danish-Norwegian Mission the previous year on February 26, 1910. Jenson, *History of the Scandinavian Mission*, 429; Woods, "Andrew Jenson's Illustrated Journey to Iceland," 114n10.

89. Jenson Journal, August 19, 1911.

90. Ibid., August 19–20, 1911. Jenson gave one more illustrated lecture on the trip, while aboard the ship *Sterling* on his way to Copenhagen. See Jenson Journal, August 27, 1911.

91. Quoted in Woods, "Andrew Jenson's Illustrated Journey," 116n27.

92. Andrew Jenson to Joseph F. Smith, Anthon H. Lund, and John Henry Smith, September 9, 1911, in SMLC, 22:732.

93. Andrew Jenson to Rudger Clawson, September 5, 1911, in SMLC, 22:726.

94. Andrew Jenson to Jacob B. Johnson, September 5, 1911, in SMLC, 22:720.

95. Apostle Joseph B. Wirthlin dedicated Iceland for missionary work and reopened the mission in September 1977. Woods, "Icelandic Conversion," 11.

96. Translated in Nelson, "History." The original quote appeared in a sixteen-page pamphlet created for the film. See *Mormonens Offer*, [12], [15].

97. Olmstead, "*Victim of the Mormons*," 205–7.

98. Translation in Nelson, "History," 28; see also *Mormonens Offer*, [1], [12], [15].

99. Quoted in B. Cannon and Olmstead, "Scandalous Film," 46.

100. Allen, *Danish but Not Lutheran*, 131–33.

101. Andrew Jenson to Joseph F. Smith and Anthon H. Lund, November 20, 1911, in SMLC, 22:879–80.

102. Joseph K. Nicholes to *Deseret News*, November 23, 1911, in SMLC, 22:885–86.

103. Jenson Journal, December 5, 1911. Around this same time, in Great Britain, Rudger Clawson attempted to unmask what he perceived to be the film's perversions in an editorial to the *Liverpool Daily Post and Mercury*. Rudger Clawson, "The Anti-'Mormon' Moving Pictures Play," *Millennial Star* 73, no. 51 (December 21, 1911): 810; B. Cannon and Olmstead, "Scandalous Film," 47–48.

104. Jenson Journal, February 9, 1912.

105. Martin Christophersen (1850–1927) served a mission to Scandinavia from 1883 to 1885. Jenson, *History of the Scandinavian Mission*, 434.

106. Jenson Journal, May 15, 1912.

107. Farewell greetings from Andrew Jenson, May 15, 1912, 3, folder 22, box 39, AJC/CHL.

108. Jenson, *Latter-day Saint Biographical Encyclopedia*, 2:108, 3: 699.

109. For missionary efforts in Russia during this time, see Mehr, *Mormon Missionaries*, 28–36.

110. Jenson Journal, May 21, 1912.

111. Ibid., May 23, 1912.

112. Ibid., May 23, 1912.

113. Ibid., June 6, 1912.

114. Ibid., June 8, 1912.

115. Ibid., June 8, 1912.

116. For histories of Latter-day Saint growth in Japan, see Neilson, *Early Mormon Missionary Activities in Japan*; and Neilson and Gessel, *Taking the Gospel.*

117. Jenson Journal, June 9, 1912.

118. For an account of the 1901 dedication of Japan, see Neilson, ed., *Japanese Missionary Journals*, 48–49.

119. Jenson Journal, June 16, 1912.

120. Ibid., June 22, 1912.

121. See Neilson and Moffat, "The Sandwich, or Hawaiian, Islands, May 1895–July 1895," chap. 2 in Neilson and Moffat, *Tales from the World Tour*, 35–87.

122. Bertha Jenson, Journal, December 14, 1909, in Jenson Journal, Book J, 198.

123. Jenson Journal, July 1–17, 1912.

124. Ibid., July 19, 1912.

125. A. William Lund would go on to serve as Assistant Church Historian for almost sixty years, until his death in 1971, three decades after Jenson's own passing in 1941. Zobell, "A. William Lund."

126. Jenson Journal, July 30, 1912.

127. Andrew Jenson to Rudger Clawson, May 14, 1912, in SMLC, 23:378–79.

128. Andrew Jenson to Joseph F. Smith and counselors, January 24, 1912, in SMLC, 23:53; Andrew Jenson to Rudger Clawson, May 14, 1912, in SMLC, 23:378; Jenson, *History of the Scandinavian Mission*, 533–36; Baugh, "Defending Mormonism," 529.

129. Andrew Jenson to Joseph F. Smith and counselors, May 10, 1912, in SMLC, 23:354.

130. Martin Christophersen to Joseph F. Smith and counselors, July 1, 1912, in SMLC, 23:526.

131. Christophersen to Smith and counselors, July 1, 1912, in SMLC, 23:527–28, 531–33.

132. Martin Christophersen to Andrew Jenson, July 2, 1912, in SMLC, 23:535; Martin Christophersen to Joseph F. Smith and Anthon H. Lund, August 28, 1912, in SMLC, 23:680.

133. See Martin Christophersen to Andrew Jenson, August 27, 1912, in SMLC, 23:676. Jenson eventually paid at least some of the attorney fees himself. However, the fine levied in the Freece case and other outstanding attorney fees remained unpaid as of November 1912. Martin Christophersen to Andrew Jenson, September 13, 1912, in SMLC, 23:730; Martin Christophersen to Joseph F. Smith and counselors, November 13, 1912, in SMLC, 23:836.

134. Martin Christophersen to Joseph F. Smith and counselors, September 11, 1912, in SMLC, 23:723.

135. Martin Christophersen to Rudger Clawson, August 29, 1912, in SMLC, 23:684.

136. Martin Christophersen to Rudger Clawson, September 4, 1912, in SMLC, 23:697–98.

137. Martin Christophersen to Andrew Jenson, September 13, 1912, in SMLC, 23:731.

138. William R. Angelo to Andrew Jenson, July 23, 1912, in Jenson Journal, August 8, 1912.

Chapter 8. Modern Record Keeper

1. Andrew Jenson to Joseph F. Smith, John R. Winder, and Anthon H. Lund, December 10, 1906, in Jenson Journal.

2. Ibid.

3. Bergera, "Commencement of Great Things," 23, 29–30.

4. HOJ, vol. 58, August 17, 1906, and vol. 59, January 1, 1907.

5. Lund Journals, August 2, 1912.

6. Jenson Journal, March 28–29, 1913.

7. Jenson to Lund, March 29, 1913.

8. See Kwolek-Folland, *Engendering Business*; and Davies, *Woman's Place*.

9. R. Jensen, "Archives of the Better World," 202–43.

10. HOJ, vol. 59, May 27, 1907.

11. HOJ, vol. 65, October 1, 1913; Jenson, "Historian's Office," 67–68.

12. Jenson to Lund, March 29, 1913.

13. HOJ, vol. 61, January 11, 1909.

14. HOJ, vol. 65, January 2, 1913.

15. See R. Jensen, "'Archives of the Better World,'" 210–12; HOJ, vol. 57, May 23, 1905; HOJ, vol. 58, June 26, 1906; HOJ, vol. 61, January 1, 1909; and Jenson, "Historian's Office," 68.

16. "Biographical Encyclopedia," *Deseret News*, May 30, 1888; K. Perkins, "Andrew Jenson," 166.

17. Jenson, *Latter-day Saint Biographical Encyclopedia*, 1:[v].

18. K. Perkins, "Andrew Jenson," 171; see also Orson F. Whitney, preface to *History of Utah*, vol. 4 (Salt Lake City: George Q. Cannon & Sons, 1904).

19. Andrew Jenson to "Dear Brother," January 1, 1901, folder 4, box 59, AJC/CHL.

20. Ibid.; Andrew Jenson to "Dear Brother," October 20, 1916, folder 98, box 20, AJC/CHL.

21. Andrew Jenson to "Dear Brother," January 1, 1901; LDS Biographical Encyclopedia Promissory Notes, folder 1, box 59, AJC/CHL.

22. K. Perkins, "Andrew Jenson," 172n14.

23. Andrew Jenson to "Dear Brother," n.d., folder 4, box 59, AJC/CHL.

24. Andrew Jenson to "Dear Brother," May 13, 1907, box 59, folder 4, AJC/CHL. See also George D. Pyper to Andrew Jenson, April 28, 1914, folder 7, box 59, AJC/CHL.

25. Jenson, "Latter-day Saint Biographical Encyclopedia Complete in Three Volumes," folder 4, box 59, AJC/CHL; First Presidency to Andrew Jenson, August 24, 1914, folder 4, box 59, AJC/CHL.

26. Andrew Jenson to Joseph F. Smith and counselors, March 17, 1915, CHL; Andrew Jenson to Joseph F. Smith and counselors, April 30, 1915, CHL; George F. Gibbs to Andrew Jenson, May 6, 1915, CHL; Joseph F. Smith, Anthon H. Lund, and Charles W. Penrose to Andrew Jenson, October 12, 1916, in Jenson Journal, October 12, 1916.

27. Andrew Jenson to Joseph F. Smith, Anthon H. Lund, and Charles W. Penrose, September 30, 1916, CHL.

28. Heber J. Grant, Anthon H. Lund, and Charles W. Penrose to Andrew Jenson, January 10, 1919, in Jenson Journal, January 10, 1919.

29. "New Books," *Deseret News,* August 21, 1920.

30. Andrew Jenson to Heber J. Grant, Anthon H. Lund, and Charles W. Penrose, January 19, 1919, CHL.

31. Jenson Journal, book K, 575–80.

32. "Biographical Encyclopedia, Printing 2000 Copies," folder 2, box 59, AJC/CHL; Andrew Jenson, memo, n.d., folder 2, box 59, AJC/CHL; Jenson Journal, book K, 580, 692. Jenson declared to subscribers that the "publication of the Latter-day Saint Biographical Encyclopedia is not a paying enterprise from a financial standpoint." Jenson, "Latter-day Saint Biographical Encyclopedia Complete in Three Volumes." For more on Jenson's estimated printing expenses and profits, see "Approximate Cost of Publishing the 'L.D.S. Biographical Encyclopedia,'" April 29, 1901, folder 2, box 59, AJC/CHL; "Estimate of profits," n.d., folder 2, box 59, AJC/CHL.

33. Andrew Jenson to Heber J. Grant, Anthon H. Lund, and Charles W. Penrose, November 26, 1918, CHL.

34. Andrew Jenson to "Dear Brother," October 15, 1920, in Andrew Jenson Scrapbook J, 1917–1920, October 15, 1920, AJC/CHL.

35. See Jenson Journal, January 26, 1915.

36. Jenson, *Church Chronology* (1914); "Special Notice," *Deseret News,* July 1, 1914.

37. Jenson Journal, December 7, 1899.

38. "Special Notice."

39. Jenson Journal, January 2, 1915.

40. Ibid., January 2, 1915.

41. Anthon H. Lund to Andrew Jenson, June 30, 1914, folder 1, box 60, AJC/CHL.

42. Oleen M. Stohl to Andrew Jenson, May 25, 1915, folder 25, box 30, AJC/CHL.

43. Jenson Journal, March 15 and 17, 1915.

44. Ibid., April 7, 1915.

45. Andrew Jenson to Joseph F. Smith, Anthon H. Lund, and Charles W. Penrose, August 20, 1917, CHL.

46. Financial ledger for Historian's Office, 1898–1905, 48–50, folder 6, box 60, AJC/CHL.

47. David A. Smith to Joseph F. Smith and counselors, December 28, 1917, folder 15, box 59, AJC/CHL.

48. Andrew Jenson to Joseph F. Smith and counselors, May 11, 1918, folder 15, box 59, AJC/CHL.

49. Exhibit C, Miscellaneous Payments to Andrew Jenson, May 11, 1918, folder 15, box 59, AJC/CHL.

50. Andrew Jenson to Anthon H. Lund, May 15, 1906, folder 15, box 59, AJC/CHL.

51. Jenson to Smith and counselors, May 11, 1918.

52. Jenson to Lund, May 15, 1906.

53. Jenson Journal, book K, 470.

54. Jenson to Lund, May 15, 1906; Jenson to Smith and counselors, May 11, 1918.

55. Jenson to Smith and counselors, May 11, 1918.

56. Jenson Journal, May 18, 1918.

57. Alexander, *Mormonism in Transition,* 101–14. See also Hobrson, "Professionals, Progressives and Bureaucratization," 639; and Wiebe, *Search for Order.*

58. Flink, *Automobile Age*, 27–39.

59. See "Reo Company"; Flink, *Automobile Age*, 35, 37.

60. Jenson Journal, October 20, 1891.

61. Ibid., July 29, 1918.

62. Jenson, in *Ninety-Seventh Semi-annual Conference*, 57.

63. "Church Officials to Begin an Inspection," *Salt Lake Tribune*, September 8, 1917; Otterstrom, "Journey to the South."

64. Otterstrom, "Journey to the South," 97.

65. See "Saints Obligated to Emulate Savior in All Good Works," *Deseret News*, December 8, 1917.

66. Jenson Journal, September 11–12, 1917.

67. Ibid., September 21, 1917.

68. Ibid., September 21, 1917.

69. Anthon H. Lund to Andrew Jenson, February 3, 1913, folder 53, box 30, AJC/CHL.

70. Richardson, "House for the Presidency."

71. "Design of General Church Office Building," *Deseret Evening News*, April 26, 1913, 1.

72. Richardson, "House for the Presidency," 236–38.

73. Anthon H. Lund, in *Eighty-Eighth Semi-annual Conference*, 10.

74. Young, "Latter-day Saints Church Office Building," 57–58.

75. Jenson, "Historian's Office," 68.

76. Jenson Journal, February 28, 1917.

77. Ibid., March 8, 1917.

78. Ibid., March 8, 1917.

79. Ibid., March 12, 1917.

80. Ibid., October 12, 1916.

81. Ibid., December 31, 1917.

82. Ibid., December 31, 1916.

83. Ibid., December 31, 1917.

84. A. Lund, in *Eighty-Eighth Semi-annual Conference*, 12–13.

85. Alexander, *Mormonism in Transition*, 95–101.

86. Andrew Jenson to First Presidency, January 19, 1919, in Jenson Journal, January 19, 1919.

87. Andrew Jenson to Joseph F. Smith, January 1, 1915, folder 4, box 3, Scott G. Kenney Collection.

88. Joseph F. Smith, in *Eighty-Ninth Semi-annual Conference*, 2.

89. Jenson Journal, October 4, 1918.

90. [Jenson], "President Joseph F. Smith Has Presided over Church 17 Years," *Deseret Evening News*, November 10, 1918; Andrew Jenson, draft, n.d., folder 98, box 20, AJC/CHL.

91. J. F. Smith Jr., *Life of Joseph F. Smith*, 479; University of Michigan Center for the History of Medicine, "Salt Lake City"; Jenson Journal, October 10, 1918.

92. Jenson Journal, October 21, 22, 23, and 27, 1918.

93. Ibid., November 11, 1918.

94. Ibid.
95. J. F. Smith Jr., *Life of Joseph F. Smith*, 479.
96. [Jenson], "President Joseph F. Smith."

Chapter 9. Explorer of Latin America

1. Jenson Journal, January 1, 1921.
2. Ibid.
3. Andrew Jenson to First Presidency, January 11, 1921, in ibid., January 11, 1921.
4. Jenson Journal, January 17, 1921.
5. "Assistant Historian Tells of Visit in Western Colorado," *Deseret News*, February 12, 1921.
6. Jenson Journal, January 18–19, 1921; Jenson, *Autobiography*, 537.
7. Jenson, *Autobiography*, 219–21.
8. Jenson Journal, February 1, 1921.
9. See A. Palmer and Grover, "Hoping to Establish a Presence"; and Tullis, "California and Chile."
10. See Jenson Journal, February 1–25, 1921.
11. For historical overviews of the church in Mexico, see Tullis, *Mormons in Mexico*; and Dormady and Tamez, *Just South of Zion*.
12. Dormady and Tamez, *Just South of Zion*, 2–5; Tullis, *Mormons in Mexico*, 13–34.
13. Tullis, *Mormons in Mexico*, 34–43.
14. Ibid., 74–84, 109–10.
15. Beecher, "Rey L. Pratt," 304.
16. See Jenson Journal, February 26–March 4, 1921.
17. Jenson Journal, March 4, 1921.
18. Ibid.
19. Ibid.
20. Ibid.
21. Ibid.
22. Ibid., March 5, 1921.
23. Jenson, *Autobiography*, 510.
24. Jenson Journal, March 9, 1921.
25. Jenson, *Autobiography*, 539.
26. Jenson Journal, March 13, 1921.
27. Jenson, *Autobiography*, 539.
28. J. F. Smith Journal, March 10 and 17, 1921.
29. Jenson Journal, March 23, 1921.
30. See Neilson and Marianno, "True and Faithful."
31. Jenson Journal, March 23, 1921.
32. Andrew Jenson to John A. Widtsoe, March 23, 1921, folder 1, box 222, Widtsoe Papers. Jenson's letter to Joseph Fielding Smith is likely not extant.
33. Jenson Journal, March 23, 1921.
34. Ibid., March 28, 1921. President Penrose had attempted to notify Jenson of the new appointments, but his letter was sent on May 24, after Jenson had uncovered the

article in the *Deseret News*. It is unclear if Jenson ever received the missive. Charles W. Penrose to Andrew Jenson, March 24, 1921, CHL.

35. Jenson Journal, March 28, 1921.

36. Jenson, *Autobiography*, 539.

37. Ibid., 540; Jenson Journal, April 30, 1921.

38. Jenson Journal, June 18, 1921.

39. In 1897, following Jenson's return from his world tour, his increased presence at the Historian's Office led to some friction with Penrose, then an Assistant Church Historian. Penrose apparently slandered Jenson to Emmeline B. Wells, who reported the remarks to Jenson. The incident nearly caused Jenson to quit the Historian's Office if he was not called as an Assistant Church Historian. He was called the next month. Apparently the two men smoothed out their differences in the ensuing years and became friends. Jenson Journal, September 13–14 and October 19, 1921.

40. Grant Journal, March 12, 1921.

41. Jenson Journal, June 23, 1921.

42. Ibid.

43. Ibid., June 26–27, 1921.

44. Anderson, "One Andrew Jenson," 787.

45. Jenson, *Autobiography*, 542.

46. Andrew Jenson to Heber J. Grant, Charles W. Penrose, and Anthony W. Ivins, July 12, 1921, in Jenson Journal, book L, 158–59.

47. Ibid.

48. Jenson Journal, October 9, 1921.

49. "Two Days Quarterly Conference Well Attended," *American Fork (UT) Citizen*, August 6, 1921.

50. Jenson, in *Ninety-Second Semi-annual Conference*, 119–20.

51. The Church of Jesus Christ of Latter-day Saints officially has no "position on the specific geographic locations of Book of Mormon events in the ancient Americas." The Church of Jesus Christ of Latter-day Saints, "Book of Mormon Geography."

52. See Givens, *By the Hand of Mormon*, 89–116. For further information regarding early Latter-day Saint missionary activity in Mexico, see Geilman, "Taking the Gospel," 8–46.

53. See Givens, *By the Hand of Mormon*, 106–7.

54. See David O. McKay to Joel Ricks, March 28, 1919, folder 7, box 1, Ricks Papers.

55. Jenson, in *Ninety-Third Semi-annual Conference*, 132.

56. Andrew Jenson, "Ancient Ruins in South American Lands Held to Be Evidence of Divine Authenticity of Book of Mormon," *Deseret News*, June 6, 1923.

57. Jenson Journal, January 5, 1923.

58. Andrew Jenson to Heber J. Grant, January 16, 1923, CHL.

59. Jenson Journal, May 8 and 31; June 14, 1922.

60. Grant, Journal, January 5, 1923.

61. Jenson to Grant, January 16, 1923.

62. Jenson, *Autobiography*, 513–14.

63. Jenson, *Latter-day Saint Biographical Encyclopedia*, 2:318; see also Page Scrapbook.

64. Jenson to Grant, January 16, 1923.
65. Jenson Journal, January 22, 1923.
66. Joseph Fielding Smith to Heber J. Grant, January 18, 1923, CHL.
67. Jenson to Grant, January 16, 1923.
68. See Joseph Smith, History, 1224; Givens and Grow, *Parley P. Pratt*, 290, 300; Bray and Neilson, *Exploring Book of Mormon Lands*, 4–7.
69. S. Larson, *Ministry of Meetings*, 320, 322.
70. Ibid., 455.
71. Excerpts from Weekly Council Meetings.
72. Bray and Neilson, *Exploring Book of Mormon Lands*, 10.
73. Jenson, *Autobiography*, 547–50.
74. Andrew Jenson to Heber J. Grant, February 11, 1923, CHL.
75. See Jenson Journal, February 19, 1923.
76. Thomas P. Page to Maud Butterfield, March 15, 1923, in Page Scrapbook.
77. Jenson Journal, April 11, 1923.
78. Heber J. Grant to Andrew Jenson, May 2, 1923, CHL.
79. Jenson Journal, May 3, 1923.
80. Jenson also apparently contemplated a trip through the West Indies, including Cuba, Haiti, and the Dominican Republic. Notes, Trip to Central and South America, folder 10, box 30, AJC/CHL.
81. Jenson, *Autobiography*, 576.
82. Jenson Journal, May 11, 1922.
83. Jenson, *Autobiography*, 581.
84. Jenson Journal, May 11, 1922.
85. See Bray and Neilson, *Exploring Book of Mormon Lands*.
86. Andrew Jenson, "Ancient Ruins in South American Lands Held to Be Evidence of Divine Authenticity of Book of Mormon," *Deseret News*, June 2, 1923.
87. Jenson's speeches are captured in short diary entries and brief notices in the *Salt Lake Telegram*. He likely gave the same lengthy discourse at the many venues he visited. The address was printed as "Ancient Ruins in South American Lands Held to Be Evidence of Divine Authenticity of Book of Mormon," *Deseret News*, June 2, 1923.
88. Round the World Club, Minutes, August 2, 1923, Round the World Club Papers.
89. Andrew Jenson to Heber J. Grant, July 11, 1923, CHL.
90. Ibid.
91. Ibid.
92. Andrew Jenson to Heber J. Grant, Charles W. Penrose, and Anthony W. Ivins, July 12, 1921, in Jenson Journal, book L, 158–59.
93. Jenson Journal, February 1, 1924; Grant Journal, February 1, 1924.
94. Jenson Journal, July 31, 1924.
95. Ibid., January 1, 1925.
96. Melvin J. Ballard, Diary, September 3, 1925, in Ballard, *Melvin J. Ballard*, 75.
97. Heber J. Grant, in *Ninety-Sixth Semi-annual Conference*, 10–11.
98. Apostle Orson F. Whitney wrote a song in Jenson's honor, paying tribute to his advocacy for missionary work in South America. It concludes with the following two

stanzas: "Thus the South American Mission / Opened was by Elders Three, / With the soul of good St. Andrew / Hovering o'er them—don't you see? // Then all hail to our three heroes—/ Melvin, Rulon S. and Rey! / And all hail to Andrew Jenson / Great Preparer of the way!" Orson F. Whitney, "How It Happened," song lyrics, folder 1, box 178, Widtsoe Papers.

99. Jenson Journal, October 7, 1925.

Chapter 10. Public Commemorator

1. Arthur Chapman, "Mormonism's Century of Strife," *New York Herald Tribune*, March 30, 1930; "One Hundred Years Find Church Grown from Six to 700,000," *Ogden Standard*, March 30, 1930.

2. "L.D.S. Church Conclave Will Attract 50,000 People," *Salt Lake Tribune*, March 29, 1930; "100,000 Mormons to Go on Salt Lake Pilgrimage," *Los Angeles Express*, March 28, 1930, in Historical Department, Journal History of the Church, March 28, 1930.

3. "Wards to Install Radios for Centennial Services," *Deseret News*, March 26, 1930.

4. "City Threatened by Rooms Crisis for Centennial," *Deseret News*, March 29, 1930.

5. *Message of the Ages*, 7.

6. Pyper, "Message of the Ages."

7. For more on ritualization, see Bitton, *Ritualization of Mormon History*, 177.

8. Jenson, in *One Hundredth Annual Conference*, 149.

9. Ibid., 149–50.

10. Ibid., 150–51.

11. See J. Lund, "Joseph F. Smith"; S. Esplin, "Lest Thou Forget"; Kimball, *Historic Sites and Markers*.

12. Upton, "Why Do Contemporary Monuments Talk So Much?," 19–20.

13. Flake, *Politics of American Religious Identity*, 109–17; S. Esplin, "Lest Thou Forget," 288–93.

14. See Gobel and Rossell, *Commemoration in America*; Bodnar, *Remaking America*, 15–16.

15. Jenson Journal, September 28, 1924.

16. Ibid., September 28, 1924; "Honor Awarded Early Pioneers," *Salt Lake Beobachter*, October 2, 1924.

17. "Stones to Mark Trail of Mormon Caravan," *New York World*, October 26, 1924.

18. Fielding, *Unsolicited Chronicler*, 119–66.

19. "Thousands Attend Dedication of Gunnison Monument," *Millard County Chronicle*, June 2, 1927; Jenson Journal, May 30, 1927.

20. "Summit Stake Erects Monument on Old Mormon Trail," *Deseret News*, July 23, 1927; "Ceremony Marks Unveiling Echo Canyon Monument," *Salt Lake Tribune*, July 17, 1927; Jenson Journal, July 13, 1927.

21. Hawkins, "Centennial of the Covered Wagon," 115.

22. Ellison, "Covered Wagon Centennial."

23. Giles, "Mormon Caravan," 739–41, 760–62.

24. "Utahns Urge Improving Old Trail," *Deseret News*, July 12, 1930.

25. Morris, "Perpetuating Our Ideals," 284.

26. Jenson Journal, June 19–22, 1931; Andrew Jenson, "Over the Pioneer Trail," *Deseret News*, June 27, 1931.

27. Jenson attended the dedication of at least two other monuments along the Mormon Trail: one in the Snake River Valley in August 1937 and another in North Platte, Nebraska, in November 1938. He was also made a life member of the Oregon Landmarks Association for his diligent work in memorializing the pioneer trail. See Jenson Journal, August 21, 1937, and November 18, 1938.

28. "Final Marker Dedicated at Rites in Park," *Salt Lake Tribune*, July 24, 1933; Jenson Journal, July 23, 1933.

29. Jenson, *Autobiography*, 635–38.

30. Ibid., 639–42.

31. Jenson Journal, May 1, 1935.

32. Ibid., May 2, 1935.

33. "Stars and Stripes Greet Wagon Party in Denmark," *Deseret News*, June 18, 1935.

34. Andrew Jenson, Scrapbook R, January–July 1935, June 3, 1935, AJC/CHL; "Stars and Stripes Greet Wagon Party in Denmark," *Deseret News*, June 18, 1935; Jenson, *Autobiography*, 647.

35. Jenson, *Autobiography*, 655; "Andrew Jenson Presents Pioneer Relic to Denmark," *Salt Lake Tribune*, July 5, 1935; Andrew Jenson, "World Proves Beautiful Place Says Covered Wagon Envoy During Travels," *Deseret News*, July 20, 1935.

36. Hilda Holmes to Andrew Jenson, April 2, 1935, folder 30, box 49, AJC/CHL; Andrew Jenson to Hilda Holmes, April 25, 1935, folder 30, box 49, AJC/CHL; Andrew Jenson, Outline for Speech, ca. 1935, folder 32, box 49, AJC/CHL.

37. Jenson, *Autobiography*, 654–55; "Jenson Presents Covered Wagon," *Deseret News*, July 4, 1935.

38. Jenson Journal, August 14, 1935.

39. Andrew Jenson, Scrapbook R, January–July 1935, June 27, 1935, AJC/CHL.

40. Doctrine and Covenants 69:7–8.

41. See Neilson, "Traveling and Standing Ministers."

42. For a history of Magellan and his inaugural circumnavigation of the world (1519–22), see Boorstin, *Discoverers*, 259–66. For a history of subsequent around-the-world travel, see Chaplin, *Round about the Earth*.

43. Jenson Journal, May 15, 1913.

44. Historian Harry Liebersohn has suggested that world explorers acted both as interpreters of foreign cultures and peoples and as mediators of ethnographic knowledge. Liebersohn, *Travelers' World*, 305.

45. Plimpton, *As Told at the Explorers Club*, xii–xiii.

46. Jenson Journal, May 15, 1913.

47. Round the World Club, Minutes, May 15, 1913, Round the World Club Papers.

48. Roll of Membership, Round-the-World-Club, September 1919, Round the World Club Papers.

49. Round the World Club, Minutes, April 3, 1926, Round the World Club Papers.

50. Round the World Club, Minutes, February 27, 1935, Round the World Club Papers; Jenson Journal, February 27, 1935.

51. Jenson, *Autobiography*, 671–72.

52. Jenson Journal, January 5, 1923.

53. "Company Formed to Preserve L.D.S. Relics," *Salt Lake Telegram*, February 25, 1927; "Jenson Family Acts in Time," *Salt Lake Tribune*, February 25, 1927.

54. Jenson Journal, February 25, 1929.

55. Ibid., March 11, 1929.

56. Ibid., March 29, 1929.

57. Ibid., March 30, 1929.

58. Ibid., July 4–5 and 10, 1929.

59. Ibid., November 16, 1929.

60. Ibid. Months later, David A. Smith, Joseph Fielding's younger brother and first counselor in the Presiding Bishopric, apparently insulted Jenson between sessions of the April 1930 general conference. Jenson recorded in his journal: "The only thing that happened during the day was an insult offered me by David A. Smith of the Presiding Bishopric at the opening of morning session of the conference. May God punish him according to his sin. It is not the first time that conceited bunch has insulted me. This time he did it once too often." Two years later Jenson had a dream that he quit the Historian's Office but was then brought back as the "Chief Historian" to serve with President Ivins. Jenson Journal, April 6, 1930, and January 2, 1932.

61. Jenson Journal, November 18, 1929.

62. William H. King to Andrew Jenson, June 24, 1929, folder 60, box 30, AJC/CHL.

63. Andrew Jenson to Heber J. Grant, January 31, 1930, folder 60, box 30, AJC/CHL.

64. Heber J. Grant to Andrew Jenson, February 1, 1930, in Jenson Journal, February 1, 1930.

65. Jenson Journal, February 1, 1930.

66. Ibid., March 5, 1930.

67. In the 1960s, staff in the Historian's Office determined to take down Jenson's memorial library, deaccessioning many of his books and discarding his field notes.

68. Jenson Journal, March 29, 1932.

69. Jenson, *Autobiography*, 623; Jenson Journal, April 2, 11, 16, 19, 23, 27, 29, and 30; Jenson Journal, May 4, 6, 7, and 9, 1932.

70. "Scandinavia's Contributions to Utah," in Carter, *Heart Throbs of the West*, 2:290–91.

71. Jenson Journal, April 22, 1932.

72. Ibid., May 10, 1932.

73. Ibid., August 18, 1932.

74. Ibid., October 1, 1932; see also journal entries for October 14, 17, 18, 25, and 27; and November 22, 1932, for details on the painting of his wall map.

75. Jenson Journal, December 10, 1932. Apparently Jenson's son Parley was the most upset by the large amount of money Jenson spent on his memorial hall. Jenson Journal, December 26, 1932.

76. Jenson Journal, December 11, 1932.

77. Ibid., September 14, 1932. After Jenson's death, the Memorial Hall was maintained by family members through the Andrew Jenson Memorial Association. In 1958, with

the hall mostly unused and in need of renovation, it was sold to Earl Olson, a grandson of Andrew Jenson, for $3,000. Jenson's artifacts and books were distributed among the Daughters of Utah Pioneers, the Sons of Utah Pioneers, and Brigham Young University.

78. See Jenson Journal, June 18, 1938.

79. W. Aird Macdonald, "Mormon Battalion Monument at San Diego Ready for Dedication Sunday," *Deseret News*, January 27, 1940; "Mormon Leader Will Dedicate Marker Today," *San Diego Union-Tribune*, January 28, 1940.

80. Jenson Journal, January 28, 1940; Van Wagenen, *Remembering the Forgotten War*, 156.

81. Heber J. Grant, "Historic Trek Memorialized," *Los Angeles Times*, January 29, 1940.

Chapter 11. Twilight Church Historian

1. "Mrs. Jenson Laid at Rest," *Deseret News*, April 19, 1937; "Rites Arranged for Mrs. Jenson, Wife of Historian," *Deseret News*, April 16, 1937.

2. Heber J. Grant to Andrew Jenson, April 12, 1937, in Jenson Journal, April 13, 1937.

3. Jenson, *Encyclopedic History*, iv, italics in original.

4. Andrew Jenson, in *Eighty-Eighth Semi-annual Conference*, 89–90.

5. O'Toole, "On the Idea of Permanence."

6. Andrew Jenson to Joseph Fielding Smith, May 24, 1926, in Jenson Journal, book M, 77–79.

7. See, for example, Jenson's general conference address in April 1918. *Eighty-Eighth Annual Conference*, 131.

8. See Hawai'i Honolulu Mission Manuscript History.

9. Francis J. Russell to Isaac Russell, quoted in Parshall "Bad Old Days."

10. Van Tassel, *Recording America's Past*, 103.

11. Future national standards for managing archival material had the reverse strategy. Modern bedrock principles like preservation of a collection's original order (*respect des fonds*) or provenance already existed within the European archival tradition, but their widespread adoption in fledgling US archives, including the Historian's Office, was slow. The uptake, however, among public archives proved swifter around the start of the twentieth century. Berner, "Historical Development of Archival Theory"; Berner, *Archival Theory and Practice*, 17–23.

12. Quoted in Berner, *Archival Theory and Practice*, 17.

13. Andrew Jenson, in *Ninetieth Semi-annual Conference*, 127–29. Jenson had also presciently anticipated a need for greater preservation at the Historian's Office years before such a project became popular nationwide during the Great Depression. Many of the techniques Jenson had employed at the Historian's Office since the early twentieth century became the norm under the guidance of the Historical Records Survey, a Works Progress Administration project to better copy, bind, and make available swaths of records in public archives across the country. McDonald, *Federal Relief Administration*, 751–56, 791–93; Noggle, *Working with History*, 1–12.

14. Jenson, in *Eighty-Eighth Semi-annual Conference*, 90.

15. Jenson, *History of the Scandinavian Mission*, iii–iv; Jenson, *Encyclopedic History*, iii–iv.

16. Jenson, *Encyclopedic History*, iii–iv.
17. Jenson Journal, March 17, 1927; Jenson, *Autobiography*, 593.
18. Jenson Journal, December 4, 1927.
19. Ibid., December 15, 1927.
20. Ibid., December 20, 1927.
21. "Missionhistorien," *Bikuben*, December 21, 1927.
22. Final Meeting of the Scandinavian Mission History Committee, December 17, 1928, folder 3, box 40, AJC/CHL.
23. Ibid.
24. See K. Perkins, "Study," 136n42.
25. Jenson, *Autobiography*, 631–32.
26. Andrew Jenson, "Day by Day with the Utah Pioneers," *Salt Lake Tribune*, April 5, 1934.
27. Jenson Journal, April 5, 1934; "Editor of L.D.S. Saga Flies over Pioneers' Trail," *Salt Lake Tribune*, July 25, 1934.
28. Jenson Journal, May 8, 1934.
29. Ibid.
30. Ibid., August 28, 1934.
31. Ibid.
32. Malmquist, *First 100 Years*, 326.
33. Jenson Journal, August 28, 1934.
34. Ibid., August 29, 1934. Jenson later noted with pride: "My articles on Zion's Camp, which were being published in serial form in the *Deseret News*, were translated into the Danish-Norwegian, the Swedish, the German, and the Dutch languages. I translated the articles for *Bikuben*, the Danish-Norwegian paper, which afterwards published them in book form." Jenson, *Autobiography*, 634.
35. Jenson Journal, September 1 and 22, 1934.
36. Ibid., September 10, 1934. It's unclear what financial remuneration, if any, Jenson received for his columns for the *Deseret News*.
37. Jenson, *Autobiography*, [iii].
38. See Andrew Jenson, in *Ninety-Fourth Annual Conference*, 136.
39. Jenson Journal, March 26, 1937.
40. Givens and Grow, *Parley P. Pratt*, 352–53; Sondrup, "Literary Dimensions of Mormon Autobiography."
41. Popkin, *History, Historians, and Autobiography*, 11–32; Freeman, *Rewriting the Self*, 5–13; Weintraub, "Autobiography and Historical Consciousness."
42. Jenson, *Autobiography*, iii.
43. Harold H. Jenson, "Addenda," in Jenson, *Autobiography*, 670–71.
44. Jenson, *Autobiography*, 667.
45. J.A.W., "Autobiography."
46. *Autobiography of Andrew Jenson*, pamphlet, folder 27, box 26, AJC/CHL.
47. Jenson Journal, June 25, 1883.
48. Andrew Jenson to Heber J. Grant, Charles W. Penrose, and Anthony W. Ivins, December 4, 1922, CHL.

49. Jenson Journal, January 1, 1930.

50. Garr, Cannon, and Cowan, *Encyclopedia*, 233.

51. Andrew Jenson to First Presidency, June 1, 1928, quoted in K. Perkins, "Study," 130.

52. Andrew Jenson to Joseph Fielding Smith, August 4, 1931, CHL.

53. Joseph Fielding Smith to Heber J. Grant and counselors, August 5, 1931, CHL.

54. Jenson, *Autobiography*, 622; Andrew Jenson to Joseph Fielding Smith, December 22, 1931, folder 29, box 22, Joseph Fielding Smith Papers, 1893–1973, CHL.

55. Jenson, *Autobiography*, 623.

56. K. Perkins, "Andrew Jenson," 238.

57. Andrew Jenson to Joseph Fielding Smith, October 21, 1932, quoted in K. Perkins, "Study," 131.

58. James E. Talmage to Joseph Fielding Smith, November 25, 1932, folder 10, box 5, Talmage Collection; Joseph Fielding Smith to James E. Talmage, November 29, 1932, folder 10, box 5, Talmage Collection.

59. Joseph Fielding Smith to Andrew Jenson, December 8, 1932, quoted in K. Perkins, "Andrew Jenson," 239.

60. Jenson Journal, December 8, 1932.

61. Ibid., February 28, 1935.

62. Ibid.

63. "It Begins Tomorrow in 'The News': The New Church Encyclopedia," *Deseret News*, March 15, 1935.

64. "Encyclopedic Church History in 'News' Ended," *Deseret News*, February 20, 1939. The series formally ended in February, but the *News* ran a series of new entries until March.

65. Jenson Journal, July 10, 1939, and September 18, 1940.

66. Jenson, *Encyclopedic History*, iii.

67. Ibid.

68. "Vital Facts about Each LDS Community Published," *Deseret News*, October 4, 1941.

69. "On the Book Rack."

70. Jenson Journal, December 11, 1935.

71. See ibid., August 11, 1901.

72. Ibid., December 11, 1925.

73. Andrew and Kirsten were married on August 30, 1875.

74. Andrew and Emma were married on December 10, 1886.

75. Jenson, *Autobiography*, 630.

76. Andrew and Bertha were married on July 18, 1888.

77. Leo was adopted by Bertha and Jenson in October 1906. Leo was born to unwed parents in Cache County, Utah, in 1905. Jenson Journal, October 18, 1906.

78. Jenson Journal, December 11, 1935.

79. Ibid.

80. Ibid.

81. Jenson, *Autobiography*, 666.

82. "Veteran Historian Receives Officials," *Deseret News*, December 12, 1935.

83. "Historian Works at Desk as Usual on 85th Birthday," *Deseret News*, December 11, 1935.

84. "Andrew Jenson Attains Age of 90 Wednesday," *Salt Lake Telegram*, December 8, 1940.

85. Jenson Journal, December 11, 1940.

86. Andrew Jenson, "Andrew Jenson Speaks, 1933, 1940," audiocassette, CHL. This is the only known recording of Jenson's voice.

87. Work, "Grandfather's Clock."

88. See box 27, folder 16, AJC/CHL, for more information on the grandfather clock built by Christian Jensen.

89. Jenson Journal, December 12–14, 1940.

90. Ibid., December 20, 1940.

91. Ibid., December 25, 1940.

92. Ibid., December 31, 1940.

93. Jenson, Journal, vol. 15, [554]–[55]. Lund's remarks, made at Jenson's funeral, were recorded in the back of Jenson's journal by family members.

94. Jenson Journal, March 12, 1941.

95. "Veteran LDS Historian Ends His First 'Real Vacation,'" *Salt Lake Tribune*, June 5, 1941.

96. Jenson Journal, October 23, 1941.

97. Ibid., November 15, 1941. The British aircraft carrier *Ark Royal* was torpedoed on November 13, 1941, by a German submarine near Gibraltar.

98. Jenson Journal, November 15, 1941.

99. Ibid., November 18, 1941.

100. "Pen Stilled," *Salt Lake Tribune*, November 19, 1941.

101. "Andrew Jenson, 90, Mormon Historian," *New York Times*, November 20, 1941.

102. "Church Heads Honor Leader," *Deseret News*, November 19, 1941.

Epilogue

1. President Heber J. Grant clarified during his administration that Assistant Church Historians were not to be presented before the twice-yearly general conference of the church for sustaining with the General Authorities. Prior to 1923, Assistant Church Historians, along with other officers in the auxiliary organizations, were presented for sustaining with the General Authorities, but Grant felt this led to many being sustained "who could not properly be regarded as belonging to the General Authorities." Heber J. Grant to Andrew Jenson, December 7, 1940, folder 34, box 27, AJC/CHL.

2. Jenson Journal, vol. 15, pp. [475], [478]. Jenson's funeral proceedings were transcribed and copied into the final pages of his journal by Eva or another family member. See also "Historian Paid Final High Honor," *Deseret News*, November 22, 1941.

3. Andrew Jenson, in *Ninety-Seventh Semi-annual Conference*, 58.

4. Andrew Jenson, in *Seventy-Seventh Semi-annual Conference*, 98.

5. Andrew Jenson, in *One Hundredth Annual Conference*, 150.

6. Matthew 28:19–20.

7. Andrew Jenson, in *Seventy-Third Annual Conference*, 69.

8. See, for example, George Q. Cannon, in *Seventy-First Semi-annual Conference*, 63–69; and Francis M. Lyman and Orson F. Whitney, in *Eightieth Annual Conference*, 31, 59.

9. Jenson Journal, vol. 15, [563].

10. Jenson, in *Ninety-Seventh Semi-annual Conference*, 58.

11. Jenson Journal, vol. 15, [566]–[67].

12. Jenson, *Encyclopedic History*, iv.

13. Jenson Journal, vol. 15, [559].

14. Jenson, *Autobiography*, 193.

15. He is buried at plot 67302 M-3-1-E-1 in the Salt Lake City Cemetery. Apostle John A. Widtsoe dedicated the gravesite after Jenson's funeral.

16. Jenson Journal, December 19, 1937; "Elder Jenson Memory Noted," *Deseret News*, November 21, 1941.

Bibliography

Throughout the bibliography, the acronym "CHL" is used for Church History Library, Church History Department, The Church of Jesus Christ of Latter-day Saints, Salt Lake City, Utah.

Newspapers

American Fork Citizen. American Fork, UT. 1914–79.
Bear Lake Democrat. Paris, Idaho Territory. 1880–85.
Bikuben [Beehive]. Salt Lake City. 1879–85.
Den Kostelige Perle [*The Pearl of Great Price*]. Salt Lake City: Deseret News, 1883.
Deseret Evening News. Salt Lake City. 1867–1920.
Deseret News. Salt Lake City. 1850–.
Deseret News 2013 Church News Almanac. Salt Lake City: Deseret News, 2012.
Deseret Weekly. Salt Lake City. 1850–98.
The Evening and the Morning Star. Kirtland, OH, December 1833–September 1834.
Historical Record / The Historical Record, a Monthly Periodical, Devoted Exclusively to Historical, Biographical, Chronological and Statistical Matters. Salt Lake City. 1882–90.
Latter-day Saints' Millennial Star. Liverpool. 1840–1970.
Los Angeles Times. Los Angeles. 1881–.
Millard County Chronicle. Delta, UT. 1910–85.
Millennial Star. Liverpool. 1840–1970.
New York Herald Tribune. New York City. 1924–66.
New York Post. New York City. 1801–.
New York Times. New York City. 1851–.
New York World. New York City. 1860–1931.
Ogden Standard. Ogden, UT. 1888–1908.
Omaha Bee-News. Omaha, NE. 1927–37.
Politiken [Politics]. Copenhagen. 1884–.

Provo Daily Enquirer. Provo, UT. 1889–1900.
Salt Lake Beobachter. Salt Lake City. 1890–1935.
Salt Lake Democrat. Salt Lake City. 1885–87.
Salt Lake Herald. Salt Lake City. 1870–1909.
Salt Lake Telegram. Salt Lake City. 1915–52.
Salt Lake Tribune. Salt Lake City. 1870–.
San Diego Union-Tribune. San Diego, CA. 1868–.
Skandinaviens Stjerne: Organ for De Sidste Dages Hellige (Star of Scandinavia). Copenhagen. 1851–1956.
St. Louis Globe-Democrat. St. Louis. 1852–1986.
Washington Post. Washington, DC. 1877-.

Other Sources

Adams, Charles P., and Gustive O. Larson. "A Study of the LDS Church Historian's Office, 1830–1900." *Utah Historical Quarterly* 40, no. 4 (Fall 1972): 370–389.

Alexander, Thomas G. *Mormonism in Transition: A History of the Latter-day Saints, 1890–1930*. Urbana: University of Illinois Press, 1986.

Allen, Julie K. *Danish but Not Lutheran: The Impact of Mormonism on Danish Cultural Identity, 1850–1920*. Salt Lake City: University of Utah Press, 2017.

———. "Parallel Promised Lands: Scandinavian Saints in Pioneer-Era Pleasant Grove." Paper presented at the Mormon History Association Annual Conference, June 8, 2019, Salt Lake City, Utah.

Anderson, James H. "One Andrew Jenson." *Improvement Era* 24, no. 9 (July 1921): 786–87.

Arrington, Leonard J. *Adventures of a Church Historian*. Urbana: University of Illinois Press, 1998.

———. *Building the City of God: Community and Cooperation among the Mormons*. Salt Lake City: Deseret Book, 1976.

———. *Great Basin Kingdom: An Economic History of the Latter-day Saints, 1830–1900*. Urbana: University of Illinois Press, 2005.

Arrington, Leonard J., and Jon Haupt. "Intolerable Zion: The Image of Mormonism in Nineteenth Century American Literature." *Western Humanities Review* 22 (Summer 1968): 243–60.

Ballard, Melvin J. *Melvin J. Ballard: Crusader for Righteousness*. Salt Lake City: Bookcraft, 1966.

Baugh, Alexander L., ed. *Days Never to Be Forgotten: Oliver Cowdery*. Provo, UT: Religious Studies Center, Brigham Young University, 2009.

———. "Defending Mormonism: The Scandinavian Mission Presidency of Andrew Jenson, 1909–12." In Neilson and Woods, *Go Ye into All the World*, 503–42.

Beecher, Dale F. "Rey L. Pratt and the Mexican Mission." *BYU Studies* 15, no. 3 (Spring 1975): 293–307.

Bell, E. Jay. "The Windows of Heaven Revisited: The 1899 Tithing Reformation." *Journal of Mormon History* 20, no. 1 (Spring 1994): 45–83.

Bennett, Richard E. "'The Upper Room': The Nature and Development of Latter-day Saint Temple Work, 1846–55." *Journal of Mormon History* 41, no. 2 (April 2015): 1–34.

Bergera, Gary James. "'The Commencement of Great Things': The Origins, Scope, and Achievement of the Journal History of the Church." *Mormon Historical Studies* 4, no. 1 (Spring 2003): 23–39.

Berner, Richard C. *Archival Theory and Practice in the United States*. Seattle: University of Washington Press, 1983.

———. "Historical Development of Archival Theory and Practices in the United States." *Midwestern Archivist* 7, no. 2 (1982): 103–17.

Bibelske henvisninger: I overensstemmelse med de Sidste-Dages Helliges tro og lærdomme [Biblical references: In conformity with the Latter-day Saint faith and doctrines]. Copenhagen: F. E. Bording, 1880.

Bitton, Davis. *The Ritualization of Mormon History and Other Essays*. Urbana: University of Illinois Press, 1994.

———. "Strange Ramblings: The Ideal and Practice of Sermons in Early Mormonism." *BYU Studies* 41, no. 1 (2002): 4–28.

Bitton, Davis, and Leonard Arrington. *Mormons and Their Historians*. Salt Lake City: University of Utah Press, 1988.

Bodnar, John. *Remaking America: Public Memory, Commemoration, and Patriotism in the Twentieth Century*. Princeton, NJ: Princeton University Press, 1992.

Bolotin, Norman, and Christine Laing. *The World's Columbian Exposition: The Chicago World's Fair of 1893*. Urbana: University of Illinois Press, 1992.

Boorstin, Daniel J. *The Discoverers*. New York: Random House, 1983.

Brackenridge, R. Douglas. "'Are You That Damned Presbyterian Devil?' The Evolution of an Anti-Mormon Story." *Journal of Mormon History* 21, no. 1 (Spring 1995): 80–105.

Bray, Justin R., and Reid L. Neilson, eds. *Exploring Book of Mormon Lands: The 1923 Latin American Travel Writings of Mormon Historian Andrew Jenson*. Provo, UT: Religious Studies Center, Brigham Young University, 2014.

Brøndal, Jørn. "Danes and Danish Americans, 1870–1940." In *Immigrants in American History: Arrival, Adaptation, Integration*, edited by Elliott Robert Barkan, 1:323–31. 4 vols. Santa Barbara, CA: ABC-CLIO, 2013.

Brown, Lisle G. "Temple Pro Tempore: The Salt Lake City Endowment House." *Journal of Mormon History* 34, no. 4 (Fall 2008): 1–68.

Buerger, David John. "The Development of the Mormon Temple Endowment Ceremony." *Dialogue: A Journal of Mormon Thought* 20, no. 4 (Winter 1987): 33–76.

Bunker, Gary L., and Davis Bitton. *The Mormon Graphic Image, 1834–1914: Cartoons Caricatures, and Illustrations*. Salt Lake City: University of Utah Press, 1983.

Cannon, Brian Q., and Jacob W. Olmstead. "'Scandalous Film': The Campaign to Suppress Anti-Mormon Motion Pictures, 1911–12." *Journal of Mormon History* 29, no. 2 (Fall 2003): 42–76.

Cannon, George Q. *The Journal of George Q. Cannon*. Church Historians Press. Accessed April 27, 2018. https://www.churchhistorianspress.org/george-q-cannon?lang=eng.

Cannon, Hugh J. Journal. Hugh J. Cannon Papers, 1891–1977. MS 28333. CHL.

Cannon, Kenneth L., II. "Beyond the Manifesto: Polygamous Cohabitation among LDS General Authorities after 1890." *Utah Historical Quarterly* 46, no. 1 (Winter 1978): 24–36.

Carter, Kate B., comp. *Heart Throbs of the West*. 12 vols. Salt Lake City: Daughters of the Utah Pioneers, 1939–51.

Chaplin, Joyce E. *Round about the Earth: Circumnavigation from Magellan to Orbit*. New York: Simon and Schuster, 2012.

The Church of Jesus Christ of Latter-day Saints. "Book of Mormon Geography." Gospel Topics Essays. Accessed April 23, 2020. https://www.churchofjesuschrist.org/study/manual/gospel-topics/book-of-mormon-geography?lang=eng.

Church Records Committee History. Collection, 1899–1908. CR 314 12. CHL.

Clawson, Rudger. Diary. Special Collections. J. Willard Marriott Library. University of Utah, Salt Lake City.

———. "Memoirs of the Life of Rudger Clawson." MS 24682. CHL.

———. "Reorganization of Financial System at President's Office, under Administration of Presidents Lorenzo Snow and Joseph F. Smith." In Boyd Payne, "Rudger Clawson's Report on LDS Church Finances at the Turn of the Twentieth Century," *Dialogue: A Journal of Mormon Thought* 31, no. 4 (Winter 1998): 165–79.

Committee on Records. "Record Keeping." Circular to "Presidents of Stakes and Missions, Bishops of Wards, and Other Presiding Authorities." February 1, 1902. M200.2 F527r 1902. CHL.

Cornwall, Marie, Camela Courtwright, and Laga Van Beek. "How Common the Principle? Women as Plural Wives in 1860." *Dialogue: A Journal of Mormon Thought* 26, no. 2 (Summer 1993): 153–67.

Cowan, Richard O. "'Called to Serve': A History of Missionary Training." In Neilson and Woods, *Go Ye into All the World*, 23–44.

"Danmark Kirkebøger, 1484–1941." *FamilySearch*. https://familysearch.org.

Davidson, Karen Lynn, Richard L. Jensen, and David J. Whittaker, eds. *Histories, Volume 2: Assigned Historical Writings, 1831–1847*. Vol. 2 of the Histories series of *The Joseph Smith Papers*. Edited by Dean C. Jessee, Ronald K. Esplin, and Richard Lyman Bushman. Salt Lake City: Church Historian's Press, 2012.

Davies, Margery W. *Woman's Place Is at the Typewriter: Office Work and Office Workers, 1870–1930*. Philadelphia: Temple University Press, 1982.

Daynes, Kathryn. *More Wives than One: Transformation of the Mormon Marriage System, 1840–1910*. Urbana: University of Illinois Press, 2001.

Derr, Jill Mulvay, Carol Cornwall Madsen, Kate Holbrook, and Matthew J. Grow, eds. *The First Fifty Years of Relief Society: Key Documents in Latter-day Saints Women's History*. Salt Lake City: Church Historian's Press, 2016.

Dormady, Jason H., and Jared M. Tamez, eds. *Just South of Zion: The Mormons in Mexico and Its Borderlands*. Albuquerque: University of New Mexico Press, 2015.

Driggs, Ken. "The Prosecutions Begin: Defining Cohabitation in 1885." *Dialogue: A Journal of Mormon Thought* 21, no. 1 (Spring 1988): 109–25.

Eightieth Annual Conference of The Church of Jesus Christ of Latter-day Saints. Salt Lake City: Deseret News, 1910.

Eighty-Eighth Semi-annual Conference of The Church of Jesus Christ of Latter-day Saints. Salt Lake City: Deseret News, 1917.

Eighty-Eighth Annual Conference of The Church of Jesus Christ of Latter-day Saints. Salt Lake City: Deseret News, 1918.

Eighty-Ninth Annual Conference of The Church of Jesus Christ of Latter-day Saints. Salt Lake City: Deseret News, 1919.

"Eleonor Reynolds." *Music News* 14, no. 3 (January 20, 1922): 21.

Ellison, Joseph. "The Covered Wagon Centennial: March of the Empire Builders over the Oregon Trail." *Washington Historical Quarterly* 21, no. 3 (July 1930): 163–78.

Ellsworth, S. George. "Hubert Howe Bancroft and the History of Utah." *Utah Historical Quarterly* 22, no. 2 (April 1954): 99–124.

Esplin, Scott C. "'A History of All the Important Things' (D&C 69:3): John Whitmer's Record of Church History." In Turley and Harper, *Preserving the History of the Latter-day Saints*, 49–82.

———. "'Lest Thou Forget': Memorializing and Marking the Mormon Pioneer Trail." In *Far Away in the West: Reflections on the Mormon Pioneer Trail*, edited by Scott C. Esplin, Richard E. Bennett, Susan Easton Black, and Craig K. Manscill, 278–307. Provo, UT: Religious Studies Center, Brigham Young University, 2015.

Esplin, Scott C., and Kenneth L. Alford, eds. *Salt Lake City: The Place Which God Prepared*. Provo, UT: Religious Studies Center, Brigham Young University, 2011.

Esplin, Ronald K. "'A Place Prepared': Joseph, Brigham and the Quest for Promised Refuge in the West." *Journal of Mormon History* 9 (1982): 85–111.

Excerpts from Weekly Council Meetings, 1849–1940. George A. Smith Family Papers. Special Collections. J. Willard Marriott Library. University of Utah, Salt Lake City.

Fielding, Robert Kent. *The Unsolicited Chronicler: An Account of the Gunnison Massacre, Its Causes and Consequences*. Bendix, NM: Redwing Book, 1992.

Firmage, Edwin Brown, and Richard Collin Mangrum. *Zion in the Courts: A Legal History of the Church of Jesus Christ of Latter-day Saints, 1830–1900*. Urbana: University of Illinois Press, 1988.

First Presidency. Letterpress Copybooks, 1877–1949. CR 1 20. CHL.

First Presidency (John Taylor) Correspondence, 1877–1887. CR 1 180. CHL.

First Presidency (Wilford Woodruff) General Correspondence Files, 1887–1898. CR 1 171. CHL.

First Presidency General Authorities Correspondence, 1887–1918. CR 1 176. CHL.

Flake, Kathleen. *The Politics of American Religious Identity: The Seating of Senator Reed Smoot, Mormon Apostle*. Chapel Hill: University of North Carolina Press, 2004.

Flink, James J. *The Automobile Age*. Cambridge, MA: MIT Press, 1988.

Freeman, Mark. *Rewriting the Self: History, Memory, Narrative*. New York: Routledge, 1993.

Frimodt-Møller, H. O. *Flyveblad mod Mormonismen* [Broadside against Mormonism]. København: Kirkelig Forening for Den Indre Mission i Danmark, 1905.

Gardner, Marvin K. "General Authorities." In Ludlow, *Encyclopedia of Mormonism*, 2:538–40.

Garr, Arnold K., Donald Q. Cannon, and Richard O. Cowan. *Encyclopedia of Latter-day Saint History*. Salt Lake City: Deseret Book, 2000.

Geilman, Matthew G. "Taking the Gospel to the Lamanites: Doctrinal Foundations for Establishing the Church of Jesus Christ of Latter-day Saints in Mexico." Master's thesis, Brigham Young University, 2011.

Gibbons, Francis M. *Joseph Fielding Smith: Gospel Scholar, Prophet of God*. Salt Lake City: Deseret Book, 1992.

Giles, John D. "Mormon Caravan to Independence Rock." *Improvement Era* 33, no. 11 (September 1930): 739–62.

Givens, Terryl L. *By the Hand of Mormon: The American Scripture That Launched a New World Religion*. New York: Oxford University Press, 2002.

———. *The Viper on the Hearth: Mormons, Myths, and the Construction of Heresy*. New York: Oxford University Press, 1997.

Givens, Terryl L., and Matthew J. Grow. *Parley P. Pratt: The Apostle Paul of Mormonism*. New York: Oxford University Press, 2011.

Gobel, David, and Daves Rossell. *Commemoration in America: Essays on Monuments, Memorialization, and Memory*. Charlottesville: University of Virginia Press, 2013.

Gordon, Sarah Barringer. *The Mormon Question: Polygamy and Constitutional Conflict in Nineteenth-Century America*. Chapel Hill: University of North Carolina Press, 2002.

Grant, Heber J. Journal. Heber J. Grant, Collection, 1853–1945. MS 1233. CHL.

Gutjahr, Paul C. *The Book of Mormon: A Biography*. Princeton, NJ: Princeton University Press, 2012.

Hales, Brian C. "Identifying Joseph Smith's Plural Wives." *Journal of Mormon History* 40, no. 3 (Summer 2014): 155–68.

———. *Joseph Smith's Polygamy*. 2 vols. Salt Lake City: Greg Kofford, 2013.

Hansen, Peter O. "How the Danish translation of the Book of Mormon originated, ca. 1885." MS 3522. CHL.

Hardy, B. Carmon. *Solemn Covenant: The Mormon Polygamous Passage*. Urbana: University of Illinois Press, 1992.

Hartley, William G. "Down-and-Back Wagon Trains: Travelers on the Mormon Trail in 1861." *Overland Journal* 11, no. 4 (Winter 1993): 23–34.

———. "The Seventies in the 1880s: Revelations and Reorganizing." *Dialogue: A Journal of Mormon Thought* 16 (Spring 1983): 70–76.

Hatch, John P., ed. *Danish Apostle: The Diaries of Anthon H. Lund, 1890–1921*. Salt Lake City: Signature Books, 2006.

Hawai'i Honolulu Mission Manuscript History and Historical Reports, 1850–1978. 9 vols. LR 3695 2. CHL.

Hawkins, Albert. "Centennial of the Covered Wagon." *Oregon Historical Quarterly* 31, no. 2 (June 1930): 115–24.

Heath, Harvard S. Introduction to *The Mormon Church on Trial: Transcripts of the Reed Smoot Hearings*, edited by Michael Harold Paulos, vii–xx. Salt Lake City: Signature Books, 2008.

Hemming, Val G. "A Voice from the Land of Zion: Elder Erastus Snow in Denmark, 1850 to 1852." *Dialogue: A Journal of Mormon Thought* 35 (Spring 2002): 131–43.

Hendrix-Komoto, Amanda. "'Playing the Whore': The Domestic and Sexual Politics of Mormon Missionary Work on Tahiti Nui and in the Tuamotus." *Journal of Mormon History* 41, no. 3 (July 2015): 58–96.

Henrichsen, Lynn E., and George Bailey. "'No More Strangers and Foreigners': The Dual Focus of the LDS Church Language Program for Scandinavian Immigrants, 1850–1935." *Mormon Historical Studies* 11, no. 2 (Fall 2010): 23–53.

Historian's Office. Correspondence Files, 1856–1926. CR 100 394. CHL.

Historian's Office. Letterpress Copybooks, 1854–79, 1885–86. 3 vols. CR 100 38. CHL.

Historian's Office Plans, 1898 and 1917. CR 100 41. CHL.

Historical Department. Journal History of the Church. 1930–2008. CR 100 137. CHL.

Historical Department. Office Journal, 1844–2012. 102 vols. CR 100 1. CHL.

Hobson, Wayne K. "Professionals, Progressives and Bureaucratization: A Reassessment." *Historian*, 39, no. 4 (August 1977): 639–58.

Horne, Dennis B. *The Life of Orson F. Whitney: Historian, Poet, and Apostle*. Springville, UT: Cedar Fort, 2014.

Howard, Susan W. "William Jarman: 'That Anti-Mormon Apostle of the British Isles.'" *Journal of Mormon History* 43, no. 1 (January 2017): 70–79.

Hughes, William E. "A Profile of the Missionaries of the Church of Jesus Christ of Latter-day Saints, 1849–1900." Master's thesis, Brigham Young University, 1986.

Iceland Mission History, 1912. In Andrew Jenson, Collection, ca. 1841–1942. MS 17956. CHL.

"Introduction to History, 1838–1856 (Manuscript History of the Church)." The Joseph Smith Papers. Accessed February 13, 2018. http://www.josephsmithpapers.org/doc/introduction-to-history-1838–1856-manuscript-history-of-the-church.

J.A.W. "Autobiography of Andrew Jenson." *Improvement Era* 42, no. 2 (February 1939): 101.

Jensen, Marlin K. "There Shall Be a Record Kept among You." *Ensign*, December 2007, 28–33.

Jensen, Robin Scott. "'Archives of the Better World': The Nineteenth-Century Historian's Office and Mormonism's Archival Flexibility." PhD diss., University of Utah, 2019.

———. "Ignored and Unknown Clues of Early Mormon Record Keeping." In Turley and Harper, *Preserving the History of the Latter-day Saints*, 135–64.

Jenson, Andrew. "Andrew Jenson Speaks, 1933, 1940." Audiocassette. AV 440. CHL.

———. Autobiography and Journals, ca. 1864–1941. MS 1230. CHL.

———. *Autobiography of Andrew Jenson*. Salt Lake City: Deseret News Press, 1938.

———. Collection, ca. 1841–1942. MS 17956. CHL.

———. Collection, 1850–1935. MSS 325. L. Tom Perry Special Collections. Brigham Young University, Provo, UT.

———. *Day by Day with the Utah Pioneers, 1847: A Chronological Record of the Trek across the Plains*. Salt Lake City: Salt Lake Tribune, 1934.

———. *Encyclopedic History of the Church of Jesus Christ of Latter-day Saints*. Salt Lake City: Deseret News, 1941.

———. "An Epitome of the History of the Church of Jesus Christ of Latter-day Saints." In *World's Fair Ecclesiastical History of Utah*, 9–164. Salt Lake City: George Q. Cannon & Sons, 1893.

———. "The Historian's Office." *Utah Genealogical and Historical Magazine* 8 (April 1917): 61–69.

———. *History of the Scandinavian Mission*. Salt Lake City: Deseret News Press, 1927.

———. *Jorden rundt: En rejsebeskrivelse af Andrew Jenson* [Around the world: a travelogue of Andrew Jenson]. Salt Lake City: n.p., 1908.

———. *Latter-day Saint Biographical Encyclopedia: A Compilation of Biographical Sketches of Prominent Men and Women in the Church of Jesus Christ of Latter-day Saints*. 4 vols. Salt Lake City: Andrew Jenson History Company, 1901–19. Reprint. Salt Lake City: Western Epics, 1971.

———. "Latter-day Saints Emigration from Wyoming, Nebraska—1864–1866." *Nebraska History Magazine* 17 (1936): 113–27.

———. "Plural Marriage." *Historical Record* 6, (July 1887): 233–34.

———. "Quincy, Adams County, Illinois"; "Hancock County, Illinois"; "Nauvoo." *Historical Record* 8, nos. 2–3 (March 1889): 733–843.

———. "Scandinavian Latter-day Saint Literature." *Utah Genealogical and Historical Magazine* 13, no. 4 (October 1922): 181–89.

———, comp. *Church Chronology: Or a Record of Important Events*. Salt Lake City: n.p., 1886.

———, comp. *Church Chronology. A Record of Important Events*. 2nd and rev. ed. Salt Lake City: Deseret News, 1899.

———, comp. *Church Chronology. A Record of Important Events*. 2nd and rev. ed. Reprint. Salt Lake City: Deseret News, 1914.

Jenson, Andrew Alexander. Journal (in possession of family).

Jenson, Emma Howell. "Christmas in Scandinavia." *Woman's Exponent* 34, no. 8 (February 1906): 51.

Jessee, Dean C. "The Writing of Joseph Smith's History." *BYU Studies* 11, no. 4 (Summer 1971): 439–73.

"Joseph Smith's Historical Enterprise." The Joseph Smith Papers. Accessed November 6, 2017. http://www.josephsmithpapers.org/doc/series-introduction-for-the-histories-series.

Kimball, Stanley B. *Historic Sites and Markers along the Mormon and Other Great Western Trails*. Urbana: University of Illinois Press, 1988.

Kwolek-Folland, Angel. *Engendering Business: Men and Women in the Corporate Office, 1870–1930*. Baltimore: Johns Hopkins University Press, 1998.

Larson, Andrew Karl. *Erastus Snow: The Life of a Missionary and Pioneer for the Early Mormon Church*. Salt Lake City: University of Utah Press, 1971.

Larson, Gustive O. *The "Americanization" of Utah for Statehood*. San Marino, CA: Huntington Library, 1971.

Larson, Stan, ed. *A Ministry of Meetings: The Apostolic Diaries of Rudger Clawson*. Salt Lake City: Signature Books, 1993.

Lee, John D. *Mormonism Unveiled; or the Life and Confessions of the Late Mormon Bishop, John D. Lee*. St. Louis: Bryan, Brand & Company, 1877.

Liebersohn, Harry. *The Travelers' World: Europe to the Pacific*. Cambridge, MA: Harvard University Press, 2006.

Light from the Home Paper of Hans Peter Freece, The "Richfield Reaper," Thursday, May 28th, 1908. N.p., 1908.

Ludlow, Daniel, ed. *Encyclopedia of Mormonism*. 4 vols. New York: Macmillan, 1992.

Lund, Anthon H. Journals, 1860–1921. MS 5375. CHL.

———. Papers, 1869–1920. MS 1256. CHL.

Lund, Jennifer L. "Joseph F. Smith and the Origins of the Church Historic Sites Program." In *Joseph F. Smith: Reflections on the Man and His Times*, edited by Craig K. Manscill, Brian D. Reeves, Guy L. Dorius, and J. B. Haws, 342–58. Provo, UT: Religious Studies Center, Brigham Young University; Salt Lake City: Deseret Book, 2013.

Lyman, Francis M., Rudger Clawson, and Andrew Jenson. Circular to "Presidents of Stakes and Missions and Bishops of Wards." March 13, 1901. M200.2 F527re 1901. CHL.

Malmquist, O. N. *The First 100 Years: A History of the Salt Lake Tribune, 1871–1971*. Salt Lake City: Utah State Historical Society, 1971.

Mauss, Armand L. *The Angel and the Beehive: The Mormon Struggle with Assimilation*. Urbana: University of Illinois Press, 1994.

McBride, Spencer. "Mormon Beginnings in Samoa: Kimo Belio, Samuela Manoa, and Walter Murray Gibson." In *Mormon Pacific Historical Society Proceedings 2006*, 50–63. Laie, HI: Mormon Pacific Historical Society, 2006.

McDonald, William Francis. *Federal Relief Administration and the Arts: The Origins and Administrative History of the Arts Projects of the Works Progress Administration*. Columbus: Ohio State University Press, 1969.

Mehr, Kahlile B. *Mormon Missionaries Enter Eastern Europe*. Provo, UT: Brigham Young University Press/Salt Lake City: Deseret Book, 2002.

The Message of the Ages: A Sacred Pageant Commemorating the Centenary of the Organization of The Church of Jesus Christ of Latter-day Saints. Salt Lake City: Heber J. Grant, 1930.

"Messages from the Mission." *Improvement Era* 14, no. 11 (September 1911): 1062.

Mormonens Offer [A Victim of the Mormons]. Aarhus, Denmark: Reklametrykkeriet [Busch & Petersen], [1911]. Copy at CHL.

Morris, George Q. "Perpetuating Our Ideals through Markers and Monuments." *Improvement Era* 53, no. 4 (April 1950): 284–85.

Mulder, William E. *Homeward to Zion: The Mormon Migration from Scandinavia*. Minneapolis: University of Minneapolis Press, 1957.

Neilson, Reid L. *Early Mormon Missionary Activities in Japan, 1901–24*. Salt Lake City: University of Utah Press, 2010.

———. *Exhibiting Mormonism: The Latter-day Saints and the 1893 Chicago World's Fair*. New York: Oxford University Press, 2011.

———. "Introduction: Laboring in the Old Country." In *Legacy of Sacrifice: Missionaries to Scandinavia, 1872–1894*, edited by Susan Easton Black, Shauna C. Anderson, and Ruth Ellen Maness, xiii–xix. Provo, UT: Religious Studies Center, Brigham Young University, 2007.

———. "The Nineteenth-Century Euro-American Mormon Missionary Model." In Neilson and Woods, *Go Ye into All the World*, 65–90.

———. "Traveling and Standing Ministers: The Commandment to Travel (or Not) in the Joseph Smith Era." *Religious Educator* 17, no. 2 (2016): 14–36.

———, ed. *Global Mormonism in the Twenty-First Century*. Provo, UT: Religious Studies Center, Brigham Young University, 2008.

———, ed. *The Japanese Missionary Journals of Elder Alma O. Taylor, 1901–1910*. Provo, UT: BYU Studies and Joseph Fielding Smith Institute for Latter-day Saint History, 2001.

Neilson, Reid L., Justin R. Bray, and Alan D. Johnson. *Rediscovering the Sites of the Restoration: The 1888 Travel Writings of Mormon Historian Andrew Jenson, Edward Stevenson, and Joseph S. Black*. Salt Lake City: Deseret Book, 2015.

Neilson, Reid L., and Van C. Gessel, eds. *Taking the Gospel to the Japanese, 1901–2001*. Provo, UT: Brigham Young University Press, 2006.

Neilson, Reid L., and Scott D. Marianno. "True and Faithful: Joseph Fielding Smith as Mormon Historian and Theologian." *BYU Studies Quarterly* 57, no. 1 (2018): 6–64.

Neilson, Reid L., and Scott D. Marianno. *A Voice in the Wilderness: The 1888–1930 General Conference Sermons of Mormon Historian Andrew Jenson*. New York: Oxford University Press, 2018.

Neilson, Reid L., and Riley M. Moffat, eds. *Tales from the World Tour: The 1895–1897 Travel Writings of Mormon Historian Andrew Jenson*. Provo, UT: Religious Studies Center, Brigham Young University; Salt Lake City: Deseret Book, 2012.

Neilson, Reid L., and Nathan N. Waite, eds. *Settling the Valley, Proclaiming the Gospel: The General Epistles of the Mormon First Presidency*. New York: Oxford University Press, 2017.

Neilson, Reid L., and Fred E. Woods, eds. *Go Ye into All the World: The Growth & Development of Mormon Missionary Work*. Provo, UT: Religious Studies Center, Brigham Young University, 2012.

Nelson, Richard Alan. "A History of Latter-day Saint Screen Portrayals in the Anti-Mormon Film Era, 1905–1936." Master's thesis, Brigham Young University, 1975.

"News from Denmark." *Juvenile Instructor* 14, no. 24 (December 15, 1879): 278–79.

Ninetieth Semi-annual Conference of The Church of Jesus Christ of Latter-day Saints. Salt Lake City: Deseret News, 1919.

Ninety-Second Semi-annual Conference of The Church of Jesus Christ of Latter-day Saints. Salt Lake City: Church of Jesus Christ of Latter-day Saints, 1921.

Ninety-Third Semi-annual Conference of The Church of Jesus Christ of Latter-day Saints. Salt Lake City: Church of Jesus Christ of Latter-day Saints, 1922.

Ninety-Fourth Annual Conference of The Church of Jesus Christ of Latter-day Saints. Salt Lake City: The Church of Jesus Christ of Latter-day Saints, 1924.

Ninety-Sixth Semi-annual Conference of The Church of Jesus Christ of Latter-day Saints. Salt Lake City: The Church of Jesus Christ of Latter-day Saints, 1925.

Ninety-Seventh Semi-annual Conference of The Church of Jesus Christ of Latter-day Saints. Salt Lake City: The Church of Jesus Christ of Latter-day Saints, 1926.

Noggle, Burl. *Working with History: The Historical Records Survey in Louisiana and the Nation, 1936–1942*. Baton Rouge: Louisiana State University Press, 1981.

Olmstead, Jacob W. "*A Victim of the Mormons* and *The Danites*: Images and Relics from Early Twentieth-Century Anti-Mormon Silent Films." *Mormon Historical Studies* 5, no. 1 (Spring 2004): 203–21.

Olsen, Eva Jenson. "The Other Mother." In *Heart Throbs of the West*, comp. Kate B., 1:286–87. Salt Lake City: Daughters of the Utah Pioneers, 1940.

One Hundredth Annual Conference of The Church of Jesus Christ of Latter-day Saints. Salt Lake City: Church of Jesus Christ of Latter-day Saints, 1930.

"On the Book Rack." *Improvement Era* 44, no. 6 (June 1941): 351, 364.

O'Toole, James M. "On the Idea of Permanence." *American Archivist* 52, no. 1 (Winter 1989): 16–17.

Otterstrom, F. W. "A Journey to the South: Gems from President Smith's Talks to the People on the Way." *Improvement Era* 21 (December 1917): 97.

Page, Thomas P. Scrapbook, ca. 1884–1933. MS 8225. CHL.

Palmer, A. Delbert, and Mark Grover. "Hoping to Establish a Presence: Parley P. Pratt's 1851 Mission to Chile." *BYU Studies* 38, no. 4 (1999): 115–38.

Palmer, Sally B. "Projecting the Gaze: The Magic Lantern, Cultural Discipline, and Villette." *Victorian Review* 32, no. 1 (2006): 18–40.

"Paper for the Young Saints in Denmark—Work Progressing in Scandinavia." *Juvenile Instructor* 15, no. 8 (April 15, 1880): 92–93.

Parrish, Alan K. "Seventy." In Ludlow, *Encyclopedia of Mormonism*, 3:1301–2.

Parshall, Ardis E. "The Bad Old Days." *Keepapitchinin* (blog), February 26, 2018. http://www.keepapitchinin.org/2018/02/26/the-bad-old-days/.

———. "Winston Churchill Investigates the Mormon Question, 1910–1911." *Keepapitchinin* (blog), June 12, 1909. http://www.keepapitchinin.org/2009/06/12/winston-churchill-investigates-the-mormon-question-1910-1911/.

Penrose, Charles W. Journal, December 1895–July 1896 and January 1897. MS 3009. CHL.

Perkins, Eric, and Mary Jane Woodger. "Administration from the Underground." In *Champion of Liberty: John Taylor*, edited by Mary Jane Woodger, 347–70. Provo, UT: Religious Studies Center, Brigham Young University, 2009.

Perkins, Keith W. "Andrew Jenson: Zealous Chronologist." PhD diss., Brigham Young University, 1974.

———. "A Study of the Contributions of Andrew Jenson to the Writing and Preservation of LDS Church History." Master's thesis, Brigham Young University, 1971.

Peterson, John Alton. *Utah's Black Hawk War.* Salt Lake City: University of Utah Press, 1999.

Pfragner, Julius. *The Motion Picture: From Magic Lantern to Sound Film.* Translated by Theodore McClintock. Folkestone, UK: Bailey Brothers and Swinfen, 1974.

Plimpton, George, ed. *As Told at the Explorers Club: More than Fifty Gripping Tales of Adventure.* Guilford, CT: Lyons Press, 2003.

Popkin, Jeremy D. *History, Historians, and Autobiography.* Chicago: University of Chicago Press, 2005.

Price, Rex Thomas, Jr., "The Mormon Missionary of the Nineteenth Century." PhD diss., University of Wisconsin–Madison, 1991.

Prince, Gregory A. *Leonard Arrington and the Writing of Mormon History.* Salt Lake City: University of Utah Press, 2016.

Proceedings before the Committee on Privileges and Elections of the United States Senate in the Matter of the Protests against the Right of Hon. Reed Smoot, a Senator from the State of Utah, to Hold His Seat. 4 vols. Washington, DC: Government Printing Office, 1904–6.

Pyper, George D. "'The Message of the Ages': A Sacred Pageant." In *One Hundred Years, 1830–1930: Centennial Celebration of the Organization of The Church of Jesus Christ of Latter-day Saints*, 45–56. Salt Lake City: Heber J. Grant, 1930.

Quinn, D. Michael. *The Mormon Hierarchy: Extensions of Power.* Salt Lake City: Signature Books, 1997.

Rasmussen, Matthew Lyman. *Mormonism and the Making of a British Zion*. Salt Lake City: University of Utah Press, 2016.

Reinwand, Louis. "Andrew Jenson, Latter-day Saint Historian." *BYU Studies* 14, no. 1 (Fall 1973): 29n1.

"Reo Company Reports Net Profits of 2 1/2 Millions." *Motor Age* 27, no. 1 (January 7, 1915): 36.

Richards, Franklin D. Journal. Richards Family Collection, 1837–1961. MS 1215. CHL.

Richardson, Matthew O. "A House for the Presidency: The History of the Church Administration Building." In *Salt Lake City: The Place Which God Prepared*, edited by Scott C. Esplin and Kenneth L. Alford, 231–57. Provo, UT: Religious Studies Center, Brigham Young University, 2011.

Ricks, Joel. Papers. MSS 2857. L. Tom Perry Special Collections. Brigham Young University, Provo, UT.

Roberts, Richard C. "First Council of the Seventy." In Ludlow, *Encyclopedia of Mormonism*, 3:1303.

Round the World Club Papers, 1913–1935. MS 2465. CHL.

Rowley, Dennis. "Inner Dialogue: James Talmage's Choice of Science as a Career, 1876–84." *Dialogue: A Journal of Mormon Thought* 17, no. 2 (Summer 1984): 114–32.

"R.S. Reports." *Woman's Exponent* 9 (September 1, 1880): [53].

Scandinavian Jubilee Album. Salt Lake City: Deseret News Press, 1900.

Scandinavian Mission Letterpress Copybooks, 1858–1920. 26 vols. LR 9332 21. CHL.

Scandinavian Mission Manuscript History and Historical Reports, 1855–1920. 17 vols. LR 9332 2. CHL.

Schwantes, Carlos A. "The Concept of the Wageworkers' Frontier: A Framework for Future Research." *Western Historical Quarterly* 18, no. 1 (January 1987): 39–55.

Scott G. Kenney Collection. Special Collections. J. Willard Marriott Library. University of Utah, Salt Lake City.

Searle, Howard C. "Historians, Church." In Ludlow, *Encyclopedia of Mormonism*, 2:589–90.

———. "Early Mormon Historiography: Writing the History of the Mormons, 1830–1858." PhD diss., University of California, Los Angeles, 1981.

Seventieth Annual Conference of The Church of Jesus Christ of Latter-day Saints. Salt Lake City: Deseret News, 1900.

Seventy-First Semi-annual Conference of The Church of Jesus Christ of Latter-day Saints. Salt Lake City: Deseret News, 1900.

Seventy-Second Semi-annual Conference of The Church of Jesus Christ of Latter-day Saints. Salt Lake City: Deseret News, 1901.

Seventy-Second Annual Conference of The Church of Jesus Christ of Latter-day Saints. Salt Lake City: Deseret News, 1902.

Seventy-Third Annual Conference of The Church of Jesus Christ of Latter-day Saints. Salt Lake City: Deseret News, 1903.

Seventy-Seventh Semi-annual Conference of The Church of Jesus Christ of Latter-day Saints. Salt Lake City: Deseret News, 1906.

Shipps, Jan. "From Satyr to Saint: American Perceptions of the Mormons, 1860–1960." In *Sojourner in the Promised Land: Forty Years among the Mormons*, 51–97. Urbana: University of Illinois Press, 2000.

Sillito, John R., and Linda Thatcher. "'Sisterhood and Sociability': The Utah Women's Press Club, 1891–1928." *Utah Historical Quarterly* 53, no. 2 (Spring 1985): 144–56.

Sjodahl, Janne M. "An Estimate of the Scandinavian Jubilee." *Improvement Era* 3, no. 10 (August 1900): 747.

Smith, Chris. "A Plea for New Appreciation of Popular History: John Clark Ridpath, a Case Study." *Indiana Magazine of History* 77, no. 3 (September 1981): 205–330.

Smith, Dennis H. "Formal Reporting Systems of The Church of Jesus Christ of Latter-day Saints, 1830–1975." Master's thesis, Brigham Young University, 1976.

Smith, Joseph. *History*. Vol. C-1 of the Joseph Smith Papers. http://www.josephsmithpapers.org/paper-summary/history-1838-1856-volume-c-1-2-november-1838-31-july-1842/396.

Smith, Joseph Fielding. Journal. Joseph Fielding Smith Papers, 1893–1973. MS 4250. CHL.

———. Papers. 1893–1973. MS 4250. CHL.

Smith, Joseph Fielding, Jr. *Life of Joseph F. Smith*. Salt Lake City: Deseret Book, 1938.

Snow, Erastus. *One Year in Scandinavia*. Liverpool: F. D. Richards, 1851.

Sondrup, Steven P. "Literary Dimensions of Mormon Autobiography." *Dialogue: A Journal of Mormon Thought* 11, no. 2 (Summer 1978): 75–80.

Stenhouse, Fanny. *"Tell it All": The Story of a Life's Experience in Mormonism*. Hartford, CT: A. D. Worthington & Co., 1875.

Stenhouse, T. B. H. *The Rocky Mountain Saints: A Full and Complete History of the Mormons*. New York: D. Appleton and Company, 1873.

Stevenson, Edward. Journal. Edward Stevenson Collection, 1849–1922. MS 4806. CHL.

Stewart-Freece, Blanche K., and Hans P. Freece. *How Mormons Recruit Abroad*. [New York]: n.p., 1911.

Talbot, Christine. *A Foreign Kingdom: Mormons and Polygamy in American Political Culture, 1852–1890*. Urbana: University of Illinois Press, 2013.

Talmage, James E. Collection. MS 1232. CHL.

———. Journals. 30 vols. James E. Talmage Papers. MSS 229. L. Tom Perry Special Collections. Brigham Young University, Provo, UT.

Taylor, John, George Q. Cannon, and Joseph F. Smith. *To the Seventies*. Salt Lake City: Church of Jesus Christ of Latter-day Saints, 1883.

Thorp, Malcom R. "'The Mormon Peril': The Crusade against the Saints in Britain, 1910–14." *Journal of Mormon History* 2 (1975): 69–88.

———. "Winifred Graham and the Mormon Image in England." *Journal of Mormon History* 6 (1979): 107–21.

Tullis, F. LaMond. "California and Chile in 1851 as Experienced by the Mormon Apostle Parley P. Pratt." *Southern California Quarterly* 67 (Fall 1985): 291–307.

———. *Mormons in Mexico: The Dynamics of Faith and Culture*. Logan: Utah State University Press, 1987.

Turley, Richard E., Jr. "Assistant Church Historians and the Publishing of Church History." In Turley and Harper, *Preserving the History of the Latter-day Saints*, 19–48.

———. "Gathering Latter-day Saint History in the Pacific." In *Pioneers in the Pacific: Memory, History, and Cultural Identity among the Latter-day Saints*, edited by Grant Underwood, 145–59. Provo, UT: Religious Studies Center, Brigham Young University, 2005.

Turley, Richard E., Jr., and Ronald W. Walker. *Mountain Meadows Massacre: The Andrew Jenson and David H. Morris Collections*. Provo, UT: BYU Studies Press, 2009.

Turley, Richard E., Jr., and Steven C. Harper, eds. *Preserving the History of the Latter-day Saints*. Provo, UT: Religious Studies Center, Brigham Young University; Salt Lake City: Deseret Book, 2010.

Turner, John G. *Brigham Young: Pioneer Prophet*. Cambridge, MA: Harvard University Press, 2012.

University of Michigan Center for the History of Medicine. "Salt Lake City, Utah." In *The American Influenza Epidemic of 1918–1919: A Digital Encyclopedia*. Ann Arbor: Michigan Publishing, University of Michigan Library, n.d. Accessed April 20, 2017. http://www.influenzaarchive.org/cities/city-saltlakecity.html#.

Upton, Dell. "Why Do Contemporary Monuments Talk So Much?" In *Commemoration in America: Essays on Monuments, Memorialization, and Memory*, edited by David Gobel and Daves Rossell, 11–35. Charlottesville: University of Virginia Press, 2013.

Van Tassel, David D. *Recording America's Past: An Interpretation of the Development of Historical Studies in America, 1607–1884*. Chicago: University of Chicago Press, 1960.

Van Wagenen, Michael Scott. *Remembering the Forgotten War: The Enduring Legacies of the U.S.–Mexican War*. Amherst: University of Massachusetts Press, 2012.

Vendsyssel Conference Manuscript History and Historical Reports, 1850–1868. LR 9723 2. CHL.

Vermeir, Koen. "The Magic of the Magic Lantern (1660–1700): On Analogical Demonstration and the Visualization of the Invisible." *British Journal for the History of Science* 38, no. 2 (June 2005): 127–59.

Vig, Peter Sorensen. *Danske i Amerika* [Danish in America]. Minneapolis: C. Rasmussen Publishing, 1907.

Walker, Ronald W. "'A Banner Is Unfurled': Mormonism's Ensign Peak." *Dialogue: A Journal of Mormon Thought* 26, no. 4 (Winter 1993): 71–91.

———. "Heber J. Grant and the Utah Loan and Trust Company." *Journal of Mormon History* 8 (1981): 21–36.

———. *Wayward Saints: The Godbeites and Brigham Young*. Urbana: University of Illinois Press, 2008.

Walker, Ronald W., David J. Whittaker, and James B. Allen. *Mormon History*. Urbana: University of Illinois Press, 2001.

Walker, Ronald W., and Richard E. Turley Jr. "The Andrew Jenson Collection." *BYU Studies* 47, no. 3 (2008): 9–44.

Walker, Ronald W., Richard E. Turley, and Glen M. Leonard. *Massacre at Mountain Meadows: An American Tragedy*. New York: Oxford University Press, 2008.

Weintraub, Karl J. "Autobiography and Historical Consciousness." *Critical Inquiry* 1, no. 4 (June 1975): 821–48.

Westergren, Bruce N. *From Historian to Dissident: The Book of John Whitmer*. Salt Lake City: Signature Books, 1995.

White, Richard. *"It's Your Misfortune and None of My Own": A New History of the American West*. Norman: University of Oklahoma Press, 1991.

Whitmer, John. "The Book of John Whitmer." Andrew Jenson manuscript copy, ca. September 1893. In Andrew Jenson, Collection, ca. 1841–1942. MS 17956. CHL.

———. "The Book of John Whitmer, 1831-ca. 1846." Andrew Jenson typescript, ca. March 1894. MS 3552. CHL.

Whitney, Orson F. *History of Utah*. 4 vols. Salt Lake City: George Q. Cannon & Sons, 1892–1904.

———. Journals, 1877–1879, 1881–1898, 1901–1903, 1905–1931. MS 1305. CHL.

———. *Life of Heber C. Kimball, an Apostle*. Salt Lake City: Juvenile Instructor Office, 1888.

Widtsoe, John A. Papers. CR 712 2. CHL.

Wiebe, Robert H. *The Search for Order, 1877–1920*. New York: Hill and Wang, 1967.

Woodruff, Wilford. Journals, 1828–1898. MS 1352. CHL.

Woods, Fred E. "Andrew Jenson's Illustrated Journey to Iceland, the Land of Fire and Ice, August 1911." *BYU Studies* 47, no. 4 (2008): 101–16.

———. *Fire on Ice: The Story of Icelandic Latter-day Saints at Home and Abroad*. Provo, UT: Religious Studies Center, Brigham Young University, 2005.

———. "Icelandic Conversion and Emigration: A Sesquicentennial Sketch." In *Regional Studies in Latter-day Saint Church History: Europe*, edited by Donald Q. Cannon and Brent L. Top, 1–21. Provo, UT: Religious Studies Center, Brigham Young University, 2003.

———. "Men in Motion: Administering and Organizing the Gathering." In *A Firm Foundation: Church Organization and Administration*, edited by David J. Whittaker and Arnold K. Garr, 197–222. Provo, UT: Religious Studies Center, Brigham Young University; Salt Lake City: Deseret Book, 2011.

Woodworth, Jed. "Mormonism and Education." In *Mormonism: A Historical Encyclopedia*, edited by W. Paul Reeve and Ardis E. Parshall, 289–98. Santa Barbara, CA: ABC-CLIO, 2010.

Work, Henry C. "Grandfather's Clock." New York: C. M. Cady, 1876. https://www.loc.gov/resource/sm1876.01869.0/?sp=3.

Young, J. D. C. "The Latter-day Saints Church Office Building." *Utah Genealogical and Historical Magazine* 8 (April 1917): 57–60.

Zobell, Albert L., Jr. "A. William Lund (1886–1971)." *Ensign*, March 1971, 75.

Index

REID L. NEILSON has served as the Assistant Church Historian and Recorder of the Church of Jesus Christ of Latter-day Saints. He is an award-winning author and editor of dozens of books on the Latter-day Saints, and coeditor of *Pacific Apostle: The 1920–21 Diary of David O. McKay in the Latter-day Saint Island Missions.*

SCOTT D. MARIANNO is an historian in the Church History Department of the Church of Jesus Christ of Latter-day Saints and coeditor of *A Voice in the Wilderness: The 1888–1930 General Conference Sermons of Mormon Historian Andrew Jenson.*

The University of Illinois Press
is a founding member of the
Association of University Presses.

Composed in 10.5/13 Minion Pro
by Lisa Connery
at the University of Illinois Press
Manufactured by Sheridan Books, Inc.

University of Illinois Press
1325 South Oak Street
Champaign, IL 61820-6903
www.press.uillinois.edu